LANDSCAPES OF THE SOUL

LANDSCAPES OF THE SOUL

The Loss of Moral Meaning in American Life

—————————

Douglas V. Porpora

OXFORD
UNIVERSITY PRESS

2001

OXFORD
UNIVERSITY PRESS

Oxford   New York

Athens   Auckland   Bangkok   Bogotá   Buenos Aires   Calcutta   Cape Town
Chennai   Dar es Salaam   Delhi   Florence   Hong Kong   Istanbul   Karachi   Kuala
Lumpur   Madrid   Melbourne   Mexico City   Mumbai   Nairobi   Paris   São Paulo
Shanghai   Singapore   Taipei   Tokyo   Toronto   Warsaw

and associated companies in
Berlin   Ibadan

Published by Oxford University Press, Inc.
198 Madison Avenue, New York, New York 10016

Oxford is a registered trademark of Oxford University Press

A version of chapter 1, "A Caterpillar's Question: Contesting Anti-Humanism's
Contestations," was previously published in the *Journal for the Theory of Social Behavior*
27 (2/3), 1997.

A version of chapter 5, "Heroes: Religion and Metanarratives," was previously published in *Sociological Forum* 11 (2), 1996.

The paragraphs from Friedrich Nietzsche's *The Gay Science*, (1974, Vintage, are
reprinted with permission from Random House, Inc.

Lyrics from "The Man of La Mandra" and "The Impossible Dream" used by permission
© 1965; Joe Darion, lyrics; publishers, Andrew Scott Music, Helena Music Company.

Library of Congress Cataloging-in-Publication Data
Porpora, Douglas V.
    Landscapes of the soul / Douglas V. Porpora.
        p. cm.
    ISBN 0-19-513491-5
    1. United States—Moral Conditions. I. Title.

HN90.M6 P65 2001
306'.0973—c21   00-061125

9 8 7 6 5 4 3 2 1

Printed in the United States of America on acid-free paper

To the next generation:
Aaron and Dara, Mandy, Jason, Nicole and Nathan,
Julie and David

CONTENTS

Acknowledgments ix

Introduction 1

CHAPTER 1

The Caterpillar's Question 25

CHAPTER 2

The Further Geography of the Soul 57

CHAPTER 3

The Emotional Detachment from the Sacred 95

CHAPTER 4

The Meaning of Life 131

CHAPTER 5

Heroes 167

CHAPTER 6

Callings, Journeys, and Quests 201

CHAPTER 7

Resources of the Self 237

CHAPTER 8

Communities of Discourse 273

CHAPTER 9

The Human Vocation 297

APPENDIX A

Theory 311

APPENDIX B

Tables 313

Notes 317

References 335

Index 347

ACKNOWLEDGMENTS

This book took me a long time to research and write, and so many people helped me at different stages along the way that I fear overlooking someone. It becomes easy to understand how Oscar winners can go on and on.

My former office mate, Barbara Hornum, first made salient to me the idea of a worldview. I wrote the chapter on heroes first and am grateful for William Sullivan's early, supportive comments on it. My gratitude also goes to Alan Wolfe, who was gracious enough to comment on that chapter and on an earlier draft of the introduction. In the early stages, many other people helped me as well, among them Caroline Chmielewski, David Kutzik, Ernest Hakanen, Darko Surin, and Amy Smith. I had originally planned to transcribe the interviews myself. After completing three of them thirty hours later, I was grateful for Sharon Gehm's intervention. Without her, I probably still would be at this task. At the library, Richard Binder was, as always, an invaluable resource Drexel University will fully appreciate only now that he has retired. Similarly, I am grateful to William Rosenberg and the Drexel University Survey Research Center for the opportunity afforded me to conduct public opinion surveys of my own. Rakhmiel Peltz corrected my Yiddish.

As I produced more chapters, I relied on other readers, particularly the tough, critical eyes of Donald Eckard and Mah Hui Lim. When a first draft of the manuscript was completed, one of my former mentors, Magali Sarfatti Larson, became a steadfast source of support. At this time, too, I was grateful to have comments on the entire manuscript from my friends in the International Association for Critical Realism, Margaret Archer, Roy Bhaskar, and Andrew Collier. Several of my undergraduate students, too, eventually read an entire draft. Philip Hough, William Johnston, and David Saidman probably have no idea how much they gave me just by continually asking to read additional chapters. I am equally grateful to my colleagues, Anthony Glascock and Wesley Shumar, for their support and help in reconstructing some of the chapters. My thanks as always goes to my mentor, Kyriakos Kontopoulos, who trained me in theory.

I am grateful to the Humanities Research Center at the Australian National University (ANU) for the time I spent in Canberra as a Visiting Fellow. As hosts, colleagues, and friends during this time, I particularly want to express my appreciation to Margot Lyon and Jack Barbalet. To Jack, I owe an intellectual debt as well. It is to his influence that my book owes much of its current cast.

While at the ANU, I became friends with many like-minded scholars from diverse fields who were all enormously supportive of my work. Among them were Mary Besemeres, Rachel Bloul, Axel Clark, Suzanne Dee, David Parker, Susan Tridgell, and Anna Wierzbicka. I must particularly single out Susan Tridgell, who read several drafts in their entirety and who, though she could also be heatedly critical, has always been an equally passionate advocate of the book. Along with Mary, David and Axel, Susan represents a distinctive, Australian approach to literary criticism that, in its endeavor to recapture literature's moral voice, deserves to be better known worldwide.

I would also like to acknowledge those involved in the book's production, especially Susan Day, Enid Stubin, and Liz Szaluta, who so meticulously copyedited the manuscript and otherwise brought the book to completion. Most of all at Oxford, I am deeply grateful to my editor, Cynthia Read, both for her abiding faith in the book and for all the work she devoted toward making it so much more friendly to the common reader.

Contrary to what our students think, few writers write effortlessly. There is a joy to writing but also pain. Like runners, those of us who write have learned just to work past the pain and even in some strange way to enjoy it. Of course, as our companions can testify, writers are not always such a joy to be around. For staying by my side and lessening the pain, I thank my generous wife, Lynne Kotranski.

My biggest debt is to the people I interviewed who willingly bared themselves to me. I hope in what I have produced they will feel I have honored their gift.

LANDSCAPES OF THE SOUL

Introduction

If you tear the heart away from God,
to whom will you then commit it? Tell me this.
Soulless is the person who has been able
to tear his heart away from God for a single moment.

Rumi

Let me begin with two personal anecdotes, each of which illustrates what this book is about and why I came to write it. I am a college professor, and both anecdotes relate to experiences in my classroom. Both, I believe, have wider significance.

I teach sociology, and on one occasion I asked my students whether or not they considered capitalism to be exploitative.

"It depends on your point of view," my students said.

I was puzzled. "What do you mean?"

"Well," my students replied, "if you were a worker, you would probably say yes, and if you were a capitalist, you would probably say no."

I pressed them further. "Well, what do you think?"

"We think," my students replied with finality, "that it's all relative to your point of view."

I am known by our students as one of the "campus radicals," as one who does not like capitalism and who does think it is exploitative. Yet, I do not believe my students were just trying to avoid disagreeing with me. I am also known as a teacher who encourages discussion and who enjoys a good argument. Even the members of the College Republicans seek out my classes as a forum where their views can be aired with appreciation.

As the late and politically conservative scholar Allan Bloom noted, there is one thing all college professors know today: Our students believe truth to be relative. Our students do not just believe that what is taken to be true is relative to the individual—which nobody would deny—but that what actually is true is up to each of us individually.[1]

Politically conservative as he was and politically left as I am, Professor Bloom and I are on one side of a divide; our students are on the other. Professor Bloom and I might be labeled "modernists." We both would hold truth an objective feature of reality, independent of what either of us happened to think is true. We both would also hold that even moral claims may be true or not. Professor Bloom and I would certainly disagree about the exploitative nature of capitalism. Yet, there is one point about which we would adamantly agree: Independent of anyone's point of view—including both his and mine, capitalism either truly is or truly is not exploitative. There is some relationship between capitalism and exploitation that is independently true.

Our students, on the other hand, represent a view that has come to be labeled "postmodern." It no longer believes in truth and is highly skeptical about moral truths in particular. Such a postmodern sensibility is widespread at the turn of the millennium.

On another occasion, I happened to notice that, like the wider society around me, many of my students did not seem to care about the suffering of others—about the homeless or the poor in general. I first noticed this during the Reagan years, during a time when, as I argued to my students and also in print, the United States was waging a covert but genocidal war in Central America, a war that was shamefully oppressing the already long oppressed peoples of Nicaragua, Guatemala, and El Salvador.[2]

What struck me at the time was that my students did not dispute the highly unfavorable way I depicted the United Sates, the disparaging portrait I painted of their country. While at the time I believed what I was saying and still do, I fully expected and wanted my students to argue with me, to tell me it all was not so. I was prepared to engage my students in argument and to persuade them otherwise.

Instead, my students calmly—even uncritically—accepted what I had to say. They believed the horrors I was relating to them were real. Their responses to me were completely different:

"Why should we care?"

"What does this have to do with us?"

Strangely, many of my students seemed morally indifferent to the plight of others, morally unmoved even when we ourselves were collectively contributing to that plight. It was a moral indifference I also witnessed then in society as a whole and that we continue to witness in society as a whole even today. My story, however, does not end here.

I ruminated about my students' indifference and about how I could inspire their moral emotions. I concluded that for my students to care about the suffering of others, I needed to connect the well-being of others with some larger picture, with my students' own larger pictures of the meaning of life. It was, I thought, with the moral values contained within my students' own religious traditions that I needed to connect, through which I could show them "for whom the bell tolls." I resolved to do so next term.

My colleagues were taken aback when the next term's book orders arrived. While my colleagues had assigned their classes the usual sociology textbooks, I had assigned books on existentialism, religion, and the meaning of life.

"No sense talking about sociology," I said to my colleagues' stares, "until we've connected with the students' values." In retrospect, I imagine I appeared as mad as the narrator of Robert Pirsig's *Zen and the Art of Motorcycle Maintenance*, who had become as obsessed by the concept of quality as I had by the concept of values.[3]

There is a Yiddish saying I often hear from my father-in-law: "Der mentsh trakht un got lakht,"—people plan, and God laughs. In this case, God was laughing at me. If my students had been indifferent to hearing about the suffering of others, they were worse than indifferent to my new talk about the meaning of life. They thought I was crazy. And they were bored—bored by talking about the meaning of life. Boring students was not something to which I was accustomed.

If I had sought to connect with the values contained in my students' own religious traditions, I soon learned that my students—whatever their religion—were somehow disconnected from those values and traditions themselves. One young woman finally did tell me that she subscribed to a meaning of life based on her religion.

"What is it?" I asked eagerly.

"Well," she explained, "I'm Catholic. So the meaning of life for me is just to enjoy ourselves."

As a practicing Catholic myself, I could only gape in wonder. My Jewish students were no different. Judaism was all about family, they told me. Nothing more. My Jewish students were disconnected from their deeper moral traditions, too.

This second anecdote, I believe, also has wider significance. If the first anecdote points to a contemporary skepticism about truth, the second anecdote points to a contemporary retreat from cosmic meaning, a retreat from larger frames of reference in which we place ourselves and our lives. The contraction of meaning—from transcendental horizons to the merely local—is a second feature associated with the postmodern sensibility.

The loss of truth and the loss of meaning are related but not principally in the manner we might suppose. We might suppose that we have withdrawn from overarching worldviews—whether religious or secular—precisely because we have become especially dubious of their truth. Certainly the erosion of faith by doubt is part of the contemporary picture. It is not, however, the most important part.

The investigation presented in this book will suggest that when it comes to withdrawal from the cosmos, to emphasize cognitive doubt puts the cart before the horse. We will see that in cognitive terms— that is, in terms of belief—there actually is little loss of faith in the sacred. Most Americans continue to believe in God. Many just do not find God someone to whom they are particularly attached. Thus, like my students, many find debates about God's existence of little consequence. What has withered is not principally belief in cosmic meaning but concern with cosmic meaning. The withdrawal from the sacred is not principally a matter of belief but of emotion. Our skepticism about any answers to life's ultimate questions is often just a way for us to dismiss the questions. Our emotional withdrawal from cosmic meaning comes first. Our skepticism is secondary.

Our emotional withdrawal from the sacred does not usually reveal itself directly. Instead, it appears in one of its most consequential effects: the loss of moral purpose. Why should we care? Why should we care about genocide in Kosovo, about the poor in our own country, or, indeed, about any remote other in distress? The question posed by my students is a question of moral purpose. It is a question that asks about the inclusiveness and nature of our purpose here on earth; the question relates to the meaning of life. At the same time, it is also a question about ourselves, about who we are and who we take ourselves to be. In moral space, who we are is primarily a matter of what we stand for.

Moral purpose is a pivotal concept, connecting our grand views about the meaning of life with our own personal identities. Moral purpose is the central concern of this book—specifically the moral identities and moral purposes of contemporary Americans. At the turn of the millennium, are there any moral purposes to which Americans commit their lives? If so, what are these purposes? Do they encompass the whole of life or do they rather tend to be much smaller? In what worldviews are these purposes grounded, and how do they relate to any sense of the grand meaning of life and to our own personal identity? At the dawn of the new millennium, this book asks, *Quo vadis?* Where are our lives each individually going? Of particular interest throughout is the difference it makes to a life—to its shape, cohesion, and identity—that it does or does not embody moral purpose of a life-encompassing scope.

METHODOLOGY

The book's investigation relies partly on national public opinion polls and on more local surveys I conducted myself through my university's survey research center. Statistics, however, cannot capture the emotional dynamic at issue here, the dynamic between what we believe and what we feel. Thus, although I employ survey data to determine certain general relationships and representative views in our society, the core of the book consists of actual dialogues. Like an anthropologist, I have done my best to keep field notes on many casual conversations on the topics under consideration. More formally, I also conducted short interviews on specific topics, which I taped and transcribed.

At the core of this book, however, are in-depth interviews with forty people from a cross-section of society. These interviews each lasted two hours and were also taped and transcribed. Although not a random sample, the forty people I interviewed represent the major spiritual views prevalent in America—and even some that are more peripheral. I interviewed people who vary in religious devotion, including—besides Catholics and Jews—both liberal and fundamentalist Protestants. A range of Jewish voices is represented, including one that speaks articulately on behalf of a spiritual Judaism. Although they represent only small minorities of the population, I interviewed political activists, avowed atheists, and some who subscribe to "new age" philosophies. In short, I interviewed people with different levels of attachment to varied discourses of ultimate meaning.

In some cases, I knew the person before. Others were at least at one remove from me, acquaintances of acquaintances. I solicited a number of interviewees, for example, from a Methodist minister friend. I asked her to identify people in her church who were not college educated, not overly religious, and willing to be interviewed on the topics of this study. Other people without a college degree and with even fewer ties to organized religion were located for me by the administrative assistant of my department. A colleague set up a number of interviews for me in his home town in western Pennsylvania so that I could hear from people in a very rural area.

To identify people to interview, I developed two grids. One grid displayed different degrees of religiosity against different religions and religious denominations. Because Jews differ so much in both religious perspective and religiosity, I oversampled them. A co-speaker at a talk I gave at a local high school was director of religious education at a synagogue. I asked to interview her because she represented a kind of spiritual Judaism uncommon among American Jews. I also oversampled atheists, political activists, and people subscribing to the newer, countercultural meaning systems. A second grid provided a breakdown of demographic and socioeconomic categories. By rotating the people I interviewed on the cells of this grid, I tried to ensure that they varied by age, race, gender, education, and income. I was fairly successful in attaining variation on most of these categories, although African Americans are somewhat underrepresented.

One or even a few voices cannot speak on behalf of everyone in a category. The point of the in-depth interviews is not to establish the proportional representativeness of views, however, but to elicit an illustrative sample of the different ways differently situated people think about life's ultimate questions. The point of the interviews, in other words, is to identify inner mechanisms of thought on ultimate matters. How representative is what people told me? This question I address by reference to the national surveys and to the smaller, random samples I was able to collect myself.[4]

Although this book is a work of sociology, it transgresses the conventional boundaries of sociology in a number of ways. One transgression is style of presentation. The sociological convention is to present the comments of interviewees in indented quotes, separate from the analysis. Conventionally, even if the actual interview was a dialogue, the interviewer's own contribution to the discussion is erased. To effect a scientific appearance, a rigid separation is maintained between observer and observed. Thus, the comments of interviewees appear as so many specimens in a petri dish over which the sociologist casts a scientific eye.

No doubt it will disconcert many of my sociology colleagues to find my interview material seamlessly interwoven with the text in the same manner as the dialogues that open this book. My colleagues will want to know: are the people I interviewed data or just conversational partners?

The answer is that the people I interviewed are both. Feminist scholars have long urged sociologists to drop the pretense of a rigid separation between observer and observed, to admit that scientific research is actually a dialogue with the world, a dialogue in which observer and observed both participate. Although this book is not specifically concerned with women's issues, it nevertheless puts into practice this feminist perspective. The interviews I conducted were dialogues rather than closed-ended surveys. By being open about my own opinions, I was able to elicit deeper responses and carry the progression of ideas further in different directions.

In the end, if my own voice enters these pages alongside those of my subjects, it is partly because I feel an obligation to be as publicly forthcoming as were the people I interviewed and partly because one party cannot be removed from a dialogue without its ceasing to be a dialogue. I hope now that readers feel invited to enter this dialogue along with us.

MORAL PURPOSE

I said that this book is centrally concerned with moral purpose, a phrase that may seem strange. Although moral purpose is something to which some sociologists and philosophers have alluded, I do not know any who has specifically named it such. Because moral purpose has gone unnamed, it has also gone unstudied. To make something a focus of study, we must first identify it, which requires that it be named.

Ultimate concern perhaps is the concept closest to what we mean by moral purpose. Named by theologian Paul Tillich, ultimate concern refers to whatever we make the central concern of our lives.[5] Our ultimate concern is that to which we are not just committed but ultimately committed—above all else—and from which in turn we derive our ultimate fulfillment. Like a moral purpose, an ultimate concern is something to which we are emotionally tied, and like a moral purpose, an ultimate concern can be more or less encompassing. From a theological perspective, Tillich suggests, it is idolatrous for us to make an object of ultimate concern anything that is not truly ultimate. I will make a parallel suggestion about our ultimate moral purposes, that they too should ultimately be directed toward what truly is ultimate.

If ultimate concern and moral purpose coincide so closely, it is because they are aspects of the same dynamic. Whereas ultimate concern is in some sense an emotional or spiritual call, moral purpose is our response to that call, the life project or moral career it elicits. If our ultimate concern in life contracts, our sense of moral purpose contracts along with it. Our examination of moral purpose must therefore encompass an examination of ultimate concern as well.

As I say, this book willfully transgresses a number of sociological conventions. Its style of presentation is perhaps its least offense. It is even more transgressive for a sociologist to adopt a theological concept like ultimate concern for purposes of sociological explanation. As a secular discipline, defensive about its scientific status, sociology prefers to keep religion exclusively an object of study and not an intellectual partner. By violating this sociological convention here and elsewhere, I hope to overcome the sociological neglect of theology—not as object of study but as co-contributor of insight.

Today, we rarely think of morality as relating to our purposes. Morality today is largely conceived as procedural. That is, we usually think of morality as concerned with the procedures or means by which we pursue our ends. We may not, for example, lie or cheat to accomplish our goals. Our means are constrained by moral considerations. Today, the conventional mark of good people is that they pursue their chosen goals without resort to immoral means.

What about the morality of our goals? There are, to be sure, some ends we are morally enjoined not to pursue. We are not to seek vengeance or cruel satisfactions. We are not to be overmuch concerned with the pursuit of money, status, or power. Yet, compared with the moral attention we pay to our means, we pay scant attention to the morality of our ends. What attention we do give to ends again focuses on negative constraints; certain goals are not to be pursued.

Morality is not only about what we should not do, however. It is also supposed to provide positive guidance as to what we should be doing. *How am I to live?* This is the most critical moral question we can ask ourselves, a moral question that addresses not any individual act but the entire course of our lives. The question fundamentally has to do with moral purpose—what it really asks is, *What purpose or purposes should my life serve?*

As important as it is, how we should live is a question we seldom ask. Because morality is viewed as procedural and as a matter of negative constraints, our course appears simple and straightforward: within the moral constraints that bind us, we are morally free to do whatever we please, to pursue whatever goals we desire. Within the moral constraints, our various purposes are regarded as morally neutral. The question of purpose is thereby largely removed from moral discourse.

Whether we devote our lives to stamp collecting or to fighting injustice appears a matter of personal preference. Popular morality tells us much that is negative about how we should not live but little about what we actually should be doing with our lives.

When it comes to the morality of our lives as a whole, neither do we receive much guidance from professional philosophy. Although academic philosophy of ethics has changed over the past decade, it remains preoccupied with moral quandaries, with whether or not particular acts—such as abortion or euthanasia—are right or wrong.[6] Like sociology, moreover, academic philosophy of ethics is a secular discipline that attempts to ground ethics exclusively in secular reason. Secular reason gives us technical rules of procedure devoid of emotion. Little in academic philosophy of ethics addresses the emotional inspiration for ethical conduct.[7]

Lately, philosophers themselves have expressed dissatisfaction with this focus on the rightness or wrongness of individual acts. Alisdair MacIntyre and Charles Taylor, for example, have recently recommended a shift away from debating what it is right or wrong to *do* and toward what it is good or bad for us to *be*.[8]

To speak of the good as MacIntyre and Taylor advise is to return to a Greek perspective on ethics. Plato and Aristotle agreed that the nature of the good toward which one's life moves is what defines who one is. We are morally defined, as Tillich would put it, by our ultimate concern.

The good moves us, Plato and Aristotle further agreed, as a final cause, drawing us to itself so that ultimately we become molded in its image. Suppose, for example, that the good that moves us is tolerance or justice. By being so moved, we become tolerant or just ourselves. Whereas in nature a mechanical cause imparts motion by pushing from behind, in the human sphere, a final cause moves by pulling us forward from ahead. According to Aristotle, we are drawn toward tolerance or justice as ideals loved, revered, or admired.[9] Thus, the attractive power of a final cause is fundamentally emotional. The fact is that moral purpose is less something we choose than something that chooses us. Before we ever choose to devote our lives to one or another moral purpose, that purpose must first move and inspire us.

Something exciting happens when we turn our attention from the morality of means to the morality of ends. Emotionality returns to ethics in a central way. In this book we will explore the ways in which people are or are not emotionally grasped by larger moral purposes. We will examine people's heroes, their journeys, their sense of calling.

We will try to identify the different sources drawing people to concerns greater than their own small circle of affairs.

Because in both academic philosophy and sociology moral purpose has gone unnamed and unstudied, neither discipline has attended much to moral emotions. Yet, moral purpose and moral emotion both have been latent not just in theology but in literature as well. Think of the emotional dynamics in the life transformations experienced by fictional characters like Ebenezer Scrooge and Jean Valjean. To take advantage of what literature has to teach, I will depart yet again from conventional sociology. I will draw not only on theology but also on literature to identify and articulate certain emotional dynamics.

Literature cannot be dismissed as just fiction. Literature is an alternative path to knowledge, to truth.[10] Part of my argument is that we have lost touch with a whole range of moral and spiritual emotions. By its very nature, this argument cannot be addressed by the intellect alone, but must also be addressed by the heart. It is not enough just to name the emotions we have lost. To appreciate these emotions, we need to feel the feelings associated with them. The emotions themselves must be evoked. Because it often presents reality in a heightened or clarified form, literature is able to elicit emotions we would not otherwise experience. With the voices of ordinary people alongside those of philosophers, theologians, social scientists, and novelists, I hope also to create one other effect: the sense of commonality in a quest that enlists ordinary people every bit as much as intellectuals, a collective quest for ultimate meaning.

Ultimately, this book is about the meaning of life. I mentioned earlier that moral purpose is the link that connects who we are individually with the meaning of life. We truly discover who we are only when we identify the moral purposes toward which our lives move. To be there to move us, however, moral purposes must originate from somewhere.

In comparative religion, our broadest, most encompassing moral purposes are said to originate *cosmogonically*, from a meaning of life.[11] The idea is that our highest moral purposes originate from what we believe the cosmos to be about and what we consider our own place in the cosmos. Rooted in a Judeo-Christian cosmos, for example, our own society thinks murder wrong because it believes that all humans are made in the image of our common creator.

When we say that moral purposes are cosmogonic, we mean that they arise from some such conception of what the universe is about and from which we derive what is good and what is bad, what is right and what is wrong. Whether we realize it or not, some such conception always underlies our ethical viewpoint, supplying its rationale.[12] There is no reason to seek social justice, for example, without some wider understanding that gives justice its importance. For the most encompassing of our moral purposes, this kind of wider understanding provides the meaning of life.

What happens when we are without any larger moral purpose? The lack of moral purpose manifests itself as a lack of moral vision. Two books that appeared in the eighties present this problem in context: *Whose Keeper?* by Alan Wolfe and *The Politics at God's Funeral* by the late Michael Harrington.[13]

Both books concern the demise of biblical religion and the task of finding a new moral direction without it. According to the biblical tradition, we are our "brother's keeper," the guardian and guarantor of the other men and women with whom we share our time on this planet. For the biblical religions, this guardianship is one of the grand moral purposes our lives are supposed to serve. It is part of the very meaning of life, rooted in a certain conception of God and of God's own purposes and interests. What happens when this biblical tradition loses its hold? What substitute vision can we draw on that might lift us from moral indifference to concern for the poor and oppressed? What else might motivate us to rise as keepers of other persons' welfare? That is to ask, with Michael Harrington, about the nature of our politics after we have lain God to rest.

Whose Keeper? and *The Politics at God's Funeral* are both strongly prescriptive works. Each advances an argument in favor of a new moral vision, a new source of moral motivation. According to Wolfe, the new vision must come from sociology, which, he maintains, continues to invoke the moral sensibilities of the biblical prophets. It is the place, Wolfe says, where the language of social morality is still to be found. For Harrington, in contrast, our new vision should be the vision of democratic socialism, a vision that Harrington himself did much to build in this country. If moral visions motivate us by telling us what we should be or what we should strive toward, then, according to Harrington, today we should be democratic socialists who collectively strive to make the democratic socialist vision a reality.

Wolfe may be right that sociology represents one of the few remaining forums in which the language of social morality is invoked, in which we are able to articulate and evaluate alternative moral visions, including the vision of democratic socialism advanced by Harrington. It is unlikely, however, that alternative moral visions will actually originate in sociology. Whatever moral visions provide the grist for sociology's mill, they will probably be imported from outside on more ultimate moral grounds. Thus, if Americans are to be brought around on moral grounds to Harrington's vision of democratic socialism, the moral motivation will likely have to come from a source beyond this specific vision.

Wolfe and Harrington both critically evaluate what remains for us sensibly to believe in. However, this raises an equally important question: What, if any, moral purposes are there to which ordinary Americans now actually subscribe? This is the question that concerns us here.

SECULARIZATION AND THE INDIVIDUAL SELF

Wolfe and Harrington are searching for new sources of moral vision, because, as the titles of their books imply, both presume the cultural death of God. Since the Enlightenment, intellectuals have assumed that secularization—the decline of religion—would be a natural accompaniment of scientific progress and widening education. As humanity matures, intellectuals have believed, we will outgrow our childish, religious beliefs.

Whether such a long-term process of secularization has in fact been underway is a complex question. It depends on what we mean by secularization and on our level of analysis. Does secularization mean the decline only of biblical religion or of all religion, including, for example, the new-age forms? At the societal level it is indisputable that church and synagogue are more peripheral today than they were in medieval times, but the societal level is not the only one to consider.

Has religion been peripheralized as well in the hearts of individual people? This question, too, is complex and can be answered only by getting inside the heads of individual people. That is where I propose we go.

The non-sociologist reader will likely be surprised to learn that it is also sociologically transgressive to propose exploring what individual people think and feel. Is this not what sociologists typically explore? No, it is not. Sociology is a discipline anxious about many things. Sociology is defensive about its scientific status, and sociology is defensive as well about its relation to psychology, which, along with philosophy, is the "Other" against which sociology distinguishes itself.

Sociology's defensiveness about psychology dates back to one of its principal founders, Emile Durkheim, who proposed a method of studying society without having to bother at all with the thoughts of individual people. Sociologists favored Durkheim's method because by following it, they could represent sociology as an enterprise completely independent of psychology. Eventually, however, they had to admit the failure of Durkheim's approach and went on to discover culture—which at least encompasses thoughts that people share.[14]

Yet, no sooner did sociologists discover culture than we began proclaiming a cultural Durkheimianism.[15] With the so-called cultural turn, it is still not the thoughts of individual people that we study but ideas that presumably float around on their own in the culture—in art and advertisements, television and film, books and magazines, and so on. Individuals may embrace these cultural ideas, but individuals themselves do not concern us. Individuals we still leave to psychology. Thus, even when we interview individual people, it is cultural "texts" or "discourses" we must profess to be after.

Sociology's dismissal of the individual has only sharpened with the ascendance of postmodernism in the humanities and social sciences. Postmodernist thinkers tell us that as individuals, we have no coherent selves. Hence, it is pointless to consider individuals. Individual selves are not really there; individuals are just fragmented sites at which disparate cultural discourses come together.

How do postmodernists profess to know this? By examining the cultural sense of self found in television and film, literature, art, and advertising, postmodernists descry a lost sense of self, selves that are fragmented and incoherent within such cultural "discourses."

Perhaps selfhood has been lost in our cultural discourses. But does this translate into a lost sense of self among actual, living, breathing people? And do not even people without a sense of self nevertheless remain selves in some more basic, ontological sense? Because moral purpose has to do with selfhood, it is part of the aim of this book to answer these questions. Both questions reside beyond what are usually considered the borders of sociology, the first belonging to psychology, the second to philosophy.

By themselves, however, discourses can do nothing. Discourses do not think and they do not feel. For better or worse, individual people are the only moving pieces on the human stage. Thus, if sociology confines itself to the analysis of media content, it forsakes causal explanation and becomes only literary criticism. Therefore, parting company with the usual sociological posse, we will not halt at the disciplinary border but continue our chase wherever it leads. It is not the questions refused that make a sociologist but the answers provided.

Although few sociologists admit to studying individuals and fewer still study morality, I am hardly alone in doing so. This book resumes a conversation begun by *Habits of the Heart*, written fifteen years ago by sociologist Robert Bellah and an interdisciplinary group of colleagues.[16]

I say this book resumes the conversation because, as important as *Habits* was widely considered to be, few sociologists have elected to engage with it, and the community as a whole has seemed desirous to quarantine *Habits* as something it was never meant to be: the last word on the subject. Perhaps this treatment has something to do with *Habits'* concern with individuals and morality. In any case, *Habits* was intended to begin—not end—a conversation. By way of resuming this conversation here, we will address certain issues, such as identity, that *Habits* did not explore; we will disentangle certain issues that *Habits* tended to merge; and we will arrive at a distinctly different diagnosis of the contemporary moral malaise.

The major thesis of *Habits* was that American individualism produces moral values that lack any shared grounding in a common national tradition. For this reason, many people regard all morality as relative, a matter of individual taste.

One important contribution of *Habits* was the concept of moral proceduralism. Yet *Habits* tended to leave murky what the alternative to moral proceduralism should be. The alternative is moral purpose, the focus of our inquiry. This focus will lead us to a different diagnosis of the problem. *Habits* attributed much of contemporary individualism to the rise of a therapeutic language of self-understanding. Before any such language can exert its claim on us, however, there must already exist a void that such language pours in to fill. The void, I will argue, originates in a prior detachment from the sacred, the emotional nature of which will be the focus of our exploration.

Bellah and his colleagues certainly were not postmodernists. Yet, by documenting the absence of any larger, nationally shared meaning, *Habits* has been widely interpreted as confirming a postmodernist thesis. The thesis is that at the turn of the millennium, we have reached the end of *metanarratives*, the end of cosmic stories through which our lives acquire meaning.[17] In a sense, the postmodernist thesis is that secularization has not only been underway but is now fully accomplished.

The end of meaning is a conclusion too hastily drawn from *Habits*. Consider one of the most famous figures to emerge from *Habits*, a woman, code-named Sheila, who reported following a religion all her own, a religion she actually named "Sheilaism."

Certainly it is amusing that someone would not just invent her own religion but also name it after herself. But is it illegitimate to do so? Because of its communitarian perspective, which locates truth and meaning in community consensus, *Habits* did in fact suggest that Sheilaism is somehow illegitimate.

There are several issues to be disentangled here. First, the absence of shared meaning does not signify the absence of all meaning. As Sheila's case illustrates, if you do not hold a shared worldview, it does not follow that you hold no worldview whatsoever. As anthropologist Claude Levi-Strauss observed, in addition to social meaning, there is also private meaning or idiolect. Whereas *Habits* examined meaning horizontally, across individuals, in search of something shared, we also need to examine vertically the worldviews people hold individually. Before we pronounce the total absence of meaning, we need to see how high our individual worldviews reach, how broad and encompassing they are, how ultimate. Such a vertical examination of private meaning will occupy us here.

Habits, finally, tended to equate shared meaning with meaning that is nationally shared. In a plural society, however, people may share all kinds of moral meanings that do not rise to the level of national consensus. Particularly in a plural society, people may share diverse, subnational, religious meanings. Although *Habits* treated religion in one chapter, religion was not a central concern of the book. Bellah and his colleagues note, however, that although they never raised religion as a topic themselves, their interviewees very often did.[18] Before we pronounce the end of meaning, we need to take a more focused look at how people individually orient themselves religiously.

National public opinion surveys are the place to begin. From public opinion surveys, we know the percentage of Americans who individually believe in God; the percentages associated with each of the various religious denominations; and even quite a bit about the content of Americans' religious beliefs.

What do the survey data tell us? About a third of the American people are Christian fundamentalists who believe the Bible is literally—word for word—the voice of God. All told, 46 percent accept literally at least the Bible's account of creation. Although another 40 percent believe in evolution, they believe it is a process guided by God. Only 9 percent believe that humans evolved without God's having any role in the process.[19] Under 5 percent of the population consider themselves outright atheists or even agnostics; 95 percent of the American people believe in God in some form.[20] Finally, if we ask Americans how important God is to them, then, in sharp contrast with other industrialized countries, over 50 percent of Americans assign God very great importance.[21]

What do these data suggest about God's presumed demise? At first sight, they suggest the presumption is completely wrong—at least in America. What, then, of those academics who speak of the death of God and the end of metanarratives? The survey data suggest they have been in the ivory tower too long, talking to themselves. The survey data suggest that at least in America, God is alive and well. And if God survives, then so must metanarratives. The postmodernist claim appears baseless. Meaning lives on.

Or does it? As the reader will have detected, I am no friend of postmodernism and only too pleased to pronounce postmodernism wrong if I can. Indeed, this book will demonstrate that the end of meaning is wrong as a philosophical thesis, a thesis about the very possibility of ultimate meaning. Against postmodernism, we will see, meaning remains not only possible but necessary to our sense of self.

The end of meaning, however, need not be interpreted as a philosophical thesis, a thesis about what is theoretically possible. Instead, the end of meaning may be taken as an empirical claim, a claim about what is now actually the case. Even if meaning always remains a possibility for us, many of us may currently be without it.

At first sight, the survey data suggest the end of meaning is wrong even as an empirical claim. First sights, however, can be misleading. In this case, I think they are. Despite the statistics, the research to be presented here will indicate something empirically true about the claim of God's death and the end of metanarratives. I have come to think of it as one of the mysteries at the turn of the millennium that many people not only go on believing in God but go on attaching importance to that belief without its having much moral relevance to their lives or giving their lives much moral direction. Mysterious as this may sound, it is all a matter of how belief in God actually functions in people's lives. It is a mystery this book will attempt to unravel.

In the vast debate over secularization, this mystery seldom surfaces. Of course, even to notice it, we must draw our attention from cultural discourses to individual people; it is within individual people that the mystery resides. Even among sociologists who study individual people, however, the debate over secularization has focuses on beliefs and behavior. Do people continue to believe this or that religious doctrine? Do they continue to attend religious services with the same frequency? At the level of the individual, these are the sorts of questions that preoccupy the secularization debate.

The secularization debate has largely overlooked religious emotion and, more particularly, religious experience. Indeed, religious experience has been neglected by the sociology of religion in general. David Yamane, one of the few sociologists to investigate religious experience, describes its study as "the road less traveled."[22] But religious emotion and religious experience lie at the heart of our mystery. The mystery we are concerned with involves a dissociation between what we think and what we feel. More properly, because emotions are not just feelings but orientations of care toward the world, the mystery involves a dissociation between belief and engagement.[23] This dissociation in turn can be traced to an absence of religious experience.

The statistics documenting belief in God do not tell the entire story. As we will see, even if we stick with survey data, other statistics reveal an emotional disconnection from God—even among those who attach importance to their belief in God. Moral purpose is what moves us to moral action. Moral movement is an emotional response, a response of moral emotions. These moral emotions are often lacking in relation to God.

For many of the people I spoke with, God is largely a cipher who stands for the meaningfulness of life. That there is a God means there is an ultimate someone to whom what we do here matters. This same someone ensures that "everything happens for a reason," a conviction, we will see, that is remarkably prevalent and comforting. For many, God's existence also founds a belief in an afterlife, which, again, most people find comforting. Finally, God remains the ultimate monitor of the kind of procedural morality represented by the Ten Commandments.

This list of psychological functions certainly involves some emotion such as a sense of security. And the list may be long enough as to make it seem unreasonable to expect more of God. Lacking, however, is any talk of experiencing God or of God as an emotionally inspiring exemplar of the good.

For us to be morally inspired by God, we would need to know more about God than is suggested above. In the mythic metanarratives of our traditional religions, God emerges as a distinct personality. In the Jewish and Islamic traditions, God is a champion of social justice who delivered Israel from slavery and who continues even now to act on behalf of the downtrodden. At the heart of the Christian tradition stands a cosmic love so great as to have offered freely the supreme sacrifice for us.

To be touched by stories of God is to be emotionally grasped by God's own moral example. It is to experience love and justice, for example, as the meaning of existence. We are touched by the stories if they elicit in us a love for the moral qualities God represents. We are touched by the stories if we experience God's own example as a call or demand, emotionally pulling us to follow. In following, our lives acquire a unity of purpose that lends them a coherent identity.

The stories, however, can cease to compel. Certainly they will not work if we are utterly turned off to all talk of God. Yet, even among those who believe in God, the stories may stop working. They may cease to function as sources of moral inspiration. We may continue believing in the God of the stories without believing in or being moved by the stories themselves. God then endures like the smile of the Cheshire cat, stripped of surrounding features. Such a God is a cipher, a "floating signifier" without referent. As we will see, this is the God in whom many Americans believe.

THE LANDSCAPES OF THE SOUL

In *Whose Keeper?* Wolfe says that "when individuals talk with social scientists, especially when they talk in any moral depth, the process should be a moral passage for both of them."[24] I think I can say the interviews I conducted were a moral passage, both for me and for many of the people I interviewed. In most cases, the interviewees were gratified that a social scientist cared about what they had to say. Many came to verbalize feelings and beliefs of which they had not previously been aware.

In several cases, certain philosophical topics actually moved interviewees to tears. I had not anticipated this reaction. My wife, on the other hand, was not surprised. She is a social scientist, too, one whose work on health care includes research on AIDS. When I started describing my interview topics to her, she wondered how I could ask such intimate questions. I was taken aback. After all, she talks to people about their sexual partners and practices. Are not these intimate matters? "Yes," she replied, "but you are asking people about their souls."

My wife was right. As the title of this book suggests, I am inquiring about the contemporary soul. If, as I have said, moral purpose connects with the meaning of life at one end, at the other end it connects with our own personal identity. Thus, this book is as much about personal identity as it is about ultimate meaning. In fact, empirically establishing the connections between ultimate meaning, purpose, and selfhood is one of my central objectives.

I spoke earlier about the postmodernist denial of the individual self. This denial is as ambiguous as the postmodernist denial of meaning. Denial of self is also often understood as a philosophical claim:

that we are not singular selves ontologically, which is to say our selves do not exist in fact. So understood, I will argue, this claim is indefensible. Our conception of ourselves must be distinguished from what we actually are in fact. Even when we no longer have a coherent conception of ourselves, singular selves are what we are and what we remain.

As with the denial of meaning, the postmodernist denial of self need not be interpreted philosophically. It can also be interpreted as a claim not about what we actually are but about how we tend to experience ourselves. It may be that although we remain singular selves in a philosophical sense, we nevertheless have widely lost the sense of our own coherence—or the ability to articulate it.

To the extent that postmodernists are denying not selfhood as such but only sense of self, their claim is no longer conceptual but empirical. In this case, its truth becomes a matter of observation. What we ultimately need to observe is what postmodernists themselves neglect: actual people, not media representations of them.

Ironically, when we examine what postmodernists themselves ignore, we find some vindication for their claim. If, as a metaphysical claim about fundamental human reality, the denial of self is philosophically mistaken, it nevertheless appears true as a phenomenological claim about how many of us actually experience ourselves. We may not truly be soulless, but many of us experience ourselves as such.

We need first to conceptualize what we even mean by a coherent sense of self. Such a concept must be larger than what sociologists ordinarily deal in. Sociologists typically see our identities as entirely constructed in what they call social space, the space in which our personal relations and group affiliations are laid out. For sociologists, our identities tend to be defined by the social categories with which we identify or in which we can be placed. We are someone's son or daughter, wife or husband. We are African American or white and European. We are members of the Rotary or of the Communist Youth League. These are all relational identifiers in social space. Who we are in social space is the intersection of all these overlapping roles.

Most sociological studies of identity begin and end here in social space. We, too, will begin in social space with questions about our personal identities. The very next chapter, "The Caterpillar's Question," begins by posing to all of us the question the Caterpillar posed to Alice: "Who are you?"

Social space is just our point of departure, however. In fact we will see that as long as we remain rooted in social space, we will never be able to give a complete answer to the Caterpillar's question. Most ordinary people also think of their personal identities solely within the realm of social space—solely, that is, in terms of their social relationships and group memberships. As a result, when asked who they are, most people are as startled as Alice was to find they have no adequate answer.

We cannot adequately describe who we are just in terms of our placement in social space. Social space is only one of the landscapes of the soul. It is not only with persons and groups that we identify. We also identify with values. As philosopher Charles Taylor argues, we are who we are not just in social space but in moral space as well, a space of alternative and competing moral values. In moral space, we are what we stand for. We are the quests we are embarked on, the callings that move us. In moral space, our souls are like arrows that point to visions of the good. To know more deeply who we are, we need to know the moral directions in which our souls are pointing.[25]

To speak of moral directions is to speak again of moral purpose. It is to speak of that toward which our lives move. Our souls may not point to anything more than the procedural morality that defines the boundaries of acceptable behavior. Yet, even within the boundaries of moral constraint, there will always be that which ultimately concerns us. With Paul Tillich, we must ask how ultimate are the concerns around which our lives revolve. As a purely empirical matter, it may be that the whole of our lives revolves around concerns that are too small—too small really to encompass the whole of life. If such is so, our sense of identity will suffer. At the extreme, our self-portrait may be a picture painted only in a corner of life's canvas, with the remaining space left blank.

In the end, the moral worth of our lives must be judged not only by the values we have chosen but also by the values we have declined. We may ignore the moral points of the compass that circumscribe our lives, but even in the values we deny, we establish who we are. At the gates of hell, Dante finds the souls not of those who chose evil but of those who morally were neither here nor there; in time of moral contention, they remained neutral.

Once we introduce moral space as a further landscape of the soul, still other landscapes are disclosed. As we have observed, moral purpose does not arise ex nihilo. Instead, moral purposes always originate from a metaphysic, a worldview that identifies our place in the cosmos. Moral space itself thus implies a metaphysical space in which our lives are also situated. We are who we are not just in social space, not just in moral space, but in metaphysical space as well. If to know who we are is always to know our position in a space, then part of who we are is our position in the cosmos. As a culture, we may fail to think cosmologically; we may fail to imagine an entire cosmos. But we cannot fail to do so without endangering our own personal sense of identity. What is closest to us individually—our very souls—is connected to what is most distant and most grand—the meaning of life.

It is much more difficult in today's multicultural climate to speak of moral space and metaphysical space. Whenever I raise moral or metaphysical issues in my classroom, my postmodernist students respond with the cry: "Who's to say?" Who's to say which metaphysical picture is right or wrong? Who's to say what the meaning of life is?

Like many more sophisticated academics and intellectuals, my students believe these questions unanswerable, permitting them to dismiss moral and metaphysical inquiry. Yet, even about ultimate matters, we will see, there are ways to establish some truths. Even about God, there are points on which a theist can persuade an open-minded atheist, or an atheist an open-minded theist.

The fact is the questions posed by my students are answerable, although they are generally surprised when I do answer them. My answer is always the same. If the question is, "Who's to say," the answer is, "The best argument." We learn the truth not from a "whom" but from a "what." To the extent that we can learn the truth, it is always ascertained by the best argument available to us.

The best argument does not create the truth. The truth always depends on the nature of reality, which is independent of whatever we believe or claim. So the best argument does not create the truth, but it offers our best purchase on the truth.

Who's to say which is the best argument? It is up to each one of us individually to judge. Yet, this individual judgment of truth is not entirely up to us. If we are open-minded, critical thinkers, then we may have to admit that the best argument is not the one we brought to the table. The best argument may belong to those with whom we initially disagreed. We may have to concede that the truth is different from what we originally thought and, more painfully, different from what we would prefer. The tendency is to think that belief in objective truth makes us intolerant of others' perspectives. It need not. What belief in objective truth should make us intolerant of are those beliefs of our own we cannot justify. Unless we subject ourselves to such rigor, we entertain no critical thought and experience no intellectual growth.

On any issue, the best argument is never something we can arrive at on our own. For example, we may believe in God for what we consider good reasons. But we cannot know whether our reasons really are good until we share them with others.

The best argument always emerges from dialogue, especially from dialogue with those who disagree with us. When we converse just with those who agree with us, we tend to reinforce our own prejudices. If believers speak only with those who believe in God, they will never doubt that God exists. It is only by listening sensitively to those who see things differently that we discover where our own arguments fall short. Diversity of opinion is important, not because there is no truth apart from our individual opinions but because only diversity enables us to find it. The more diversity in a conversation, the surer we can be that our considered judgment reflects the best argument around.[26]

The search for truth therefore is not a solitary enterprise. It is something we can accomplish only in community with diverse others also seeking the truth. Within such communities, we collectively create what I call "critical space," the space of argument.

Critical space is an amazing human creation. It is an invisible space that consists only of arguments and counterarguments. In critical space, it does not matter "who" made an argument. All that exists is the argument itself, detached from its maker. Critical space confronts us whenever we enter a conversation with diverse others about the truth—whenever, for example, atheists and religious believers sit down to talk.

Critical space is the final landscape of the soul. Just as who we are is determined by our location in moral space and metaphyical space, so are we also distinguished by where we stand in critical space. We are distinguished by the arguments we accept and by the ones we reject. But we are also distinguished by our relation to the argumentative process itself. We may be someone who believes in argument and who therefore weighs all that is said. Alternately, we may be one who takes no argument seriously but who loves to argue just for the sake of argument. We may be intellectual heroes, daring to accept painful truths, or intellectual cowards, shutting our minds when the truth is insufferable. We may be closed-minded dogmatists, impervious to argument because we are already sure we have truth in hand; alternately, we may be intellectual sojourners still on the road. These are all possible postures in critical space. They, too, define who we are.

Because critical space arises only from the dialogues we have in community, community is vital to the search for truth. Yet, truth and critical space both exceed the confines of any one community. Truth is determined by the strength of argument, not community consensus. Even the consensus of any given community may be wrong. Any given community may remain ignorant of certain arguments, refuse to hear them, or evaluate them improperly.

Who's to say if this is the case? Again, this is a decision each of us must make individually for himself or herself. We make our judgment, however, not on whim but on honest evaluation of the arguments, always knowing that we ourselves may be the ones who are wrong. We make our judgment by being ever open to new arguments, especially to arguments originating from communities other than our own. In the end, we must find our conversational partners in the universal community of humanity as a whole. This makes the search for truth long and difficult. Yet, it is part of our life's work, part of what we are all here to do. We can refrain from the search for truth; we can choose to die with the beliefs we were born with. In that case, however, our identity in critical space will be only a void.

Social space, moral space, metaphysical space, and critical space: these are the terraced landscapes of the soul. It is part of the objective of this book to demonstrate empirically the value of viewing our lives from this framework. I have compared this book to a dialogue. I would also like to compare it to a journey, to an exploration of terrain that although previously traversed by others still retains its wild, uncharted nature. This book is a kind of traveler's report. The various spaces I have identified are the maps I have drawn along the road. They are my maps of the contemporary soul.

Now is an especially appropriate time to take this journey and reflect on who we are. We are at the turn not just of a century but of a millennium. How ironic that the second millennium closed with a postmodern loss of meaning. In the first century, by contrast, the common era began with a plenitude of meaning. Besides the birth of Christianity and Rabbinic Judaism, there were also in Israel the independent movements of the Essenes and the Baptist. In the far east, Buddhism had just crossed over from India into China. And throughout the Roman Empire, there were mystery cults for the many and, for the intellectual few, the high philosophies of Stoicism, Cynicism, and Epicureanism. All addressed the question, *How am I to live?* Then, perhaps, there were too many answers; today, there are too few. Today we have lost even the question.

According to Tillich, each millennium experiences its own distinct spiritual anxiety. In the first century and the centuries preceding it, the major spiritual anxiety was over death and mortality. The great spiritual question was how to live knowing we are certain to die. For much of the ancient world, according to Tillich, that question was definitively answered by Socrates, who exemplified "a courage which could affirm life because it also could affirm death." In the tenth century and the centuries that followed, the spiritual anxiety concerned guilt: How do we justify our existence in the face of moral culpability? At the end of the twentieth century, our major spiritual anxiety is about meaning: How do we continue to affirm meaning despite the press of meaninglessness?[27] Dealing with this question as it does, this book is a product of its time.

CHAPTER 1

The Caterpillar's Question

To many, it is not given to hear of the Self. Many, though they hear of it,
do not understand it. Wonderful is he who speaks of it.
Intelligent is he who learns of it.

Blessed is he who, taught by a good teacher, is able to understand it.

—The Upanishads

SOCIAL SPACE

When she tumbles down the rabbit hole, one of the first characters Alice meets is the Caterpillar. Reclining dreamily on a mushroom, the Caterpillar stops smoking opium long enough to ask a disconcerting question: "Who are *you?*"

To her surprise, this is a question Alice finds she cannot answer. Part of the problem, surely, is that by the time Alice meets the Caterpillar, she is no longer quite the same person she was when she began her day. At the time of their encounter, Alice has shrunk to roughly the same size as the Caterpillar. A more fundamental problem, however, is that Alice and the Caterpillar do not share the same social space, the arena of personal connections and relationships. It is through social space that we first begin to identify who we are.

I once posed the Caterpillar's question to Aaron, a thirteen-year-old boy about to make his bar mitzvah. "Who are you?" I asked.

Although Aaron knew I was asking a philosophical question, he mischievously replied, "I'm your nephew."

Aaron's was not the answer I was seeking, but it was nevertheless a perfect sociological response to my question. After our names, we first identify who we are by locating ourselves within a network of social relations. My nephew had not just identified himself to me; as I only had one nephew at the time, he had identified himself uniquely.

Uniqueness is integral to identity. To speak of our identities is to speak of who each of us uniquely is. Two things are said to be identical if one cannot be distinguished from the other. Identity is thus linked to differentiation. We are uniquely who we are because in ordinary life, (1) we cannot differentiate our own self from ourself, and because (2) there are always ways of differentiating our own self individually from everyone else's self. Only I am myself.

Already, we begin to see why the postmodernist denial of ontological identity is incoherent. The ability to distinguish ourselves from each other is necessary for social life to go on. Socially, our unique identities are the objects to which unique experiences, thoughts, and actions are attached. Socially, we need to distinguish whether it is Uncle Harry or Aunt Sue who enjoys fishing, hates the Democrats, or believes in UFOs. Experiences, thoughts, and actions all need to be assigned to specific somebodies. There are no disembodied experiences, no free-floating thoughts, no actions without actors. For us even to conceptualize experiences, thoughts, and actions, they all must belong to somebody in particular—to Uncle Harry or to Aunt Sue or to whomever. Experiences, thoughts, and actions that are all unique in space and time must be matched with equally unique identities. Thus we need to distinguish one unique identity from another.[1]

Our identities are the objects of our own self-consciousness. We humans are said to possess self-consciousness, our most distinctive trait. Self-consciousness is the ability to make our own selves the object of our consciousness. Implicit in the very concept of self-consciousness is a self or identity we are self-conscious of.[2] Thus, again, for us to make sense of our lives, we need a concept of our own unique, personal identities.

This conceptual need is recognized even by Hinduism, according to which our socially distinct identities are an illusion. Upon enlightenment, Hinduism tells us, one recognizes one's true self, the Atman, which is distinct from the ordinary self of social life. Thus, there is, according to Hinduism, a level of consciousness at which I am not the self I think I am. I must distinguish my true self from my illusory, social self. According to Hinduism, my true self, the Atman, is at one with everyone else's true self. Thus, in Hinduism, there is no distinction between my true self and yours. Our true selves are all equally a manifestation of the one, "no-self" self of the universe, what the Upanishads call Brahman or Om. Consequently, with Hindu enlightenment, we realize that our true selves are not distinct but, rather, all one.

Hindu enlightenment, however, is a transcendental experience that leaves ordinary life behind. Outside that experience, we remain caught in the web of distinct identities. Within some Buddhist traditions, it is partly because ordinary social life requires our having unique identities that the search for enlightenment is primarily an older person's pursuit, undertaken only after one is able to retire from social demands.[3]

The implicit uniqueness of our identities is signified by our names. Our names are the very first way we identify ourselves. They are the first piece of information offered in introductions, and we are liable to suffer embarrassment if we forget the name of someone we should know. To forget someone's name is an offense against identity. It raises the possibility that the nameless one is an identity we do not consider significant.

Between our first and last names, our identities are often if not always uniquely fixed. I doubt there is anyone else in the world who has ever lived who has the same first and last name as I. (I have never quite understood what possessed my parents to affix a Scottish first name to an Italian last name.)

Many full names of course are not unique. Presumably, there are other Jim Joneses besides the notorious one associated with the suicide cult in Guyana. Nevertheless, within the social circles that matter—the local ones within which we operate—our names are generally unique and, therefore, suitable enough to fix our identities. That is why, of course, to protect my subjects' identities, all their names have been altered. The only exceptions are my nephew, who wanted to see his name in print, and a biblical critic we will later meet in the capacity of an expert witness.

There are some cultures that deliberately name their children after those who have gone before. In some tribal societies, children are named after a deceased ancestor or mythic hero. The point of such nominal identity is to indicate that the contemporary bearer of the name is the embodiment of the forebear's identity. In this way, the forebear is in some sense thought to live on in a new incarnation.

Something of this sensibility survives even in our own culture. Sometimes children are given the exact names of a parent (usually the father) to establish a historical continuity of lineage. Through the children and grandchildren, who are usually distinguished by the appellations *junior* and *the third*, a transhistorical connection is affirmed.

Among the people I interviewed, three were Sannyasins, disciples of the Bhagwan Sri Rajneesh. They had joined thousands of others at Rajneesh Purim, the Bhagwan's extensive compound in Colorado. This was a place that stirred considerable controversy in the eighties, enough to become the subject of a *60 Minutes* broadcast. Speaking with these people, I had difficulty understanding what all the furor was about, why the Bhagwan himself had become a target of government harassment. It is true that in the *60 Minutes* segment, the movement's spokesperson revealed herself to be alarmingly anti-Semitic. The three people I spoke with were not. They all assured me that such anti-Semitism is not characteristic of the movement as a whole and was specifically not characteristic of the Bhagwan, who died in 1990. As far as I can gather, the Bhagwan's message is an innocuous, eclectic variant of Hinduism.

One of the Sannyasins I interviewed, Prem Prakash, was a retired schoolteacher and a former Protestant minister. Twice divorced, he now lives alone. The other two, Veet Raj and Anand Naveeno, are a younger, married couple who run a small business. Veet Raj is an African American man, formerly from Jamaica. Anand Naveeno came to Rajneesh Purim from Germany, where she joined the movement.

None of the Sanskrit names that these Sannyasins now go by is original. When one becomes a Sannyasin, one is initiated into a new identity that breaks with the past. This is signified by a new name, which is accompanied by a poem. The poem elaborates on the meaning of the name. The meaning of the names is significant. Anand means bliss, Prem means pure love, and Veet means beyond.

According to an American Sufi healer I spoke with, "When a spiritual teacher gives you a name, it is because he sees something in you or something you should aspire to be." Something similar transpires with certain Catholic religious and, more generally, with all Catholics when at confirmation they take on the name of a saint, a role model they are meant to emulate.

Even at birth some people are given the names of virtues: Hope, Prudence, Faith, and Charity. In expressing such qualities, names extend beyond social space. They reach out into moral space and, as in the case of Emmanuel or "God with us," into metaphysical space as well. If Emmanuel means God with us, the implication is that there is a God, a God who is both able and willing to be with us.

Names carry other freight as well. They are usually gendered. Hope, Charity, and Faith, for example, are all usually associated with women. Emmanuel is a name normally reserved for males, perhaps reflecting a metaphysical assumption that God is a he. Likewise, names vary by social class and by ethnicity. They also vary by generation. In my age cohort, for example, there are few women with the names Bertha, Hazel, or Sadie. To me, those names have always conjured images of older women.

What is in a name? Much, actually. That is why today so much of our politics is preoccupied by what we are to call each other. "Colored," "Black," "Afro-American," or "African American," each designation conveys something different. Each connotes a distinct identity. The so-called politics of identity has consequently become one of our most contested political battlefields.

Among some peoples, the connection between a name and the identity which it denotes is thought to be so close that one's true name is kept secret. To know someone's "true name" is to have magical power over him or her.

Even for us, a magical power may reside in our true names. When I ask Catholic Sister Marge O'Hara who she is, her voice fills with emotion.

"I am...Patricia Margaret. When I say I am Patricia Margaret...that feels...I am...It's funny. I have a really good friend, who calls me Patricia Margaret with a way that..."

"Is that your real name?"

"Yeah, that's my baptismal name, Patricia Margaret. I've been called Marge my entire life. But when she called me Patricia Margaret when everyone else was calling me Marge, it was like...When she calls me Patricia Margaret, she calls me from, like, a place of unconditional love. I could never understand her love for me. I didn't teach her. I didn't do anything for her. I didn't prove anything. She just...loved me. And the way she says, 'Patricia Margaret,' I've grown to feel that that is...me...loved. You know? And I'm Patricia Margaret."

For all the meaning that names can bear, they are but our entry points to social space, the first dots on the map. To identify more fully who we are, that map needs to be filled in. Presumably it would not have done the Caterpillar much good if Alice had merely identified herself as "Alice." Presumably, the Caterpillar would then have asked, "And who is Alice?"

We speak of locating or placing ourselves within a network of social relations. The words *location* and *place* invoke a spatial metaphor. That spatial metaphor is reinforced by the way anthropologists and sociologists often depict social networks. We draw maps. Traditionally, the first thing an anthropologist in the field would do is draw a kinship diagram. Sociologists draw sociograms. Kinship diagrams and sociograms both consist of points and lines. The points represent people; the lines represent relationships. In kinship diagrams, the relationships depicted are either marriages or genealogical ties. The relationships depicted by a sociogram can be almost anything: who talks to whom, who is a friend of whom, and so forth. It was by sociographically depicting who had sex with whom that a sociologist at the Centers for Disease Control was able to identify the "patient zero" of the AIDS epidemic.

The points and lines of social connection are laid out in a space. Such social spaces even have their own topographies. In sociograms, there are peaks and valleys, places where the lines of connection are dense and places where they are sparse. Cliques are mountains of connectivity, separated by valleys of isolation.

To capture our location in social space fully, many such maps need to be overlaid. We have one place in a genealogy, another place in a friendship network. We have still another location in a job structure, something often represented graphically as an organization chart. We also have a nationality in a field of nationalities, a religion in a field of religions, a race in a field of races. We have a marital status, a gender, and a sexual orientation. We occupy positions or roles in a whole assortment of different organizations. We have class positions in a hierarchy of classes and various statuses in social hierarchies of status. Who we are in social space is our placement simultaneously within all these relationships. In social space, we are the unique intersection of all our social positions.

The various social positions we occupy are not all equally essential to who we are. To some social roles we bring a previously established identity and take that identity away with us when we leave the role. Our demographic characteristics are generally more essential to our identities. They are what sociologists sometimes refer to as "master statuses," statuses so constitutive of our social identities that they overshadow the other social positions we occupy only contingently. Our gender, our race, our sexual orientation are all essential in this way. We would be fundamentally different people if we differed in any of these master statuses. We would not be who we are now.

The significance of these master statuses is not entirely up to us. These master statuses were already significant to the society into which we were born and which imposed their significance on us at birth. They determine how we will be raised, some of what we will value, and for which other social positions we will or will not be eligible. Ordinarily, by the time we reach adulthood, these master statuses are so deeply inscribed in us as to set the definitive parameters of our identities.

By the time we reach an age at which we can critically reflect on who we are, we are already somebody we did not choose to be. We begin self-reflection on an identity that has been pre-given to us. When we first look at our identities, we find an identity already there. This is the experience that the German existential philosopher, Martin Heidegger, refers to as "thrownness." When we first examine ourselves in the world, we discover ourselves already having been "thrown" into the world, ready-made.[4]

We can certainly change our original characteristics, even some of our fundamental characteristics. The point, however, is that when we emerge in the world as self-conscious beings, we do not arrive without predicates. From the very beginning and thereafter, our social selves at their very core are not disembodied, transcendental egos. Instead, our egos are, among other things, fundamentally gendered, raced, and sexually oriented.

At issue in the politics of identity is the fact that our selves enter the world not just with demographic predicates but with demographic predicates that carry different moral and metaphysical values. To be a man is not just to be a man but in some societies a warrior or "bread-winner" as well. Manhood has certain metaphysical meanings attached to it, which vary from society to society. With those meanings come moral rights and privileges, duties and obligations. Social space is itself embedded in a moral space and a metaphysical space.

Some people begin life with identities already negatively valued. Negative values are attached to identities with the "wrong" skin color, the "wrong" sexual orientation, the "wrong" social class, and a host of other "wrong" identity markers. The underlying point of the politics of identity is not just to open the social space so as to include these identities equally but to change the negative values that are attached to them at the start.

The problem is that social space is already itself incipiently a moral and metaphysical order. The relationships that make up social space are themselves made up of moral norms and meanings. There is something it metaphysically means to be a mother. By virtue of that metaphysical meaning, there are moral norms governing what good motherhood entails. The same is true of every social position and role we occupy.

Thus, to challenge social space is at once to challenge the moral and metaphysical order as well. It should come as no surprise, therefore, that even those oppressed by the current social arrangement may offer some resistance. What the oppressed are being urged to surrender is not just their chains but their place in a cosmic order, an order in which they themselves may be both morally and metaphysically invested. To many, that is to surrender the cosmos and yield to chaos.

This is poignantly illustrated by Kazuo Ishiguro's novel, *The Remains of the Day*.[5] One need not be a Marxist to find the British class system deeply troubling. That some people should live their lives as servants to others seems demeaning, particularly to us in America. The household staffs of the British aristocracy are seemingly oppressed.

Oppressive or not, in its heyday, the British class system was a cosmic chain of being, in which even servants had a deeply meaningful place. In the novel (unlike the movie version), the story of *The Remains of the Day* is told from the butler Stevens's point of view. It unfolds as his moving and sophisticated philosophical treatise on what it means to be "a great butler."

To us today in America the very phrase "a great butler" may seem an oxymoron, a grandiose triviality. Ishiguro's accomplishment is that we close his book with a different attitude entirely. We have learned that to be a butler is to possess a calling and a profession, one that comes with colleagues and professional disputes, with professional journals and ideals. It is with these ideals that the book is concerned.

Despite Anthony Hopkins's sensitive performance, we might come away from the film thinking of Stevens as a person so repressed, so caught up in a petty social role that he renounces the love of his colleague, Miss Kenton, and insists on remaining at his station in the dining room even as, in the servants' quarters above, his father lies dying.

To attribute Stevens's behavior to personality flaw is to do him an injustice and to miss the entire point of the book. Stevens's behavior stems from his commitment to his station. To remain at one's station despite all adversity is, according to Stevens, the essence of greatness. "'Dignity,'" he says, "has to do crucially with a butler's ability not to abandon the professional being he inhabits," not to abandon that being even when one's "betters" egregiously let down *their* side.

Stevens's commitment to his calling is not unthinking. Behind it, there lies a substantive moral vision, a deep moral purpose. It is not his betters that Stevens ultimately serves but, through them, human betterment. We learn that like all truly great butlers, early in his career, Stevens was at pains to attach himself to a "great household." Stevens dismisses those in his profession who equate the greatness of a household with such superficialities as lineage or titles. For Stevens, the greatness of a household inheres in its moral stature. By moral stature, Stevens is not referring to the conduct of the household in its private affairs. Instead, a great household is one in which the members are publicly involved in "the progress of humanity." By serving great employers in that endeavor, a great butler makes his own small contribution to that cause as well.

In Lord Darlington's household, the fate of Europe seems to hang in the balance—who knows what damage may ensue from even one disgruntled guest? To ensure the smooth running of the backroom politics underway, Stevens's efforts in their own small way approach the heroic. It is for this reason that Stevens seems almost committed to celibacy, and it is for this reason as well that in the urgency of the moment, Stevens remains at his station, allowing the father he idolizes to die without him.

In the end, there is in Stevens's selfless behavior a nobility of purpose even a Marxist might honor. The tragedy of the novel is that the cause Stevens serves is a misbegotten one. In the end, he has to admit the truth about his employer, that as Darlington's critics had maintained, he was just a political amateur in over his head, that his lordship's misguided efforts served only to abet the cause of Hitler. At the remains of the day, Stevens's own lifelong selflessness has left nothing but the waste of what might have been.

The larger tragedy perhaps is that it is not until the end of his life that Stevens ever rises to a critical reflection on the social order itself. It is not until then that Stevens ever scrutinizes the dehumanizing constraints imposed on someone in his station. By that time, Stevens inhabits his station so completely that it is still only within the parameters of that identity that he can go on to absorb his new insight.

Whatever might have made Stevens change his ways earlier in life, it certainly could not have been a simple, socialist appeal to self-interest. For Stevens, the social order as a whole and the particular social being he had come to inhabit would have held too much moral meaning for that to have worked. Stevens did not so much *inhabit* a particular "professional being" as *become* a particular professional being.

Stevens had no social identity apart from that of being a butler. Being a butler is as essential to Stevens's identity as his race and gender. To renounce the butler's role would be to renounce his social self.

In addition to our unchosen demographic characteristics, there are thus other social positions we can adopt that will be every bit as essential to who we socially are. Marriage and parenthood come immediately to mind, but as in the case of Stevens, a profession can confer essential social being as well. To be a teacher, physician, or lawyer, for example, is not just to fill a role but to adopt a moral career that grows into an identity.[6]

To fault Stevens therefore raises an interesting philosophical difficulty. If we are to fault Stevens, we must fault him for remaining who he was. Throughout his life, Stevens remains true to the moral purpose of his calling, even heroically so. Yet, in the face of what Lord Darlington was up to, Stevens himself comes to recognize a higher ethical demand that transcends the obligations of any one profession, any one social position. It is an ethical demand Stevens encounters in the persons of Miss Kenton and in Darlington's nephew, Mr. Cardinal. It is a universal ethical demand that addresses Stevens not as a butler but as a human being.

Who is the self addressed by this universal ethic if it is not some specific, social identity? If Stevens is to be faulted for remaining himself in the face of this higher ethical demand, who is the self that might have chosen to become someone new, a self that would endure across such a transmigration from one incarnation to another? Evidently we are confronting here a self above the social self, a self independent of our social position. With that more fundamental self, we leave social space behind.

BEYOND SOCIAL SPACE

We have observed that when Alice encounters the Caterpillar, she and the Caterpillar do not share the same social space. Presumably the Caterpillar knows nothing of the human distinctions that operate in the world above the rabbit hole. Accordingly, it would have availed Alice little to have identified herself as the daughter of Dean Liddell of Christ Church College or as the favorite companion of the mathematician, Charles Dodgson.

Because Alice and the Caterpillar do not share the same social space, the Caterpillar's question immediately becomes existential: Who are you essentially? Who are you in and of yourself? It is this question Alice finds she cannot answer. In this postmodern era, we may not be surprised at Alice's loss for words. Instead, we may find it absurd that such a question is even asked.

It is night, and I am sitting in the living room of Jason Fishman. An extremely intelligent man with degrees from Columbia and Harvard Universities, Jason works for a private, nonprofit research organiza-

tion. Jason has a long history of political activism, and during the
eighties he traveled to Nicaragua and El Salvador as part of the movement in opposition to U.S. foreign policy.

"Okay," I say, "We're almost at the end of the interview. Now I
would like to ask you an existential question: Who are you?"

Jason laughs long and hard, and I laugh with him. Finally, he collects himself. "Do you," he asks, "I mean, do you get good responses to
that question?"

I tell him that in truth I usually do not get good responses to this
question.

"I'm a plain, ordinary man," one respondent tells me.

"Who am I?" wonders another, a wife and mother of two grown
children. "Oh, I don't know. If I could figure that out, I would be one
step ahead of the game.... I just am who I am. I don't know."

I point out that this is who God claims to be in the Bible.

She brightens. "I am who I am. That's it! This is it. What you see is
what you're getting. That's it. It doesn't get any better."

"Who are you?" I ask an African American man about my age.

"Lawrence Patterson," he tells me. We are sitting in an all-you-can-
eat diner, trying not to be distracted by the food and the noise.

"And who is Lawrence Patterson?"

"Lawrence Patterson is a fearless, strong, independent, self-
assured black man who has struggled most of his life to arrive at the
definition I just gave you."

"That's great."

"He's also...."

"Wonderful with words?"

Lawrence laughs. "Shit. He's also a frightened, fearful, insecure,
very dependent person. And depending on where he's at any given
day, you will see either one or both of those people."

"Who are you?" I ask Melinda, a quiet housewife I meet in rural,
western Pennsylvania. "How would you answer that?"

"Hmm."

"I want to know who you are and how you see yourself."

"Hmm. That's probably the hardest question so far. Let's see. I suppose a good listener. If somebody asked me for help or to do something, I probably would if I could. Better with kids a lot of times than
adults. I wish I could say patient, but I can't."

I interview Iris Barbuda at her office in the Federal Reserve,
where, without a college degree, she has worked herself up to a high-
level position. Due to a misunderstanding, I arrive a half hour late,

and Iris is initially miffed. In the course of the interview, however, we establish a good rapport. I begin to broach the subject of identity.

"These are," I start again. "Most people find these questions difficult."

"Who am I?"

"Yes, exactly," I say, pleasantly surprised to have been anticipated. "Who are you?"

"This is a very interesting question. In fact, I've been doing a lot of searching about it lately, because I always thought that I was some kind of independent person that had a good life and could get things done, and then my husband died. And it was a stupid thing, but I'm…and it sounds silly, but, like, after three and a half years, I find…I feel like I'm finding myself again. I'm starting to get there. And to me, when I sit back and look at it and I'm thinking to myself, well, when my husband died, I went through an awful period for a long time. I thought of myself as kind of worthless, unattractive…and then…and I felt like somehow I was losing my mind. I was very disconnected."

"Well, your identity was very bound up with another person."

"Uh-huh."

"After all those years."

"Yeah."

"And it's really…"

"But to me it was amazing that I…I did. I lost all my self-confidence. I mean, to me, I thought I was probably the most self-confident person I had ever met. And I still loved people, and I, I'm bubbly and everything around them, but deep down I was with this horrible struggle with myself, like I wasn't contributing anything. I didn't have any good ideas any more, and all those things. So anyhow, lately I feel like I'm coming back into myself again and I'm starting to feel good about myself again."

Who is Iris now? I never did learn from this line of questioning who Iris rediscovered herself to be. In fact, none of the above responses really answers my question. In each case, elicited is an aspect of self but not a definitive identification of self, an identification that fully captures the unique self I am addressing. Eli Cohen may be an ordinary man, but that does not help me much to distinguish the ordinary man he is from countless others.

Like the sociologist Manfred Kuhn, I could perhaps have asked the question "Who are you?" twenty times over, each time eliciting some new trait. That, however, is a tiresome way to proceed—particularly for the respondent, and what would I have when I was done? Whatever our selves may be, they are not going to be lists of attributes, however long.

I am not so dull as to have expected the people I interviewed all to be existential philosophers. Although I hoped for more, I fully antici- pated that most people would not be able to define themselves on the spot. Consequently, I had prepared a number of further questions that I hoped would help people articulate who they are.

I asked people if they thought of life as a journey and if so, where this journey was taking them. I asked if they thought of life as a story, and if so what would the story of their lives be about. I thought asking peo- ple what epitaph they would like to see engraved on their tombstones might be a more concrete way to elicit who they were. Sometimes these questions worked well, and sometimes they did not. In no case, however, did I learn who people uniquely were by asking such questions. While I did learn some of the things that were important to them, I did not learn their identities. In many cases, my respondents were just as flus- tered by my more concrete questions. My exchange with Gerry Storr, an anthropologist with a doctorate, is typical.

"So what would you like on your tombstone? What would you like it to say?"

"I don't—I won't have a tombstone."

"Well, if you had to choose."

"Oh, I don't know."

"Suppose you had a tombstone."

"Well, 'He's lived his life. He lived his life the way he wanted to.' I don't know. I really don't know. I've never thought about it."

Melinda likewise had no idea how her epitaph should read. "I don't know. I wouldn't have the foggiest idea of what I would want writ- ten on my tombstone."

When I ask Iris Barbuda, she says, " 'Here lies a basically good per- son.' I have to get more creative than this, but basically 'a person that knew how to enjoy life.'"

Two other responses were a bit more revealing.

"Oh, God," says

Lawrence. "Here lies Lawrence, a good brother to his sisters, a good man to his people and a friend. I don't know, something like that."

Julie Cates, a young, single, Americorps volunteer who has just graduated from college, replies similarly. "Oh, Jeez. Something like, 'She was a great Mom. She accepted everyone for who they were.' Something like that."

Revealing or not, the answers to my questions do not really tell us who these people are. The philosophical question is: Why not? Do not these people have unique identities that can be expressed in words?

Do any of us? Here we are on the terrain of the French existentialist Jean-Paul Sartre and sociologist George Herbert Mead.

HUMANISM AND ANTI-HUMANISM

According to Mead, when we speak of the self, we must make a distinction between the "I" and the "me." We are each uniquely an "I" and each uniquely a "me." Our me is who we are now. It is our socially created self, the product of our various social positions, various social influences, and our own past choices. In each moment, however, our selves always transcend our me. Our selves are also always an unqualified I, which can self-consciously reflect on the me and move beyond it.[7]

What is this mysterious I? According to Sartre, the I is our capacity to transcend the material laws of cause and effect to make freely chosen responses to ethical choices. As such, the I is what Sartre calls a "nothingness," and this nothingness is part of our being.[8]

When Sartre says that the I is a nothingness, he does not mean that it literally is not there. He means that it is a "no-thing-ness." In other words, our true or authentic self is not a material thing alongside other things in the world, things governed by causality. Instead, we are really something immaterial that has free will. If what we truly are is immaterial, it is impossible to state what we authentically are in words. The authentic I we are is ineffable. This comes close to the wisdom of the Upanishads.

> The Self beyond all words is the syllable OM…The self is OM, the indivisible syllable. This syllable is unutterable, and beyond mind. In it the manifold universe disappears. It is the supreme good—One without a second. Whosoever knows OM, the Self, becomes the Self.[9]

This self beyond words, Svetaketu is told by his father in the Chandogya, "That Art Thou."[10] Indeed, according to the Upanishads, this self is, for each one of us, our common, true self. It is the non-linguistic, no-minded consciousness we experience in meditation, the enlightened self we otherwise encounter along the eightfold path. It is the self at our center, which underlies all our experience.

Echoing the Upanishads, Sartre argues that our true vocation on earth is to become who we really are. Who we really are is someone more fundamental than any social role we play. For Sartre, it is existential "bad faith" to confuse who we essentially are with our various role performances. The I is always capable of reflecting on and transcending any social self we adopt. Not to do so when required, to deny that we are more than our role performances is the essence of what Sartre means by existential "bad faith."

It is of such existential "bad faith" that the butler Stevens is ultimately guilty. Stevens denied to himself that existentially he was anything more than a butler. Accordingly, he failed to liberate himself from the confines of his narrow role. He failed as well to respond to an ethical imperative that was addressed not to Stevens, the butler, but to Stevens, the self behind the butler's performance.

In Mead, Sartre, and the Upanishads, we have a humanist answer to our question: Who are we existentially? The answer is that we are each a transcendental ego, above and beyond whoever we socially are at the moment. If so, then it is no wonder that neither Alice nor any of my respondents can find the words to describe existentially who they are. Existentially, we are a transcendental "nothingness" beyond words. This is a humanist answer, meant to affirm what is special about humanity. As morally responsible centers of conscious experience, we each have a sacred identity.

There are serious problems with such a transcendental conception of self. Whatever the spiritual experience of cosmic unity may reveal about our deeper place in the universe, a purely transcendental conception of self does not do justice to our routine selves on life's surface. Even in our routine existence of daily life, our selves exhibit a distinctly human capacity for conscious self-reflection. While self-reflection is a capacity the I-me distinction is meant to affirm, the distinction actually rends it asunder. If the I is so totally other than the me, then when the I reflects on the me, it is no longer reflecting on itself but on something other than itself. For Sartre and the Upanishads especially, what the I reflects on is not the self but a false self, a simulacrum.

Not even Mead's more moderate formulation of the I-me distinction escapes this dilemma. Is the I conscious of itself or just the me? Either the I has a reflexive "blind spot" of its own or the original problem just resurfaces, threatening infinite regress.[11] Clearly the I and the me cannot be so divorced without compromising what is meant by genuine self-reflection. For genuine self-reflection, what we need is not a transcendental I reflecting on a me but a me reflecting on a me.

Given the philosophical problems associated with the I-me distinction, it becomes vulnerable to its complete opposite. Lying but a hair's breadth away from this humanist conception of self is its antihumanist twin. Begin with the I-me distinction and merely deny that there is any I beyond the me, merely deny the existence of any kind of disembodied, transcendental ego. We then end up as nothing but a me. As the I-me distinction has been formulated, this means we are nothing other than our various social performances. When the show is over and we look behind the curtain, we find no one there.

We thus arrive at postmodernism's antihumanist explanation for why my respondents cannot articulate who they are. My respondents cannot identify their selves because they have no selves. Selfhood is just an illusion. This view might seem to coincide with the Upanishads, but the humanist Upanishads affirm a true self that is identical with the no-self self of the universe. Contemporary anti-humanism does not. Contemporary antihumanism is thus a kind of deprived Hinduism in which only false, illusory selves exist. In the absence of any real selves, the entire ground of moral significance collapses into nihilism.

Postmodernist antihumanism originated in France, which since 1968 has been wrestling with Sartre's ghost. It was from French thought, preoccupied with postmodernity, that we first heard the announcements of "the death of man," "the dissolution of the self," "the disappearance of the actor." What began with French post-structuralists and deconstructionists is now being celebrated throughout America's academic disciplines, from literary theory and history to anthropology and sociology. Outside the academy, the postmodernist denial of identity has paradoxically become the theoretical expression of political identity movements.[12]

It was in the early seventies that the postmodernist current first reached our shores in the work of the French Marxist philosopher Louis Althusser. Althusser explicitly declared Marxism "an antihumanism." Althusser was intent on creating a Marxist theory from which all traces of human agency were expunged. According to Althusser, capitalism is an autonomous mechanism operating on its own without input from human actors.[13]

Human actors are, according to Althusser, merely the placeholders of social positions, just the "carriers" of social structure. There is no unified human agent. Instead, each one of us is a different illusory person in each social position we occupy. The illusion of a unified self is, according to Althusser, a trick of language. The trick originates with our names. Althusser maintained that it is because we are bestowed with names by which we are "hailed" that we come to think of ourselves as coherent subjects of action. It is a trick society employs to allow itself to operate. The true agent is no longer human beings but society itself.

Althusser's emphasis on language is shared by all the postmodernists. For the postmodernists, language is no longer a tool humans employ for social cooperation but an autonomous mechanism that operates according to its own logic. We are but the nodes, Jacques Derrida tells us, through which language autonomously passes. Thus, language is not the vehicle through which humans become persons but rather something totally other from us, which only fools us into thinking we are selves.[14]

Taking on the I-me distinction directly, the psychoanalyst Jacques Lacan argues that the I can never truly be self-conscious of the me as the me is in and of itself because the I can grasp the me only through the imposition of linguistic categories. Separated thus by the gulf of language, the prelinguistic me will always elude the grasp of the I. Accordingly, the very possibility of self-reflection fractures.[15]

The I itself, Lacan argues, is a linguistic chimera. According to Lacan, it is not just through our having names that language fools us into supposing we have coherent identities. Language is replete with "subject positions," which we discursively adopt. We adopt the subject position of the speaker or the spoken to. As if we were really there, we refer to ourselves in discourse through the pronouns *me, myself,* and *I*.[16]

According to Michel Foucault, the very idea of our being coherent identities coalesced only recently with the Enlightenment. Michel Foucault is the historian of the postmodernist movement. We become convinced we have selves, Foucault argues, only because of the rise of vast discourses positing a self, discourses associated with such institutions as clinics, prisons, and the Catholic confessional. In the Catholic confessional, for example, a whole vocabulary arises, naming previously nonexistent, secret, interior states. As Catholic penitents confess these secrets out of their depths, they mistakenly come to accept the depths of the soul as something already there before the disciplinary apparatus was erected, and as with the confessional, so with prisons, schools, and clinics. The expansion of the self is actually a modern by-product of advancing disciplinary technologies. Selfhood is, accordingly, a symptom of culturally diffuse power arrangements.[17]

Without a "true" or "core" self, our identities effectively become congeries of social roles and personae. Since our social roles and personae are often disparate, our identities lose their coherence. A heterosexual black male in Jamaica—my respondent Veet Raj, for example—will find it difficult to locate himself coherently. In terms of race and nationality, he can count himself among the oppressed. In terms of gender and sexual orientation, he is numbered with the oppressors. Our identities are consequently fragmented and fluid.[18]

Such fragmentation is particularly acute in a postmodern world in which, in contrast with traditional society, we function as so many different personae in ever multiplying circles of social interaction. As our circles of social involvement proliferate, we reach the stage of the "protean" or "saturated" self.[19] With one persona on the internet, another at political meetings, still others at home and office, it is no wonder that Gilles Deleuze and Felix Guattari cite the schizophrenic as the postmodern emblem of self.[20] Socially fragmented as we are, we find ourselves no longer speaking with a single voice. Instead, at the end of the second millennium, we are like the Gadarene demoniac encountered by Jesus: "My name is Legion: for we are many."[21]

Postmodernism does not just describe this ghastly postmodern condition. It also seems to celebrate it as reflective of the actual, transhistorical nature of the self. Strangely, this antihumanist conception of self appeals to many in the women's movement, the gay and lesbian movements, and other movements associated with political identity.[22] These movements are supposed to be liberating. Yet, with a postmodern conception of self, one wonders who or what is to be liberated. Subject positions? One can well imagine liberating an oppressed person but not an oppressed social role.

Here is one place where a specifically religious voice can correct secular social science. When we respond to the moral claims of the oppressed, we do so because we encounter the oppressed other as a "thou," as a "who," a coherent self who addresses us. It is only in the context of what Martin Buber refers to as the "I-thou" relationship that we respond to the moral call of the other. Only a thou can address us with moral claims, and in response to that address, we are called to be thous ourselves, to respond equally, self to self.[23]

Contrary to Foucault, an appreciation of the I-thou relationship hardly had to await the Enlightenment. The parable of the good Samaritan was told and understood in the first century, and eight centuries before that the Upanishads were already wrestling with a surprisingly modern conception of self. Even before Descartes, thous were compassionately responding to other thous in distress.

The I-thou relationship is fundamental to the social being of the material creatures we are. We are creatures who live cooperatively, and language is largely a tool toward that end. The exorbitant heights to which postmodernists elevate language cannot itself account for the origin of language.[24] Language could have evolved only because of the cooperative advantage it conferred. Conceptually, linguistic cooperation implies human actors using language to coordinate their actions.

Coordination in turn requires an ability to reliably specify our own future actions on the basis of our self-knowledge of our own mental states.

A singular something commits to showing up at the office every day, and sure enough, that singular something does indeed show up. What is this something if not a self? By reference to their own mental states, selves can evidently predict their own behavior better than any social theory can. Language and selfhood cannot be as separate as postmodernist theory maintains.

Indeed, if language is a means of communication among cooperating selves, it is also more than that. It is through language that we become selves in the first place. Language is not just a means to express thoughts we might have independently. The more complex thoughts unique to humans are possible only once we have language. Not even in our own minds, for example, can we wonder what is moral to do without the language to formulate morality.

Language is the whole basis of our human self-consciousness. Although what it means for us to be self-conscious can lead to tortured formulations, at one level it is very simple. At one level, self-consciousness is simply our linguistic ability to identify for others—and ourselves—both our actions and the mental states that motivate us to perform them.[25] We become able to do this by being raised in a community of language users. Our acquisition of language is what elevates us beyond the mere consciousness of animals to fully self-conscious selfhood.

Lacan's putative dilemma therefore never arises. There is no prelinguistic me, unalterably separated by language from a prelinguistic I. Instead, the selves we become are thoroughly linguistic in the first place.

I have been speaking of our *being* selves rather than of our *having* selves. The self is not some interior entity inside us, some "ghost in the machine." A self is not something we possess but something we bodily become. As Emile Durkheim noted long ago, socialization is the process through which selfhood becomes "incarnated and individualized in each one of us."[26] Socialization is the process through which God has evidently chosen to make us souls.

Formulations like the I-me distinction are highly misleading. They have misled both humanism and antihumanism into debating the twin sides of an untenably idealist position. Both have looked inside our bodies to find the self. Humanists claim to find there a unitary self, and antihumanists claim to have found instead a whole crowd of interior selves. Both idealistically treat the self as some ghostly entity inside us. From a more materialist perspective, however, selves—as opposed to self-concepts—are not something we possess but something we are bodily.

All the confusion disappears if we just come to think of the self as another word for person. A person is a material being that exhibits self-conscious behavior. This self-conscious behavior is what makes the material being not just a material being but also a self. Thus, a self is a person and a person is a self. Just as persons occupy the same space as their bodies, so do selves.[27]

One major virtue of equating selves with incarnate persons is that it solves at a stroke the referential problem of consciousness that plagues the I-me distinction. It is the singular, incarnate person who has mental states and the same incarnate person who, able to report those mental states, thereby displays what we mean by self-consciousness. Instead of an I reflecting on something it is not, we have rather a person self-consciously reflecting on the person he or she is.

We have been speaking here of the concept of self, which is different from our individual self concepts. Although postmodernist philosophy generally confuses the two, they must be kept distinct. It is one thing to suggest that our self concepts today are fragmentary or weak. Whether or not that is so is an empirical question. It is quite another matter to deny that human beings are selves ontologically or in reality. That claim is philosophical rather than empirical.

To the extent that postmodernism denies not just the vibrancy of contemporary self-identities but also the very concept of selfhood, it collapses into conceptual incoherence. Without at least the concept of self, postmodernism forfeits all ability to conceptualize self-consciousness. It cannot account for the ways we worry about ourselves, monitor ourselves, and plan our own futures, all of which imply a self that is monitored, worried about, and planned for. Nor can postmodernism accommodate human action, since action conceptually implies an actor. Thus, although postmodernists like to speak of our behavior being strategically managed, the very concept of strategic management implies a strategic manager. Conceptually, postmodernism cannot have one without the other.

More fundamentally, in its denial of any center of conscious experience, postmodern theory makes conceptual orphans of feelings, thoughts, experiences, desires, beliefs, and intentions. Although postmodern philosophy fails completely to notice, such mental phenomena cannot be unmoored. For mental states to be individuated, for them even to be conceptualized at all, they must be attached, must belong to some specific center of experience.[28]

In the course of my interviews, there is amusement, there is recollection. There is wonderment about who we really are. These mental states do not float in the air.[29] They all belong to specific personal identities. It is Jason Fishman who laughs with me. It is Sister Marge who recalls a friend. It is Iris Barbuda who wonders who she really is.

In each case, who is it experiencing these emotions? Is it only one of Iris Barbuda's many ego-identifications that does the wondering while the others are complacent? Is it just one of Jason Fishman's many personae who finds my questions funny? Is it only a subject position Sister Marge adopts and not Sister Marge herself who is moved by a remembrance?

Just to raise such questions is to provide their answers. Emotions, feelings, and other mental states are coherently ascribed neither to person-parts nor to person phases, aspects, positions, or performances but to persons themselves. Persons and their mental states can be defined only in relation to each other. Just as what it means to be a person is virtually defined by the range of mental states attributable to persons, those mental states have meaning only as predicates of persons. If, then, we cannot describe the social world without reference to experiences, emotions, feelings, and myriad other mental states, we cannot do conceptually without the centers of experience to which such mental states are attached. As thinking, feeling subjects of experience, our identities as incarnate persons cannot be denied.

BACK TO THE CATERPILLAR'S QUESTION

We have come a long way to recover a coherent concept of identity, a concept of identity as embodied persons. Yet, what we have recovered is only the ontological concept of identity and not our own phenomenological sense of identity. Thus, in recovering our ontological identity, we have also recovered our initial problem as well: Why are Alice and my respondents unable to articulate who they are? If there really is such a thing as our own personal identity, why is it so difficult for us to describe it?

It may well be that while postmodern thought is incoherent as an ontology of the self, it is nevertheless accurate as a description of the phenomenological state of the self at the turn of the millennium.[30] While we remain coherent selves ontologically, we may not experience ourselves as such. Indeed, at the turn of the second millennium, we do appear to find ourselves utterly without a vocabulary of the self, without a way of talking about who we are. By the end of the twentieth century, our experienced sense of self does appear weak. As a description of that weakness, the label "postmodernity" is not inapt.

Why should our sense of self be so weak at this time? Among the people I interviewed, we find perhaps one clue. There was at least one type of person who had a very clear sense of self, a type of person who could answer my questions deeply. If you ask these people who they are, they will tell you immediately that they are children of God or disciples of Jesus Christ. I am speaking of Christian fundamentalists.

Although my conversation with two fundamentalists, Matt Bennett and John Wasserman, was typical, they themselves are not. Both in their early twenties, Matt had majored in "appropriate technology"— engineering suitable for the Third World. He has already applied what he learned in Guatemala and Ghana and has also been to Peru, where he helped run Bible studies. John has also been abroad—to Zambia, where he worked with missionaries. He is now employed by the Billy Graham Crusade.

Matt and John live together with five other Christians in a collectively owned community house. Although the community members belong to a conservative Presbyterian church in the suburbs, the house itself is in the Philadelphia inner city. The oldest resident, Frank, is thirty-one and in college had majored in sociology and urban studies. He is now completing a divinity degree. In the community's terms, Frank is the "most mature" Christian and in that sense the leader. The others try to learn from him.

There are several engineers in the house, which the community is rehabilitating itself. One of the rehabilitated rooms is a chapel, simple but beautiful. All sleep together in one large room with triple-deck bunk beds. There are two bathrooms, a large kitchen, and two large living-room spaces filled with books, homey furniture, and attractive photographs from travels abroad. The large and impressive deck outside has already been redone. The group has talked about buying and rehabilitating other houses in this disadvantaged area with the intention of renting them out for a "fair" price and bringing in revenue at the same time.

All in the house pool their money so that not all of them need to be engaged in paid employment at the same time. Instead, some can thereby be freed for schooling or ministry of various kinds. The group lives simply, and when I expressed pleasant surprise at the set-up, Matt welcomed me to "Utopia."

Delighted with my interest in them, Matt and John had invited me to dinner for this interview. We sang a Christmas carol and said a prayer before sitting down to a simple but pleasant meal. The community buys its food in bulk and tries to cut costs in both food and household maintenance so as to develop a surplus that can be shared with the poor. For all the community members, a simple, non-materialistic lifestyle is very important.

After dinner, we conduct our interview. "Now," I say, "I have some questions on identity. Who are you? How would you define yourselves?"

John answers first. "The only way to define myself is as a follower of Christ. And just anything else I think of is…actually by far secondary to that."

Matt nods. "Yeah. A son of God. First, because I am created by God. Second, because I've been redeemed, saved from rebelling against God. So now I'm really following him and have been re-adopted into his family. I'm part of a family of God."

"Okay," I laugh. "I expected you guys to say that. I mean, I'm happy you said it. Let me just follow up, though. What makes you…I asked you to define yourselves. But who are you? You're a Child of God, a follower of Christ."

I look from one to the other. "If you're both that, what makes you two different? You're not the same person."

They both smile. John answers. "Okay. I mean, there's two pieces to that. First is that in one very real sense, I really am very much like Matt and very much unlike those who would not identify themselves as followers of Christ. So, in a very basic sense, I very much agree with that and say, 'Yeah.'

"The fact that both of us give a similar answer, and you might say, 'Well, jeez, you're…that makes it sound like you're the same person.'"

He laughs and continues. "I'd say, 'Yeah.' In another sense, Matt and I are much different in many ways. In terms of some of the things we like to do, the types of personality we have, some of the gifts. I mean, God does give different types of gifts to different people for different tasks. In that sense, I would define myself as someone who has been gifted in terms of administration, one that very much has a burden for students and ministering to them, working with them. So in some of those things, I am somewhat different from Matt. But that's more secondary. I'm a follower of Christ, and Christ has gifted me slightly differently than, say, Matthew."

"Now, wait. Bear with me here."

"Okay. Sure."

"What would you like to see written on your tombstone that sort of summarizes your life? Presuming you will have a tombstone."

John is right with me. "No, right. right. There's two answers to that. I'll answer your question and then the deeper one.

"I think what I'd like on my tombstone would be something to the effect of 'Here's someone who has loved Christ and has been an exemplary model.'

" More important than my tombstone, though...If I've really done that, my tombstone could end up being that somebody's crucified me and doesn't care what's on my tombstone. In that case, I would say, the more important piece that underlies your question is that at the end of my life what I'd really want to hear is Christ say, 'Well done, good and faithful servant.'"

I'm impressed with this answer and nod solemnly. I then turn to Matt and laugh. "You're not going to say the same thing. Are you?"

"I was going to attempt to say something like, 'My tombstone would say that they could see Christ in me.' It has to do with that."

"Hmm." I nod. "These are good answers."

"Do you want me to talk about that?"

"Yeah!"

"All right, identity again. Something I've learned more recently is to be content with this idea that you don't have to have an individual identity that's primary. And I think that's the popular thing, especially in America: to find yourself, figure out who you really are, to express yourself and things like that. So ultimately that is not as important.

"First, it is important just to submit to Christ and be like him. To identify yourself in the community of Christians and in the body of Christ. To put down pride, which might really be the thing that motivates people to put themselves forward or try to have their self-identity. I mean, there are plenty of things that make me unique and things I like to do; things that describe my personality and the gifts that I have; things I want to do with my life; but ultimately I don't want those to be the things that form my identity, but just to be content to be united with Christ."

John and Matt may not be typical fundamentalists, but the articulateness of their answers does not distinguish them from other fundamentalists I interviewed. For example, Brad Caldwell, young and only recently "born again," was quite ready for my tombstone question.

" Man, it just struck me because I'm reading a book that kind of...yeah, I mean, that kind of brought that question forward, and I wrote some stuff down: 'What would you want to have on your tombstone?' And that's what I'm trying to think of...I thought I had it with me, but I don't."

"Oh?"

"I guess, trying to remember, what I wrote down is something like, 'A man who was saved by grace, a man who knew God's grace, a man who…yeah…lived by the joy and the peace that only God's great grace could offer.' It was something like that I wrote down."

"So who are you?"

"Who am I?" Brad coughs. "I mean, my identity? What?"

"That's what I was asking."

" My identity is found in the person of Jesus Christ. I would say I'm a person who is still far from as perfect as Christ, but I'm a person who is imperfect, and there's still sin in my life that is yet to be…that I still struggle with and all. But who I am, I mean…I place…I guess, who I am…my identity is placed in Jesus Christ. That's where I place my security. That's where I find myself. I'm not sure if you're looking for different characteristics of who I am or…"

I assure Brad that he is indeed telling me what I am asking to hear. We academics are used to disparaging the intelligence of fundamentalists. I myself am neither a fundamentalist nor uniformly sympathetic to fundamentalism. Elsewhere, for example, I have rather severely criticized the Christian right.[31] Yet, there is no gainsaying the fact. When it comes to matters of identity, there is in the answers I receive from fundamentalists a depth and articulateness that is generally lacking from the answers I receive from those in what we think of as the mainstream of American culture. If nothing else, this articulateness is indicated by the more extended discussion on identity it is possible to have with fundamentalists.

The difference in responses is not due to education. Admittedly, in contrast with some of my respondents, the fundamentalists do have college degrees. Yet, even compared with other college graduates, the fundamentalists' answers tend to be deeper. They tend to be deeper even than the answers of others with postgraduate degrees.

Nor is the difference due simply to the involvement of the fundamentalists in a community or movement, although, I suspect, that is part of what makes the difference. As political activists, Jason Fishman and Lawrence Patterson also belong to movements or communities. If I ask either of them questions about political economy in general or capitalism in particular, I will receive very sophisticated and penetrating answers. They are, however, much less assured when it comes to describing their own identities. In contrast, the fundamentalists belong to very specific kinds of communities that offer a vocabulary for identity construction.

It is not only fundamentalists who offer me easy answers about identity. Others on the spiritual margins of postmodern culture, likewise, seem to have a more profound sense of who they are—my Sannyasins, for example. When I ask Prem Prakash what he would like to see written on his tombstone, he, like the fundamentalists, is more than prepared for my question.

"It's interesting you should ask. I want to be cremated, but anyway—or buried at sea and let the fish enjoy it."

Prem then gets a bell from his shelf and holds it with the opening up. "You know, a bell can be a cup. If you fill it up...let's say one person, let's say the person's meant to be a bell, but his parents and everybody says, 'You're a beautiful container. You should be a cup.' You know. And he lets people fill him up that way. And whether it's like this or it contains a liquid, it doesn't have the sound it was meant to have.

"And I was writing something and getting more into writing poetry. Near the end of the poem, it says I'm...my tombstone when I'm dead should read, 'Let it never be said that he never rang.'"

I nod solemnly.

"If I'm meant to be this" —Prem turns the bell over so that it is back to being a bell, then flips the bell so that it is once again a cup— "and not this thing filled that everybody else says I should be." Prem wants to be what he was meant to be, his authentic self.

Closer to the cultural mainstream, Hannah Gottlieb also has a clear sense of personal identity. Hannah is the director of religious education at a Conservative Jewish synagogue in the suburbs.[32] Her voice resonates with a quiet, almost sensual spirituality that cannot be conveyed on paper. Hannah's words will have to speak for themselves.

"What," I ask her, "does Judaism mean to you? What does it mean to be Jewish?"

"It defines everything I touch...and think...and believe...and do. And that is what Judaism is. It's both a link with tradition...and it's also a window opening countless opportunities for interpretation. Because as much as Judaism has its really strong tradition, you could ask a question and get thirty answers to the same question, which allows me, today, to root myself in tradition, pick of the thirty, and then know that I am also capable of adding my own layer: thirty-one."

"So it's alive."

"Very alive. I hear the voices very...I hear lots of voices, and one of the voices I hear is the voice of tradition, guiding me in what I do."

I ask Hannah what the other voices are that she hears.

"I hear my mother. My mother died when she was forty-two and I was nineteen. She is alive and well with me. Very much she is with me, and so I very much believe that souls live on. I mentioned my grandmother and the women before me. I very much feel connected to the women, the Jewish women who came before me—my grandmother and my great-grandmother. I very much feel their strength and their life force. What they accomplished in their lives is with me. I hear my husband. I hear the rabbis. I hear lots and lots of voices."

The postmodernists maintain that ours is an age without "metanarratives," an age without overarching schemes of meaning or tradition within which to place ourselves. That may be true for many today, but in people like Hannah Gottlieb, a communally shared, historical quest for meaning lives on. In them, the great journey continues. I ask Hannah if she ever thinks about what she might like written on her tombstone.

"Yes!" she exclaims, leaning forward for emphasis.

"You do?"

"No," she laughs. "That's the answer."

"Yes?" I laugh too. "What does that *mean?*"

Hannah laughs again. "No, I've never thought about it. I know that yes, I want to be able to say 'I lived!' That's very important to me. 'Yes!' I experienced it. I do a zillion things at once, and people often say to me, 'Hannah, I don't know how you can do all you do and beh, beh, beh.' I do it because I need it and I want it and it's really important. It's just experiencing. I want to know life. I want to feel it and experience it and that's what I do. And I have four sons. And all this meaning business...you know...it's absolutely integral with that I'm the mother of four sons and I have a family and a husband and I'm always growing and learning. It is like this...that's how I feel. Like, I go through...I'm experiencing life, and that's really important."

In one respect, Hannah's response thus far differs little from those of others who also enjoy life. In another respect, however, Hannah's passion already accords a depth and sanctity to life that reflect a very Jewish affirmation of our existence. According to Friedrich Nietzsche's doctrine of the "eternal return," we should each live our lives in such a way that we could positively affirm what we have done should we have to relive each moment of our lives countless times.[33] Hannah's cosmic "Yes!" is precisely such an affirmation. As she continues, Hannah's response assumes further cosmic dimensions.

"But it's not only just to be this selfish...you know, I'm not just taking. It's all connected to...these are the Jewish words: Becoming One. That's the Jewish vocabulary.

"'Hear, O, Israel, the Lord, our God, the Lord is One.' What does that mean? It means that I can become One. And the promise we offer the kids—the possibility; I won't say promise—the possibility that we offer is that there's a way to become One. And that way is communion: communion with God, communion with self, and communion with community.

"And that's what I'm trying to achieve. So there are lots of pieces: my family, my writing, my learning. It's all helping me, I think, to become One. And that might be becoming true to myself...oh...becoming One, becoming whole."

I stop Hannah for clarification. "Do you mean this in two senses: whole yourself—One—an integrated person, yourself? And also One with the world? Okay, maybe three senses. And becoming One with God?"

Hannah nods vigorously at each one of these questions. She does in fact mean wholeness in all three senses. Cosmic Oneness or wholeness is the moral project of her life: *Tikkun olam*, rebuilding the whole of our broken world.

What distinguishes the fundamentalists, the Sannyasins, and Hannah Gottlieb is that they all locate their identities within cosmic dimensions. They fix their identities within a moral space and a metaphysical space that transcend locale. They fix their identities in relation to an "axis mundi," a nonarbitrary centerpoint of the cosmos, in terms of which their identities are meaningfully grounded in the cosmos itself. In the cosmos itself, their identities have a meaningful place.

To be known and identified by the cosmos itself is the ultimate ground of identity. To be so identified is an aspiration exemplified in Thornton Wilder's play *Our Town*. In the course of that play, one of the characters tells of a letter her friend, Jane Crofut, received from her former minister in another town. The envelope arrives with an unusual address:

Jane Crofut
The Crofut Farm
Grover's Corners
Sutton County
New Hampshire
United States of America
Continent of North America
Western Hemisphere

Earth
The Solar System
The Universe
The Mind of God[34]

With that address, the minister's letter surely will reach its destination even if, as many physicists now maintain, our universe is but one of countless others. By addressing his letter this way, the minister reassures the recently displaced Jane Crofut that she can never truly lose her place in the cosmos. Her identity will always be known. We are ever addressed by what Buber calls the "Eternal Thou."[35]

It is no wonder that as long as sociologists remain fixed on our identifications in social space they find only fragmented identities. Nor is it any wonder that as long as ordinary people themselves remain fixated on social space, they will find themselves unable to experience themselves as coherent wholes. The social spaces we inhabit are too contingent, too fragmented, and too disconnected to provide a global sense of self. By itself social space does not sufficiently ground who we are. That perhaps is a realization Alice came to as she confronted the Caterpillar.

Beyond social space, Christian fundamentalists, in their commitment to Jesus, orient themselves in relation to a moral purpose, a life-long moral project. So do the Sannyasins in relation to awakening and Hannah Gottlieb in relation to Oneness. Possession of such moral projects does not necessarily make anyone any more moral than anyone else. Indeed, the life of the butler Stevens was likewise oriented by a moral purpose, and we have already seen that his life was morally flawed. Much depends on the moral project one adopts and how one pursues it.

Nevertheless, there is something distinctive about the moral purposefulness of the fundamentalists, the Sannyasins, Hannah Gottlieb—and even Stevens. For them, morality is not just a matter of proper procedures, a matter of moral ways to pursue morally neutral ends, ends that are not themselves either moral or immoral but just desired. For such people, it is not just how they pursue their goals that is moral or immoral. Instead, they have life goals that, whatever we may think of them, encompass a moral vision. It is very clear that these individuals define themselves within what Charles Taylor refers to as a space, the horizons of which are marked by alternative moral purposes. If, as a philosopher, Taylor makes the point in the abstract, we begin to see here how it empirically applies.

Clearly the fundamentalists, the Sannyasins, and Hannah Gottlieb are all religious. They are all religious in a way that is not rote. They have penetrated to the heart of their different religious traditions and found there a vision of the good by which their lives are grasped. Insofar as each of their lives is oriented toward their respective visions of the good, they experience a unity of purpose that, as Hannah Gottlieb puts it, offers their identities the possibility of unification.

It is not exclusively religion that provides this kind of purpose. Indeed, as we will see, some of the other people I interviewed—Jason Fishman and Lawrence Patterson, for example—also possess a life-encompassing unity of purpose. Jason Fishman and Lawrence Patterson are committed activists, drawn to dedicating their lives to a vision of a just society.

There is, however, yet another trait that distinguishes the fundamentalists, the Sannyasins, and Hannah Gottlieb. By virtue of their religious traditions, their moral purposes are metaphysically grounded. Their purposes arise cosmogonically from what each sees as the very nature of the cosmos. Their identities thus assume a position not just in moral space but in metaphysical space as well.

Again, it is not only religion that can serve this function, although perhaps whenever our understanding begins to approach ultimate matters, we ineluctably enter a realm that borders on religious philosophy. If religion is not the only way to ground ourselves metaphysically, it is at least the purview of religion to offer a life-encompassing vision of the good and a vocabulary through which to understand and reflect on it metaphysically. Such a distinct vocabulary may be more spiritually necessary than our secular age acknowledges.

I said earlier that the fundamentalists and the Sannyasins may provide a clue as to why it is so difficult today to articulate who we are, that they may provide a clue as to a language of self we have lost. Like Hannah Gottlieb as well, the Sannyasins and the virtually premodern fundamentalists still occupy a moral space and a metaphysical space in which they can confidently identify who they are. It may take moral space and metaphysical space to do that. Yet it may well be precisely a strong sense of moral space and metaphysical space that has disappeared for many of us at the turn of the millennium. This absence is what the postmodernists mean by the end of metanarratives.

As a description of this predicament, the label *postmodernity* may again be apt. By the turn of the millennium, both moral space and metaphysical space seem to have receded. If we require those spaces to identify ourselves fully, then it may not be surprising if many of us no longer know who we are. A century that at its midpoint declared the death of God ends by proclaiming the death of the self, an intellectual journey, as it were, from deicide to suicide. We need to push our investigation further.

CHAPTER 2

The Further Geography of the Soul

"All right," said Deep Thought. The Answer to the Great Question..."

"Yes!"

"Of Life, the Universe and Everything..." said Deep Thought.

"Yes...!"

"is..."

"Yes...!!!...?"

"Forty-two," said Deep Thought, with infinite majesty and calm."

—*Douglas Adams,* The Hitchhiker's Guide to the Galaxy

In chapter one, we observed that sociologists and the lay public both tend to situate identity entirely in social space. By the end of the chapter, however, we began to suspect that truly to know who we are, it is insufficient to remain in social space. Instead, as Charles Taylor argues, our selves also acquire their identities in moral space and metaphysical space. Taylor's point is abstract and philosophical. As such, it remains unassimilated, either by sociologists or by lay people concerned with their own identities. We need to see how such philosophical constructs apply empirically to the concrete details of lived experience. Here, then, let us depart from the usual sociological approach to identity and explore the further geography of the soul: moral space, metaphysical space, and critical space.

Moral space is where we find moral purpose, but moral purpose must be emotionally and conceptually grounded in some larger worldview. Our worldviews are the domain of metaphysical space. Because worldviews make claims about what is, they ineluctably raise questions of truth. These move us into the space of critical argument. In each of these landscapes of the soul, we have a distinct identity.

It is perhaps part of the condition of postmodernity that in metaphysical space and critical space, most of us have only null identities. We so lack any articulated worldview that arguments about the cosmos strike us as ponderously irrelevant. Today, we shy away from thinking cosmically. In fact, we tend actively, through humor, to distance ourselves from cosmic concerns. What is the meaning of life? In answer, we quote Douglas Adams or Monty Python and laugh. Whereas the existentialists engaged seriously with the moral implications of meaninglessness, for many of us today, the very question of life's meaning is no more than a joke. Yet, while the jokes are certainly funny, something larger is at stake. After the laughter dies, we do well to consider the vocabularies and the emotions we continue to lack.

MORAL SPACE

Charles Dickens's *A Christmas Carol* opens with a portrait of the miser Ebenezer Scrooge. Scrooge's life revolves around money. In fact, Scrooge is an ideal type, personifying the ethos Max Weber referred to as "the spirit of capitalism."[1] For Scrooge, the making of money, accumulation is a moral end in itself. Scrooge does not accumulate in order to spend. Rather, we discover, he lives quite frugally.

For Scrooge, accumulation—not enjoyment—is the purpose of life. Anything that distracts us from that purpose, anything—like Christmas—that threatens productive efficiency is immoral.[2] Thus, Scrooge contemptuously dismisses the poor as so much surplus population. They deserve not charity but poorhouses and debtors' prisons. Accumulation matters; people do not.

Because emotions can be altered by altered beliefs, they often can be dissipated through argument. When, however, our emotional attachment is to an ultimate concern, argument alone may not prevail against it. Then, as in the case of Scrooge, what is required is an emotional exorcism.

Scrooge receives such an exorcism when he is visited by three ghosts one Christmas Eve. The three ghosts do not engage Scrooge in ethical debate. Their strategy instead is to reawaken in Scrooge a panoply of emotions he has managed to stifle, emotions such as loneliness, sorrow, joy, and social solidarity. In particular, Scrooge is brought face to face with the poor he has dismissed as surplus population. Scrooge does not learn any new facts, but he does come to appreciate the import of the facts. The facts finally come to matter to him.

There is, as Aristotle observed, a distinction between an emotional way of knowing and a way of knowing that is only cognitive.[3] When we know something emotionally, we know in a way that engages us and orients us toward what is known. Our emotions are orientations of care toward the world and, as such, judgments of the heart, practical judgments by which we state with our lives how it is we personally stand in relation to the objects of our emotions.[4]

By the time the ghosts are done with him, Scrooge is no longer a detached observer of poverty. He comes to know poverty in a way that finally orients him toward it. The knowledge Scrooge acquires is knowledge he now feels. Thus, by experiencing emotions beyond its compass, Scrooge starts to detach himself from accumulation as an ultimate concern.

Ultimately effective in Scrooge's reclamation is the displacement of his old vision by a new one. His new, life-guiding vision is an idealized vision of Christmas. Along with the Moslem Ramadan and the Jewish high holidays, Christmas is one of the few occasions in modern life when profane time is interrupted by sacred time, a time when, if it so affects us, it is still possible to experience ourselves transported to what Eliade calls *illo tempore*, the time of aboriginal myth.[5] Sacred festivals like Christmas do not simply commemorate the mythic past. They reinaugurate it in feelings of transcendence. For those to whom the Christmas festival speaks, it is as if shepherds once again sing and angels walk the earth. Unlike profane time, sacred time is not linear but recoverable, repeatable. It is not superseded or lost. It is the experience of eternity.

Ideally, then, at Christmas, profane existence is transcended. The profane market economy is replaced by a moral economy of the gift. Christmas is a time of excess and largesse. The earth's bounty is celebrated by parties and feasts. People "shop 'till they drop." Status distinctions disappear or are reversed as those of higher social station bestow gifts on those of lower. The family unit is thus enlarged. Even the poor and neglected are to be welcomed back into the momentary realization of the "cosmic communitas," the cosmic community.[6]

Sacred time has emotional power, and it is this emotional power that Christmas exerts on Scrooge. As it does, Scrooge is ethically transformed. This transformation has nothing to do with utilitarianism or deontology or any other form of secular reason that preoccupies professional philosophers. Scrooge's ethical transformation is religious. It is cosmogonic. It is emotional.

In coming to love ultimately a different good from the one he had loved ultimately before, Scrooge's phenomenological identity changes. We miss the point of *A Christmas Carol* if we just think that Scrooge had a selfish personality before the ghostly visitations and came to have an unselfish personality afterwards. What changed was not Scrooge's personality per se. What changed was Scrooge's ultimate concern, the moral purpose by which he is emotionally grasped.

In moral space, our identities are arrows that point toward one or another vision of the good. In moral space, we are what we stand for. In these terms, I am one who considers such and such important. I am engaged in this life project. I am embarked on that quest. My life points in that moral direction.[7]

There is an ineluctable connection between selfhood and morality, between who we are and what we take to be the good. Scrooge had a vision of the good before the ghosts arrived. The good for him was money and accumulation. As we know what had significance for him, what had importance, and what was trivial, we know who Scrooge was as an identity.

We likewise know who Scrooge became after the ghostly visitations. When his moral compass shifted so as to point now to Christmas, Scrooge became someone new, someone so new that his acquaintances thought he had lost his mind, that he was not himself. It was the moral significance Scrooge attached to things that had changed. What had been morally significant to him before became insignificant, and what had seemed trivial before now assumed central moral importance. With respect to his orientation in moral space, Scrooge truly was no longer who he had been.

THE GOOD

In philosophical circles, talk of "the good" goes back to the Greeks, to Plato and Aristotle. For Plato and Aristotle, the good is that toward which our activities point, that for the sake of which we do anything. In the *Nicomachean Ethics*, Aristotle makes a distinction between instrumental and ultimate goals. Instrumental goals are goals we pursue not as ends in themselves but because they are a means to some further, ultimate goal.[8] Commodious living and survival are ultimate goals, undertaken not for some further purpose but as ends in themselves. Ultimate goals need not be so overarching, however. Merely dancing and enjoying a ball game are likewise ends in themselves, undertaken for no other purpose beyond themselves. Before the visitations, accumulation was such an ultimate goal for Scrooge.

According to Aristotle, any activity we undertake, we undertake either because it is good in itself and is hence an ultimate goal or because it serves something that is good in itself and is hence an instrumental goal. Being good involves loving something and not just doing something. In whatever activity we pursue, the good emotionally draws us toward itself and shapes us in its image.

By knowing what someone takes to be good in itself, we learn what that person stands for and who he or she is. Goods are thus another name for values, values that constitute who we are in moral space. They constitute who we are by being that toward which our lives aim, that which makes our lives worth living. In any life, there are multiple goods we might pursue as ends in themselves.

Herbert Bauman is a professional philosopher, specializing in metaphysics. In his mid-fifties, Herbert is one of the avowed atheists I interviewed. Herbert does sometimes attend synagogue, but he describes himself as more a "gastronomic" than a religious Jew, meaning he cares about Jewish culture but rejects Jewish religion. For Herbert, the good is simple: it is family.

"This question for me has a very easy answer, and it is not informed by any philosophical theory whatsoever. For me, there is one highest good: having healthy and happy children. I know with Cartesian certainty what my priorities are: children first; then my wife; then my brother and sister and mother; then perhaps my work; then perhaps listening to music; and then...everything else. But far and away, my children come first.

"We have childless friends who travel, dine out, attend theater, etc., far more than we do. But I am not jealous of them. Quite the contrary, I pity them. They cannot possibly have experienced the transcendent joy we derive from our children. There is nothing in this life that remotely approaches it.

"I know that Jewish mothers are expected (stereotypically) to talk this way. Okay, so I'm a male 'Jewish mother.' On the day our oldest child was born...the moment I laid my eyes on her, I had the most profound reaction of my life. Unfortunately...it was ineffable. It was at that moment I became a feminist."

Herbert's vision of family is in its own right an emotionally transcendent experience of the good and, as such, life-orienting. For Tom Brown, somewhat younger and single, the good turns out to be similar.

"Okay," I ask Tom, "What would you say your values are?"

"My values? Well, I think my most important value is to treat other people the way I like to be treated."

"Go ahead," I urge him.

"And I guess to live a good life."

"So what does it mean to treat other people the way you like to be treated? What way is that?"

"Well," Tom replies. "Respect. You know, not to intimidate, humiliate."

"And," I continue, "to lead a good life, what does that mean? What's a good life?"

"Well, treating other people the way you like to be treated is part of it."

"Okay."

"And..." Tom falls silent.

"And what?"

Tom remains silent. I try to urge him on. "Yeah. You can take your time. The tape's got two hours on it." Actually, Tom was probably not reassured hearing that I had up to two hours of conversation planned. I try again to put him at ease. "We won't take two hours."

"Oh."

"So what did I ask you?"

"Oh, you asked me, 'What are your values?'"

"Yeah," I say. "You told me. Oh, what...what else is, what is a good life? Part of it is treating other people with respect."

"Yeah."

"Is there any other part? Well, let me ask you a different question. What would you say...Philosophers sometimes talk about 'the good.' Assuming the good—what the good is can differ from person to person, for some people the good can be money, the good could be God, the good could be, you know, it could be anything."

"Mm-hm."

"You see what I mean by the good?"

"Uh-huh."

"What would be the...what would you define as the good? Like, what are the good things in life?"

Surprisingly, this more philosophical formulation of the question finally strikes a chord with Tom. "Oh. Family, friends. Friends...all right, that brings something else up about values. I value friendships."

"Friendships?"

"Highly."

"And why do you...what does friendship mean to you that you value it?"

"Well," Tom says, "an ability to confide things you wouldn't ordinarily confide to just anybody and not feel uncomfortable about it. The ability to tell somebody anything, things you wouldn't just tell other people."

"And you would say family, too?"

"Yeah."

I finally put Tom out of his misery. "Okay. So family, friendships, and treating people with respect?"

"Uh-huh. You know, just, yeah. If I had time to think more about it, I'd come up with other things."

Like Tom, Ellen Smith, an accountant and middle-level manager for a multinational corporation, has difficulty expressing the values she lives by. "I want to start," I say to her, "by asking you what you would say your values are. Everybody has a difficult time with this one, by the way, so I can ask it in different ways."

After a moment's reflection, Ellen responds. "I think, you mean things like you should treat people the way you want to be treated?"

"Okay."

"That kind of thing?"

"Yeah," I nod.

"Well, I mean, I guess I just don't know how to..."

I try to prompt her. "Is that..."

"Normal values," Ellen asserts.

"What are normal values?"

"Things that you should think are good."

"Like?"

"I think are good."

"Like what?"

"Like being honest and treating people the way I want to be treated and...I think you should work, work for what you get and, you know, try not to be stingy."

"Okay," I say.

"You know?"

I nod. "Normal values."

"Yeah."

Family, friendship, honesty, work, and the golden rule. As other studies confirm, these are fairly typical values people say are important to them.[9] More largely, Tom and Ellen's difficulty articulating values empirically supports Taylor's contention that modern culture emphasizes what is right or wrong to do as opposed to what is good or bad to value or be. This cultural inarticulateness about values bears a cost. If it is our values, our sense of what is good that constitutes who we are in moral space, then inarticulateness about values results in inarticulateness about self.[10]

THE HIERARCHY OF GOODS

The values Herbert, Tom, and Ellen cite as most important are all goods. Parenthood is a good. Friendship is a good. Work is a good. If there is a problem with these as ultimate values, it is hardly that they are not good in themselves. We might say that these particular values reflect American individualism, but that is merely to apply a label. It names but does not explain the condition. How did Americans end up with values we describe as individualistic? Individualism is itself a residue that reflects the absence of something else. What is that something else?

We begin to gain some purchase on the problem when we notice that what looks like individualism here is actually an ultimate concern with values that are not truly ultimate. As important as they are, friendship, family, and work all stand in need of moral grounding in prior, more fundamental values. They are all values that point to something more. The something more is what is absent.

Like Herbert Bauman, Hannah Gottieb considers parenthood a centrally important value. Yet, because Hannah is more emotionally connected with Jewish religious thought, she is able to place parenthood within a larger sense of purpose.

"I would say," Hannah tells me, "that no matter what I accomplish in life, the best...at the top of my resume, I want it to be that I'm a good mother to my children. That, to me, is the most important role I take.

"And to be a good mother—that means that I need to be a good person, and I need to be the best person I can be, and I need to keep growing, and it's not only that I meet the needs of my children."

I tell Hannah that I am struck by the connection she makes between being a good mother and being a good person. I ask her if she can elaborate.

"Oh, yes," Hannah replies emphatically. "I'm the role model for my kids! If I'm not a good person...I'll go out, and people will say, 'Your children are really *mensches*, your kids are really...' And they are. My kids have a really good...soul. And that didn't come from nowhere.

My husband is a good man, and I think of myself as a good person. We're not perfect, and that doesn't mean we don't do stuff we shouldn't, but that's something that is part of the backbone of our family: Being a *mensch*, being a good person, being fair.

"And living with four boys, we're always saying, 'Is it fair?' And whatever. But this notion of trying to be just and good is really an important backbone of our family. And obviously and as the rabbis teach, you can't say that to your children if you don't live it and do it."

Hannah's position on parenthood coincides with that of the ancient Greek philosophers. Plato and Aristotle thought deeply about friendship and family, which they too considered to be among life's most important goods. But family and friendship, the philosophers reflected, are morally contingent on prior values, values such as truth and justice, which are not specific to such relationships. Plato and Aristotle would have made the point along much the same lines as Hannah suggests. To be a good friend or a good parent, one first needs to be a good person.

Family and friends are extolled in modern society—and not just by the Christian right, which has made so much of the phrase, *family values*. Some commentators have argued that as we have become disconnected from what is more ultimate, the tendency today is to make the family itself an object of worship. Indeed, survey data reveal that for many today, holidays such as Christmas and Passover are less celebrations of religious meaning than of family togetherness. If so, then it is not the decline of family values that is the problem today but rather their apotheosis.[11]

Can an unjust person be a good parent? A good friend? The Greek philosophers would have said no. According to Plato and Aristotle, good friendships—and by extension good families—depend upon a prior commitment to ultimate good.

Judaism, Christianity, and Islam have always understood this, which is what makes the apotheosis of family values by the Christian right so peculiar. Jesus, himself, expected his message to divide rather than unite families—including his own. Did Jesus not demand that we go beyond our filial ties to follow him? "What credit is it to you," Jesus asked, "if you love only those who love you? Even the tax collectors do that."

Judaism makes the point even more starkly. One of the central stories in the Torah comes in the twenty-second chapter of Genesis. It is not only recited annually as part of the regular Jewish liturgy; it is the designated Scripture reading for the second day of Rosh Hashanah and it opens the morning prayer service each day. The story is of Abraham and Isaac.[12]

As the story goes, long after Abraham's wife, Sarah, had passed menopause, God granted the previously childless couple a son, Isaac. Subsequently, to test Abraham's devotion, God commands Abraham to take Isaac to a mountain top and there to make of Isaac a burnt offering to God. Abraham proceeds to follow God's command. Fortunately, at the last minute, convinced that Abraham's priorities are in order, God stays Abraham's hand and provides a ram for him to sacrifice instead. Through Isaac, the steadfast Abraham becomes the father of Israel.

Like many modern readers, I always found this story ghastly. I would be appalled if I believed for one minute that God ever commanded Abraham to make any such sacrifice. It is reassuring to learn, therefore, that the rabbinic tradition has also had problems with this central story of Judaism. Some rabbis even argue that by complying with such a command, Abraham actually failed God's test.[13]

There is, however, a certain interpretation that allows us to appreciate the story as a powerful metaphor affirming the very point we have been discussing. According to this interpretation, even that which we love most, even the family is morally subordinate to something higher—if not necessarily to some divine person, then at least to those personal attributes that the philosopher, Ludwig Feuerbach, described as divine: love, justice, and mercy.[14]

Poet Richard Lovelace puts it succinctly. In "To Lucasta, Going to the Wars," the poem's persona explains to his lover why he cannot remain at her side, why he must go away to fight the good fight. "I could not love thee, dear, so much," he tells her, "loved I not honor more." Even if for honor we substitute some other virtue, the point is the same as that made by Plato and Aristotle two and a half millennia ago; it is the same point made by Hannah Gottlieb today: our very capacity to love rightly and well is dependent on the prior values that make us a good person.

As much as the miserly Scrooge strikes us a character, his values predominate today as we begrudge the poor what little they receive in welfare. Macroeconomic growth or accumulation has become an end in itself—just as it was for Scrooge—quite apart from its cost to people. "The poor are not our business," we say. As a people, perhaps, we still need to hear the words spoken to Scrooge by Jacob Marley's ghost: "Mankind was my business."

If in moral space our selves are constituted by the goods or values to which we point, one danger is that the whole of our lives may point to goods that are too small. We may take as objects of our ultimate concern goods that are not truly ultimate. We then find ourselves without any moral motivation when larger issues command our attention. If who we are in moral space is not to be a truncated self, we must beware lest we draw our moral compass too narrowly.

Whatever it means to be a good person, it must include values that encompass the whole of life. The whole of life is not encompassed by friendship or family or even both taken together. They do not even encompass the whole of Herbert Bauman's life. Herbert was once an engaged political activist, and he became politically active once again subsequent to my interview with him. When I press him, he acknowledges that justice is very important to him. Yet he did not list social justice at all among his priorities. The reason, he speculates, is that he is used to thinking morally more in terms of obligations than in terms of "the good." As a philosopher, Herbert is of course familiar with the concept of the good, but he has not applied it to his own life. The contemporary moral focus on obligations obscures even from us the deeper values we hold.

Lawrence Patterson is more in touch with his activist side. Although he too places great importance on family, the vision of the good he articulates is more encompassing. Lawrence was raised by his grandmother in Chester, a city just to the south of Philadelphia known for shipping and manufacturing; Chester's shops, music and cinema once made it "the place to be" on Saturday night. With the deindustrialization that began in the late sixties, Chester is now the second poorest city in the United States. Wandering its downtown today, you might think you were in Chechnya; its bombed-out buildings make it appear worse than even the worst sections of Philadelphia.

As a poor African American raised in this milieu, it is not surprising that Lawrence's early life was troubled. With male role models who, as he puts it "were all drunk," Lawrence soon found himself strung out on heroin and sleeping on the street. He was finally caught in the process of robbing an ice cream parlor, at which point the police pinned another rap on him—a savings-and-loan robbery he says he did not commit. Convicted of both crimes, Lawrence served five years in prison.

During his prison years, a seed was planted in Lawrence's life that would eventually change it. Lawrence "walked the yard" with Jack Johnston, who introduced Lawrence to Marxism and dialectical materialism. Marxism explained to Lawrence why his people "were always getting their asses whipped." For Lawrence, Marxism became a metanarrative that both made sense of life and offered a vision of the good.

If it is not surprising that Lawrence ended up in prison, it is surprising how his later life turned out. Lawrence eventually got off drugs by attending a twelve-step program and became a drug counselor himself. He began working with troubled adolescents and joined the Socialist Workers Party, which sent him as a representative to the People's Republic of China. At the time I interviewed him, Lawrence had just completed a combined bachelor's and master's degree in social work and had been promoted to a managerial position in a nationwide drug counseling organization. Given Lawrence's lifelong struggle with himself, his answer to my first philosophical question is not surprising.

"What do I love most in life? Life. The fact that I'm breathing is what I appreciate. For so long, I couldn't even say that. All my life I've just appreciated the fact of being here. I really just—just was happy being here, being me, you know what I'm saying? I don't know how else to say it. I'm glad I'm a human being and not a chair, you know, or not a tree or something, you know, and I just feel real good about being here, being alive, being human."

"What are you most committed to?"

"Eating, like I said. I'm most committed to—there's different...I guess I feel there's different levels to that."

"Yeah."

"Personally, I'm committed to being the best person that I can be."

"What does that mean: being the best person that you can be?"

Lawrence thinks a moment. "That means, for me, that means for me trying not to hurt anyone...trying not to hurt myself, accepting that I have strengths, weaknesses, limitations. Ah, accepting that I have real strong and good qualities that I can pass on to others.

"Personally, being part of the whole structure of human existence and trying to change what was for me for a long period of time in my life left unchanged. For example, relationships with family members and friends. Trying to be more of a friend and being more of a family member on a personal level. That's a strong commitment for me.

"Socially being a part of changing those things within my community and my sphere of influence. Being able to change those things that I can change and working with other people to do that. For example, having...being involved in community activities, maybe setting up town watches—I don't know what, but being involved in a community and community settings and community movements and stuff like that.

"Politically, to begin to be more of an active activist and to be more of...more involved with people who feel and think the way that I do about change in this country. And that has different levels as well.

Because there's certain things that being an African American, being black, I must do in order to see that happen. But I believe that the struggle against oppression and the struggle politically for what's right has to be fought on a lot of different fronts. And I've learned through my existence to be flexible enough to be able to fight on those fronts. Before I wasn't. It was one way or the highway."

The good life for Lawrence Patterson is thus quite encompassing. It includes a right orientation toward himself, his friends, and family; community involvement; and political engagement. The Greek philosophers would have pressed Lawrence further. Lawrence himself speaks of the various aspects of a good life as being on different levels. The Greeks would have asked Lawrence what the good is that inheres at each of these levels. In what way are his commitments at each level all a manifestation of a unified life?

HYPERGOODS

For Plato and Aristotle, every finite good points to a larger good beyond it. The smaller goods are good because they participate in or are instrumental in serving a larger purpose. Each good draws us, moves us to rise higher on the ladder of ever more encompassing goods. At the end of the chain is goodness itself, what Aristotle termed the "unmoved mover," which does not serve any further purpose but is in itself the ultimate end of all our actions.[15]

Although Aristotle referred to the unmoved mover as God, Aristotle's God was not the "living God" of Judaism, Christianity, and Islam, who acts in history. Instead, Aristotle's God was a vision, so entirely and perfectly self-sufficient as to require no action of its own. Yet every level of creation was moved by it to become more like it and thus to return to it. There is a kindred idea in both Judaism and Christianity that one might be so moved with awe by the example of God's goodness that one is drawn to emulate it. Thus the movement of which Aristotle speaks is the emotional movement effected by an ultimate good that morally inspires us.

Philosopher Charles Taylor refers to such an ultimate good as a hypergood, a good above all other goods. Tillich, a theologian, refers to it as the object of ultimate concern. Both Taylor and Tillich agree that when one is grasped by such a hypergood, all other goods become subordinate to it. The hypergood becomes the ultimate purpose of life.

The particular image associated with the hypergood varies. For Judaism, it may be the image of a broken world made whole. For

Christianity, it may be the "reign of God" and for Islam the community at Medina. For secular Marxism, it may be the vision of communist society. All such images are utopian. All are abstract enough to encompass the whole of life. All encompass such abstract qualities as justice, mercy, and love—the "divine" attributes.

Whatever the images we associate with the hypergood, they all demand that we do something, that we take on a life's task. Hypergoods not only provide ultimate purpose to life, they demand our lives in return. They demand our adoption of the hypergood as the ultimate purpose served by our own lives, even at the expense of the lesser goods associated with ordinary life. It is the widespread lack of emotional connection with any hypergoods today that leaves behind the narrower concerns that look like individualism.

Hypergoods are subversive, and the modern world distrusts them. Individually, hypergoods are subversive because they relativize the significance of the lesser goods around which ordinary life revolves. Collectively, they are subversive because they also relativize and challenge the established order we take for granted. This is certainly true for Lawrence Patterson. When I ask him what the good is, he instead tells me what is bad.

"What do you think?" I ask. "What's your sense of the good? What's the good in life?"

"I believe that there's enough resources in this world to take care of the world, and I don't care how many people you put on the planet, we have enough resources so that everyone could have that—everyone could live comfortably. Lavishly, even. But because of the way it's distributed, because those who control the wealth and control the resources have made certain determinations about the quality of life for other people...we have problems.

" My sense of right and my sense of wrong in all that is that no one person has the right to make that determination for someone else...Owning property and owning water and owning electricity somehow is crazy to me. I don't believe in owning electricity and owning water and owning the dirt. I believe that it's here for general consumption, and whatever we have the ability to produce and whatever quality of life we have the ability to maintain or enhance for people should be promoted and not stripped away.

"You know, poverty, poverty is the result of someone saying, 'Look, there ain't enough for everybody to go around, so you can have this and *you* can't.' And setting up structures and systems and institutions that promote that. And this is not just in today's time, this is going back to, you know, to the beginning of time. You see, you had kings and queens and serfs and landlords and you had barons, land barons and all that kind of stuff. That's the whole idea of someone having more stature, someone being more important than someone else. And I just totally disagree with that. That's what I think is basically and fundamentally wrong; that some human beings think that they're more important or that they have more right than other human beings. And they don't."

Lawrence has just told me what is bad. "So the good would be what?"

"The good would be for all people, all men and women, all human beings to be treated equally. Not different, not better, not worse, just equally."

I ask Lawrence if he feels as if his life has meaning.

"Uh, yeah, yeah."

"So what's the meaning of your life?"

"You set me up," he growls. "Um, I don't know. To fight for truth, justice and...I don't know...I think that, I guess, really, why I'm here, the meaning of my life, I don't know. I just feel like I can do a lot more to make the world a better place and that, you know, I just want that to be my life's meaning, my life's work, whatever...You know, just try to make things better for people. I don't want the accolades—you know what I'm saying? I don't want to be a big muckety-muck or nothing like that, you know? I do want to be seen as someone who tried and gave it their best. I want to be remembered as someone who fought against what was wrong."

If the Greeks had actually pressed Lawrence to provide the unifying theme of all aspects of his life, they would have received their answer: "To fight for truth and justice, to be remembered as someone who fought against what was wrong." The words truth and justice particularly would have resonated with Plato and Aristotle. For them as well, *truth* and *justice* were constitutive of the ultimate good.

To speak of the ultimate good is to speak of that good that concerns us ultimately, the good that constitutes the ultimate purpose of our lives. The problem in the modern or postmodern world is a pervasive loss of emotionally moving contact with a good that is ultimate, a contact that was once provided by the sacred. We are still emotionally moved by goods, but they tend to be goods that are less than ultimate—family, friends, and material possessions. As a consequence, the whole of our lives is without any overarching moral purpose. There is a lot of talk today about our loss of vision, and that is what the loss of overarching moral purpose entails. This hardly means that we are all immoral. It does mean that our sense of morality has become largely procedural.

PROCEDURAL MORALITY

To say that modern morality is mainly procedural is to say that it focuses on the means we adopt to pursue our ends.[16] Such "instrumentalism" is already evident in the mention of the golden rule made by both Tom Brown and Ellen Smith. So many of my respondents make reference to the golden rule that we will have to return to it for a fuller treatment. Here, however, it may be observed that for both Tom Brown and Ellen Smith, the golden rule appears to be a procedural ethic, constraining our behavior in certain ways. For Tom Brown, the golden rule means respecting others as he goes about his business. For Ellen Smith, it means not lying, cheating, and so forth. It also means that she should not always think of herself. If we think of morality in terms of procedures, then, contrary to the Christian right, there is little evidence that Americans have become more immoral. All indications are that Americans remain very concerned that they pursue their ends in a moral way.[17]

The problem with a morality that is largely procedural is that it does not identify any moral purpose we ought to fulfill with our lives. The procedural constraints tell us what we should refrain from doing but offer little moral vision as to what we actually should be about doing. A morality reduced to procedural constraints is summed up by the sixties refrain, "Do your own thing as long as you don't hurt anyone." In the absence of hypergoods, that morality is dominant today. It is the morality articulated by Joe Barboso, a young physics major, when I ask him what governs his actions.

"I think that everybody has a right to do what they want in the world and, like, I try to do whatever I want, as long as it doesn't conflict with what somebody else wants. Like, I can do...I think I can do whatever I want as long as it doesn't harm anybody else, like, physically or mentally and, like, I would try to, I would try to set that up. I mean, I know that ideal, but, like, I try to do everything I want but I...I consider others first. So my main value would be to do what you want but don't step on anybody else's toes."

Joe is hardly immoral. As he says, he tries to consider others first and not harm anyone. Beyond that, he feels we should all be free to do "our own thing." That is fine, but what should "our own thing" be?

A morality reduced solely to the way we pursue "our own thing" totally removes "our own thing" from moral discourse. For such a morality, whatever "our own thing" is, it will by definition be amoral. Whatever ends we choose to pursue within the moral means will have the appearance of morally neutral preferences.

The problem is that it is the purposes we pursue and not just the ways in which we pursue them that give our lives meaning. To ask about the meaning of life is to ask about life's ultimate purpose. Where only our means are considered a matter of morality and not our ultimate ends as well, we may be procedurally moral and yet morally purposeless.

METAPHYSICAL SPACE

In researching a topic as basic as what people think about the meaning of life, data are likely to surface anywhere—in even the least likely of settings. One morning while I was sitting in my dentist's chair, the desalivator in my mouth, my dental hygienist and I embarked on a discussion of Tibetan Buddhism. Knowing my hygienist to be a practitioner of yoga, I had mentioned that I was going to use Zen breathing techniques to distance myself from the unpleasantness I was about to experience. She in turn hailed me as "a new-age kind of guy" and, as she scraped my teeth, proceeded to tell me about her own beliefs.

According to my hygienist, compassion is one of the highest values of Tibetan Buddhism, which even offers various exercises one can practice to intensify it. What most struck me, however, in what she was saying was the cosmogonic origin of that value, the way compassion arises as a value from a particular metaphysical worldview. According to Tibetan Buddhism, we have all been here before countless times. Over the course of our many past lives, we all have had the opportunity to be each other's parents and children, sisters and brothers.

It is on this view precisely because we have all been emotionally much closer to each other in the past than we may now appear that universal compassion is both a possibility and an ideal. Whether or not one accepts this metaphysical assumption is beside the point. What is illustrated is the close connection between a life-encompassing value and an underlying metaphysic. It is from a certain metaphysical conception, from a particular way the cosmos is experienced that a life-encompassing value arises. My dental hygienist, a Tibetan Buddhist, knows what life is about because she knows where she stands ontologically in relation to the whole.

In relation to the whole, furthermore, my dental hygienist acquires an identity in metaphysical space. It is an identity that transcends any contingent social position she happens to occupy to place her in intimate connection with every other human being on the planet. In the metaphysical space of Tibetan Buddhism, my hygienist knows who she is essentially.

We can trace a similar connection between cosmos and morality in Judaism and Christianity. Rooted in both traditions, our own Declaration of Independence holds the following truths to be self-evident: "That all men are created equal. That all are endowed by their Creator with certain inalienable rights."

In the Judeo-Christian tradition, too, morality arises cosmogonically. In the Judeo-Christian tradition we each have inalienable human rights because of who we are in the cosmos. Each of us is a distinct child of God, each made equally, as Genesis tells us, in the image of God. For better or worse, it is because the Judeo-Christian tradition sees the image of God as borne distinctly by humans that we within that tradition attach much greater moral significance to the life of a human than to the life of a dog. Within the metaphysical space of Judaism and Christianity, we know who we are in relation to ultimate reality. It is by virtue of that essential identity that we hold ourselves to have fundamental human rights.

A close reading of the Declaration of Independence indicates that the rights to which it refers are not simply human conventions. They are not just the rights that happen to be legally honored by one given society. Indeed, the Declaration was penned precisely because in the society in which it was written, those rights had not been acknowledged. The Declaration considers the rights it enumerates to be ontologically grounded in the nature of the cosmos, whether acknowledged socially or not.

Today, talk of fundamental human rights has become almost universal. Yet in the secular humanist discourse that is the language of the public forum, no reference is made to the ontological grounding of those rights.[18] Indeed, it is hardly a secret that within secular discourse, no such metaphysical grounding is offered.

Secular humanism has been attracted to Judeo-Christian morality, but it has scrapped the Judeo-Christian cosmos that underlies it without putting anything in its place. Without such metaphysical grounding, rights talk threatens actually to become the empty rhetoric that postmodernist philosophers suppose it to be.

We hear, for example, that China is violating human rights. What do we mean by that? Just that China is not behaving nicely to its people or perhaps that it is behaving very unnicely? Alternatively, do we mean just that the Chinese government is not behaving the way we know and like our own government to behave? When morality is detached from all metaphysical moorings, it is no wonder that it all begins to appear relative. If, in particular, talk of human rights is not rooted in any metaphysic and refers only to what society conventionally chooses to acknowledge, then it is hard to know what to make of a charge that a particular society is in violation of human rights. Such a society, like all societies, acknowledges the rights it acknowledges, and in that society those are all the rights there are.

As I talk about rights with Robert Zimbruski, a middle-aged engineer and father of two, it occurs to me that he ultimately stands on no shakier ground than many of us who think about rights for a living.

"Okay," I say. "I want to backtrack and maybe talk about your values now. Do you have...a set of values you live by, and if so, how did you come by these?"

"Well," Robert answers. "values, to me, values are...I value the rights of other people."

"Hm-hm."

"That's one of my biggest values. I moved out to where I am now because I enjoy peace and quiet. The neighbors are mostly real nice. And I don't believe that other people should take advantage of somebody else's rights. I think, well, like I said, people's rights to me are my greatest value. And if somebody treads on my rights, that's when I get angry."

"Rights defined by society?"

"Yes, which I feel are my legal rights."

"Okay," I say. "Do you think that there are other rights, other than legal rights? I mean, as you well know, different societies believe in or have different rights and have different values. Do you think there's...Well, let me ask you this: Do you think there are right values and wrong values? Or..."

"I think each person has their own set of values. When you have three people living in a neighborhood, they'll have different sets of values. I mean, you know, my one neighbor...I mean, everything is right as far as—as long as you don't bother him. I mean, he could burn trash, he could ride his motorbikes any place he wants, but as long as you don't report him or, you know, tell the township, it's right as far as he's concerned. But I look at: No, you're violating my rights and you're violating the neighbors' rights, too. So each person, I think, has...there's, like, a set of values, but the degree to which each person looks at those, is, like, totally different."

I nod. "Okay. Where do you think you came by your values?"

"I was brought up with these values. My parents, they respect everybody else's property and they taught me to respect property."

"Do you think that possibly in addition to how you were brought up by your parents and the education system—I am assuming that you received some of your values there as well, that you came by some values from your own experience or from..."

"I think common sense; it also creates some values."

I nod.

"If you sit and look at a situation and say, 'If I do this, this is going to be the consequence and this will be the result, and the consequences outweigh the result,' I think from that you might develop some values. That doesn't necessarily have to be pointed out to you: If you do this, this is going to happen to you. You know, if a person sat down and thought about a situation before they did anything, a lot more right decisions would be made."

Robert Zimbruski greatly values people's rights. He further believes that these rights are objective, that they exist even if someone like his neighbor is unaware of them or otherwise fails to acknowledge them. Yet, like professional social scientists and philosophers, Robert is unsure as to where those rights originate from. Although in the passage above Robert seems to conflate human rights with the rights that society conventionally honors, when I push him further, he acknowledges that entire societies can fail to recognize our human rights. He is prepared to admit, for example, that this was the case in Hitler's Germany. He further speaks as if our understanding of human rights has grown so that today we have a better comprehension of human rights than in the past when, say, slavery was still an institution.

If our understanding of human rights has actually grown and not merely changed, the implication is that such rights are ontologically objective and independent of what we think about them. In other words, it is not simply that moral fashions have changed. Rather, the implication is that we have come to a better appreciation of human rights as an independent reality.[19] Yet, when I ask Robert about this point, he reverts in postmodern fashion to a subjective or cultural relativism: values and rights differ, depending on the individual or society. How, then, could Hitler's Germany have been in violation not just of our own sensibilities but of something independent we refer to as human rights?

It does not occur to Robert that his own concept of rights requires independent metaphysical grounding. When I ask Robert how he arrived at his own particular values, his answers are instructive. In essence, he offers three distinct accounts.

Robert's first answer is that he has the values he has because they were instilled in him by his parents. That Robert has been socialized to have the values he holds comes as no surprise. Yet, on moral and metaphysical matters, socialization is not a satisfactory explanation of our values. The problem is that the explanation is entirely causal. By referring to socialization, Robert is telling us that he was caused to have his values as an object acted upon by outside social forces. To the extent that Robert was merely caused to have those values, he himself is not the author of them. He has not come to own them by evaluating them critically. If Robert has merely inherited the values he holds without examining them critically, without deciding for himself that they are justified, then he has not assumed the role of a subject in relation to them. What we want from Robert as a human subject is the justifications he offers himself for the values he holds.

Robert does offer us something of the kind. As a second explanation of his values, Robert suggests that any "rational agent" would arrive at similar values just by thinking about things. As he puts it, one thinks about one's actions and their consequences and just sees what is right. Here Robert is offering what professional philosophers would refer to as a consequentialist approach to ethics: right and wrong are evaluated by consequences.

It is not entirely clear whether the consequences Robert refers to are exclusively consequences to himself—whether, that is, his view is strictly egoistic. Presumably it is not, for he castigates his neighbor for thinking only about himself and not others. If, however, we are to include the consequences for others in our moral calculations, how much and in what way can we do so? What and how much do others deserve? The answer seems to require us to possess the prior notion of rights, the nature of which we are seeking in the first place. The calculations of which Robert speaks can be made only after we already know the rights to which people are entitled.

Robert's final answer is that what our human rights are is just common sense. Robert is not the only one to think so. My students, for example, often tell me that all morality is largely just common sense. I try to point out to them that what they are calling common sense is actually the cultural legacy of Judaism and Christianity. We imbibe the morality of Judeo-Christianity as common sense because ours is largely a Judeo-Christian culture.

Yet, like my students and many others, Robert has accepted the basic morality of Judaism and Christianity while abandoning their metaphysics. Robert himself was raised in a strict religious home by devout Catholic parents. Yet, while he continues to think there must be some supreme being, for Robert the supreme being has now become remote. Robert neither practices his religion nor thinks much about God. In contrast with the writers of the Declaration of Independence, Robert specifically does not root his conception of human rights in our ontological status before God.

What Robert is missing is precisely what Charles Taylor suggests is missing from our culture as a whole: a moral ontology or underlying picture of the cosmos that would provide our moral principles their rationale. Instead, the secular tendency of our culture makes us think we can get on without situating ourselves in any kind of metaphysical space. And generally we can get on—until we are asked to justify our moral principles and values. At that point, we find ourselves at a loss.

Our problem is not simply a cultural individualism that precludes consensus on the nature of the cosmos. Even a cultural consensus on morality can lack metaphysical grounding. Conversely, each of us individually could ground his or her moral principles and values in an individual, personal conception of the cosmos. To do that, however, we need at least an individual, personal conception of the cosmos. The general problem is that such a conception of the cosmos is missing. The cosmos of Judaism and Christianity has just been abandoned without replacement. As a result, it is the cosmos itself from which people find themselves disconnected.

This cosmic disconnection surfaces again in my exchange with Peter Nighting, a recent graduate in information science. Unlike Robert, Peter was raised in a nonreligious home.

"Okay," I say to Peter, "so what would you say are the principles or values you live by?"

"Values, uh, well, I don't know...sort of the basic values that we're taught as we grow up, you know? Be kind to others, be happy with...do things...There's a whole value system, such as the society, you know, laws and what not, don't break laws, that type of values, as well as personal values like family is very important to me, and to my family as well as being courteous to perfect strangers, and feelings. Feelings are important. Other people's feelings, my feelings—that's a value."

Like Ellen Smith and Tom Brown, Peter's values include family and the golden rule. I ask Tom what he means by being "courteous to perfect strangers."

"Well, I, I was always raised to be nice. I mean, to give people the benefit of the doubt: Don't discriminate, don't ever talk down to anybody even though they may have lesser knowledge or something. That's just courteous."

"And what about feelings? What do you mean by feelings? Can you elaborate on that?"

"Feelings are important. A person's feelings. You don't specifically just choose some action without looking at the consequences of how it might affect somebody. And when I go through the reasoning before I do an action, one of my reasons is, well, how is this going to make somebody feel who's involved? How's it going to make me feel? You know, life. If it makes me feel great or it works for me, but it makes somebody else feel bad, then you have to take all that into consideration."

As for others we have heard from, aside from family, for Peter moral principles are mainly procedural. They relate not to the purposes he pursues but to his means of pursuing them. Like Robert, Peter weighs the consequences of his actions on others. Unlike Robert, Peter says he evaluates how his actions will affect not just the rights of others but also their feelings.

Because Peter's sensitive concern for others is so laudable, it is disconcerting to find his values trivialized by the metaphysical grounding he gives them. I ask Peter why he feels he should treat people as he does. "You said you were raised to treat people like this?"

"Right."

"Okay, that sort of explains why you have those values..."

"But why were they taught to me?"

"No. Not why they were taught to you, but do you think those are values...I mean different people are taught different values, right?"

"Right."

"Somebody else might be taught a different set of values..."

"Mm-hm."

"Than what you were taught...so do you think your values are right rather than...do you think those are the right values to have?"

"I don't know if it's really a matter of right or wrong. I think it's more of...well, that's what I would like to be. It's how I would like to be treated, and that's how I treat other people—by these values. That's how I live and that's how I think other people should live. Now, is it more right than some other way? I don't know. I can't tell you, but if given a choice I would use my set of values."

"Do you think your values are like preferences? I mean, like certain types of ice cream? You like vanilla ice cream. I might like chocolate. How are your values different from that? Or do you think they're not that much different?

"Oh, I don't think they are much different. As a society, we determine values, and we create laws so that you can follow those if you want to live in that society, but I see values very much like preferences. I mean, my values are what work for me and how I think they should be, but that doesn't necessarily mean that somebody else's values aren't true. I mean, take for instance these neo-Nazis, who specifically believe that only the white race...should be allowed to live and what not. I don't agree with that. I think it's wrong, but they are somebody else's values, and I can't really condemn somebody for those values, but in society those values don't work and we have laws against that and I will uphold those by living in society."

"Why do you say neo-Nazi values don't work?"

"Well, it's not that they don't work. I mean, if you want to believe that one race is superior to another, that's fine. But when you take it to a physical action and get violent, that's where society stops you. Society's values stop you, which also happen to be my values."

"I understand what you're saying." What Peter is saying is that his sensitivity to others is just a preference and as such no better or worse than neo-Nazi preferences. It is just fortunate that society shares Peter's preferences and imposes its preferences legally on all. Peter's reduction of his own commendable values to arbitrary preferences is what I meant earlier when I said he himself trivializes them. Yet the view articulated by Peter is found also in the most sophisticated of postmodernist philosophers. Like Peter, postmodernist philosophers totally neglect metaphysical space and, as a consequence, see no way to ground values objectively. Values, then, become preferences, and societal values just imposed preferences. Actually, this view is in its own way a metaphysical position as well, one that makes the assertion of values simply an exercise of power.[20]

Even this postmodern metaphysic gives rise to certain life-encompassing values: tolerance, equality, and respect for diversity. These values arise from the unavoidable metaphysic that remains even when metaphysics is denied. Peter's own respect for diversity itself seems grounded in his metaphysical reduction of values to preferences.

"I do," Peter says, "consider the two very similar: values and preferences. Just because some values aren't mine, that doesn't mean they're wrong or mine are more right than others."

"So," I press him, "You wouldn't say that somebody who, who is a neo-Nazi...neo-Nazi values...You wouldn't say those values are wrong?"

"Well…"

"Any more than you wouldn't, you wouldn't say that I'm wrong if I didn't like vanilla ice cream, actually…"

"Exactly…I'm going through the definition of how I see wrong in relation to my values. Believing in my values, neo-Nazis are wrong, but, I mean, who's to say? It's kind of difficult. I would say yes and no on that. Neo-Nazis are not wrong, but in my value system they're wrong."

In its reduction of values to preferences, postmodern philosophy, ably articulated here by Peter, mistakenly conflates tolerance with unwillingness to judge. Tolerance of others does not require us to confer equal validity on their claims. We can countenance the expression of opinions we judge objectively incorrect. Civil libertarian that I am, I may defend the rights of people to hold neo-Nazi values, but is it just a matter of subjective preference whether or not we judge all races equal? Is there really nothing objective we can say about this? Why, then, do we even bother doing social science?

The question is whether postmodernism's metaphysical reduction of values to preferences really honors the full truth about our values. "Who's to say?" Peter asks. Who's to say whether or not neo-Nazi values are better or worse than any others? Certainly, if values are equated with taste, no one can say. The comparative validity of our different values is an issue we address in critical space, the space of arguments and counterarguments. In that space, it is the weight of argument that decides the comparative validity of our values. We enter that space, however, only if we have one or another metaphysic to debate. Our own metaphysics are the initial chips we lay on the table to play the game of argument. Without any metaphysical position to begin with, there is nothing to argue about.

The problem with our failure to situate ourselves in any kind of metaphysical space is not simply that our morality needs to be metaphysically grounded somehow. The problem is not simply philosophical. It is also emotional. Robert Zimbruski and Peter Nighting may be emotionally connected to their values even without any kind of metaphysical underpinnings. Many others, however, may find themselves a good deal less emotionally connected to their moralities. If our reverence for human rights, for example, historically originates in a certain conception of who we are in the cosmos, then our present profound lack of clarity about our cosmic status can only diminish the sanctity we accord human beings.

I ask Michael Fields, for example, why it is wrong to take the life of a human but not the life of a cow. Michael muses over this question and offers that it is no more wrong to take the life of a human than a nonhuman animal. Our tendency to think otherwise, he suggests, is a form of speciesism. It is just us against them.

There are of course radical vegetarians or vegans who would share Michael's conclusion. For vegans, however, this is a position arrived at through reflection that leads to an active reverence for all life. Michael, however, is neither a vegan nor even a vegetarian. Michael has just lost touch with the metaphysical ground underlying conventional morality. Thus, when he thinks through the issue logically, he experiences no emotional connection to the vision behind the morality that might prompt him to resist the philosophical dismissal of that morality.

If we need some worldview in metaphysical space to tell us who we are cosmically, to ground and to emotionally connect us to our moralities, that worldview need not be specifically religious. Kurt Vonnegut's *Breakfast of Champions* is a deeply irreverent book that lampoons both conventional morality and religion. Yet, within is a profound vision of who we might cosmically conceive ourselves to be.

At one point in the book, the main character, Kilgore Trout, enters a restaurant bathroom. On the mirror he sees the question scrawled: "What is the meaning of life?" Trout, a rather eccentric character, picks up a pen and scribbles back,

> To be
> the eyes
> and ears
> and conscience
> of the Creator of the Universe,
> you fool.[21]

Let us delete Trout's reference to the Creator. Let us suppose he had only written, "To become the eyes and ears and conscience of the universe." That one line would still offer a profound sense of who we are and a profound sense of the human vocation. We are, it would be saying, the universe become conscious of itself. We are the universe seeing and hearing. In that understanding, there is a reverence for who we all are, and in that reverence a vocation. The vocation is to become as well the conscience of the universe, its moral guardians.

Trout's mad ravings are not so mad. Even with Trout's reference to the Creator deleted, they offer a way for us to bestow ultimate meaning on our existence, a nonreligious way for us to conceive a human project. To derive meaning from nonmeaning was the specific task of the existentialists, of Sartre, Camus, and Nietzsche. All confronted an empty sky, which seemed to make our own existence pointless and absurd.

It was the emotional experience of cosmic absurdity that drove the existentialists' reflections, an experienced need for cosmic purpose and the failure of the universe to answer it. The existentialists' anguish can well be appreciated even by theists who do not find the universe so silent. It is much harder to appreciate for those, whether theistic or atheistic, to whom a felt need for ultimate purpose is foreign.

Out of his own cosmic angst, Albert Camus reconsiders the myth of Sisyphus, who was condemned forever to roll a rock up a hill, only to have it always roll back down again.[22] If Camus can extract some meaning for Sisyphus in this situation, then perhaps there is hope for us as well.

And Camus does extract some meaning. "If this myth is tragic," says Camus, "that is because its hero is conscious. Where would his torture be, indeed, if at every step the hope of succeeding upheld him?"

> The workman of today works every day in his life at the same tasks, and this fate is no less absurd. But it is tragic only at the moments when it becomes conscious. Sisyphus, proletarian of the gods, powerless and rebellious, knows the whole extent of his wretched condition; it is what he thinks of during his descent. The lucidity that was to constitute his torture at the same time crowns his victory. There is no fate that cannot be surmounted by scorn.[23]

To Camus, it is the very consciousness of Sisyphus that makes his purposeless existence such a tragedy. Camus means for us to feel for Sisyphus in this situation. In feeling for Sisyphus, however, we are simultaneously to feel for all humankind, for we are similarly placed. Thus, already in Camus's existentialism, a moral, humanistic emotion arises in response to our shared cosmic fate.

Camus, however, takes us even further. We are not just to feel pity or protectiveness toward Sisyphus, for Sisyphus has the capacity to conquer his plight by means of the same consciousness that is the cause of it. Sisyphus can defy his fate by scornfully embracing it, by refusing to allow the painfulness of consciousness to make him surrender consciousness. It is in the steadfast commitment to consciousness on the part of Sisyphus and ourselves that the nobility of consciousness is affirmed and human dignity established. For atheistic existentialism, too, morality is cosmogonic. For existentialism, morality requires that we remain conscious of the absurdity of life, that we confront our finitude, and not relapse into what Sartre calls the "illusion of eternity."[24]

Just as for theistic worldviews, the moral stance of the existentialist requires us to attend to who we really are in the cosmos. It requires
us to identify our authentic selves. It requires us finally to live lives worthy of those authentic selves. The complaint of the existentialists is
that we normally do not live as the beings we authentically are; our
ordinary lives do not honor our authentic selves.

If we do not live authentic lives, the reason is not, contrary to the
way authenticity is now popularly understood, that we are not in touch
with our inner feelings. It is, rather, that we are not in touch with our
true place in the cosmos. Instead of lifting our gaze to the cosmic
dimension, instead of orienting ourselves in metaphysical space, we
are so enthralled by the world's lesser goods that we fail to turn our
attention to more ultimate goods. Buddhists have a name for this condition; they call it *avidya*.[25] As the Transcendentalist philosopher
Henry David Thoreau understood, we are possessed by our possessions. Accordingly, we live, said Thoreau, what is not life, and so when
we come to die, we discover that we have not lived.[26] Because he
believed our lives are "frittered away by detail," Thoreau went to the
woods to experience what life is essentially, to orient himself stripped
down in metaphysical space and thereby recover his authentic self.

Avidya acknowledges the attractive pull of proximate goods, block-
ing concern with what is ultimate. The concept is an old one, but it is
religious rather than sociological. As such, it lies beyond sociology's
ken. Yet, if we are looking for mechanisms to explain what looks like
individualism, then *avidya* cannot be ignored. It is a concept to which
sociologists can add their own insights. After all, consumer capitalism
is, if anything, an economic system that functions not just by fostering
avidya but by producing even surplus *avidya*. It encourages us to seek
our identities in what we buy as opposed to what we morally stand for.[27]
It is no wonder, then, that as individuals so shaped, we are estranged
from our true selves.

As part of the culture of late capitalism, postmodernism, curiously,
shares common ground with the positivism it repudiates. Both, for
their own reasons, reject metaphysical discourse. Both are empiricist,
taking the apparent for the real.[28] For both positivism and postmodernism alike, there is no sense in speaking of an authentic self distinct
from the fragmented selves we may experience ourselves as being. It
must be that for both positivists and postmodernists, a certain emotion
is absent, a certain longing for cosmic purpose. For those who possess
that emotion, who feel that longing, metaphysical space cannot be so
blithely abandoned.

CRITICAL SPACE

On a national survey, the Gallup Organization once asked people to evaluate on a scale from one to ten how certain they were that Jesus rose from the dead. On this scale, one indicates absolute certainty that Jesus *did not* rise from the dead, and ten indicates absolute certainty that Jesus *did* in fact rise from the dead.

Not all Christians would regard this question as important. An Episcopal priest was something of a mentor to me. Throughout his life a committed political activist, he was the one who initially led me to a life of political activism. Back in the 1980s, we found ourselves together at a march in Washington to protest U.S. involvement in Central America.

As we walked, I mentioned reading some books of biblical criticism that examined the historicity of Jesus's empty tomb and the resurrection appearances. My friend was incredulous. Why, he wanted to know, was I reading that?

I explained that insofar as the resurrection is the foundational event of Christianity, it seems important to question it. It seems important to know as much as we can about its historical truth.

"It is not important at all," my friend replied. "You Catholics are too hung up on historicity." What is important, my friend said, is the story. The story is what we are to live by, whether it is historical or not. Thus has the liberal Protestant theology of my friend's generation separated "the Jesus of history" from "the Christ of faith." According to that theology, it is the mythic Christ proclaimed by the church community to whom Christians are supposed to relate, not the actual Jesus of history. In such a sociological theology, the question of historical truth does not surface at all.

Most Catholics of course are not as "hung up" on historicity as I am, but it is not only Catholics who are. In the so-called third quest for the historical Jesus currently underway, there are many Protestant exegetes who similarly see the importance of connecting the Christ of faith more closely with the Jesus who actually lived.[29]

Whether Protestant or Catholic, however, most Christians are neither exegetes nor theologians. Outside the narrow circle of liberal theology, most Christians would share my assumption that it is vitally important to Christianity that something qualifying as a resurrection did occur.

If most Christians would agree with me on the importance of this point, they evidently would not share my doubts. I asked my wife, a non-Christian, how she thought I would have answered the Gallup poll question. How certain did my wife think I was about the resurrection?

Knowing its importance to me, my wife supposed that on a scale of certainty from one to ten, I would probably place myself at eight. I told her I was not even that certain. Instead, I would probably place myself at a certainty level of six. I am more inclined than not to think something remarkable happened—although not necessarily the reanimation of a corpse.[30] Even so, I have substantial doubts.

Judging from the results of the Gallup poll, I am part of a distinct minority within American Christiandom. With regard to certainty about Jesus's resurrection, 64 percent of respondents to the Gallup poll placed themselves at level ten. They indicated absolute certainty that Jesus was raised from the dead. They have no doubts whatsoever.[31]

No doubts about something like that? A colleague of mine, more expert than I at public opinion research, counsels against accepting this finding at face value. Respondents know the game, he tells me. To affirm their values, people frequently choose the most extreme response available. People are not as doubt-free as the Gallup findings suggest. I am sure my colleague is right. Yet even if we allow for some overstatement of certainty, surprisingly little doubt is expressed.

Perhaps the absence of doubt is not so surprising. Christians after all are admonished to have faith. Perhaps it is Christian faith the Gallup findings reflect. I do not deny a proper role for faith. However, faith becomes problematic when it so privileges a belief that the belief becomes immune to question or argument, when faith leaves no room for doubt. At that point, faith threatens to stifle critical reflection and intellectual growth.

Consider that it is not only in Jesus's resurrection that we are admonished to have faith. Various communities call us to faith in the literal truth of the Bible, the infallibility of the pope, or in Muhammed as the greatest of the prophets. While we all will want to argue against some of these objects of faith, we cannot do so consistently while preserving from debate our own objects of faith.

The problem gets worse. Consider racists, sexists, or those who are homophobic. We really cannot fault people for having been raised to hold intolerant views. If we fault them, it is for retaining their intolerant beliefs, for not subjecting them to critical scrutiny. Yet how can we fault others for not questioning their beliefs when we exempt our own cherished notions from critical scrutiny? On this point, consistency demands that we speak as one with the postmodernists: No belief is privileged; all must be equally open to question.

Although our religions may be among our most cherished beliefs, it is precisely our most cherished beliefs that we should be prepared to question. When we do question, we open ourselves to critical space, the space of argument and counterargument. In that opening, there is the danger we may lose our faith, but there is also the prospect that the faith we attain will be sounder and more sophisticated. In neither case do we lose. If our faith is sound to begin with, it will withstand argument. If it is unsound, we are better off moving onto firmer ground.

Critical space is the terrain we must travel in order to grow not just intellectually but even religiously. We embark on this terrain only when we encounter diversity, when we engage another with a different faith. We can of course establish a mutual nonaggression pact in which we do not question the other's faith and the other does not question ours. That is generally what we do. Yet, this nonaggression pact leaves us with nothing to say to one another about our most important beliefs. No one's faith is ever threatened, but, likewise, no one's faith ever intellectually grows.

There is a better way. We can become for each other what the Jewish tradition calls *haverim. haverim* are religious study partners who gently and lovingly challenge each other's claims to truth. By prodding each other to more reasoned positions, *haverim* turn their diversity of opinion into an epistemic asset, a way of leading each other toward sounder beliefs.[32]

If we are to allow others to identify the gaps and flaws in our own reasoning, then we must prepare to give and to receive arguments. We must further assume that arguments matter; that, contrary to postmodern relativism, some arguments are better than others; that there are such things as gaps and flaws in the ways we reason.

Generally, we do not serve each other as *haverim*. Instead, in postmodern fashion, our tendency is to leave each other's beliefs alone. Without *haverim*, we all remain mutually unaware of the doubts we should have about our own beliefs. Perhaps it is this condition that the Gallup finding reflects.

I am again in western Pennsylvania in a small coal-mining town, speaking to Melinda Ratzschall, a Lutheran housewife. "Okay," I say to her, "Um, Jesus. Do you think he was divine? God? Do you think he was a good man, just a really good man? Or do you think he was divine? Do you think...what do you think about him?

"I think he was God."

"Oh, okay. Okay...Do you think he rose from the dead?"

"Yeah."

I nod. "You think he was resurrected. Do you ever doubt that? Maybe he wasn't?"

"No."

"You don't?"

"No."

If Melinda has never doubted the resurrection, perhaps it is because she has never had to. She tells me she "never knew anybody that was an atheist." The absence of diversity in Melinda's world means that she would never encounter anyone who might call her views into question. In order to have a *haverim* relationship, we first must find our *haverim*.

I have a similar exchange with Frederick and Martha Schmidt, a couple in their seventies. Although, like Melinda, Frederick and Martha are not fundamentalists, they, too, are conservative Lutherans, who accept literally much of what they read in the Bible. I ask them whether they have any doubts that God exists.

"No," says Martha.

"I don't," Frederick replies.

Martha continues. "No. Too busy to start worrying about stuff like that."

"Really?"

"Sure, we have a busy life. We're collecting rocks. He's out doing gardening, mowing grass. Who has time to worry about that? We're doing stuff that God wants us to do, and we'll just keep away from there."

Frederick echoes his wife. "We do a lot of things."

"Yeah," Martha continues. "Idleness can be bad for people. They can sit and imagine stuff that they shouldn't even be thinking about...That's one main thing that people shouldn't be thinking about."

"Huh?" I had to switch the tape around. "Can you say that again? You were saying idleness is—is bad?"

This time it is Frederick who picks up the thread. "'Idleness is the devil's workshop,' is the way I've heard it stated."

"Right. Right." I'm familiar with the adage. It is not the first time in my interviews that I am struck by how much stock people place in adages, by how frequently proverbs serve as organizing parameters of our lives.

Martha goes on. "Well, okay, idleness is the devil's workshop. People that just sit around and worry about stuff that they shouldn't be thinking about. They don't have time to think about something they shouldn't have their mind on at all."

Certainty is one orientation we might adopt in critical space. Instead of conceiving ourselves on a journey, a quest for truth, we might view ourselves as having already arrived, truth in hand. There are differences among those who are certain. We might be certain because, like Melinda, it just never occurs to us to question. Or, like Frederick and Martha, we might even think it is not good to question the "truths" we have received.

Alternatively, we might be certain because we prematurely decide that we have examined and assessed all the arguments there are. That seems to be the case with Iris Barbuda. "Why," I ask her, "do you think...do you never doubt that God exists?"

"As I said," she answers, "God in some form—no, I never doubt that he exists."

"How come?"

"I think I said before that I don't think all of this could be an accident."

Iris means that the whole universe is too complex, too stupendous, too orderly just to have been an accident. Iris is stating what philosophers call "the argument from design." Not a philosopher herself, Iris has arrived at it independently through her own critical reflection. Iris thus stands in contrast with many others. Many others report that they were caused to believe in God by external forces such as socialization. To that extent, they remain objects acted upon. In contrast, Iris acts as a subject, judging for herself which beliefs are rationally justified and which are not. In this way, she becomes the author of her own beliefs.

Without *haverim*, however, Iris has not been pushed farther into critical space. An atheistic *haver*, for example, might object that the argument from design has been called into question, first by philosopher David Hume and even more sharply by Charles Darwin. In light of that objection, Iris would have been pressed to further examination.

The publicly constructed arguments of critical space take a long time to conclude. For a long time, every argument seems to be met by a counterargument, including even the counterarguments themselves. So the conversation, the journey, continues. In the academy, for example, many are convinced that Hume and Darwin have demolished the argument from design. This, too, is a premature certainty. Although, as Hume shows, the argument from design cannot prove the existence of God with mathematical certainty, no empirical claim can be proven with the conceptual certainty of mathematics. Outside of mathematics, all we can do is marshal better or worse arguments. Thus, the argument from design cannot be dismissed as it often is on the grounds that it is not a mathematical proof. Admittedly, even on less stringent standards, the argument from design was definitely set back by

Darwin. Yet, as we shall see, the strength of the argument is undergoing fresh reevaluation in light of the so-called anthropic coincidences of physical cosmology.

Because the arguments of critical space seem to go on forever, because the book can never be closed on them with absolute certainty, many people conclude that we cannot ever know anything. In contrast with absolute certainty, skepticism becomes an alternative orientation in critical space. That alternative is illustrated by Betty Enders. I ask her whether she believes there is any such a thing as the truth of a matter.

"What matter?"

"Well," I say, "let's say we were just talking about whether or not there is a supreme being."

"Okay."

"Do you think that there is...I have my opinion, you have your opinion. Do you think that one of us could be right and the other could be wrong?"

"Sure."

"Both of us could be wrong?"

"We could both be right."

"Oh," I agree, "and we could both be right."

"Well, exactly. I mean, you know, but that...that's what this world is made up of: different people with differences of opinions."

"And how do we arrive at the truth?"

"I have no idea. I think if we knew that, we'd be the supreme being."

Although also not a philsopher, Betty has independently articulated a major philosophical position. That there is no "God's eye view" of reality is one of the central principles of postmodernist philosophy.[33] Instead of a God's eye view, all we can ever attain are diverse, humanly situated eye views. Because our view of reality varies with our social placement, it is presumptuous, the postmodernists tell us, even to speak of truth—of what putatively corresponds to reality. At most, there are only local truths, socially constructed truths that hold only locally in each of our diverse human communities. Truth, then, according to postmodernism, is relative to society or even the individual.

From the accurate insight that we are without any unquestionable (or "privileged") epistemological foundations, postmodernists conclude that ultimately we are without anything we can call truth. Even to speak of truth in this circumstance is just an exercise of power, an attempt by one community to impose globally its own local truth on all others. The very word *truth* in postmodern circles has consequently become suspect. The so-called hermeneutics of suspicion is today a widely prevalent orientation in critical space.[34]

The postmodernist suspicion of truth is meant to replace the modernist view, of which postmodernism often paints a caricature. Contrary to the way it is often presented by postmodernism, modernism, too, denies any privileged epistemological foundations that are unquestionable. Yet, in contrast with postmodernism, modernism maintains that we can still arrive at something approaching if not a God's eye view of reality, then at least a "view from nowhere," a view of reality that is larger and more warranted than our own initial, individual perspective. We arrive there through discussion, through argument and debate.[35]

According to modernism, if we allow everything to be debated—including our initial, foundational assumptions—then better or worse arguments will emerge. While the book on those arguments may never close and all truths may remain provisional, we can nevertheless, by evaluation of the arguments so far, draw certain conclusions about objective reality. While some beliefs may remain in dispute, the arguments in favor of others will far outweigh the arguments on behalf of their contraries. Those aware of the arguments, therefore, those alert in critical space will be in possession of what so far has the best claim to truth.

This modernist orientation in critical space is exemplified by Sandra Moreno, who is an evangelical Christian and a highly respected physicist. She tells me that while much about current physical cosmology remains in dispute, some things seem firm.

"Do, do we know...Is what we learned about dinosaurs just a game? I don't believe so. Just in astronomy, we have learned that the sun is at the center of the solar system and not the earth. I don't think that that's going to change. That is firm. We've learned that the sun is in the outer reaches of the Milky Way galaxy. I believe that's firm. We've learned, you know, about the distribution of matter around our self. Yes, these are not, I don't believe, likely to change."

Postmodernists might ask why Sandra "privileges" these "truths" of science. Why should they be accepted uncritically? The point, however, is that these truths should not be accepted uncritically. These truths remain provisional and can be overturned in light of new arguments and new evidence that powerfully call them into question. Yet, for the truths Sandra cites, no such argument, no such evidence is anywhere on the horizon. That is why Sandra says these truths currently seem firm.

The scientific "facts" Sandra cites have not in fact been privileged. They had to fight their way to their current truth status in equal argument with opposing views. Their current claim to truth does not derive from privilege. It has been earned. To see that, to know that, one of course must be aware of the arguments in critical space. Not everyone is so aware. We return to my dialogue with Frederick and Martha Schmidt.

"And," Frederick tells me, "they have —and this is something I don't quite agree with either: they have a bunch of professors that are instilling ideas in their students that I don't think is good."

"Like?" Like me, I suppose.

"Well, you get back to this evolution again, the Scopes trial..."

Frederick and Martha do not believe in evolution. I ask them. "You don't believe in evolution?"

Frederick answers. "I sure don't. I think it's the way God made things, not the way evolution says. With Darwin and his theory on...no, under any conditions."

"So what do you think? If you don't agree with that, what do you think?"

"I think," says Frederick, "it's the way the Bible says it."

"Exactly?"

"That's right."

"So..."

"Man is not related to a bird in any way or a frog or anything like that."

Finally, Martha finishes the point. "God created the heaven and the earth. Then he put into it everything that's there, and he didn't make me out of a cow or you out of a bull. I mean, you know?"

I know that Frederick and Martha express a faulty understanding of the theory of evolution and that in terms of that faulty understanding, evolution does seem incredible. I know, further, that Frederick and Martha are unfamiliar with the wider arguments that have earned Darwin's theory its truth status in critical space.

Frederick and Martha belong to a community of Christian believers for whom, the postmodernists would say, creationism is a local truth. I, in contrast, belong to a scientific community for whom the local truth is evolution.

But what does it mean to call creationism and evolution local truths? It can only mean that Frederick and Martha's Christian community believes in creationism and that the scientific community—which includes such Christians as Sandra Moreno and me—believes in evolution. But we do not need postmodernism to tell us that there are different beliefs about the world. Calling such diverse beliefs local truths suggests that the Christian community and the scientific community literally—and not just figuratively—inhabit different worlds. On that construal, Frederick and Martha actually got here through God's instantaneous creative act, and Sandra and I got here through evolution. This is an example of the epistemic fallacy, failing to distinguish our beliefs about the world from the world itself.

Curiously, we do not find postmodernists championing the right of conservative Christianity to present creationism in public schools. But why not, if creationism and evolution are coequal as merely local truths? Is it simply that from a postmodern perspective, religion in general and creationism in particular are not politically correct? Is there not some kind of unexamined moral privileging operating here?

Postmodernism is against privileging any one local truth. Paradoxically, however, the postmodernist position actually does privilege such views as creationism. By declaring all beliefs equal, a consistent postmodernism would place creationism, which has done little to earn a universal claim to truth, on a par with evolution, which has forcefully earned its position in the critical space of argument. When the merits of two claims are unequal, it is not those who recognize the inequality who are engaged in privileging but rather those who would privilege the lesser claim by elevating it without warrant to an unearned equality of status.

Curiously, for all its love of discourse, a consistent postmodernism silences discourse. Postmodernism celebrates "difference" and diversity. But what do those of us from diverse communities of belief have to say to one another? We can listen attentively and respectfully to one another as I believe I have done with Frederick and Martha, but what then? We can march in each other's cultural parades, but what then?

When we find that those of us from different communities hold divergent beliefs, postmodernism seems to counsel respectful silence. Yet we can do better than silence. We can enter critical space together in a shared examination of our previously unquestioned assumptions. We can challenge each other to arrive at ever more warranted beliefs. We can concede where we find our own arguments wanting and accordingly modify our views, reformulate them, adopt more sophisticated positions. That is what is what is entailed by a "liberal" discourse. That is what is meant by an examined life. That is how we avoid dying with the beliefs we were born into. That is how our own identities intellectually grow.

That intellectual growth, that cross-community dialogue assumes that despite our opposed beliefs, it is the best account of a common world we are after, a common world in which we all either originated from a special act of God on the sixth day or evolved equally from lower forms of life.

Critical space of course has many internal boundaries. There is a critical subspace of political arguments, a critical subspace of moral arguments, and so on. Today, the critical subspace of metaphysical argument is not one many choose to enter. Postmodernism itself seems to accept uncritically the condition it accurately describes: that when it comes to metaphysics, all is beyond critical inspection, all is just a matter of faith; diverse belief systems are incommensurable, and cross-community discourse impossible.[36]

If we are to enter critical space, our own articulated positions must be placed on the table. In order to examine critically what we believe, we must first believe something. When it comes to metaphysics, however, many of us do not know where we stand. Transfixed by *avidya*, caught in the details of daily life, we experience part of our postmodern condition as alienation from the cosmos. We have already begun to suspect that this alienation is largely emotional. The emotional detachment from the cosmos is what we now need to explore.

Chapter 3

The Emotional Detachment from the Sacred

Have you not heard of that madman who lit a lantern in the bright morning hours, ran to the market place, and cried incessantly: "I seek God! I seek God!"—As many of those who did not believe in God were standing around just then, he provoked much laughter. Has he got lost? asked one. Did he lose his way like a child? asked another. Or is he hiding? Is he afraid of us? Has he gone on a voyage? emigrated?—Thus they yelled and laughed.

The madman jumped into their midst and pierced them with his eyes. "Whither is God?" he cried; "I will tell you. We have killed him—you and I. All of us are his murderers. But how did we do this? How could we drink up the sea? Who gave us the sponge to wipe away the entire horizon? What were we doing when we unchained this earth from its sun? Whither is it moving now? Whither are we moving? Away from all suns? Are we not plunging continually? Backward, sideward, forward, in all directions? Is there still any up or down? Are we not straying as through an infinite nothing? Do we not feel the breath of empty space? Has it not become colder? Is not night continually closing in on us? Do we not need to light lanterns in the morning? Do we hear nothing as yet of the noise of the grave diggers who are burying God? Do we smell nothing as yet of the divine decomposition? Gods, too, decompose. God is dead. God remains dead. And we have killed him....

...The madman fell silent and looked again at his listeners; and they, too, were silent and stared at him in astonishment. At last he threw his lantern on the

ground, and it broke into pieces and went out. "I have come too early," he said
then, "my time is not yet. This tremendous event is still on its way, still wandering; it has not yet reached the ears of men."

—*Friedrich Nietzsche,* The Gay Science

Here is how to make yourself into the madman of Nietzsche's parable:
Stand up in front of a classroom in any large, metropolitan university,
preferably on one of the coasts, and read aloud to the students the epi-
graph that begins this chapter. Read it with feeling as if you too are
moved by the enormous loss conveyed by Nietzsche's powerful
imagery. When you finish and look up, you will find the students
regarding you with blank stares. Should you probe them for a reaction, any reaction, they will humor you with the response accorded
Nietzsche's madman. The students will consider you, too, a bit mad.

If Nietzsche's madman concluded that he was too early, that his
time had not yet come, you might conclude that you have arrived too
late, that your time has passed. It might seem as if God has been so
long dead and buried that no one remembers what all the fuss was
about. The stench of the corpse is completely faded.

In intellectual circles of course, if you try this now, you literally will
have come too late. The intellectual furor over the so-called death of
God took place in the 1960s, at which time it was big news, reported
on in all the newspapers.[1] The sixties were likewise the heyday of
French existentialism, of the attempt of Sartre and Camus to come to
moral terms with an empty universe. Now, even existentialism appears
passé, like a dressing meant for a wound already healed. With the healing, both the pain and the incident that inflicted it are forgotten. If
religion once served as a sacred canopy of meaning, we since seem to
have grown quite comfortable living under a naked sky.[2]

Actually, as we have seen, reports of God's virtual demise are premature. Public opinion polls consistently show that between 89 percent and 95 percent of the American public profess belief in God.
Only 2 percent claim to be atheists. On closer inspection, not even my
students are atheists. Their indifference to Nietzsche's parable then
becomes something of a mystery. It is not as if my students do not react
to anything. True, they are often similarly unmoved when I call their
attention to the poor or oppressed, but should I go on to attack
America or the capitalist system, my students become thoroughly
engaged. In contrast, talk about God and other ultimate matters leaves
them cold.

Thus, if God is not exactly dead, God is not exactly well either. Something has happened to the Old One. The question is what. This question bears directly on our inquiry. We have observed that really to know who we are, who we are existentially, it is not enough to place ourselves in social space. We need to orient ourselves in moral space and metaphysical space as well. We need to locate ourselves within a morally meaningful cosmos.

At issue in Nietzsche's parable is whether the cosmos that served the West for two millennia continues to function for us as a morally meaningful cosmos should. It is one thing to believe in God. It is another for that belief to be operative in our lives. Do we experience God? Does that experience provide us with moral meaning and metaphysical direction? God may not be dead, but he may be "hidden," "eclipsed," or "silent."[3] The postmodern end of metanarratives is more an affair of the heart than of the head.

Whether or not we are less religious today than we were, say, two hundred years ago is a much debated question.[4] On some dimensions, we may actually be more religious today. Church membership and church attendance in the United States, for example, appear to be greater today than before the Civil War.[5] Of course, church membership and attendance represent just one dimension of religiosity—and not necessarily the most important one. If we go back further, back one millennium or perhaps two millennia, it seems clear that substantially more of us today than then inhabit a desacralized or disenchanted world. If we truly want to understand what we have lost, if we truly want to understand what Mircea Eliade refers to as *homo religiosus* (literally, "religious man") in his and her natural habitat, then it may be back two millennia that we need to go.[6]

For *homo religiosus*, the world was very different from what it is for those of us living at the centers of modernity or postmodernity. Even many of the religious among us tend to live out our lives on a single, profane plane of existence. In the profane space and profane time we occupy, no point has any greater cosmic significance than any other. Consider how we just commemorated the millennium. Considering that we were marking the passage of a thousand years, the media attention was, at least until the last moment, surprisingly subdued. Yet many were repelled even by the modest attention the millennium did receive. It is all arbitrary, they protested, nothing to make a fuss about. The secular attitude is to treat each time like all other times, each place like all other places. Profane space and profane time offer no point of cosmic reference.[7]

For *homo religiosus,* however, profane existence was always punctuated by the sacred. There were fissures in space and time through which the sacred poured. In space, there were sacred rivers and cities; sacred mountains that inspired awe; sacred groves, filled with numinous dread. Temporally there were sacred festivals, which did not just commemorate the mythic past but which actually reinaugurated it as the extraordinary time of "the eternal now." For *homo religiosus,* there were sacred rites, objects, and incantations, all filled with power.[8]

Homo religiosus effectively walked two worlds, the sacred and the profane. Of the two, it was the sacred world that was the more real, the more filled with being. It was from the sacred plane that profane existence drew its sustenance. The sacred was consequently experienced as the ground and source of being. It was the origin of meaning.[9] It was for this reason that *homo religiosus* was ever drawn to the sacred, ever making pilgrimages to holy shrines, ever consecrating with sacred rituals the otherwise mundane events of human existence.

Although *homo religiosus* still survives, it walks a world foreign to the modern, secular imagination. For the completely secularized person, the numinous emotions associated with the sacred are not often felt.[10] In our secularized culture, for example, we now tend to think of dread simply as intense fear, but religiously, dread is a distinct emotion. It is the creepy, uncanniness of encountering that which is totally other, what we might feel if we encountered a ghost, a Nazgul, or a Darth Vader.[11] Dread is the emotional reaction before the utterly unapproachable. It is the same emotion experienced in confrontation with "the holy."

The holiness of God is not mere perfection. It is the wholly other perfection of that ground of being who announces, "My ways are not your ways." *Yahweh* means literally "I am who am," and it is literally as "am-ness," as the ground of being that God speaks. The dreadful aspect of God survives in both Jewish and Christian liturgy as when God is pronounced "Holy, holy, holy, Lord of hosts," but many today do not know what the words mean, let alone feel the sentiment.

From what might be considered their premodern perspective, Christian fundamentalists continue to experience the holiness of God. Holiness, Brad Caldwell says, is one of the attributes that most attracts him to God. When I ask him what holiness is, he tells me.

"What I've learned is that holiness is something which as humans we cannot truly understand. It is something that is totally foreign and alien to us. God's holiness is, I guess, what I see as…It's something that is so far different from you and I that we can't…It's something we can't understand, but it's something we want to understand more and more because what it does is it gives us a glimpse of who we are and how much sin there's really in our lives."

Brad Caldwell speaks of being attracted by God's holiness. If dread were the only emotion associated with the holy, this attraction would be difficult to understand. In addition to dread, however, the holy also inspires awe. *Awe* is another word originally associated with the numinous that has lost its power as our sense of the numinous has faded. Today, we use the words *awed* or *awesome* mostly in connection with feats, feats we thereby intend to designate as impressive.

Numinous awe, however, is primordially not a reaction to doing but to being. It is, in the first place, total otherness that inspires such awe, an awe that Steven Spielberg attempts to capture in his film, *Close Encounters of the Third Kind.* Close encounters with extraterrestrial aliens inspire awe because as the very word *alien* connotes, those who visit the earth from space are totally other from us. We speak today of the mystery of the unknown, but it is not the unknown as such that inspires awesome mystery but the unknowable, the unfathomable, the wholly other.[12]

In the scientifically disenchanted world we now inhabit, outer space represents one of the few remaining sites from which such awesome otherness may emanate. The compelling attraction of the now uncommon experience of awe may explain why so many people are fascinated by UFO's. Consider Ellen Smith, for example, the accountant who, in the last chapter, found it difficult to articulate her values. Ellen finds it less difficult to talk about UFOs. She is, in fact, an avid but critical reader of UFO literature. I try to find out why.

"I think," Ellen says, "maybe because I tend to like these things to be true, except..."

"Why would you like them to be true? You have—you have reasons and you seem to have done some reading and seem to be..."

"Well, frankly, though, some of the accounts I've read make me wish, make me where I'd become glad if they weren't true. Some of them are frightening."

"Uh-huh."

"But, I guess...well, it's exciting to think that these things..."

"Why? Why would they be exciting?"

"I don't know."

"What's exciting about them?"

"How can you *not* think they're exciting?"

"Well..."

"If somebody said to you, 'I'm going to introduce you to somebody from another planet,' and they could guarantee one hundred percent that this person is from another planet, you wouldn't find that exciting?"

"I would find that exciting. I just wonder…"

"I mean just the fact that they'd be so different from us. That seems so incredible. That makes it…I just think it's, I think, it's an unknown. It's a mystery. And so that's just fascinating."

The wholly other is already entrancing and captivating in itself. The sacred, however, is more than just wholly other. It manifests itself as a fullness of being that inspires veneration and reverence as well as awe. In at least certain experiences of epiphany, we encounter the sacred as that before which we recognize ourselves as just "dust and ashes."[13] What attracts us in this experience is not the sense of our own cosmic insignificance but the contrasting sense of proximity to that which *is* cosmically significant. Cosmically, *to be* is *to be meaningful.* The sacred is filled with being precisely because it is charged with meaning.[14] Thus, when we are close to the sacred as we are, for example, during the Jewish Days of Awe, spanning Rosh Hashanah and Yom Kippur, we are simultaneously close to the source of our own being and our own meaning. This is particularly true for the monotheistic religions, in which God is experienced as the one ground of all being and all meaning.

This is how God is experienced by fundamentalist John Wasserman. "The reason that I am attracted to God," John tells me, "isn't because of goodness or compassion or those kinds of things, although those things are obviously there, but, rather, the fundamental part is, he's God. He's truth. And that he's the one who by being such defines what is good, defines how people act, defines all those kind of things. So, in one sense, it is, you know, his compassion, his love, and his mercy that I love, that I enjoy. And yet, there is a more fundamental thing, which is that he is God. And with that comes the truth behind everything. And I think that that's, that's kind of the key."

John describes God as truth. From a secular perspective, this may seem a peculiar thing to say. In secular discourse, we treat truth as a formal relation that holds between our claims or beliefs and reality. If our claims and beliefs correspond to reality, we say they are truthful or the truth. Yet when John describes God as truth, he means not merely that God is a reality. Instead, John seems to speak of truth in the same way as Jesus when Jesus declared himself to be the truth. Truth in this sense refers not just to a reality but to ultimate reality, the ultimate source of meaning. Philosophers have a word for this connotation of truth. It is truth as *alethia*, the Greek word for the reality that ultimately discloses itself.[15]

I follow up with John to find out whether he really is invoking an alethic sense of truth. "Well, when you say 'truth,' it sounds like...When you say God is the truth, to me, what you're saying is that that is more fundamental than love, compassion, patience, justice. And it also sounds like when you say 'truth,' you do not mean...you mean something different from simply not telling lies."

"Right."

"It sounds like what you are saying is that God is rock-bottom reality."

"Right."

"And that's what? The source of all being?"

"Exactly, and that it is God that has brought everything that there is into being. And he is in control. He is bigger than everything else that there is. And, therefore, things like, you know, goodness, love, all those other things flow out of God and are defined by God."

Being, meaning, and morality: cosmically, the three coincide. Contemporary philosophy of ethics attempts to found our moral obligations entirely in the profane sphere of existence. For utilitarianism and other forms of consequentialist ethics, for example, what is right is determined by abstract calculations determining which actions will bring about the greatest good or the greatest happiness for all. The calculations, however, are ungrounded in any larger cosmic order. As a consequence, contemporary philosophy of ethics often appears lifeless and devoid of feeling. It does not connect ethics with emotion. On the contemporary philosophical account, ethics inspire no moral passion. In contrast, for *homo religiosus*—for people like John Wasserman and Brad Caldwell—the moral sense arises from an emotional encounter with the sacred. For them, morality is cosmogonic. It is from the experienced moral meaning of the cosmos itself that certain actions become good or bad, right or wrong.[16]

I ask Matt Bennett, "What if God were malevolent?" Would he and John Wasserman then still love God, just because God is the creator of the universe? Suppose rock-bottom reality were evil?

"Well," Matt responds, "I think that the way you define what is good, though, is what God is. God is good. Good is God. You ask what if God were malevolent? It seems an unanswerable question. But it is not like there are some principles of good and evil, and God's a player within that system. It is God who defines morality, and some of his attributes that we think of as good are his love; his patience—even with people who rebel against him; his justice—that he will eventually punish sin; his forgiveness. He will take people who have rebelled against him and continue to bring them back to himself. His mercy. And the way he loves us is our model for the way we are to love other people."

Matt's last sentence is foundational. At its core, Christian ethics is not based on obedience to commands but on an experienced call to respond to God's own unconditional, selfless love by emulating it. As the parable of the Good Samaritan makes clear, we truly respond to this call only when we extend a Godlike, unconditional love to all the other, concrete thous we encounter.

One need not be a fundamentalist to share this view. In fact, it is in no small part because many Christians find certain biblical passages unloving that they reject a literal, fundamentalist reading of the Bible. For such Christians, the lovingness of God, however much it might shine through the Bible, is itself higher than the Bible. When love and the Bible seem to conflict, as, for example, in attitudes towards gays and lesbians, it is the Bible that must take second place.

What fundamentalist and liberal Christianity are at least supposed to share is both the centrality of love and the cosmogonic origin of that ethical principle. We love others, the author of the first letter of John tells us, because God first loves us. Whereas for Hinduism, fundamental cosmic reality is emotionally experienced as an identity of the individual self with the self of the universe, for the monotheistic religions of the West, fundamental cosmic reality is emotionally experienced as an I-Thou relationship. Christian morality is born out of this religious experience of the sacred. As expressed through the New Testament, God's unconditional love for us is experienced emotionally as so transcendent that emulation becomes the only appropriate response.

This moral dynamic lies at the core of Victor Hugo's novel, *Les Miserables*. In *Les Miserables*, the life of the miscreant Jean Valjean is completely transformed when the "good Bishop," whom Valjean has just robbed and whose murder he has just contemplated, treats Valjean with a generosity that Valjean emotionally experiences as wholly other. It is Valjean's awed response to that numinous generosity that calls him from then on to live a life in imitation of the good Bishop. Although Christian ethics is often caricatured as an authoritarian obedience to God's commands, for many the motivating force is not obeisance to God's authority but a call to respond emotionally to God's example.

The call to emulate God's example is the cosmogonic origin of Jewish ethics as well, a point made by Rabbi Daniel Gordis, who calls his fellow Jews to a more spiritually infused Judaism.

Parashat Kedoshim, the Levitical Holiness Code, gives a rationale for all of Jewish religious life; it begins with a statement that
because God is holy, we, too, should be holy. Religious life, it
suggests, is about trying to imitate God. It is not the essence of
Judaism to live life in accord with God's command simply
because God has commanded. The Torah suggests that *mitzvot,*
or Jewish behaviors, are actually a means to an end. They are
designed to create holiness. Jewish life is about creating holiness by providing guidelines for imitating God.[17]

Religious Jews and Christians thus are called to emulate God. For
those, like Jean Valjean or Rabbi Gordis, who emotionally experience
such a call, life takes on moral purpose. Morality, then, is no longer
just a matter of constraints on the pursuit of private, morally neutral
ends. Life itself becomes a moral project with a comprehensive purpose and meaning. Such a life immediately takes on a definite orientation in moral space. It is emotionally centered around some vision of
the good. As in the case of Jean Valjean, we know what such a life
stands for, what it points to. In that pointing, in that committed direc-
tionality, an identity emerges in moral space.
    Yet it is not just in moral space that an identity emerges. Insofar as
the moral purpose pursued is ontologically grounded, grounded in
the very nature of the cosmos, such a morally oriented life is cosmically oriented as well. It is oriented toward what the cosmos itself
reveals as *alethia.* Thus, in relation to the sacred, we ourselves acquire
a fuller, deeper identity beyond our position in social space. We
acquire an identity in moral and metaphysical space as well.
    It is the loss of all this that Nietzsche laments in his proclamation
of the death of God. It is the loss of all moral purpose he fears, the
utter collapse of moral and metaphysical space. It is the specter of
nihilism that Nietzsche beholds, a universe in which we no longer pursue any moral vision—or if we do, it is like the moral vision pursued by
the butler Stevens, one that possesses no cosmic grounding. Insofar as
orientations in moral space and metaphysical space are foundational
to our identities, it is ultimately for our own souls that Nietzsche fears.
    Nietzsche blames our predicament on 2,000 years of Christianity.
He has a point. The desacralization of the world began with monotheism. In the efforts of Judaism, Christianity, and, later, Islam to stamp
out idolatry and paganism, all the plural manifestations of the sacred
were absorbed into the One God. In their shared affirmation that
"God is One," none of the monotheistic religions would tolerate any

other source of sacred meaning. Metaphysically, all our cosmic eggs were placed in one monotheistic basket. Such a metaphysical strategy could only ensure that when the reality of God was undermined toward the end of the second millennium, we would be left without anything to ground ourselves morally or cosmically. According to Nietzsche, that is the predicament we face today. That, according to Nietzsche, is why, individually or collectively, we no longer know what we are about, where we are going, or what our lives mean.[18]

Now, as we end the second millennium, we find the postmodernists making a similar, Nietzschean claim. According to the postmodernists, it is characteristic of our age that we are not only without God but also without any substitute for God. According to the postmodernists, ours is an age without metanarratives, without any overarching cosmic meaning that can supply our lives with an encompassing moral purpose.[19]

We need to ask whether this postmodernist claim is really justified. Is it really true that people today feel their lives to be without purpose and meaning? As a preliminary measure, we might look to the data collected by public opinion polls. What does the American public tend to say about such questions when asked?

In one such poll, the Gallup Organization asked a nationwide sample of adults, "How important to you is the belief that your life is meaningful or has a purpose?" The comparative frequency of responses is listed below.[20]

Very important	83%
Fairly important	15%
Fairly unimportant	1%
Not important	1%

Evidently the vast majority of people in the Unites States still consider it important that their lives possess some ultimate meaning or purpose. As we observed earlier, contrary to Nietzsche's announcement of God's demise, an even greater majority of the American public still profess belief in God. Given how important the sacred traditionally has been to moral meaning, we might expect that if people still consider life meaningful, then God will figure prominently in whatever overarching purpose most Americans attach to their lives. If we expect that, however, we will be surprised. Consider the distribution of nationwide responses to a question asked by the National Opinion Research Center (NORC).[21]

Do you agree or disagree with the following: To me, life is meaningful only because God exists.

Strongly agree	23%
Agree	24%
Neither agree nor disagree	24%
Disagree	15%
Strongly disagree	10%
Can't choose	5%

People may believe in God, but God evidently is not the primary source of meaning in many people's lives. If we accept these numbers at face value, about half of Americans would consider their lives meaningless if they believed that God did not exist. For the other half of the population, the meaning of life is not rooted in God.

Such public opinion data give us the general lay of the land. They help us to judge how representative more anecdotal information may or may not be. In a sense, the public opinion data give us breadth. The disadvantage of such data is that they lack depth. It is difficult to know what the respondents actually mean by their responses. For this reason, public opinion data need to be complemented by the sort of in-depth interviews we have been examining.

It may be that the NORC respondents did not really understand the question. It may be that their responses mean something different from what they appear to mean. At least preliminarily, however, we need to take seriously the possibility that for up to half of Americans—theistic or not—God and meaning are decoupled.

A very large number of Americans may believe in God without that belief's functioning as we might expect. Whatever other functions God may serve for them, for many people, God may not function at all as the ultimate ground of meaning. This may begin to explain why my students in particular are so indifferent to God's state of health. God just is not vital to the meaning of their lives. Their lives revolve around other suns.

Public opinion data provide even further indication that God and meaning may be decoupled. In this case, the detachment obtains between religion and morality.

Do you think your outlook on religion affects your ethical and moral behavior a great deal, or affects it somewhat, or has little to do with your ethical and moral behavior?[22]

A great deal	52%
Somewhat	27%
Has little to do with it	19%
Don't know	2%

Again, for about half the population, morality is strongly grounded in religion and, presumably, God. For almost as many, however, religion and morality show some degree of separation. For almost twenty percent, the separation between religion and morality is pronounced: their religious outlook has "little to do" with their moral outlook. Again, for a great many people, God does not function as we would expect. God does not serve as the ground of ethics. Perhaps we have the beginnings of an understanding of what has happened to God. If God has not died, God may simply have become more detached from our lives. This seems to be the case for quite a number of the people I interviewed, including those who believe in God.

THE VARIETIES OF RELIGIOUS ALIENATION[23]

Conversations with individual people shed some light on the numbers examined above. Fundamentalists and many other religious people experience a fulfilling, personal relationship with God. But many other people do not share this experience. It is not surprising for this experience to be absent in atheists and agnostics or in those who have found some nontheistic path to meaning. We know, however, that the overwhelming majority of Americans identify themselves as theists. Presumably, therefore, in the responses examined above, many theists indicate only a weak connection to God.

While it may be interesting to explore why atheists do not experience God, it is even more interesting—and more relevant, given the theistic character of America—to explore how and why theists, too, may be alienated from God. Many people may believe in God, and God may represent a very important element of their universe. Nevertheless, for a variety of reasons and in a variety of ways, their connection with that ultimate reality is distant or troubled. For such people, God is not what provides either meaning or moral inspiration. The role God plays in their lives is other than that.

Quite understandably, some people find my endless questions exasperating. Eli Cohen is one of these. I interview Eli in his living room, while his wife, Guzia, works in the kitchen. Both in their seventies, Eli and Guzia are Jewish survivors of the Holocaust. He was at Dachau and Auschwitz, she at Bergen-Belsen. They met after the war at a displaced persons' camp.

Eli has just told me what he is committed to in life: his wife, his children, Israel, and the United States.

"What about God?"

"God?" Eli asks. "I am a great believer."

"In?"

"I'm not a religious person."

"What do you mean, you're not a religious person?" Eli's assertion confuses me because Eli attends synagogue on the High Holy Days, fasts on Yom Kippur, and abstains from leavened bread during Passover. In comparison with many Jews, Eli seems observant.

Eli continues. "A religious person is...observes a lot of, you know? Things, you know? He goes to the synagogue...three times a day."

"Three times a day?"

"Absolutely."

"When do they find time to work?"

"Well, I'll ask you. In the morning, in the afternoon, and at night. And he does a lot of things. Studies a lot. I am not like that. I am...I respect the person that does it, but I'm not like that. But I am a great believer that somebody above is watching us."

"Why do you believe that?"

"Because I've...I feel in me...in me that God follows me. Whatever I do, I feel...I have something in me that God...watches over me. Whatever I do, I say to myself, 'Thank God.' And this is not a story. I really mean it."

"I believe you."

"I really believe it," Eli says again. "I'll tell you the truth. I do it my way. Since I'm here, and anything I've done in my life till now, I feel that somebody was watching me. From the first day that I came to this country."

"Not before?"

"Depends. When I was in concentration camp, we give up everything...we lost all the hope."

Having previously written about the Holocaust, I am staggered to be sitting so close to a man who once stood equally close to Rudolf Hoess, a man who once waited for the turn of Hoess's thumb to determine whether he would live or whether he would die. "Did you feel like God was watching you then?"

"No, I was...I didn't feel like there was a God around there. I thought that...we lost our God. Because if he could see what was going on, and he didn't help us...we gave him up. The only ones who believed in him was the real, real religious Jews, like the rabbis. They still believed in him in some way. Why, I don't know."

"But you didn't?"

"No, I didn't."

Like most people, though unlike the rabbis of whom he speaks, Eli is neither a theologian nor a philosopher. Eli meets God—or fails to—not through the intellect but through personal experience. For many Jews like Eli, if God truly existed, he certainly seemed to have abandoned them at the camps. One need not be a Holocaust survivor to be similarly impressed by the problem of evil. Theologians have struggled to reconcile the image of God as at once both all powerful and all good. Many regard the evil in the world as prima facie evidence that no such God exists. I am inclined to agree. For Eli, however, this is not just an academic argument but lived experience.

"When I was in concentration camp, we had a rabbi's two sons. They were—they were ready to be rabbis, too. They was beautiful, honest, nice people. They were twins. And they took them away, and they killed them. In front of us. How could I believe that there was a God then? I couldn't believe it. Even I couldn't believe that!

"I ask myself a question. If a God is there, and such good Jews that they gave their life away just for being religious and to teach somebody else, and God doesn't help them, and they take them away, so what is it? What, that's…what a good question to ask, but nobody could answer. Until now, my question is still the same thing: Why did they took away little kids, infants, and killed them for nothing? Why? But this 'Why?' nobody has answer for it. And if it would be a God, like everything like they, they…He could do something and he didn't do nothing."

There it is, the theological problem of evil, more powerfully posed than it could possibly be by any abstract argument. If God truly is there, perhaps it is God's own fault that people doubt God's existence.

At the risk of exasperating Eli, I press him further. "Why aren't you religious?"

"Because this is my way of living. Not everybody's got to be the same way."

"But do you have a reason for not being religious?"

"Yeah, yeah. I have, I have a reason. One reason is I wasn't brought up to be real, real religious. And the second reason was the concentration camp, what we went through. It's going to be fifty years."

"Right."

"It's…eh…the thirty-first is going to be fifty years since I lost all my family. Fifty years. I mean, that's…eh…this is the reason. If you go through something like that…a guy like me, you lose everything. You lose, you lose your hopes, and you lose beliefs and everything else. Sometime, I wonder how we, how I bounce back in life. Me and millions like me."

Yet, if it was in personal experience that Eli failed to find God, it was also in personal experience that God and Eli eventually did meet. Eli now experiences his life as if "somebody" were watching over him. "But do you think God helps you?"

"I told you. While I was in concentration…I was all against him."

"Right."

"But this, I'm saying so. The, the rabbis they didn't say noth—they didn't say that. They said that we got, that we're punished for something. This was their, their idea. And I heard from one rabbi. But average people like me, we gave up the hopes completely, but religious…But then, when I came here, and I started building up a family and building up a life, I said to my wife a lot of times, "Everything I do is with somebody's help. Somebody above us is watching us."

"Why did you think that?"

Eli practically shouts at me. "This is my belief!"

"Yeah, but why did you believe it?"

"Because I believe in something."

"Even…okay."

"I believe in something!"

"Do you remember when you first had that…belief?"

"Yes, since I came here. I'm telling you."

"What…Can you describe, though, the incident?" I'm pressing my luck.

"The incident? Yes, when my kids was born."

"That was the first time you started to believe in something?"

"That's right. That's right. It was a miracle. I start building…what we lost in the old country. I start building a new generation. I lost them already. I lost my brothers and sisters, my mother and everybody else. This was to me, like, to me and my wife, it was the first miracle in our lives."

Popularly, a miracle means something that defies the laws of nature. Classically, however, a miracle is just a sign of God, a sign that God is present and active in our lives. It was a miracle Eli personally experienced that made him believe if not in God then at least in "somebody" above.

"Tell me about God. What, who is God?"

"You know, you can't carry on a conversation about God, because nobody knows actually, but it's a might that…You gotta believe in something. A person, a normal person…if he's not a Communist, you gotta believe…You can believe in a lamp or you can believe in something else, but you gotta have a belief. A person that doesn't have a belief is not a person."

Through his personal experience, Eli has come to believe in something supernatural watching over him. If pressed, he will acknowledge that something as God. Yet Eli's relationship with God remains complex and ambivalent. For Eli, God is still a mysterious other, about which he knows little. Given God's own history with Eli, God is not particularly a moral inspiration.

"Is God good?"

"Well...he wasn't too good to us, the Jewish people, during, during the war, because he, he...they killed the biggest rabbi, the biggest people with brains, Jewish people. They went to kind of die. So how could I say he was good?"

"So God isn't good?"

"He wasn't...not...He occasionally, he gives us a lesson. I think he gives us a punishment. Why? I don't know."

"You think the Jews were being punished?"

"The people, the real religious people, they—they said something happened that we were punished for a while."

"Do you believe that?"

"No, I don't."

"Why did God let that happen, then?"

"I have no idea."

"Do you love God?"

"I respect him."

"But do you love him?"

"You can't love something that you don't know what it is. It's a...you love a person, you love a piece of furniture, but you..."

Eli ends in laughter, but I persist. "But you don't...love God?

"I don't hate him!"

That probably is as much as God deserves and as good as I am going to get from this line of questioning. I have been arguing that moral purpose derives from a vision of the good and that by representing such a vision, God may call forth our love and, through that love, our emulation. It is clear that for Eli Cohen, God does not function this way. For Eli, God is principally a mysterious somebody who now watches over him.

Yet, even for Eli, God is also something more than that. As emotionally conflicted about God as Eli is, God also seems to represent for Eli a placeholder for meaning. It is very important to Eli for one to believe in something—unless, of course, one is a Communist. While for Eli, no meaningful content may originate from God, God remains at least a cipher who stands for the place that meaning ought to occupy. By believing in God, Eli believes in meaning. As we will see, God functions this way not only for Holocaust survivors.[24]

Since, despite his protestations about not being religious, Judaism remains important to Eli, I try finally to find out what Judaism means to him. "What does it mean, what does it mean to you to be Jewish?"

"Very important. I believe different..."

"What does it mean to be Jewish?"

"To be proud of yourself."

"But what does, what does it mean—"

"To be born this way. To be raised this way." It is Eli's wife, Guzia, who calls this in from the kitchen.

Eli echoes his wife. "I was born and raised this way."

"But what way? What is, what is Judaism?"

"Judaism is—"

Guzia interrupts again. "We believe in God."

Again Eli affirms his wife's comment. "We believe, believing things."

"Believing in things? Well, you think...I believe in things, but I'm not Jewish."

"So it's, you can believe..."

"So what makes you different from me?"

"I don't say you're different."

"Well, what does it mean to be Jewish?"

"We believe in a different religion."

"Well, what do you believe?"

"I believe..." Eli chuckles and calls to his wife. "He asks certain questions. It's hard to answer."

Guzia answers instead. "Yeah. You respect each other. Even you are not Jewish, but we respect you."

I nod. "Yes."

Guzia continues. "Because you are not Jewish, and you are going this way..."

"You got a lot of religions," says Eli. "You got Moslems, you got all kinds of religions."

"Yeah," I reply. "Well, I could tell you about Christianity. I could tell you what I believe."

"Go ahead," says Eli. "You tell me what you believe so maybe you'll give me a hint. I'll give you an answer from my..."

"Um..." I find myself strangely embarrassed to speak of my own religious beliefs, but fair is fair.

"Go ahead," Eli tells me.

"I believe in…Jesus. I believe that…uh…God is good, that there's a God who made the universe."

"That's right," replies Guzia. "One God is for everybody."

Now Eli is the interviewer. "Go ahead."

"And I think that God is good, and that he put us here for a purpose. And I think that God is *not* all powerful. Because, I think, I don't think that the Holocaust was punishment. I think that God…it wasn't in his power to do anything. So I think it was human beings who did that. So I don't agree with the rabbis who say that God punishes…was punishing the Jews. I don't believe that. I think that God himself was crying during the Holocaust."

"They believe," Eli begins. "The rabbis believe that God is upstairs and that he does everything what is going on here. And he…If he's so mighty, if he's so strong…"

"I don't think he is so strong…I don't think God is so strong." I am offering one standard theological solution to the problem of evil. Forced to choose logically between God's goodness and God's omnipotence, many theologians choose goodness.[25] I concur. It is goodness, not power we should worship.

Eli continues as interviewer. "If you don't, if you don't think he's so strong, who told you that he's not strong? How do you know better than me?"

A fair question. "The Holocaust," I reply. "I think God is good. You say God isn't good. I say God is good. You see, you say God is strong. I say, 'He's not strong, but he's good.'"

"I say," Eli replies. "I say that you got to believe in something."

"I do believe in something."

"So we all believe in different ways."

"Okay, but now I'm asking what you believe." I persistently remember the question we began with. "I told you what I believe. Now, what do you believe? What is Judaism? I told you what it means to me to be Christian. I believe that God is good. You have to be good. And sometimes, sometimes you fail."

"Well, this question," Eli finally says. "It's hard. I tell you, you keep on talking about religion, and you're not going to get the right answer from nobody. Not only from me but nobody."

Although Eli is not completely right—some people can provide more of an answer to the questions I am asking—his assessment is at least frequently correct. Even among those who never experienced anything like the Holocaust, people may believe in God without deriving much concrete purpose or meaningful content from that belief.

Like Eli, Iris Barbuda also tells me she is not very religious, and in her case, too, her statement is somewhat surprising.

"Now," says Iris, "my daughter-in-law's Catholic. I go to her Catholic church. I have no qualms about taking communion in her church. I mean, I'll go to the Catholic church. In fact, when I was...right after my husband died, I was in Washington, D.C., and I still contribute to the basilica there. And it did a lot for me. It was soothing. I think religion is sometimes..."

"Soothing?"

"Soothing," Iris affirms.

"You don't go to the Lutheran church regularly?"

"No."

"Okay."

"I'm a member, and I go."

"You're a member?" I'm surprised because membership in a church is a greater commitment than just attending a church. Iris had led me to believe that she wasn't very religious.

"I am a member," Iris affirms.

"Of a Lutheran church in this area?"

"Hm-hm."

"Uh, okay. You say you're not religious. Why? What does that...what does that mean when you say you're not religious?"

"Well, I guess maybe going to church. I'm not a churchgoer."

"Okay."

"And I don't...I certainly know religious people, and I don't espouse some of the same beliefs that they do."

"Like..."

"I'm not sure that there is...I think there's a God. There has to be a supreme being. What he's like or...I have no idea."

As we saw in the previous chapter, Iris believes there must be a supreme being because, as she reasons, someone had to have created the universe and everything we see. If Iris is hesitant here about acknowledging the existence of God, it is because, like Eli, she has little sense as to who or what God is. Clearly, if Iris has little sense of what God is like, God can do little to inspire her morally or give her life meaning. For Iris, too, God is at most a cipher who simply holds a place for meaning.

The same is true for Tom Brown. "Okay," I say to Tom. "Now, you said you believe in God?"

"Yeah, I believe in God...but I have doubts. You want to ask why. I don't know. Now you're going to ask why I believe in God."

When we first encountered Tom, my questions had made him

nervous. Now that he has me figured out, he evidently can conduct the interview without me. "That was going to be my next question."

"I believe in God because I was taught to believe in God." As we have seen, many people say they believe in God simply because they have been socialized to believe in God. The belief is not something they arrived at on their own but rather something that has been programmed into them. While many who inherited their belief in God may still be emotionally invested in it, others, like Tom, may doubt its validity without considering it important enough to actively examine.

I press Tom further. "Do you ever feel..."

"You know, I don't see, I don't see any physical evidence of God."

"Hm-hm."

"You know, I was taught that there is a God. If I grew up in an environment where I was taught there wasn't a God, I'd probably believe there wasn't a God."

"Well, knowing that..."

"But I still have doubts."

"Well, knowing that, why do you believe at all?"

"If I have doubts?"

"No, no. I know you have doubts."

Tom nods.

"But why aren't you an atheist then? Why don't you just say, 'Well, I was taught to believe in God or if I was brought up in some other way, I wouldn't believe—I would have been taught to believe in something else.' So if that's the only reason you have to believe in God, why do you still believe in God? In other words, you said you believe in God, but you have doubts. Why didn't you..."

"I have doubts. I mean, I'm not..."

"I understand you have doubts."

"I'm not sure a hundred percent. I have reservations."

That Tom has doubts has registered with me. "Well, why do you believe at all?"

"Well, I guess the only answer I can offer is what I just gave you. I was brought up that way."

"Okay. Do you ever..."

Tom shrugs. "If somebody was asking me to give logical and tangible evidence, I couldn't do it."

"Hm-hm."

"I just couldn't."

I decide to go with the flow. "So, all right, tell me about your doubts. How did you...is it just that you just look around and see that we could have been brought up differently and that there's no evidence…"

"Yeah, I don't see any visual, tangible evidence. I don't see any scientific evidence. You know. I don't see God. I can't touch him."

I nod. Although Tom reads about and otherwise investigates issues that interest him, he has not really gone out of his way to examine what physical evidence there might be for God's existence. Tom talks about the lack of physical evidence, but probably more important is the lack of experiential or emotional evidence. If Tom does not experience God in his life, then God's existence will not likely loom as a compelling question for him.

"Do you ever feel like you have an experience of…did you ever experience God's presence?"

"No. I know people who have said…people who were born-again Christians have said they experienced…You know, they can pinpoint the day they were 'saved.'"

"Hm-hm."

"Frankly I wonder if it's all in the mind."

"Hm-hm. So you don't feel that you've had any experience of God?"

"No…no…no."

"No personal relationship?"

"No."

"Now, you went to Catholic school?"

Tom nods.

"When did you…Can you tell me at what age you decided that…where you began to think…I mean, I'm sure it didn't happen overnight…that when you first began to think that God was just maybe made up by human beings, and what prompted that?[26]

"It might have been before high school, but it definitely was not after high school. It was before…"

"Earlier than high school. Earlier than graduation from high school?"

"Right. I can't pinpoint. It might have been in junior high, I don't know. I can't pinpoint. I can't remember."

"Was God ever important to you before that?"

"Well, not the most important."

"What was most important?" Tom remains silent, and I say, "Well, okay, nothing comes to mind…"

Tom finally responds. "Well, family."

"Family," I repeat.

"Family. I guess God was important to an extent, but not, you know...He wasn't the center of every...of my life."

If God was not the center of Tom's life then, neither is God at the center now. Although Tom continues to believe in God, Tom probably would not be unduly upset if it were conclusively announced that God is dead. Although Tom is a believer, it is difficult to imagine his strongly affirming in response to a public opinion question that, "To me, life is meaningful only because God exists." We can easily imagine Tom responding, "Neither agree nor disagree."

We first encountered Joe Barboso in the previous chapter. He is the young physics major who believed that we should each do our own thing as long as we do not hurt anybody. Although Joe's belief in God is shaky, he does tend to believe.

"I think," says Joe. "I think, just in general, on the average, I think that of the many schools of thought, I think I lie somewhere between God created the world and is running it like an experiment he's not into playing and between God created the world and is actively participating with, like, signs or whatever."

"Right." Joe positions his beliefs somewhere between the traditional "living God of Israel" who acts in history and a Deist conception such as was held by some of America's founding fathers. According to Deism, God initially set up the universe and then left it to its own devices. Deism has a strong affinity with empiricist mechanism—that is, with a clockwork conception of the universe. Thus, it is not altogether surprising that this view would be attractive to a young physics major.

In Deism, God truly is alien or disengaged from the world. If God designed the world with a purpose, that purpose is inscrutable. God's purposes therefore offer scant moral direction for our lives. Instead, we must find purpose on our own. Thus, again, in Joe we find morality coincident with cosmogony: each of us must find his or her own purpose in life because the universe itself gives no independent project to achieve. As Joe continues, it becomes clear that Joe's God is the so-called God of the philosophers, an inert answer to a philosophical question that does not offer any emotional linkage or moral direction.

Joe continues. "I'd lie somewhere in between that. I'm pretty sure there's a God, but that can change tomorrow...I mean, that can change in a couple of hours. If this interview took place later, I might give you a different answer. So I'm very up in the air about whether God created the universe right now, but what's important for me is...we just talked about...what was that thing you said about..."

"Your existence...the purpose of existence."

"Oh, yeah, the purpose of existence. I don't think that's something that God gives to you or anybody gives to you. I mean, I don't think that's something that some higher being gives to you. You might create it by what you see in life or what you see on TV or read in books or hear your friends talk about. You create your purpose, your purposes, your goals in life. That might be how they're created, but I don't think some higher being gives them to you. But, my purpose is just to try to do what I do...try to like make sure I get everything done..."

"Right."

"I don't think there's a purpose to life in general, because I think everybody's purpose in life is specific to that person. You know what I mean? Like, I mean, life is something that we try to quantify to like everybody, but you can't. I mean, the purpose to life doesn't mean anything when you say it in a general sense because life is different to everybody."

"Right."

"I mean it's not like the purpose of this in-and-out tray that might...This has a purpose because this is a solid thing. Everybody comes in here and says it's maroon. It has an "in"; it has an "out"; and the purpose is to get the messages in and then get the messages out. It's a concrete thing. Life is different to everybody. Therefore, you can't say it has one definite purpose. I mean, you can't generalize like that. I think the purpose of life, if you have to say something, is to see what everybody's individual purpose in life is."

I nod. In sociological terms, Joe is saying that the purpose of life is subjective and individual. There is no common sacred canopy that covers us all. Instead, the purpose of life is whatever we individually determine it to be. The purpose or meaning of life is not something to be discovered but something to be chosen. For Joe, too, ultimate meaning is totally detached from the God in whom he believes.

"That's the purpose in life," Joe finishes. "The purpose of life is a five-billion-part thing."

I am back with Ellen Smith, talking about the values she says are "normal."

"Okay," I say. "Um, how did you happen to have those values?"

"I think it was the way I was raised."

"Okay. And why did you think those values are...why people...People grew up in different ways, right?"

"Hm-hm."

"So, I mean, some people did not grow up to have those values. So why do you...do you think...Why do you think those are the right values? Or do you think those are the right values?"

"Well, I do. I think everybody would agree with that."

"You think everybody would agree with that?"

"Hm-hm."

"So you think your values are typical of most people?"

"For most, what most people consider are good values...Maybe not everybody has them, because of the way they're raised, but..."

"But everybody would think that those are good values."

"I would think so. Most people."

"Do you think those are...It's common sense to have those values?"

"Uh-huh. Yes."

"And why are those good values?"

"Why wouldn't they be?"

"Um, I guess, what I'm asking..." It occurs to me that the reason many respondents to the public opinion questions say that their values derive only partly from religion is that they tend to regard their values as just common sense. For them, the salient origins of their values are either common sense or the way they were raised. Because they experience their values as just good common sense, they do not feel the need to seek deeper metaphysical justification. Accordingly, the religious roots of their values are less salient. In this variety of alienation, one is alienated from one's own religious grounding. I pursue this line of inquiry with Ellen.

"Do you think those values come out of religion?"

"Partly."

"Partly, but not completely?"

"Oh, because there's a lot of people who have those values who aren't religious." This is an interesting answer, suggesting a possibility I had not considered. Religious respondents to the public opinion questions may look around and see that their values are not unique to those who are religious and therefore conclude that those values are not specifically religious.

"So where did the nonreligious people get those values from?"

"From their upbringing, I think. I think it stems...That's where it all came from, the upbringing. And your upbringing may have had a lot of religious overtones in it, but it may not have."

In retrospect, I see that, as so often happens in my interviews, Ellen and I are talking at cross-purposes. I keep searching for the deeper, philosophical grounds for the values Ellen holds. Ellen, like many of my interviewees, keeps offering me sociological answers in terms of naturalistic causes. What I want are the justifications for Ellen's values that Ellen offers herself.

"But for you did the values come from religion?"

"Probably."

"What part comes from religion?"

"Uh, well…I learned the same kinds of things from religion that…from my family, but I guess I felt that the part of it that comes from religion is wanting to be a good person and go to heaven. I guess when I was younger, I wanted to do the things that would be looked upon well in God's eyes."

"Okay. And how do you think now?"

"It's hard to still think like that except that it's more, you know, you…I guess I just think that you should be a good person and live your life and try to…I guess I believe that there is a God and an afterlife and that I believe that when I die, I'll be reviewing my life, and I don't want to be, you know, ashamed or set aside all the bad. I mean, I know of course there are the bad things, but I'd rather have more good things than…because I think that's what I'm supposed to be doing here among other things so I guess that's in the back of my mind."

So Ellen does have some sense of an order, upheld by God, which includes an afterlife, and which in some way charges her with doing certain specific things here on earth. There is some sense of purpose in Ellen's life that is related to God.

"Okay, so you said you're religious. Would you say you're…you said you believe in God?"

"Hm-hm."

"Would you say you're religious?"

"Not if it's…not an organized religion. I mean, I don't go to church."

"Why don't you go to church?"

"I've never gotten anything out of it. I find it boring." I can understand Ellen's reaction. Different kinds of religious services appeal to different kinds of people, and it can be difficult to find the kind of service that speaks to us. For rituals to speak to us, we first must penetrate them so as to understand them from the inside. As long as we remain outsiders, rituals appear empty, formulaic behaviors, devoid of meaning. Perhaps it says something about our secular age that this is how the word ritual is colloquially understood.

Returning to Ellen, I say, "Okay. So would you say you're religious, would you say…"

"I still would say I'm religious…in my own way. I mean, not in an organized fashion, but, yeah, I still think I am religious." Unlike Eli Cohen and Iris Barbuda, Ellen does not equate religiosity with attendance at religious services.

"In what way are you religious?"

"Because I believe in God, and I believe in an afterlife." So religiosity has a cognitive dimension too. It is partly determined by what we believe.

"Okay."

"And I believe in, you know, trying to be the kind of person I think that God wants me to be." And religiosity also has a behavioral or ethical dimension. We can here appreciate that religiosity is a multidimensional concept.

"What does God want you to be?"

"He wants me to be a good person and to, you know, I think to make some kind of contribution and to treat others the way I would want to be treated."

Again, Ellen hints at some sense of cosmic purpose. In contrast with Joe Barboso, Ellen hints at a common, divine purpose to life that is distinct from the purposes we might just come up with on our own.

"You said make some kind of contribution. What do you...What kind of contribution does God want you to make?"

"To society, you know?"

"Like?"

"You know, like people that work...that help other people that are disadvantaged or..." For Ellen, God's purpose for us is a social purpose. To the extent that we attend to that purpose, God lifts our sights beyond our private concerns to matters of charity and justice. Yet, if that is what Ellen believes is God's purpose, she remains somewhat alienated from it.

"Are you doing that?

"No."

"So you're not doing what God wants you to do?"

"I mean we give some—some to charities but not that much, I don't think."

"So are you not...is that..."

"Yeah, I guess I...I really haven't found my...where I can contribute yet."

"But you feel like you should make some contribution?"

"Yeah, I do feel like that."

"So you're going...Part of what you do is you live...you keep an eye out..."

"Right."

"...for where your niche is."

"Yeah."

My argument in this book is not that we all must develop a relationship with God. What I am arguing for is the need to connect with some vision of the good that lifts our moral horizons beyond our selves and our own small circle. I am further arguing for the need to engage in more metaphysical thought than we typically do. In short, I think it important for our own sense of self that we conceptualize our place in the cosmos.

At the moment, however, we have been struggling with a more narrowly sociological question: How and why it is that while most Americans profess a belief in God, many nevertheless seem strangely disconnected from the God they believe in. We generally think that the major dividing line in religion is between those who believe and those who do not. We tend to think that the major differences in religion are a matter of the mind.

We tend to overlook how much of our differences in religious orientation are an affair of the heart. In the U.S., where most people are Christian and almost all are theists of some kind, the principal division may not be a matter of belief. Instead, the principal divide may be between those who somehow experience God and those who do not. The people we have just heard from all believe in God. Yet, for a variety of reasons and in a variety of ways, they find themselves emotionally detached from God. In his parable, Nietzsche tells us that many of those listening to the madman did not believe in God. Perhaps it would have been more apt to say that the God in whom they believed had already become so remote that God's life or death mattered little to them.

The postmodern detachment from the sacred manifests itself even in sociology. Twenty-five years ago, Peter Berger accused the sociology of religion of a kind of "methodological atheism," of avoiding not just the possibility of a transcendent reality but even people's reported experience of such a reality.[27] Although the sociology of religion has changed since then, its studied avoidance of transcendence has not.[28]

What makes some people religious and others not? To answer this question, we need to look beyond the cognitive and behavioral dimensions of religiosity and pay more attention to the experiential role of God in a life. Because so many intellectuals are themselves unused to thinking about God, to them, the emotional disconnection from God we have just been examining may not seem remarkable. Intellectuals, instead, may wonder how it could be otherwise. Perhaps, therefore, this chapter should end with a clear example of a contrasting life.

THE FAITH OF A PHYSICIST

The title of this section is also the title of a book by John Polkinghorne, a physical cosmologist and Protestant theologian.[29] If Tom Brown really wants to begin investigating the tangible evidence for God, he might start with that book.

If, among academics, social scientists are the least likely to be religious, physicists, it turns out, are among the most likely to be religious.[30] Recently, in fact, the findings of physical cosmology have completely reopened the argument from design cited by Iris Barbuda.

It turns out that if any of a whole host of fundamental physical constants had been even minutely different, intelligent life such as ours could never have evolved. The so-called anthropic coincidences involved are so many, so varied, and so individually and collectively improbable that if this is the only universe there is, it appears amazingly as though it had been specially designed for our eventual appearance.[31] The lament of astrophysicist Robert Jastrow has now become famous.

> For the scientist who has lived by his faith in the power of reason, the story ends like a bad dream. He has scaled the mountain of ignorance; he is about to conquer the highest peak; as he pulls himself over the final rock, he is greeted by a band of theologians who have been sitting there for centuries.[32]

As we will see, the story has not yet ended, and the theologians' triumph appears less certain than it did even a few years ago. As I talk with physicist Sandra Moreno about these matters, she counsels me against placing any theological bets on physics.

"Yeah. Yeah," Sandra comments. "I mean, there could be something horribly wrong about part of our understanding that when we see it, we're going to see the whole thing in a totally different light. We have to keep that in mind, and it is unwise and, I think, some really wrong thinking to base your theology on what we know about science."

"Hmm." I see Sandra's point, but I do think that science and theology need to be in dialogue. Theology at least must always be informed by what science uncovers.

"Science is provisional," Sandra tells me.

"So..."

"I don't worship science. My faith is not in the big bang. My faith is in God. Because I believe in, and so for myself, I worship God. And I believe that God created the universe and the physical laws and that science is a good thing to do. We're understanding more. And we will continue to understand more, but science is just a part..."

"Well, let me ask you this because, actually...So you, you're a Christian?"

"Yeah."

"And when...were you always Christian?"

"Oh, no. I was, well, I was raised a Catholic."

"Oh, okay."

"But I went through a rebellion against God as a teenager and it's very strange because I think—I know—I became an atheist, but it never occurred to me that God didn't exist. That was not where I was going. I just didn't want any part of God, and I thought, you know, that I could have this life separate and that God exists, so?"

Sandra has just identified the very experience of the alienated believer I have been trying to describe.

"Well," I say. "I think that's what a lot of people..."

"You know?"

"They're not atheists," I tell her.

"Really?"

I proceed to tell Sandra about my research, about how people do not seem to be atheists, that it is more how much people care about their belief in God.

This resonates with Sandra. "How, how...that's right. That's right! I mean, I rejected God because I...My image was that it was not what I wanted in my life, and that it said things about my...I think this is where a lot of people get into...I think this is a critical issue. And I went off for very many years, and I only became a Christian—I only turned to Christianity about six years ago."

"And can you...I don't know. How did that happen or..."

"Personal life crises. Physical science is not going to..."

"No."

"That's the problem. And some people...I remember I had a very, very devastating thing occur, and I couldn't handle it. And I was shocked that I couldn't handle it. I was thirty-five, and I was successful. A scientist, had grants, everything. Yeah, I think I was even tenured. Have I been tenured that long?

"I was, you know, I was, I was doing well by the world's standards, and yet, when this one particular thing happened, I dropped to my knees and prayed, and I had not prayed in eighteen years. So it was a long time there, and I remember I stood up, and I was so embarrassed. I thought I was such a coward. I can't handle this. I was embarrassed, and I...for a long time, I wouldn't even discuss it with anybody because I thought that...that the ultimate act of cowardice is praying. And I realize that that was the best thing I ever did, and I'm glad that I'm a Christian. It meant...I checked out other religions. I really wanted...I needed something, and I had been searching, and Christianity met me where I was."

"Hmm." Tom Brown kept asking for tangible evidence for God. If anyone is in a position to examine the tangible evidence, it is Sandra, who has devoted her life to cosmology. Yet, it was not the tangible evidence that had mattered for her. What eventually mattered was the experiential evidence in her own personal life.

"And," Sandra continues. "I believe Christianity showed me the truth. And so I placed my faith in Jesus and went on with my life. And it was quite a change for me because I was this physicist...But as I have reached a more peaceful plateau and come back and look at these things, I find that I think one of the problems is that people worship science and expect that science will provide—I mean, scientists, I don't know if other people have these problems, but they expect science will provide all the answers. In other words, science is supposed to provide not only an observation concerning the big bang but science has to explain the big bang itself."

"Well," I respond. "It also seems that for a lot of people like Weinberg and some of the other cosmologists, science is also a source of meaning in their lives. And I think for Einstein, too, it was, which I can understand."

"It's fascinating," Sandra continues. "Physics is absolutely fascinating. And people, physicists work all the time, and you can't pry people away. And it's not that we're doing it because we have to. It's because we can't stop. People love it. I love what I do. It's wonderful, and I think it's because my belief is, because we're staring at the creation."

"Well..."

"This is it! This is, this is the creation. It's beautiful. It's wonderful, and it's pure, and it's simple, and it's not messed up with feelings, touchy-feely stuff. It's not messed up with people or even...You know, biology's kind of messy. We're talking pure atoms."

I nod, although Sandra is certainly conveying a lot of feeling.

"Galaxies, very simple systems, and we've made a tremendous...We've made a tremendous, tremendous advance since Newton, for example, realizing that the same force that dropped an apple to the ground is the same force that holds the sun and the earth together. That's a tremendous leap. And so in physics we see that laws that are simple on the earth can be extrapolated into the far reaches of the universe, and there's no evidence or compelling reason to think that that is wrong."

Having a strong interest in physics, I actually could go on listening to Sandra talk about cosmology for hours. However, I have a task to complete, so I bring her back to the topic. "Do you doubt...do you ever doubt that...Do you ever doubt your belief in Christianity—that maybe it's wrong?"

"No. No. Because there's, there's, there's all this evidence but, again, that is not...I mean you can look at all the biblical evidence, but for myself the most concrete...the thing that I hang onto and that is undeniable to me—although it's not at all scientific—oh, well, maybe for sociologists it would be—is the change in my life.

"It's made a difference in my life. It has made a difference in my outlook. My mom was so amazed at the change in me that she asked me, 'What...what's happened to you?' And I told her about how I...how I started praying and reading the Bible, and I told her about Jesus and she started reading the same. And a couple of months later, she decided she wanted to get born again. And so—my mom's and my relationship had been terrible. I mean, really, I hadn't seen her in many years...

"We were very, very estranged, and in less than a year, that was totally transformed. And my mother's personality is totally different now. This is a woman who astonishes me because this is not the mother that I knew. A lot of those things that were a problem in the past for me, they're not present in her character any longer."

"Hm-hm."

"And there are things that were hard for me to make testimony about myself because I know that I'm better now, but I..."

"I understand."

"I have the direct experience of how nasty I was. But there are things that were in my character before. They are not present in my character anymore. They're gone. Attitudes that I had are gone."

"Hmm."

"And they've been replaced with peace. A totally different attitude. And they've been replaced with a lot more success, a lot more productivity because I'm not dealing with so many other problems and, and—you know, I guess for a physicist, these are not objective type things and so..."

"Well, even for a—I mean..."

"But...but in terms of behavior, there has been a measurable change in my behavior. There's been a measurable change in my outlook and in the behavior of other people I know who are Christians and who were not always in their past. And so...um...I know that God has made a change in my life. It's incontrovertible."

"You feel like you have a personal relationship with God?"

"Oh, definitely."

"That you know…"

"Oh, yes. Oh, yes."

"And that's really the—so you never doubt the existence of God?"

"Oh, no. Absolutely not."

Sandra's faith in Christianity does not rest solely on her personal experience. Sandra is too good a scientist never to have shared at all Tom Brown's suspicion that her personal experience of God might just be in her mind. Sandra, accordingly, has done some reading on biblical criticism.

Sandra wonders whether her personal experience has any sociological significance. Actually, it is both philosophically and sociologically important that Sandra's religious beliefs derive principally from her personal religious experience. Religious belief is often thought not to be rationally motivated. Sandra's case helps us see that this view is mistaken. On the contrary, many people come to religious belief rationally.

We need to consider what makes a belief rational. The first thing to notice is that we do not determine the rationality of beliefs the same way as we determine the rationality of actions. Because actions are goal-directed, we determine the rationality of an action in relation to its goal. If the goal is rational and if the action effectively leads to that goal, then the action is rational. In contrast, rational beliefs are not goal-directed. We do not ask, for example, what goal someone is trying to achieve by believing the world is round rather than flat. Generally, it is irrational when a belief is motivated by a goal.

If not a goal, what kind of reason does motivate a rational belief? Rational beliefs are motivated by epistemic reasons, considerations that bear on a belief's truth. As Tom Brown himself recognizes, that he and Ellen Smith have been raised to believe in God has no bearing on whether or not God actually exists. Their upbringing is a nonepistemic reason for their belief. In contrast, epistemic considerations are evidentiary. The argument from design is an epistemic reason for believing in God because it functions as supporting evidence for God's existence. We hold our beliefs rationally when they are warranted by strong evidentiary considerations.

Almost everyone would agree with Tom Brown that if we consider just the objective evidence—evidence we can all examine together—it is inconclusive whether or not God exists. The inconclusiveness of this evidence is what can make religious belief appear irrational. If the evidentiary considerations are inconclusive, why then do religious people believe in God? Their belief seems based on insufficient reason.

To fill this gap, sociology has long tried to lend religion some rationality by treating it as an action rather than a belief. Specifically, sociology has tried to show that religion serves some function or purpose. Sometimes, the function or purpose is social as when it is claimed that religion serves to bind a society together. Sometimes, as in current rational choice theory, the function is psychological as when it is claimed that religion fulfills a human desire for immortality. By so arguing that religion serves a purpose, sociology tries to portray religious behavior as a rational choice.

However, it follows from the distinction between actions and beliefs that sociology's effort fails. In fact, by treating religion as an action rather than a belief, sociology actually portrays religious behavior as an irrational choice. It may well be that religious beliefs serve to bind a society together, but that is not an evidentiary consideration bearing on their truth. Similarly, it may well be that we have a desire to be immortal, but this personal desire is no evidence for our truly being immortal. Thus, to the extent that sociology portrays religious beliefs as motivated not by evidentiary considerations but by nonevidentiary, social, or psychological functions, it actually represents religious belief as irrational.[33]

Sociology's mistake is to concede the philosophical ground too early. It does not follow from the inconclusiveness of the objective evidence about God that we all rationally should be atheistic or agnostic. As Sandra's case demonstrates, there is also the subjective evidence to consider.

Although atheists and agnostics rightly assess the objective evidence for God as inconclusive, they tend to forget that the objective evidence is not the only evidence anyone brings to the case. Even atheists and agnostics are also entering into evidence their own personal experience. It is just that in *their* personal experience, God is absent. As Tom Brown notes, it is not only the inconclusiveness of the objective evidence but also the fact that he does not personally experience God that makes him doubt God's existence. Tom's experience of God's absence is also an epistemic consideration.

To be sure, our experiences are sometimes mistaken. We may think we have experienced something when we have not or that we have not experienced something when we have. In general, however, our experiences are a good guide to reality. We would not survive very long were it otherwise. Therefore, it is quite rational to begin with trust in the reality of what we powerfully experience and to relinquish it only in light of compelling counterconsiderations.[34] Given the inconclusiveness of the objective evidence and Tom's own experience of God's absence, he might rationally stop believing in God altogether and become atheistic or agnostic.

It is otherwise for people like Sandra Moreno. Although Sandra's reasons for believing in God are varied, they include a personal experience of God's presence. It is as epistemically rational for Sandra to trust her personal experience as it is for Tom to trust his. Accordingly, if Sandra experiences God, it is rational for her to presume that God exists. Were the counterconsiderations compelling, rationality might demand that Sandra abandon this presumption. However, the counterconsiderations are not compelling. We have already agreed that the objective evidence is inconclusive, pointing no more against Sandra's experience than against Tom's. Until the objective evidence somehow changes, it is as epistemically rational for Sandra to believe in God as it would be for Tom to disbelieve in God.[35]

It is not the truth that is relative here but the evidence. The truth is that God either exists or does not. We are just not in a position to say conclusively which. Rationally, then, we all can only go by the best evidence we have, and that is relative—relative to our personal experience.

This point is as much sociological as philosophical. People likely believe in God for a variety of reasons. Many, like Tom Brown, believe just because they were raised to believe. Others may well believe because the belief serves some psychological function. Yet, in addition to these nonepistemic reasons for religious belief, a good many people believe in God because they feel they experience God. If so, then they believe in God for an epistemically rational reason that sociologists cannot ignore.

Not to ignore religious experience means to take it seriously, and that means taking the object of the experience seriously. The object of religous experience is not taken seriously when it is treated as something that can be excluded from analysis—as if the object of an experience contributed nothing to the content of the experience. Nor is the object of religious experience taken seriously when only the experience of God is subjected to social explanation and not also the failure to experience God. In the end, when the experience and nonexperience of God are treated symmetrically, a truly penetrating sociology of religion may not be able to sequester itself from theology.

Religious experience is sociologically important for a final reason. It lies at the heart of our contemporary malaise. It is the experience of

God that breathes life into the belief in God. Thus, if the experience of God fades, belief in God becomes de-energized. The problem is that in a monotheistic culture, God is what lifts our ultimate concern and anchors it at the transcendental horizon. Hence, if our emotional attachment to God attenuates, our moral horizons recede as well. Has this happened? We have already seen some evidence that it has. More awaits us.

Chapter 4

The Meaning of Life

What is the meaning of life?
You're born.
You die.
And do something in between.

—Dara Davis, age 12

I said before that our inquiry is primarily vertical rather than horizontal. If moral purpose originates in ultimate concern, then we need to examine how high our individual ultimate concerns reach. With a fading experience of God, has our concern with cosmic significance faded as well? Is there a more general unraveling of the ties connecting us to what is ultimate?

In this and the next two chapters we explore heroes, callings, and the meaning of life, three links to more ultimate concern. We must see what remains of them. Of the three, concern for the global meaning of life is most basic. Surprisingly, what people think existentially about the meaning of life is a question psychologists and sociologists have not previously thought to investigate empirically.[1] Perhaps this neglect is itself indicative of academic lack of interest in ultimate matters. We will have to begin the investigation ourselves.

Philosophically, to ask about the meaning of life is to ask about its purpose, the purpose if any for our being here.[2] Are we here for a purpose? Is there a reason for our existence? These are perhaps the most basic questions we can ask ourselves. In asking and answering them, we simultaneously search for our identities, for to answer these questions, we need to answer still others: Who are we? Where did we come from? Why are we here?

It is perhaps a commonplace of sociology and anthropology that all cultures seek to provide collective answers to these questions. From hunters and gatherers on, the cultural answers to those questions determine who each people thinks it is.[3]

It comes as something of a surprise that in our modern or postmodern world, so many of us individually not only are without answers, but we never seem even to ask the questions. Instead, as individuals, many of us seem to live quite contentedly without at all considering life's ultimate questions.

Such a finding seems powerfully to confirm the postmodern diagnosis of our times. It is not so much that metanarratives are no longer possible as that evidently we no longer seek them. Of course, we may also, as a consequence, no longer know who we are. The fragmentation of self that postmodernist philosophy takes to be a brute, ontological fact of our existence may, rather, be a result of a temporally specific disconnection from metanarratives. If metanarratives are ultimately cosmic, then our emotional disconnection from metanarratives—our disconnection from the very question of life's meaning—is further confirmation of an alienation from the cosmos even among those who are religious.

Our pervasive disconnection from ultimate matters is not immediately apparent from a superficial inspection of public opinion polls. According to one such poll, many people seem at least to think a good deal about the meaning of life.[4]

How often, if at all, do you think about the meaning and purpose of life?...

Often	48%
Sometimes	36%
Rarely	12%
Never	4%
Don't Know	1%

According to the results of this poll, almost half of Americans often think about the meaning of life and 84 percent think about the meaning of life at least sometimes. One problem with this question is that what "the meaning of life" refers to here is very ambiguous. There are different ways to think about the meaning of life.

In particular, when we say we are thinking about the meaning of life, we may mean only that we are thinking concretely about the meaning of our own individual lives. Is what I am doing at the moment what I want to do? Is this work I am doing meaningful to me? These are important questions to ask, but they are not at the existential level of asking about the meaning of human existence in general. If the people I interviewed are at all representative, then it is the more concrete, less existential meaning of life that people tend to think about.

Betty Enders is a religious Lutheran who believes in God and thinks we are all here for a reason. When she says "all," however, Betty is not thinking about humanity's collective, cosmic project but, rather, about the individual reasons each one of us is here.

"I sit, and, it's funny, I sit and think, 'Well, we're all here for a reason.' Whatever that reason is, I don't know. But I think we're all here...I believe that we're all here for a reason and to serve a purpose. And I think it just takes time for all of us to realize what that purpose is."

"And do you have any idea...Do you mean we each have a different purpose?"

"Oh, I definitely think we all have a different purpose, I really do. You are a teacher. I'm not a teacher, but I have been known to be very helpful in different ways to different people and I think for just...We all have a certain purpose in life, and I think we're all here to serve that purpose, and it just takes time for each one of us to realize what our part in this scheme of things is."

"Do you think it is a grand scheme, and that all these purposes fit together for some overall purpose?"

Betty hasn't thought about that. "I don't know. I've never really sat and thought about it. I really don't know."

"Okay. You say that we're all here for a purpose. Where does that purpose come from, our individual purposes?"

"I don't know that either. You know what I mean? I sit and I think about this, and I think, oh God, you know? Why am I here? Why is this happening? Why is that happening? And I think, well, I feel everything happens for a reason, and it just takes time and different events that lead up, I guess, to the main object. I don't know. But different things in my life, you know, I feel that happened, it made me a stronger person and have changed...made me what I am today."

We have seen that for many people, God may function as a cipher. In such cases, although God has little content, God at least serves as a placeholder for an absent meaning. In Betty's remarks, we see that the same function may be served by God's shadow—cosmic purpose. It is important to Betty that her life and all our lives have some cosmic purpose—not just a purpose we choose for ourselves, but a purpose cosmically assigned to us. Yet, Betty does not know what that purpose is. For Betty, an unspecified, cosmic purpose seems sufficient to affirm at least the fact if not the content of life's meaningfulness.[5]

When I ask Adam Schuster about the meaningfulness of life, he, too, responds by speaking about his own life individually.

"I mean, I feel like my life is meaningless right now. What I'm doing…I'm just using my time now as a tool to get myself somewhere else—hopefully. It's meaningless. I really don't…I really don't give a shit whether these documents go out today or get faxed or we didn't dot the *i* or the prices are wrong or whatever. You know what I mean?"

I know what Adam means. I also have worked at my share of meaningless jobs.

Adam continues. "The interesting thing I find about my job is, like, finding about equipment, you know? Like, well, this is the container of this size and you can fit this many pounds in the bag packed this way, like, the physical way, you know? And this is how they load it on the ship, and that kind of stuff.

"I like that logistical end, whether you can use the equipment for this and that stuff, you know? But I really don't care. I mean, it's just, like, a bunch of God damned paper. You know how much we throw away? They…It's meaningless, you know? And these people get so upset about it. Well, so God damned upset."

When asked to think about the meaning of life, Iris Barbuda also tends to think about her own personal life.

"What do you think the meaning of life is?" I ask her. "Or do you—do you think that life…Does life have a meaning?"

"I've thought about that, you know? Particularly in down times. You think, 'My God, here I am: I'm born, I'm going to die,' you know? It's like, well, what is this all about? And so more and more, and, I don't know, but more and more, I'm convinced that you have to make the most of what you have here. You're given a brain, so you should utilize those things that you have to make the best life that you can. And, hopefully, along the way be able to give somebody else something back."

"What does it mean to make the best life? What is the best life?"

"Well, I think the best life for you. I don't think every…see, I don't believe in Communism, so I believe that everybody is different. So what's best for me may not be best for somebody else. For me, I like things like…I like to have wonderful family and friends; I like to travel; I like to have a good job; I like to feel like I can contribute…"

"Contribute?"

"To life. I mean really, I feel like I like to make a contribution to my job, to my family, that I'm…that I'm there, and I'm worth something. You have to be worth something."

"Well, okay. That's interesting. What does it mean to be worth something?"

"It means that you have…To me, it means that you add value to the things that you are doing. You contribute. You add value to your children's life. You add value to the job that you are doing. You bring something to it that they can, that somebody else can take away from."

"Something somebody else wants?"

"If they want it. But, for instance, hopefully you can make some kind of change in what's happening to improve the process, to improve the work environment, to improve relationships even. So…even to create diversity in the workforce. Because that's really the excitement in life for me, the diversity of people."

The people we have just heard from are all engaged in important reflection on the meaning of their lives. Yet, that reflection remains concrete and personal. It does not rise to a more abstract, universal level; it is not reflection about who humanity is in general or about what humanity in general should be doing here on earth. It is not reflection about humanity's collective, cosmic purpose.

The responses to the public opinion question considered above indicate that almost half the public thinks often about the meaning of life. However, we do not know whether it is the individual meaning of their own lives people are thinking about or whether they are thinking about the possible cosmic purpose of human existence in general.

A PHILADELPHIA SURVEY

To get a better sense of this distinction—and, again, to check the representativeness of the people I interviewed, I worked with the survey research center at my university. Through random digit dialing, we asked a random sample of 280 Philadelphia residents, first, how often they think about the meaning of their own, individual lives; and, second, how often they think about the meaning of human existence in general. An introduction to these two questions clarified the distinction drawn. The comparative results are listed on the next page.

	How often Philadelphians think about the meaning of their own lives.	How often Philadelphians think about the meaning of human existence in general.
Never	3.3%	5.2%
Rarely	5.1%	11.8%
Sometimes	25.9%	39.1%
Often	39.1%	26.6%
Always	26.6%	17.3%

The responses to the Philadelphia survey question are not strictly comparable with the responses to the the national survey question we first examined. First, the Philadelphia survey clearly sampled just Philadelphians whereas the national survey sampled Americans as a whole. Second, the Philadelphia survey included an extra prompted response: "always" thinking about the meaning of life. Could anyone always be thinking of the meaning of life? No, although one might always be oriented toward what one considers the meaning of life to be. The "always" response was added to capture any such stronger affirmations of the importance of the meaning of life.

The results of the Philadelphia survey indicate that people are in fact less inclined to think about the meaning of human existence in general than about the meaning of their own, individual lives. Only 17 percent of Philadelphia respondents say they always think about the meaning of human existence in comparison with 26 percent who say they always think about the meaning of their own lives.[6]

In response to the human existence question in the Philadelphia survey, almost 44 percent of the sample say that they "often" or "always" think about the meaning of human existence. This percentage is not very different from the 48 percent of the national sample who say they "often" think about the meaning of life.

In the national sample, however, many people who say they often think about the meaning of life are probably thinking about their own lives rather than human existence in general. Thus, although Philadelphians are hardly representative of America as a whole, we might expect that even for America as a whole, less than fifty percent of the public often think about the meaning of human existence. How much less? Whatever people tell us over the phone, I actually found very few people who spent much time thinking philosophically about human existence.

Table 4-1. Attitude Toward Meaning of Life

Question: Which of the following statements best describes your attitude toward the ultimate meaning of human existence?

Percent Agreeement	Statements
5.2%	There is no real meaning to our existence. We are just lucky to be alive.
27.2%	Our existence must have some meaning, but I don't know what it is.
40.1%	We are here on earth for a purpose, and I feel I have some sense of what that purpose is.
19.7%	We are here on earth for a purpose, and I feel I know what that purpose is.
7.1%	I have some other attitude toward the ultimate meaning of human existence.

100% Total   N = 593

What answers do people come up with when they actually have been thinking about this question? To find out, the Philadelphia survey also asked what people have concluded about the meaning of life. This question was asked again in a second Philadelphia survey six months later. Combining the results of the two surveys, almost 600 randomly sampled people responded to this question.

The survey results (see Table 4-1) present a range of responses. About 27 percent of respondents affirm that there is some meaning to human existence but confess they do not know what it is. Presumably, the people we heard from above would be among those who answered the question this way. Another 41 percent answered not only that we are here on earth for a purpose but that they have at least some sense of what the purpose is. Twenty percent of the respondents felt they actually know what the purpose of our existence is.

The survey provided two additional answers to choose from, neither of which attracted many responses. About five percent of the respondents answered that there is no real meaning to our existence and that we are just lucky to be alive. Another seven percent indicated that they have some other attitude toward the meaning of life. What other attitude might there be? As we will see, among those who might answer the question this way, we find some of our more diverse perspectives on the meaning of life.

As I indicated, one reason for conducting the phone surveys was to ascertain the representativeness of the people I was interviewing. In turn, however, the in-depth interviews illuminate the deeper thinking that may lie behind respondents' answers to the survey question.

What the in-depth interviews disclose is a pervasive lack of interest in global purposefulness, a pervasively weak sense of cosmic calling. Surprisingly, as we will see, the lack of larger purpose is found even in many with a strong religious belief in God. Although many people firmly believe that God created the universe, seldom do they ask why God did so and what God's purpose for humanity might be. What collective purpose does God want us to achieve now that we are here? Most people seldom ask themselves this question.

Although we will see exceptions, and those where we might least expect them, not even religion provides much sense of collective moral vision. It does not have to be this way. Liberation theology, for example, speaks powerfully of a collective human project to realize the "reign of God" on earth, the reign of equality, justice, peace, and truth. In Latin America, this collective human project is widely and articulately embraced even by uneducated peasants who are hardly theologians.[7] In the United States, neither this project nor anything approaching a collective human purpose receives much attention, even from religion. People affirm that life has purpose, and they wait to discover what their own individual purpose might be. Perhaps they will continue waiting until they connect their own individual purpose with some collective mission for humanity as a whole.

Sociologist Anthony Giddens argues that intense self-reflection is one of the hallmarks of late modernity.[8] Giddens is attending to the proliferation of self-help manuals and guides. He is distinctly not attending to actual people, from whom we gain a balancing perspective. Actual people may also be self-reflective, but their self-reflection remains at the most concrete level. There is little reflection that is existentially abstract. Now that sociologists have discovered "discourses" and "texts," we court the danger of a cultural version of the "ecological fallacy," the mistaken attribution to flesh-and-blood individuals the properties of aggregate society. We turn now to my interviewees, whom I categorized according to the survey responses on the meaning of life.

THERE IS NO REAL MEANING TO OUR EXISTENCE

For many people, it is depressing to think that the cosmos offers us no objective meaning or purpose for our lives and that whatever meaning we extract from life is entirely our own creation. Yet that was the "truth" that the existentialists admonished us courageously to confront. Of course, courage is only necessary if objective meaning matters to us. If it does not matter, then the existentialists' truth may be taken in stride. One person who takes it in stride is Gerry Storr, the anthropologist we last heard from in chapter one.

I ask Gerry, "So what do you think is the meaning of life?"

"Are you asking what is the meaning of life or is there a meaning?"

"All right, is there a meaning?"

"On a grand scale?"

"Yeah."

"No. On an individual scale, it's the meaning you make of it for yourself."

"And what's the meaning you make of it?"

"Family. Entertainment. Enjoyment. Pleasure," Gerry laughs, "not always sexual, but it's right up there. At the top."

"So that—that is the meaning?"

"Personally?"

"Personally."

"Well, it's changed. My meaning has changed."

"In what way?"

"I don't know. I gave...I went through my 'save the world' phase."

"And what happened to that?"

"I can't save the world. I don't want to save the world. I don't care about the world. I've reduced my...my scale, okay? I'm not sure one becomes more conservative as one ages, although I think that happens to a lot of people, and maybe it's happened to me. But I've reduced my scale. I wanted freedom. I wanted equal rights for all African Americans, blacks, whatever they were at that point in time. I wanted NATO to be disbanded, and I wanted peace in Southeast Asia, and I worked very hard for that, okay? And I worked very hard to end the war and all that."

"Why...why were you into all that stuff?"

"Because I thought it was very important. I thought it was wrong. I thought war was wrong. I thought that—that, you know, if people did-n't take action to change the world, the world would never be changed, and—you know—it was the sixties. For a long time my desire was on a more global scale, okay? And that's always become...You know, I did draft counseling and I did all this other stuff, okay? And then slowly I said, 'Okay, it's my family, certain individuals I choose to help.'"

"And this brought the scale down? You said...did you once think that life had meaning? Greater meaning?"

"No. No, I think I've been an existentialist in that way since I was in high school. Well, I went through my religious exploration period."

"What was your religious exploration period?"

"I was confirmed a Lutheran, baptized a Presbyterian, then went to a Methodist church. I didn't miss Sunday school for seven years or something, went every week. But at about the age of twelve or thirteen, I began to question obviously a lot of things and then, as I went into my teens, I went...I went and spoke to Catholic priests, went to rabbis..."

"Why?"

"Because none of this basic, mainline Protestantism made any sense to me."

"Why?"

"First, I never believed—as far as I can recall, I never believed in anything like the virgin birth or...or the divinity of Jesus. I mean as young as I was, I just never, never—I don't remember ever believing any of that."

As we have seen in previous chapters, to care about ultimate meaning or purpose, one must first have some emotional connection with it. Even the existentialists—even Nietzsche—mourned the silence of the universe because they experienced themselves longing for cosmic purpose. That is why they thought courage was required to confront the purposelessness of our existence. That is why they sought to replace the purposelessness of the cosmos with a collective human purpose of our own device. For cognitive reasons, perhaps, Gerry Storr seems never to have been emotionally attached to any grand design or purpose. Thus, while unlike others Gerry admirably questioned the meaning of our existence, it seems not to have been traumatic for him to accept that our lives are cosmically meaningless.

In chapter two, when we were talking with Robert Zimbruski about rights, I noted that although Robert believes in God, God has become very remote to him. I argued that it must therefore be difficult for Robert to derive much moral inspiration from God. Here we see that this assessment was apt.

I ask Robert, "What do you think is the meaning of life?"

"It has different meaning to different people. I think life is just this finite amount of time spent on Earth. I don't really put any meaning into it. You're here and probably just try to make the best out of what you can during that short span of time."

"Do you think you're here for a purpose?"

"I was put on Earth for a purpose? No, I really don't."

"Do you think humanity in general has a purpose for living, for life?"

"No. I don't think there's any purpose."

Existentialists are not the only ones to think that there is no cosmic purpose for our existence. Atheistic Marxists think that as well. Lawrence Patterson, we remember, believes in dialectical materialism. While Lawrence does not believe in any cosmic purpose, his dialectical materialism nevertheless provides the kind of collective human project that does not occur to most people.

I ask Lawrence how the universe came into being.

"Well, it wasn't made in seven damn days."

"So where did it come from?"

"You ever hear of that dialectic stuff?"

"Yeah."

"Vaguely?"

"Yeah!" Of course I have heard of it. I am a comrade, too.

"I have a belief in dialectics. I'm a materialist, and I think that the world evolved. I think things evolved to be where they are. I think certain conditions were present—you know, energy, you know? The world is made up of energy and matter. So I think at certain times, certain conditions exist that when you put different elements together, they create a new element or a new existence or a new thing. That's really, basically, how I believe the universe came into existence."

"Do you think that our existence here on earth collectively—do you think that was just, say, a natural accident of dialectics or do you think there was some purpose behind it?"

"What do you mean?"

"Well, I mean, the dialectics. You say it all happened from dialectics?"

"Evolution."

"Okay, but was it just an accident? It happened accidentally that human beings appeared or..."

"No," Lawrence replies. "No more accidental than someone getting cancer is accidental. I mean, if certain conditions exist, they're going to give rise to other conditions. I don't know if you can call it an accident or just say that they exist."

Because I am carefully trying to ascertain Lawrence's position, Lawrence probably thinks I am dense. I ask him, "Do you think there's a purpose behind it?"

"No. No more than I think that there's a purpose behind cancer. Or no more than I think that there's a purpose behind a snowstorm. I mean, shit happens."

"And our existence here just happened?"

"I think it just happened because of the conditions that existed at the particular time."

I finally change the subject. "Well, are human beings important?"

"Yeah."

"Why?"

"What do you mean why?" Lawrence is not the first person to become exasperated with me.

"What's so important about human beings?"

Lawrence sighs. "We have, you know, so much intelligence and so much potential to go further than the planet that we live on that it's important for us to explore the rest of the universe—to stretch our world as far as we can stretch it. To find out what is out there, you know? Birds don't have that capacity. Elephants can't. Whales—hell, you get them out of the water and they're done. But man—human beings—can travel in all of those elements: under land, under the earth, under water, in the air. I mean, we have the capacity to stretch beyond the limitations of the planet that we're on and go to other planets. So we can connect; we can make the universe more connected. You know, not for our own, you know, not to exploit or to use but just to see. You know? That's why I say, 'Give me a rocket because I want to see.' I want to be a part of it. Do you know what I'm saying?"

I know what Lawrence is saying, but I had not expected this answer. Lawrence has already told us that he is committed to the human struggle for truth, equality, and justice. I suppose I expected to hear more of the same. Instead, Lawrence's answer is almost mystical: Through humans, the universe might become more connected, more conscious of itself. Lawrence almost sounds like Kilgore Trout. It is ironic to hear such a profound sense of life's meaning from one who asserts that there is no meaning.

THERE MUST BE SOME MEANING, BUT I DON'T KNOW WHAT IT IS

I am back in western Pennsylvania, speaking with the theologically conservative Lutherans, Frederick and Martha. From them, at least, I am hoping to hear something about the collective human purpose God has intended for us.

"So what do you think is the meaning of life? What's life all about, then?"

Frederick answers first. "That's a good question."

According to Martha, "We're all here for a purpose and the reason I'm not dead yet is because God has something for me to do yet. It's what I feel."

Like others, Martha has once again reduced the question of our collective human purpose to God's individual purpose for her. I try to make certain of her position. "Now, and when you say that we're all here for a purpose, you mean we each individually have a different purpose?"

"That's right," says Martha. "I think…"

"Yeah," Frederick echoes. "We each have a purpose to be here."

"And do you know what your purpose is?"

"No," Frederick replies. "I wish I did. I wondered about that a lot."

Martha has a different answer. "Well, I'm nosy, I have to see how many more great-grandchildren I'm going to have and what's going on in the world."

I try to bring the conversation back to God's collective purpose for us. "Why do you think that God…You think that God created human beings?"

"That's right," says Frederick.

"Do you think God had a plan?"

"That's a good question. I don't know."

"Did you ever think about that?"

Martha answers. "I think he did. I think that everything that everybody does is God's plan, except if they do something against his will."

"Well what do you think his plan is? Do you have any idea what his plan was?"

"Uh, no," Frederick replies, "but they have some things…It's in the Bible. Do you read the Bible?"

"Yes."

"Do you know the Bible?"

"Yes, actually."

"Okay," Frederick continues. "The Old Testament. Well, that shows that people were Israelites, the children of Israel. And God set down a series of laws for them to live by and they didn't do it. When they strayed, God destroyed them, thousands of them. And according to Revelation, there's only going to be—and there are millions of Jews, you know, over the centuries…but the book of Revelation only mentions twelve thousand from each tribe. Or a hundred and forty-four thousand."

"Right." I am familiar with the belief among Seventh Day Adventists and some other fundamentalist groups that when Jesus comes again, there will be exactly one hundred and forty thousand Jews who will be saved by their conversion to Christ.

"They're going to die of AIDS," Martha asserts.

Frederick immediately quashes this idea. "No, they're not."

"Yes, they are."

"No, they're not."

I attempt to understand this apocalyptic argument. "The Jews are going to die of AIDS?"

That is not what Martha means. "I mean everybody. The nation."

"Oh."

Frederick does not accept even this. "No, that's sort of stretching your imagination a bit, too. I don't believe that either."

Although Frederick is dismissive of his wife, I am actually relieved to hear him pounce so strongly on the view that AIDS is a punishment from God. Yet I want to be certain that I understand him correctly. "Why don't you believe that?"

Martha, however, answers first. "It says in the Bible that people can destroy themselves."

"No," Frederick responds. "Where does it say that at?"

"Oh, I don't know."

"That's right," Frederick concludes. "You don't know."

Neither Frederick nor Martha seems to know what God's ultimate purpose is in putting us here. Less religious, Tom Brown believes in God despite his doubts. Yet, like Frederick and Martha, he has no idea what God's purpose for us might be.

"Well," I ask Tom, "did God...you think that God created the universe?"

"Mm-hm."

"Did God have some purpose in mind, do you think, in creating the universe?"

"Well, I'm sure he...I'm sure if he created it, he must have had a reason. But I don't really know what it is."

"You don't know what it is? And you never wondered..."

"I'm not God, so I don't know."

"So do...you don't think that human beings are here for any kind of purpose?"

"Well, they might be."

"God didn't have any sort of master plan?"

Tom thinks about this. "Well, I—I could say yes because it would seem as though he would have a master plan. I'm not God. So I—you know, I don't like to...I don't like to say, 'Yeah, I know where, I think I know what God thinks.' Or what, you know? If you...If you're going to say, 'Well, what's your best guess?' I'd say yeah, he probably did have a master plan."

"But then if I asked you what the master plan was, you would have no idea?"

"No, I wouldn't."

Lee Ann Singer is a born-again Christian who is completely devoted to God. She, I thought, should have some idea about the meaning of life.

"So, what do you think is the mean...the mean...This is probably..."

"The meaning of life?"

I considered it auspicious that Lee Ann had actually anticipated my question. "Yeah. What's the meaning of life?"

"Oh, great. You tell me."

Not an auspicious answer, but perhaps Lee Ann is just being flippant. "Well, I would expect that you've answered it. A relationship with God..."

"It's to do God's bidding. It's to do his purpose. He put me here for a reason."

"And do you know what that reason is?"

"That reason right now—right now is for me to be praying."

"Well, I don't mean right now."

"Oh, you don't mean right now."

"I mean you have—you have specific purposes in life. God called you to stop drinking. He may call you to talk with others. Those are specific things he may call you to do in your life. But, that's not the...none of those things is the reason he put you here."

"Hm-hm."

"He put you here for a reason. Do you know what that reason is?"

"The sum total of what the reason is?"

"Yeah."

"Yeah. I don't know."

In the end, Lee Ann knows only that we are here to do God's bidding. The larger purpose behind that bidding remains a mystery.

I HAVE SOME SENSE OF WHAT THE PURPOSE OF LIFE IS

To check specifically what the various responses to the phone survey might have meant, I gave a tape recorder to a student who had been assigned to me for work study. I trained him first to ask his classmates the survey questions and then to find out what people meant by their responses.

Judging from the responses my student brought back to me, saying that one has some sense of the purpose of our existence does not guarantee that the purpose will carry much content. In my student's interviews, there were two cases in which someone said he or she had some sense of the purpose of human existence. Asked to elaborate on what that purpose is, one respondent said, "It's just—you know, just take it as it comes." The other respondent said the purpose was, "To be good to people and just live a good life and be happy."

To be good to people is at least something of a purpose. It is what I heard as a purpose as well from some of the people I interviewed more in depth—Melinda Whiting, for example.

I ask Melinda, "Did God create us for some purpose, coll—you know..."

"Collectively?"

"Collectively as human beings. I mean, do you think he...had something planned, or..."

"Well," Melinda replies, "just something very, I suppose, elementary: I think probably to maybe support each other and take care of each other and all the nice little things that people like to talk about."

I get a bit more of a sense of the meaning of human existence from Julie Cates, whom we met in chapter one. Julie, remember, is a young Americorps volunteer with a lot of experience in service learning. She is a committed social activist and in college co-founded a chapter of Amnesty International.

"Well," I ask Julie. "What about the meaning of life?"

"Why we're put here?"

"Well," I back up. "You think we were *put* here?"

Julie is silent for a while and then finally speaks. "Yeah."

"Because you believe in God?"

Julie nods.

"Well, do...do you think our existence here on earth is a pointless accident or is there some purpose behind it?"

"I don't think it's an accident. I don't necessarily think it's...ugh...For me a purpose would imply a higher goal."

"Yeah."

"And I don't know whether...well, I don't know what I think."

"Does God have a master plan?"

Julie sighs. "I guess I do believe in a purpose. Because I think God has a master plan on getting us somewhere else."

"Where?" I am excited finally to hear from someone who thinks God wants humanity as a whole to go somewhere, to achieve something.

Julie laughs. "I haven't thought about these things before. Um…I guess it would have to be better than we are…more equality and more…focused on the important things in life…like family. And I really believe that love is a really important thing for everybody and that…you know, all the wars aren't good for all of that. And so I guess I really do believe that there's a purpose."

"Do you think historically we're moving closer toward that purpose?"

"God, no. I don't at all."

"We're no closer today than…in Roman times?"

"I think we're probably further away."

HUMAN EXISTENCE HAS A PURPOSE, AND I FEEL I KNOW WHAT THAT PURPOSE IS

In the Philadelphia surveys, 20 percent of the respondents said not only that human existence has a purpose but that they knew what this purpose is. Among the people I interviewed in depth, very few people expressed such a sentiment, and those that did tended to be very religious, social activists. Presumably, not all who would answer the question this way have the same depth of vision as Sister Marge and Stephen Hertz.

Sister Marge O'Hara is a Catholic nun and social activist. "So," I ask Sister Marge, "what's the meaning of life?"

"Well, now that my mother died so recently, I've had to think about that more, and I feel that especially with my mother, that we're given a very short time to express our gifts, the gifts that we've been given, for the good of the whole universe.

"I mean I'm now learning all about the new cosmology and how everything's all so connected, but I can use my mother as an example. I think we're here for a short time to do with this life as much as we can to live to the fullest ourselves, to be happy, to be fulfilled as much as we can, but then to be with each other; to be a presence; to be a catalyst or some kind of support to others; to be for those who are less fortunate or less, you know, under depression and all; and to move on from this life into another phase of existence with God forever."

So far, Sister Marge may just be saying in more articulate, more religious language what some of the interviewees tried to express. Then, again, Sister Marge's clarity of purpose may demonstrate precisely the advantage that religious language affords. But Sister Marge is not done.

"And I really—I can see that this life, which is meant to be lived to the fullest, to the potential of our gifts and help others, is—is not all there is. So I've been thinking a lot about life in this form and its purpose. And I think its purpose is to make a contribution to the good of the whole."

"The whole?" By this time I am struck by how unusual it is to hear a holistic conception of our purpose here on earth.

"The whole universe," Sister Marge continues. "The whole of humanity."

"Do you think that human history is going somewhere as a direction?"

"Well, I really am fascinated and interested in the new cosmology..."

"What's the new cosmology?"

"Well, it's the understanding of the universe as a living organism and as the development of consciousness as the human evolutionary phase we're in now. I really believe that we are becoming more connected, and that I mean the whole..."

It is amazing to me that Sister Marge's vision of an increasingly interconnected and conscious universe is almost the same as that articulated by the secular Marxist Lawrence Patterson. I press Sister Marge further. "This is like Teilhard?"

"Yes. Yes." The reference is to the paleontologist and Catholic priest Teilhard de Chardin, who also outlined a collective, evolutionary destiny for humankind.[9]

"Well that seems to suggest that the universe had, has a history in itself."

Sister Marge nods in affirmation. "Yes. Yes."

I ask Sister Marge to elaborate on what she thinks humanity is supposed to accomplish, what its collective project is supposed to be.

"Well, I can see that we have, as humans, made lots of mistakes because of our faulty understanding of the earth as a living organism. And when we try to meet our needs by taking resources from those who will follow us, I mean, we learned that was a bad mistake. I guess, ultimately, if everything went along...or, you know, that there was a plan, maybe there would be more harmony, maybe there would be more caring, more gentle living on the earth. Like the native people, and yet, you know, we looked at them as uncivilized and unproductive and backward.

"They had a certain natural, gentle way with the universe that we're learning now may be more in keeping with the plan of God or a hope of God, a dream that we would be more in harmony. The violence now that's erupting may be one of the effects of our going in the other direction or making choices that were poor choices."

For Sister Marge, then, the plan of God—or, at least, the hope of God—is that humanity as a whole will eventually realize a socially utopian vision: a way of living in which we are more in harmony with each other and the earth. That vision is not far removed from what is envisioned by a feminist, ecologically minded Marxism.

Although Stephen Hertz employs a different vocabulary, his idea of God's purpose is even closer to the utopian vision of Marxism. A proficient accountant by day, Stephen's evenings are spent either working with the poor in the inner city or taking classes at a fundamentalistic Protestant seminary. Although Stephen comes from a fundamentalist tradition himself, he experiences major conflicts at his seminary, and we will very quickly see why.

"I asked you whether history..."

"Oh, that."

"...had a direction."

"Well," Stephen answers, "I think the quest is for a culmination of God's kingdom. I think that's at the end. That is like the perfect state of living of life."

Stephen goes on to explain that God's kingdom is built here on earth through our becoming obedient to Christ. I ask him what it means to be obedient to Christ.

"Okay," Steven says, "a lot of Christians probably wouldn't say this. I see Christ preaching a kingdom, this kingdom of what the world, what our dealings with one another are really supposed to be about. To me, foundational to the kingdom are justice and righteousness. By obedience, I think what I mean is that Christ calls us to follow him into this kingdom and work for the same things that he worked for, which are—you know, justice, righteousness, love, peace."

"What does that mean, justice and righteousness? I would say... see, most Christians wouldn't say that, what you just said."

"I guess most of the people in my tradition, the born-again tradition, wouldn't say that."

"No, I agree."

"I mean, they would strictly focus on the forgiveness of sins, which—well, I guess, I'd say lets you off the hook for working for real change today—for standing up for, you know, the homeless, the orphans, the oppressed, the widows, peoples whose voices aren't heard that need to be heard from."

In the tradition of the biblical prophets, *widows* and *orphans* are the code words for the poor and oppressed more generally. Like the prophets, Stephen believes we are divinely called to end poverty and oppression. I ask him whether what he has just told me is what justice and righteousness mean.

"Yeah. Standing up for the rights of the poor so they don't...they just don't get walked on."

"So does the kingdom of God have a political dimension?" At the time I was doing this research, I was also teaching a mini-course on the politics of the Bible at a neighboring senior center to a largely African American audience. Although the senior center had requested this activity, the center's participants were at first extremely suspicious of mixing Christianity and politics. The reason, it turned out, was that they considered politics to be dirty and God not to be associated with anything dirty. The class loosened up after we spoke of Martin Luther King Jr. and the civil rights struggle as simultaneously religious and political.

"I think so," Stephen answers me. "Christ is called a king. So, I mean, throughout history, kings have been political figures. So I think Christ has this program, and it's a program of the kingdom, and it needs to be adhered to. There's this program that Christ calls us to follow.

"What's especially distressing to me is these born-again people who have had such...this supposedly incredible religious transformation but don't see this kingdom. They seem more to be stuck on working for the kingdoms of this earth. I mean, when I say the kingdoms of this earth, I mean wealth, power, prestige, and social standing rather than giving up those things, renouncing those things and working for others as Christ would have done and did do."

For Stephen Hertz, the purpose of human existence is to realize collectively the reign of God on earth, the reign of justice, righteousness, love, and peace. That is what Stephen thinks God wants from humanity as a whole. That, certainly, is an expectation more worthy of an infinitely majestic creator than for us all just to find something or other to make our lives individually happy.

For many American Christians, Stephen's politically charged reign of God is strong stuff. Yet, if there is one point of consensus among contemporary biblical scholars, at least in the theologically liberal tradition, it is that the historical Jesus truly did speak of building the reign of God, a reign that for Jesus, too, did imply social equality, love, and justice.[10] If so, then contrary to American sensibilities, religion cannot legitimately be separated from politics.

I HAVE SOME OTHER ATTITUDE ABOUT THE MEANING OF LIFE

In the Philadelphia surveys, only 7 percent of the respondents answered that they have some other attitude toward the meaning of life. Although it is impossible to know what most might have meant by this response, in my in-depth interviews there were several people whose views might be characterized as belonging to a different framework from that assumed by the survey question.

The way the survey frames the question, cosmic meaning is equated with cosmic purpose. Thus, those who say there is no cosmic purpose to human existence seem also to deny that our existence has any cosmic meaning. Yet, some people may reject the equation of meaning and purpose. They might deny that our existence has any purpose but still affirm that it has meaning in some other way.

Among the people I interviewed, several held a such a position. All were deeply influenced by Eastern philosophy, by various mixtures of Taoism, Buddhism, and Hinduism. Jason Fishman's views are representative, although in his case there are elements of classical Stoicism as well.

We begin with my asking Jason whether he believes in God.

"Yeah, in a sense...Not in a sense of...Do I believe in the Bible? No. But in the sense that God is sort of...Is there a sort of order to the universe? Yeah."

"What do you mean...by an order to the universe?"

Jason laughs. "Well, I guess...it sort of gets back to, you know, some sense of values and...what is justice and stuff.

"I mean, the fact that there is some kind of order in the universe, that there is evolution, that the circumstances are—are right on the earth for, you know, animal life, plant life, whatever, human life...I guess I don't think that looking at it as an accident is the right way to look at it. I'm not sure it matters if it's an accident.

"The fact is that there is sort of a whole set of conditions that exist in the universe. And which has given rise to life and to human beings and to planets, and whatever. And that part of the intellectual or maybe spiritual...quest that people have is to figure out that order."

"Oh, you think that's true?" Again, I am surprised to hear someone use the language of a collective spiritual quest.

"Yeah," Jason affirms. "I do think that's true. And I think that, you know, one of the...we talked before about, What is justice? I think that, you know, maybe some of the clearest things...When you look at like, you know, the massive environmental degradation...that seems pretty clear to me that...we're messing up that order.

"That's sort of problematic in that all human existence and, you know, agriculture...architecture...all those kinds of things really sort of mess up the natural environment. And it really is...one of those large problems for humanity is to figure out how to do that and not be in such conflict with the natural environment. But there is conflict...That conflict is inherent, and that's what poses, I guess, a theological problem. If, like, the conflict is inherent, you know, what does that mean about...like what is this order? I mean, are people supposed to like...crawl around and behave like animals?" Jason laughs. "Probably not."

"What do you mean by an order in the universe...though?"

"I mean, the existence of that order, I think, is, is really awe-inspiring to people."

"Yes." Awe, as we have observed, is one of the ways we emotionally connect with the ultimate. That seems to be the case for Jason.

"And," Jason continues, "I don't think there's a purpose in the sense of design or, I mean, you know? But the fact that we're not the point of the universe...in some ways is so...central. I mean it's...We're already here. I mean, the point is to figure out what sort of...How are we going to organize ourselves and relate to the rest of the universe? The question is figuring out what this process is that is unfolding and how we relate to it, rather than what was the intent of that process."

When I ask Jason about the meaning of life, he tells me that the question is one that has impenetrable depth. I ask him whether he thinks we can make any progress on the question or whether he is saying that life has no meaning after all.

"I guess if you put it that way...I mean, I haven't thought of it that way before. I would answer that it's the former: It's the impenetrable depth, but you keep making progress. That you become, if you struggle, you become more self-aware and more aware of the, the sense of order around you. How things relate to each other. How you relate to other people and other processes around you. And, I mean, that in a sense is what wisdom is."

RELIGIOUSITY AND THE MEANING OF LIFE

Throughout this book we have been attending to a culturally pervasive lack of orientation in metaphysical space, an inability to place ourselves meaningfully in the cosmos. One consequence, we have observed, is an equally pervasive void in our own sense of self. If to know who we are is to know our place in the cosmos, then we cannot lose our place in the cosmos without losing ourselves as well.

In the previous chapter, we began to press the point that our cosmic disorientation is itself a consequence of an emotional disconnection from the sacred. It is a consequence of our estrangement both from a certain range of emotions and from a vocabulary through which those emotions might be understood. Both the emotions and the vocabulary, we have observed, are ultimately religious in nature. Yet, as we have also seen, this religious alienation holds even for many who subscribe to religious beliefs. Religious beliefs do not necessarily coincide with either religious emotions or a facility with a religious vocabulary.

We have already observed a pervasive disconnection, even among the religious, from any sense of ultimate purpose, a disconnection from any larger moral vision. We can now examine some evidence that the prevailing disorientation in metaphysical space results—at least in part—from a postmodern lack of religious sensibility.

When we ask people how often they think about the meaning of life, it turns out those who say they *always* think about it are different even from those who say they *often* think about it. Another question asked in both the Philadelphia surveys was how religious people consider themselves to be. The possible responses were: Not Religious at All; Not Very Religious; Somewhat Religious; and Very Religious.[11]

This question is not very precise; as we have seen, religiosity is a multidimensional concept. Thus, we are not entirely sure what people mean when they tell us how religious they are. We do not know if they are referring to how often they attend religious services or whether they are referring to the strength of their beliefs or to something else.[12] Unfortunately, the survey constraints limited us to a single question on religiosity. But the question actually asked probably is as helpful as any single question on religiosity could be. Presumably, at least in those who say they are very religious, multiple qualities of religiosity are strongly present. Our confidence in this hypothesis is borne out by the results, for if, as I have said, those who always think about the meaning of life are different, so are those who describe themselves as very religious. In fact, they often turn out to be the same people.

Fifty-five percent of those who say they always think about the meaning of life also describe themselves as very religious. In contrast, only 22 percent of those who often or sometimes think about the meaning of life and under 13 percent of those who seldom or never think of the meaning of life also consider themselves very religious.

It probably is not the case that those who always think about the meaning of life became very religious by thinking so diligently about our existence. More likely, the reverse is true: the very religious tend much more than everyone else to think about the meaning of life. About a third of the very religious always think about the meaning of life in comparison with less than 13 percent of those who are only somewhat religious and less than eight percent of those who are not particularly religious (see Table 4-1 in Appendix B).[13]

Clearly, even among the very religious, not all or even most people always think about the meaning of life. That should not surprise us. We have already heard from a number of very religious people—Lee Ann Singer and Frederick and Martha Schmidt, for example—who do not think about the meaning of life very often. Conversely, we heard some of the more profound reflections on the meaning of life from those like Lawrence Patterson and Jason Fishman who do not consider themselves religious.

Religion is only one path to the meaning of life and does not guarantee to get everyone to that destination. What the numbers indicate, however, is that religion remains one of the more important such paths we have. The very religious are much more likely than everyone else to feel they know what the meaning of life is. Over 40 percent of the very religious say they know what the meaning of life is as compared with 14 percent of those who are somewhat religious and under 7 percent of those who are not very religious (see Table 4-2 in Appendix B).[14]

Why should the very religious distinctly feel they know the meaning of life? A textbook explanation immediately suggests itself. When we look historically and cross-culturally, we see that all traditional societies provide some overarching, religious answer to life's ultimate questions. We conclude that there is a universal, cognitive need to answer these questions and that it is the function of religion to do so. Thus, as it is the very function of religion to provide the meaning of life, it is no surprise that the very religious feel they are in possession of this meaning.[15]

Unfortunately, this pat explanation does not quite work. First, if the meaning of life were just some simple proposition, we would expect the moderately religious to feel equally in possession of it. They do not. More fundamentally, if this chapter has documented anything it is that answering life's existential questions is not a universal cognitive need. Many people not only can but do live their lives contentedly without even considering such questions let alone answering them. Even for many of those who are religious, the questions go both unanswered and unraised. Clearly, what such individuals are getting out of their religion is something other than answers to life's ultimate questions.

Sociologists and anthropologists of course will immediately translate the explanation to the societal level. Perhaps, they will say, the individual has no cognitive need to answer life's ultimate questions, but society does. Does it? What are the answers provided by the United States as a whole? By France or Great Britain? Not even societies as a whole seem compelled to address life's existential questions.

Challenging what is almost a truism in social science, we must question whether it really is the function of religion to provide the meaning of life. Instead, I suggest, the meaning of life, the value of which I do not discount, is an important by-product of religion rather than its primordial function. In no society do the wise determine that they need answers to life's ultimate questions, devise some stories, and produce religion. More likely, some sacred reality is experienced first that, by its emotionally compelling nature, so orients life as to become its meaning.

This causal ordering carries over into our own day. Today, there is a chasm between those who are and those who are not concerned with the existential meaning of life. Those concerned with the meaning of life wonder how anyone cannot be thinking about it. Those unconcerned wonder why anyone would be obsessed by such an unanswerable question.

What distinguishes the people in these two categories is not a difference in reflectiveness. It is not as if, in contrast with the unconcerned, those concerned with the meaning of life make it their business to find it and eventually do. Instead, it is more accurate to say that some meaning of life finds them. A great purpose emotionally grasps them, and when it does, their lives align with it like a magnet to metal. So grasped by larger purpose, such people cannot imagine being unoriented to life's ultimate meaning. Those not similarly touched generally feel no need to search out life's ultimate meaning. At most, continuing to live within what I have called God's shadow, they believe in the bare meaningfulness of life; only occasionally do life circumstances prompt them to ask what the content of that meaning is.

Ultimately, we have to do here with more than just differential exposure to discourses of meaning like religion, humanism, or Marxism. For larger meaning, there must be a discourse, but for a discourse to take hold, the reality behind the discourse must also be experienced.[16] Such experience, I suggest, is what tends to distinguish those who describe themselves as very religious and at the same time what attunes them to life's overall meaning.

THE BANALITY OF GOODNESS

Melinda Ratzschall told us that if there is some purpose to our existence, it is something elementary such as being good to each other. For many people, meaning and morality coincide in the golden rule. Yet, the golden rule is mainly a procedural norm, constraining us not to think just of ourselves, not to cheat or otherwise harm others. As such, the golden rule tells us how to go about pursuing our various purposes but not what our ultimate purpose should concretely be.

What explains American instrumentalism, American emphasis on moral procedure as opposed to moral purpose? In *Habits of the Heart*, Bellah and his colleagues attribute our ethical instrumentalism to a disconnection from America's founding moral discourse. Charles Taylor instead speaks philosophically of our lack of a moral ontology, of a recession from transcendental horizons.

There is something to each of these diagnoses, but as explanations, also something unsatisfactory. Even if Americans are disconnected from America's founding moral discourse, why do they not find higher purpose in their own individual religious traditions? Individualism merely labels the condition without explaining it. We are similarly still just naming the problem when we speak of the lack of a moral ontology or of a recession from transcendental horizons. What makes Americans individualistic? Why have they retreated from transcendental horizons?

We are after a mechanism, a social psychological mechanism that explains the effects we observe. I have been suggesting that one important mechanism is an emotional disenchantment, a loss of experiential contact with the sacred. The sacred may come to us mediated through our communities and their discourses, but it cannot be equated with either. We can remain in our communities and talk their talk and still be severed from sacred reality.

We have seen a disconnection from the sacred in the remoteness of God and in the recession of any larger purpose. It comes into further relief in connection with the golden rule. The instrumentalism and individualism now associated with the golden rule are what is left when an originally charismatic ethic is routinized. When a charismatic ethic is routinized, contact with the sacred disappears, and what remains is banal.

The word *charisma* has religious roots. Today we associate charisma with personal charm or appeal. Originally, however, the source of charismatic appeal was specifically religious. It was from special contact with the sacred core of our collective being that a charismatic leader manifested compelling authority. Sociologists know from Max Weber that with the passage of the original leader, authority in a charismatic movement tends to become routinized.[17] Consider, for example, the routinization of church authority after the death of Christianity's charismatic leader.

When authority becomes routinized, the charismatic charge disappears. Although sociologists have not similarly noticed it, this can happen not just with authority but with an ethical ideal as well. Thus, it was not only Jesus's charismatic authority that became routinized over time but his original charismatic ethic as well.

Let us begin with Gerry Storr's precise recitation of the golden rule. "What," I ask him, "are the moral principles you live by?"

"Very, very individualistic. Very, very narrow. The golden rule: Do unto others as you would have them do unto you."

"The golden rule?"

"Yeah. But that's not a...that's not the religious golden rule." Gerry, remember, is an existentialist. Gerry grew up in a poor, rough-and-tumble, working-class neighborhood, and his answer, some twenty-five years later, reflects the continued importance of his formative experiences. "My principle always was 'Don't lay hands on anybody, and no one lays hands on you.' Is that the golden rule?"

"Yeah," Gerry continues. "I treat people the way I want to be treated. I'm not going to hassle, I'm not going to threaten you, but don't threaten me. Okay? That's how I've always lived my life. I mean, from day one."

Iris Barbuda offers a less macho understanding of the golden rule, but her understanding is equally procedural—concerned with how we are to proceed in life as opposed to the purpose of the proceedings.

I begin with Iris the same way. "So the first question I would like to ask is, what would you say are the moral principles you live by?"

"The moral principles I live by? I guess I try to live by the golden rule: Do unto others as I would have them do unto me. Morally, I try not to be judgmental, particularly, to stay out of other people's lives as long as they're not hurting anybody...I think that you should live ethically as well. I think you should, if you're working, you should give eight hours' work and you should live big on ethics, and you should treat people fairly and not judge them, and moralistically...diversity. I don't think we should be judgmental of other people. I think we should be able to accept people as they are.

"Oh, it's something, you don't even have to call it the golden rule. To me...it is, you should treat other people as you want to be treated."

The understanding of the golden rule shared by Gerry and Iris is procedural in nature. For them, the golden rule places negative constraints on our behavior. As Iris understands the golden rule, for example, it counsels us to stay out of other people's lives and not to judge them.

Actually, although Gerry and Iris both recite the golden rule, technically, what they actually ascribe to is not the golden rule but the so-called silver rule. The silver rule is not to do to others what you do not want others to do to you.[18] The silver rule is just the negative form of the golden rule.

Because the golden rule is associated with Jesus whereas the silver rule had already been enunciated by Rabbi Hillel and, some five hundred years before even Hillel, by Confucius, considerable ink has been spilled debating whether the golden rule is a moral standard superior to the silver rule. The silver rule, say some, merely counsels us to depart from iniquity, to avoid blame, whereas the golden rule admonishes us more positively to exercise virtue, to actively pursue the well-being of others.[19]

Until I conducted the research presented here, I had agreed with those who saw little intended difference between the silver and golden rules as isolated sayings. Semantically, the distinction seems too fine to be consequential. This assessment seems vindicated when we find those who say they live by the golden rule actually describing the silver rule. There is often some discrepancy between what people say and what they mean, so perhaps we should not make too much of the exact words by which such rules are expressed.

On the other hand, existentially, in the way we live our lives, there is a definite difference between a life lived according to the golden rule and a live lived according to the silver rule. As those who see a distinction maintain, one life will be more morally passive and the other more morally active. This difference becomes clearer when we examine Melinda Ratzschall's more active account of the golden rule.

I ask Melinda the same question I asked Gerry and Iris. "What would you say are the moral principles you live by?"

"Like I said before, not always just thinking about yourself, having respect for other people. Respect."

Melinda uses the word *respect* for the proper orientation toward other people. I was surprised how frequently respect is cited in this connection by those I interviewed. Respect is a weaker word than love; it was love for others that Jesus enjoined us to adopt—and, before Jesus, the Jewish Levitical code.[20] Yet, again, we must appreciate the discrepancy between what a person says and what the person actually means. Although Melinda uses the word *respect*, which evokes the silver rule, she actually seems to have in mind the golden rule.

I ask Melinda why she thinks we should treat people with respect.

"Well," she answers. "I think if you have respect for people and things, you're not going to abuse them…"

"Okay."

"…or use them…"

"Okay."

"…just to meet your own needs."

"Okay." So far, Melinda has still articulated the silver rule. But she goes on.

"And I think that everything else after respect will…Once you have respect, you can have love, and you can have kindness, and you can have generosity."

Melinda has now added some of the stronger qualities that distinguish the golden rule from the silver rule: love, kindness, and generosity. If we adopt these qualities, we will not be content just to leave others alone, to refrain from hassling or judging them, but will actively seek their good. Thus, however small the intended difference between the golden rule attributed to Jesus and the silver rule attributed to Hillel and Confucius, there is a great, consequential difference in the lived moral postures epitomized by these two rules.

The discrepancy between what people say and what they mean is again apparent when I speak with Eli Cohen. Although he too uses the word *respect* to convey his moral posture toward others, we will see that what he means ranges all the way from the golden rule to the so-called tinsel rule. The tinsel rule is to treat others as they deserve.[21]

"What," I ask Eli, "does Judaism teach?"

"I told you what it teaches: to respect next person."

"Is that the most important…"

"Main! Main importance."

"But what does Judaism teach?" Even I no longer know what I was after here.

Eli's wife, Guzia, calls in from the kitchen. "To be nice with people, honest…" To be nice to people sounds like the golden rule.

"That's right," Eli affirms.

Then Guzia calls in again. "And respect people if they deserve to be respected." Guzia now has precisely stated the tinsel rule. It is probably the tinsel rule that most of us actually live by. We tend to be good to those who are good to us and treat those who are bad as we think they deserve. The golden rule, the silver rule, and the tinsel rule are all varieties of reciprocity. They differ only in how they tell us to reciprocate the behavior of others.

I turn again to Eli. "Respect is the most important teaching of Judaism?"

"The most important thing," Guzia answers.

"The most important," Eli affirms. "The most important thing."

"More important than being religious?"

"Yeah," Eli says. "Yeah."

"Is it more important than going to synagogue?"

Eli nods vigorously. "Yes! Yes. I agree with that. You got some Jews that go to the synagogue, I wouldn't give you two cents for them. You know why? Because you ask some Jews to do you a favor for somebody, they're not going to do it. They go in synagogue just to show off that they going to synagogue, but that don't mean nothing. It's better being a...a good Jew and a good person instead of being a Jew and a religious bad person. You know what I mean? The main important thing in life, you gotta be good to the next...to your brother, to your neighbor, and to your family. This is it. This basis is main, important thing."

Eli has now fully articulated the golden rule: To be good to others. Just as there may be a discrepancy between what people say and what they mean, there may also be a discrepancy between what people say or mean and what they actually do. People like Gerry Storr and Iris Barbuda say they live by the golden rule or the silver rule, but their actual behavior may either exceed or fail to meet these principles or, more likely, span a wide range. We will see that Eli often exceeds even the golden rule, going the extra mile for people. At the moment, however, Eli is about to tell us a story in which he conforms more to the tinsel rule.

"Certain things, you know...eh...I was mad, let him rest in peace, I shouldn't say that, but Stein, the butcher...He had a fight with me. I wasn't so mad because he fight with me, but I had a fight with him because he was saying bad things about my wife and the kids. See what happened, he was jealous because they went to college, and his kids didn't went to college. So any opportunity he had, he used to laugh. And this thing—we had a fight, and I didn't bother with him for years and years and years. This is one—one thing what I don't like people like that. This is my feeling about life. You must respect the next person. I never had fights with nobody."

From the kitchen, Guzia's final commentary on the story again restates the tinsel rule. "You have to deserve to be respected."

Popularly, the golden rule is a celebrated ethical standard, but when counseled to treat others as we would like to be treated, much depends on our desires for ourselves. To the extent that the way we would like to be treated may not be so morally commendable, neither, then, will be the way we opt to treat others.[22] I recently had a student who sought to justify inequality. She told me she favored inequality precisely because of the competitive advantage it afforded her. As she told me she also subscribed to the golden rule, I pressed her to justify inequality in terms of the golden rule. As is clear in the following extract from her term paper, she succeeded in doing so.

> There are different interpretations of the Christian beliefs that may put a different spin on one's interpretation of society. The Christian faith believes that love thy neighbor as thyself means to treat every individual as you would have them treat you. They assume you care to have every individual treat you in a particularly friendly manner. Others who are not quite as idealistic may interpret this differently. If you wish to have someone not acknowledge you, it must then mean that you have the right not to acknowledge them. Justice, then, may not mean to treat everyone equally as the Christians believe but could mean to treat people in the way that you treat others within their same stratified category.

Even on a more idealistic understanding, the golden rule can remain an ethic of conventional reciprocity. As such, it still represents an ethic designed for ordinary life to operate smoothly. Consider why Iris Barbuda says she follows the golden rule.

"Why? It pays off. First of all, it gets you self-satisfaction. It gives me satisfaction to make somebody feel good to tell you the truth. And I don't always do that, I mean, because I can be very blunt, and I can...Some people think I'm nasty, and I really don't try to be nasty, but, I mean, that's the way I come across sometimes.

"But I like to be treated a certain way and with respect. So if you do that to somebody else, you get it in return. If you don't, you get their anger in return and some kind of retaliation. So it kind of just really makes common sense. And that's really what it is, it's just plain old common sense."

As we have observed before, what Iris calls common sense is actually the diffused cultural legacy of Judaism and Christianity. Again, it is striking that Iris, like others, uses the word *respect*. It is striking as well that Iris justifies the golden rule both in terms of utilitarian calculation and the language of self-fulfillment. Iris follows the golden rule, first, because it pays off, and, second, because it makes her feel good.

Sociologist Robert Wuthnow has also documented how, even for "acts of compassion," people often draw on utilitarian language to offer a banal account of their motives: it makes them feel good.[23] Why should utilitarian language have displaced the language of altruism? Again, it is insufficient just to say that one discourse has supplanted another. We need to understand how the original discourse lost what had once made it emotionally compelling.

In the golden rule, we glimpse part of the answer. The United States is over 85 percent Christian, and most Christians believe that the golden rule both goes back to Jesus and epitomizes his ethical teaching. Yet, the golden rule does not call us to any kind of extraordinary goodness. It instead represents the banal goodness of ordinary life and ordinary time. If the golden rule truly epitomized Jesus's teaching, we may wonder why his early followers found it so inspiring.

Although the gospels do place the golden rule on Jesus's lips, many biblical exegetes doubt the saying is authentically his. According to the scholars of the so-called Jesus Seminar, for example, the golden rule has none of Jesus's characteristic speech, expressing "nothing that cuts against the common grain, or surprises and shocks, or indulges in exaggeration or paradox."[24]

Whether or not the golden rule does go back to Jesus, the golden rule as familiarly understood was certainly not the main thrust of Jesus's charismatic ethic, which was far more radical. In contrast with the ethics of ordinary time, based as they may be on payoff or self-fulfillment, it was to an ethic of sacred time that Jesus called his followers, an ethic founded cosmogonically on a profound experience of God.

Christianity is essentially an eschatological religion, born in an eschatological milieu. At the time when Jesus made his public appearance during the reign of Tiberius, Rome was merely the most recent of foreign, imperial powers to occupy Palestine. Whereas Israel had previously been hellenized, it was now being romanized, particularly among sectors of the aristocracy. With blatant disregard for the proscription against graven images, Herod the Great had scandalized many by placing a Roman eagle at the entrance to the sacred Temple in Jerusalem. It had been torn down by militant Pharisees, who were subsequently executed. Thirty-five years later in 27 C.E, Herod's son, Herod Antipas, likewise violated Jewish taboo by building his new capital, Tiberius, on what had previously been the hallowed grounds of a cemetery.[25]

For two centuries, Jewish eschatological thought had been accumulating. Just as God had once delivered Israel from the Egyptians, many were now expecting God's imminent intervention once again. So-called zealots expected the messiah, a political champion who would militarily reclaim the sanctity of what had been profaned.

Qumran Essenes were awaiting the return of their "Teacher of Righteousness" and a last apocalyptic struggle between good and evil. In the desert, a new figure, John, in the likeness of the ancient prophets, was proclaiming the end of time and the need to prepare for it by a baptism of redemption.

It was in this eschatological context that Jesus began to preach, and what he preached was not just the coming but the actual advent of God's reign. Jesus considered himself the beginning of that reign, and if people could not recognize it, they were advised that the reign of God was like a mustard seed, which begins imperceptibly but grows mighty in the fullness of time.[26] Since Jesus preached the reign of God already in some sense present among us, his was an eschatological ethic, an ethic for the last days. Although biblical scholars have known this for decades, its significance has not been much appreciated outside those circles.[27]

With the arrival of God's reign in the eschatological moment announced by Jesus, we move from ordinary, profane time to sacred time. In sacred time, we leave ordinary life behind. Thus, the eschatological ethic that Jesus preached and practiced was supererogatory. Therein, undoubtedly, for Jesus' first century listeners, lay the source of its charismatic appeal.

Supererogation is a term generally found only in moral philosophy and, to be sure, not often even there. It means performance beyond the call of duty, beyond our conventional social obligations. Supererogatory acts may be morally commended, but conventionally, they are not morally required. The failure to perform them is not morally blameworthy. We speak, for example, of the heroism of a soldier who jumps on a grenade to save his or her comrades. Such an act is supererogatory, for as commendable as it is, no one will be morally faulted for not performing it. The supererogatory, hence, is the moral standard of saints and heroes.[28]

Yet it was to a supererogatory standard that Jesus called all his followers. They were not, for example, to insist on their rights but rather to deliver more than what could rightfully be asked of them.

> But if anyone strikes you on the right cheek, turn to him the
> other also; and if any one would sue you and take your coat,

let him have your cloak as well; and if any one forces you to go one mile, go with him two.[29]

The Romans frequently impressed civilians into corvée service. Thus, the first mile Jesus mentions "renders to Caesar the things that are Caesar's; the second mile, by meeting opposition with kindness, renders to God the things that are God's."[30] Whether or not the three admonitions above were meant literally, which is doubtful, in all three, Jesus is exhorting his followers to exceed the social obligations expected of them and to respond instead in a supererogatory way. Jesus's followers similarly were to lend money not only without excessive interest, not only without any interest at all, but even, finally, without any expectation of repayment. Likewise, they were to refrain not only from adultery but also even from adultery in their hearts. Jesus's ethic was as charismatic as he was, radically intensifying the conventional prescriptions.[31]

The starkest admonition of Jesus also reveals something of what motivates it.

But I say to you, love your enemies and pray for those who persecute you, so that you may be sons of your Father who is in heaven; for he makes his sun rise on the evil and on the good, and sends rain on the just and on the unjust. For if you love those who love you, what reward have you? Do not even the tax collectors do the same? And if you salute only your brethren, what more are you doing than others? Do not even the Gentiles do the same? You, therefore, must be perfect, as your heavenly Father is perfect.[32]

This passage is widely regarded as among the most authentic of Jesus's sayings. According to the Jesus Seminar, "The admonition 'love your enemies' is somewhere close to the heart of the teachings of Jesus to the extent that we can recover them from the tradition. The Jesus Seminar ranked the admonition to love enemies the third highest among sayings that almost certainly originate with Jesus (the other two included the complex about turning the other cheek, Matt 5: 39-42, and the cluster of beatitudes, Luke 6: 20-22)."[33]

It is clear that in the admonition to love our enemies, what Jesus demands radically exceeds the golden rule. We are not just to respect all others but actually to love them. We are not to love just our kin. We are not to love just our neighbor. We are to love so universally as to include even the enemies who persecute us. We are to go out of our way to love.

Something else is clear from the passage above: the cosmogonic origin of Jesus's ethic. What Jesus instructs us to follow is the very example of God, whose sun rises on both the evil and the good. For Jesus, God is our moral exemplar. Thus, if Jesus's ethic were to be formulated as a rule, that rule would not be, "Do unto others as you would have them do unto you," but rather, "Do unto others as God does unto you."

It is God's excessive goodness, not our own banal goodness, that is to set the moral standard of behavior. Of course, for God to be our moral exemplar, we must emotionally experience God in a certain way. Like Jean Valjean in *Les Miserables*, we must experience with numinous awe, wonder, and reverence the excessive goodness of God or at least the like goodness of those behaving in godly ways. It is our emotional experience of such goodness that calls forth our own responsive emulation.

Now, perhaps, we can better appreciate the social psychological mechanism that in a predominantly Christian culture has produced what Taylor identifies as our loss of transcendental horizons, what has produced as well an ethical orientation that appears both instrumentalist and individualistic. What we witness is not just one discourse supplanted by another or, as Bellah and his colleagues suggest, the triumph of an individualistic, therapeutic culture that frames everything in terms of self-fulfillment. Before any such transformation can occur, the original discourse must already have weakened; we are now in a position to see how it did.

What Jesus originally preached was a demanding, charismatic, ecstatic ethic, resting on a vivid experience of God's own moral example. Because Jesus himself modeled that ethic in what he taught and what he did, he himself was experienced as divine. If what is left of that ethic today is a pale shadow of what it once was, it is because, like an excited atom returning to its stable state, all the energy dissipated in the transition from charisma to routinization. The golden rule is but a residue, an important ethic but tame, a bourgeois ethic designed for ordinary life to go on.

When we lose Jesus on the cross forgiving those who nailed him there, we lose the numinous exemplar of an otherworldly goodness. Standing in his place is a wise teacher of ordinary virtue, urging us all to get along. Nice, but not a reality to inspire passionate emulation.[34]

Without either Jesus or God as exemplars of the heroically good, the Christian ethic atrophies into a banal norm of reciprocity, what we now call the golden rule. No wonder other discourses, those of utilitarianism or self-fulfillment, encroach on it. Such encroachments represent secondary rationalization, attempts to explain the ash when the flame has expired.

The routinization of Jesus's charismatic ethic did not originate with American Christiandom. The competing impulses toward ethical routinization and resacralization have been with Christianity from the beginning. As a kind of detente in the third century, the Catholic Church formally instituted an ethical double standard. While everyone was expected to conform to the conventional standard of goodness codified in the "precepts," only a moral elite were called by the "counsels" to uphold a higher, supererogatory ideal.[35] The moral elite eventually became institutionalized as clergy. They alone were expected to be the "charismatic virtuosi" who would carry on the charismatic ethic of Jesus to its full supererogatory extent.[36] Everyone else, as Stephen Hertz might put it, was let off the hook.

Of course, the clergy ceased being charismatic virtuosi themselves, ceased upholding a supererogatory ideal. They became corrupt. For that, they were rightly denounced by the Protestant Reformation. The Protestant Reformation, however, did more. It also abolished the ethical double standard, potentially subjecting all Christians once again to the higher standard. The unintended consequence, however, was to flatten or level moral sights. Instead of applying to everyone the supererogatory standard once to have been upheld by the clergy, to everyone was applied the lesser moral standard that had always been expected of the laity. With the Protestant Reformation, Christianity's moral emphasis shifted from transcendental horizons to the valorization of ordinary life. With the coincident rise of capitalism and consumer society, our attention further turned away from ultimate matters to an exclusive preoccupation with ordinary concerns: family, commerce, work, and eventually leisure.[37]

In *Whose Keeper?* sociologist Alan Wolfe, taking note of postmodernity's cultural lack of transcendence, argues that we now need to find a non-heroic ethical vision to replace the more heroic ethical visions we have lost. Perhaps. It seems to me, however, that non-heroic ethics are what we now have. We have ethical standards we find relatively easy to uphold, that do not require us to stretch morally. Wolfe's concern is that we learn once again—if we ever did know—to guard the well-being of the other souls on this planet. Our current non-heroic ethical visions are not accomplishing this end. Contrary to Wolfe, I would argue that we need emotionally to reconnect with more transcendent ethical standards that call forth the heroism in all of us.

CHAPTER 5

Heroes

Andrea (in the door): "Unhappy is the land that breeds no hero."
Galileo: No, Andrea: "Unhappy is the land that needs a hero."

—*Bertolt Brecht,* Galileo

The fate of the hero is linked to the secularization and disenchantment of the modern world. Ours is said to be an age without God,
without heroes, and, ultimately, without selves. We have already seen
the element of truth in two of these claims. We may not have lost our
belief in God, but even among many believers, God has become emotionally remote. As a consequence, for a great many, God no longer
functions as the ground of meaning, a source of moral inspiration.
Thus, God may still live but be disabled.

Similarly, we may not really have lost our selves in any metaphysical sense. Metaphysically, we remain the same selves who converse with
one another, who act for one another, and who act for and converse
internally even with ourselves. Phenomenologically, however, a great
many of us have lost our sense of self. Like Alice in Wonderland, we
are unable to articulate who we are.

Finally, we often hear the lament that ours is an age without heroes
or an age in which heroism is reduced to mere celebrity. Sometimes
this means that there is nobody today who can serve as a hero, nobody
whose virtues can withstand the public gaze. Instead, publicly all we
have are celebrities. Without such cultural heroes common to all,

heroes who represent the ideals of the group, we may lose a common sense of what binds us so that our culture itself begins to fragment.

Sociology neglects the individual actor and so focuses almost exclusively on group heroes. Indeed, when I began the research for this book, I could find no previous study by a sociologist on personal as opposed to cultural heroes. Yet, in addition to cultural heroes, we may also speak of personal heroes, heroes representing not the culture's ideals but our own. Our personal heroes are figures with whom we identify individually to represent who each of us is or aspires to be.

To say that personal heroes represent who we individually aspire to be does not mean that we want to be our heroes rather than ourselves. If, as happens to be the case, Henry David Thoreau is a hero of mine, this does not mean I want to have been Thoreau rather than who I am now. It means, rather, that what Thoreau stood for in moral space is what I now consider myself to stand for and what I aspire to stand for more fully.

One may have personal heroes without worshiping them or ignoring their faults. Instead, heroes are like moral beacons. They function in much the same way as, according to Eliade, sacred space and sacred time function for a religious sensibility.[1] For a religious sensibility, sacred times and sacred spaces orient the world, establishing points around which existence is focused. Similarly, heroes serve as centers of moral space. They signal to what one's life is called or committed.

Instead of thinking of personal heroes as idols of worship, they are better conceptualized as an idealized reference group, a group that transcends any actual group to which one belongs but to whose standards one strives to live up to. Indeed, those with heroes frequently have not just a single hero but an entire pantheon of heroes. Each heroic member of that assemblage calls out or represents a different aspect of self.[2]

Heroes are more than figures we just admire. Those we admire generally exceed the much smaller subset who constitute our heroes. For a figure to be a hero for us, it is not enough that we just admire him or her. In some way, we emotionally identify with a hero. Those who are our heroes are so because they are farther along on our own journey, because they have responded to the same call to which we respond.

We seek to stand with our heroes, to uphold the values they uphold. Heroes thus are one mechanism we use to tell ourselves what it is we stand for. For those who have them, then, heroes are an important inner marker of identity. They are a part of the landscape of the soul.

If it is true that we have also lost our sense of heroic calling, then the three losses—the loss of God, the loss of heroes, and the loss of selves—seem to go together. God, heroes, and selves all partake of the sacred while the central tendency in the collective life of modern or postmodern culture is profoundly profane or secular.

Second, as we have already seen, moral vision is integral to self-hood and cannot disappear without an experienced loss of self.[3] Traditionally, in the West, God was the source and foundation of the good. When Nietzsche proclaimed the death of God, he knew that he was proclaiming the death of "what was holiest and most powerful of all that the world has yet owned."

For Nietzsche, the death of God meant the death of higher purpose and meaning in life, the death of what until then our culture had conceived to be "the good." "Whither are we moving now?" Nietzsche asks. "Are we not plunging continually? Backward, sideward, forward, in all directions? Is there any up or down left?" In order to counter what he saw as the coming abyss of nihilism, Nietzsche attempted to fashion a new myth and a new hero: Zarathustra, "the overperson."[4]

Nietzsche's instinct was that human heroes could replace God as exemplars of the good, and so he attempted to foster a secular, heroic myth. The problem is that the heroic, like the mythic, is itself closely tied to a religious sensibility, a sensibility, we are seeing, that seems on the wane. The word hero comes from the Greek *heros*, meaning "God-person," the person charged with the charisma of the holy and sacred, the very ground of being.[5] It is from their connection with the ground and core of our being that heroes derive their charisma. Heroes are not simply role models but charismatic role models.[6] What happens to heroes in an age that no longer responds to any transcendental ground of being?

THE JOURNEY OF THE HERO: FROM DEMIGOD TO CELEBRITY

In the absence of empirical research on personal heroes, what we have is speculation. Just as many thinkers presume a universal need for cosmic meaning, many presume a universal need to identify with heroes. Thus, Marshall Fishwick asserts that "the search and need for heroes is inherent in human history."[7] Psychoanalyst Ernest Becker assumes a "constant hunger for heroes."[8] Joseph Campbell laments the loss of the heroic dimension in the modern world. If real, its loss demonstrates that not everyone at all times feels the need for heroes.

Campbell's own argument that all the heroes of different cultures represent variations on a single monomyth militates against this, however.[9]

Explanations for the putatively universal need for heroes vary. For sociologist William Lloyd Warner, heroes are needed to personalize and concretize our abstract values and principles.[10] For Ralph Waldo Emerson, the heroism of great individuals affirms the potential for heroism in all of us.[11] Becker sounds a similar theme: "Our central calling, or main task on the planet, is the heroic." Indeed, for Becker, "the hero's deed is in effect a denial of death."[12]

All this may be true without every individual feeling the need for heroes. Even if Becker is right that our central calling on the planet is the heroic, callings may nevertheless be missed. Indeed, in the disenchanted and bureaucratized world in which we now find ourselves, it becomes increasingly difficult for us to hear the call to a heroic life. This was part of what Max Weber meant when he described bureaucratized modernity as an "iron cage."

Our modern culture is frequently indicted for its lack or trivialization of the heroic dimension. It is said to be a shallow, morally bankrupt culture without ideals. "We still agree with Carlyle," says Daniel Boorstin, "that no sadder proof can be given by a man of his own littleness than disbelief in great men."[13] Arthur Schlesinger Jr. seconds this judgment: "Let us not be complacent about our supposed capacity to get along without great men. If our society has lost its wish for heroes and its ability to produce them, it may well turn out to have lost everything else as well."[14]

In Charles Glicksberg, we see reference to the three sacred losses—God, heroes, and selves—all at once. According to Glicksberg, the problem is that "if man has usurped the place of God, he does not know for what purpose he exists." Instead, "alienated from Nature and God, bowed down by his own spiritual impotence, modern man has shrunk ignobly in stature...He cannot assert himself for he has no self to affirm. What is wrong with our age," says Glicksberg, "is that it has lost its faith in the greatness or the capacity for greatness of man."[15] The three sacred losses are all evident as well in Campbell's commentary on the modern predicament.

> There is no such society any more as the gods once supported. The social unit is not a carrier of religious content, but an economic-political organization...Then all meaning was in the group, in the great anonymous forms, none in the self-expres-

sive individual; today no meaning is in the group—none in the world: all is in the individual. But there the meaning is absolutely unconscious. One does not know toward what one moves...Where then there was darkness, now there is light; but also, where light was, there now is darkness. The modern hero-deed must be that of questing to bring to light again the lost Atlantis of the co-ordinated soul.[16]

What has happened? According to Marshall Fishwick, heroes have become increasingly attenuated with secularization. Whereas in ancient times heroes were demigods, by the middle ages they were merely God's representatives. In the Renaissance, heroes were truth-seekers and in the nineteenth century self-made "men." Today, suggests Fishwick, our heroes are ordinary people just like ourselves. There has in effect been a kind of leveling of heroes concomitant with the rise of capitalism and democracy. The charismatic hero, the hero bespeaking transcendental horizons, is as dead as God.[17]

There is almost a Marxian theme in Fishwick's explanation: heroic consciousness varies with modes of production, political systems, and social institutions. That theme becomes more pronounced in Leo Lowenthal's classic analysis.[18] Lowenthal documents a shift during the early twentieth century in the kind of heroes celebrated by the media. Whereas before, American capitalism lauded what Lowenthal calls "idols of production," people who actually do something in government or the workplace, after World War II, media heroes become mere "idols of consumption," athletes, movie stars, and entertainers in general. This shift, Lowenthal suggests, reflects a greater cultural orientation toward our leisure lives.

If there is a hint of a Marxian explanation in Fishwick and Lowenthal, Boorstin anticipates contemporary postmodernist thought. According to Boorstin, celebrities have replaced heroes in modern culture. Whereas heroes were famous because they were great, celebrities are great because they are famous. "The celebrity," says Boorstin in a now-familiar definition, "is a person who is known for his well-knownness." As such, celebrities, unlike traditional heroes, are morally neutral.

According to Boorstin, celebrities are "human pseudo-events." In contemporary postmodernist language, we might say that celebrity, like God, is a "floating signifier," a sign without a referent. A celebrity as a celebrity stands for nothing. Celebrities are not moral beacons that "fill us with purpose," says Boorstin but empty "receptacles into which we pour our own purposelessness." Celebrities, therefore, are fitting heroes for an age without "metanarratives."[19]

Boorstin points to the *Celebrity Register* where in alphabetical order "the Dalai Lama is listed beside TV comedienne Dagmar" and where Bertrand Russell is followed by Jane Russell. Boorstin even anticipates postmodernism's attention to reflexivity. He suggests that insofar as celebrity refers back only to celebrity, the "fabricated" celebrity-hero is "like the woman in an Elinor Glyn novel who describes another by saying, 'She is like a figure in an Elinor Glyn novel.'" In the end, Boorstin echoes and anticipates Baudrillard's accusation that under the postmodern tyranny of the "sign," today all is empty "spectacle."[20]

This, then, is the journey the hero is seen to have traversed: from demigod in ancient times to empty celebrity today. At the level of our collective, cultural discourse, there is no doubt that celebrity is what is venerated today. Again, however, we must recall that on their own, discourses are inert. In particular, the heroes culturally venerated are inoperative unless they somehow operate personally on us.

So is celebrity similarly valorized at the individual level? Do individual Americans choose celebrities as their heroes? We know only if we ask. When we do ask, the news is both good and bad. The media may promote mere celebrity, and in many ways, individual Americans may buy into it. American adults, however, do not typically choose celebrities as their heroes. That is the good news. The bad news is that most American adults do not have heroes at all. If they do, then typically their heroes are not transcendental figures exemplifying larger vision. Judging from their heroes, what individual Americans typically stand for is ordinary life.

DO YOU HAVE ANY HEROES?

One of my first surprises when I began my interviews was that so many of those I interviewed denied having any heroes. Over and over, I received the same negative response.

"Do you have any heroes?" I ask Ellen Smith.

"I don't think so," she answers.

"You never had any?"

"Yeah, I mean there's people I admire, but I wouldn't say I have any heroes."

I heard similar answers from others. "Do you have any heroes?"

"No," says Peter Nighting. "Not really."

"Heck no!" Frederick Schmidt answers.

I ask Iris Barbuda. "Do you have any heroes you model some aspect of your life around?"

"No."

"No," I repeat. "Okay..."

"There's one pastor," Iris goes on, "that I had...so much respect for. He was a Moravian pastor. He was probably one of the nicest people I ever met. He had a wonderful sense of humor. He was a very religious man but was realistic about it, and he was the one who convinced me that the Moravian church was wonderful. But he was just a real good human being."

I have a fuller conversation about heroes with Jason Fishman. "Do you have any heroes?" I ask him.

"Probably not."

"Okay."

"And I've actually thought before like, 'Do I have any sort of role models'...I mean, there are people I've learned a lot from..."

I nod.

"...from working with personally, but I wouldn't even say there are any role models who I think can serve successfully...People I know who have successfully dealt with...you know, professional success without being sort of consumed by their careers and political activism and, you know, sort of their personal relationships, and family issues, and sort of integrated all that."

"Hm-hm."

"I don't know anybody who's done a really good job. I mean," Jason laughs, "I think everybody's sort of floundering around on their own."

I tell Jason that he need not try to come up with heroes if he really does not have any.

"No, no," he replies. "I don't think so. It used to bother me, I think, when I was younger. You know, you'd read about people who had like these mentors, who really like...taught them stuff."

"I don't necessarily mean someone in your circle."

"Yeah, well, certainly there's nobody outside of my circle that I would hold up."

"No dead white males?"

Jason reflects. "There's lots of people I admire in different ways. I mean, you know?"

"Like?"

"I have a picture of John Brown on my wall at work."

I brighten. As crazy as he was, John Brown is one of my own heroes. When I tell Jason this, he laughs. I press on. "You have a picture of him?"

"Yeah," Jason laughs. "I used to go to Harper's Ferry when I was growing up, and Sarah and I were there a year ago. Now, he's very remarkable. I mean, he's...nearly psychotic."

I admit this.

"He led this doomed uprising with no sense of strategy, you know? Got himself and most of his family killed. And all of his followers. And in his lifetime, got nothing really accomplished. Although, he may have been...in retrospect, he may have been a focal point for a lot of organizing in the Civil War. Is he somebody you want to pattern your life on?" Jason laughs. "I don't think so."

"See," I say. "I think you're more of a rationalist than I am. I'm more of a romantic." Now, I laugh. "I guess I tend to pattern my life after psychotics."

Jason continues laughing. "John Brown was an...you know, he was quite amazing, and having not only been a radical abolitionist who, you know, attacked and destroyed a U.S. armory, but...you know, he's now like considered a national hero. And there's John Brown National Park, Harper's Ferry National Park, and all that stuff, and he's treated with all the respect of like a, you know, a real American hero. There aren't a lot of heroes who, well, attacked a U.S. arsenal."

I finally talk to Gerry Storr. "Do you have any heroes you model some aspect of your life around?"

"That's interesting," Gerry responds. "I've thought about that. I haven't thought about it for a long time, but I thought about it once. I don't know how it came up. Someone asked me about it. I guess it was a show on heroes. I don't know. Something triggered it. And I realized: no."

"You don't?"

"I don't. I went back. I went back to people I respect. I went back and thought about...I actually did this, and I went back and asked as I grew up, did I have heroes? People I wanted to be like?

"I had a lot of...There were some athletes...Al Kaline for the Detroit Tigers, Willie Mays. I mean I—I didn't want to be Willie Mays. I couldn't be Willie Mays. Clearly, I couldn't be Willie Mays. He was too gifted. Teachers. There were some teachers I admired, but there were none that I wanted to be like, you know? It wasn't like, oh God, I want to be, you know, Professor Kulbor or whatever in high school or whatever. I thought about that, and I realized in high school where I think there's a time, you know, early adolescence in particular, apparently, people get heroes. I had none."

"Actually," I say, "most people don't seem to have heroes."

"Seriously? Now that's interesting. I thought they would. Is that what you're finding?"

"Hm-hm."

"Did that surprise you?"

"Very much."

"Yeah, I'm...gee, then I feel better."

There was something else that surprised me. When people did have heroes, their heroes were often not charismatic figures of history or myth. They were often not figures representing transcendental metanarratives. Instead, as Fishwick had speculated, people's heroes tended to be ordinary folk like themselves.

Martha Schmidt, for example, has a hero: her sister.

"My sister was in World War Two and in Berlin, and they bombed the hospital where she was working, and her and two doctors from Johnstown jumped under the operating table, and Dr. Blume, he got knocked out. When he come to, she was standing there crying, and when Memorial Hospital celebrated their hundredth year, her name was the only name mentioned in the whole book."

"I don't understand. What did she do?"

"She's an RN. She's a nurse."

"Because she stayed at her post?"

"She graduated from a school of nursing, and then she went to Philadelphia to work, and then she joined the service. The war was going on in nineteen forty-two, and she joined the army, and she met a man who was a captain and she got married to him, and while she was there a month, they brought him in injured for her to help operate on him."

"But what is it that you find heroic about her?"

"Because they honored her for..."

"For serving her country?"

"Well, she was three years in the Peace Corps."

"Ah."

"And she served three years in Honduras, and when she was in World War Two, this hospital that was bombed, they—they had to not care about their own lives but try to save those who were in the hospital."

"I see."

"You know what I mean?"

I do understand. Now, however, I want to find out what it means to Martha to have her sister as her hero. "What does the word *hero* mean to you? When you say she's your hero, what does that mean to you?"

"Well, she risked—she gave up a lot to help somebody else."

"Well, that's why she's a hero, but what does that word mean? Is it like someone you look up to or just someone...I mean, what does it mean to say that she's your hero? Do you understand what I'm asking?"

"Oh, yeah. I don't know. I always looked up to her. She's just a little bit older than me, and we grew up together."

"Okay."

"We dressed alike and everything. So to me, she's my hero."

Family members are among Sister Marge O'Hara's heroes, too. "I think," says Sister Marge, "that my parents are heroes in my eyes, that I was very proud of the behavior of my father and mother...in the world. I mean, I saw them as public figures and then only later, you know, did I start to kind of resent that they were more out there for the whole world than...you know? Maybe I wanted some personal attention from them.

"I came in touch with that later, but it was sort of like now that they died, I kind of put it all together and I say they were doing the best that they could do emotionally on a personal level, but I'm still very proud of how they lived in society."

"Can you explain that? I mean, how did they live?"

"I feel they contributed beyond the family from the get-go. I mean, my whole life, I felt that my parents...I was proud of my parents because they invested themselves in the community."

"In what way in the community?"

"Well, for Dad it was, through scouting, which I would consider a contribution to, you know, in that day, you know, the environment, to character of, you know, men and to specific organizations.

"They were on the boards of public libraries. They were on civic organizations of, you know, Goodwill. They were on there. They were leaders in their alumni association, president of the alumni association. Then Dad got involved in St. Vincent de Paul Society. He got involved in Rotary. He's, and he was always a leader, you know? To me he lived a model of investment in civic affairs, people-oriented affairs. He gave himself to leadership in the community."

"Mm-hm."

"And he expected that of us. He expected that we would make a contribution. So there's some of that, you know? He was an usher in church, but in those days when there wasn't a parish council, I mean, an usher was the leader."

"Oh, yeah, I remember that."

"So that was like a leadership position, you know? My mother became the first woman parish council president. I mean, she was socially...she was always in the interfaith dialogue over women in the Middle East. She was volunteering for Call to Action on the radio, you know?"

I nod. Call to Action is a Catholic reform movement.

"You know, she'd refer people, she would...she'd run bloodmobiles, but she was also a spokesperson in writing letters to the editor, writing to her congresspeople, making her thinking heard. And as a college graduate, I used to think I was proud of her, that she was a hero in my eyes.

"A woman who in nineteen forty, you know, said to my father that she didn't—she didn't clean and she didn't iron. Now she had seven children, but I mean it was like she saw her position as a woman, an educated woman, not just bound to the house but somebody who was going to use her talents for something broader than just domestic work. And that was kind of an image for me of a woman who was outspoken and critical of the church, critical of politics, critical of society's values in a way that was toward the poor.

"She would always have kind of a partnership...We lived in the suburbs, but she connected us with a family in Center City. She had kind of a partnership family and she knew Mrs. Johnson, and we would go there and meet the Johnsons, who were black, and here we were in an all-white suburb. This was something that I think she felt was important for us: to be linked."

Sister Marge's parents—her mother particularly—were remarkable people. They set for Sister Marge an example of citizenship that she has followed herself. Yet, her parents were not the first people Sister Marge mentioned when I asked about her heroes. The first person she mentioned was Dorothy Day, the founder of the Catholic Worker movement, who also greatly influenced Harvard psychologist Robert Coles.[21]

"Well, I say Dorothy Day right away because I met her and, you know, I was in her presence for three years.

"I feel very connected with her, you know? I treasure that relationship, that proximate relationship. And then, of course, she became almost a mythical hero that she never wanted to be. She didn't want to be that easily dismissed. She said don't make me a saint, 'cause then people can dismiss me, can dismiss the message."

Earlier, we observed that for someone to become our hero, it is not enough for us to admire him or her. We must establish some emotional connection with that person as well. Sometimes, as in Sister Marge's case, that connection comes from actual proximity. On the other hand, we do not make heroes of everyone with whom we come into physical contact. It is important as well that the hero points the way along the journey we experience ourselves as taking. Dorothy Day seemed to do that for Sister Marge.

"When I was off from teaching, I'd just spend time at the Catholic Worker, and that was, I guess, a conversion experience for me. Because I had philosophically always believed in helping the poor, advocating for the poor, but never…I never was physically with the poor.

"So this was my transformation in terms of learning who the poor are and the diversity of the poor. Learning what that did to me, you know? Suddenly, I was speaking with people, and then I actually met Dorothy Day—just as, you know, one of the people who were in the house and not wanting to be distinguished from them as a staff person.

"There's no such thing as staff in the Catholic Worker, just brothers and sisters. And just the whole idea of her total acceptance of her human condition and the human condition of others…The way she openly complained about discomfort and smells fascinated me because I had idealized people who work with the poor. I had, you know…I thought Cecelia Bryant was a saint. She was one of the Catholic Workers coming over to get a rest, and I used to think she was a saint. Well, when I went over there and was with her, I saw her and all her imperfections, and saw Dorothy Day, and how they treated her, and I was shocked because my hero was an ordinary person."

"What did Dorothy Day represent that made her your hero?"

"She represented for me an identification with Christ that was incredible. I mean, it was like she lived what I attempt to live. It seemed like she sacrificed, well…voluntary poverty, let's say. In choosing to live side by side with the poor, she gave up her privacy, her comfort, and chose a life of identification with those who were suffering the most.

"To me, it represented where Christ would be today. He would seek those most vulnerable, most oppressed. And not just from afar, but actually identifying with them. And I saw—I saw that as admirable, and I am always moving inch by inch toward that, wanting that, but not wanting it, you know? Seeking it, but then saying I need this and this and this, so, you know, that's all right for Dorothy Day, but I'm not Dorothy Day, so…"

I begin to protest. Sister Marge hardly lives a life of luxury.

"…Or Oscar Romero, who was a person a lot more like me in his…before his conversion. I feel like he's a hero because when he got it, he put himself out there. Now, I feel those are people that I want to emulate, you know? I want to move toward more credibility.

"You know, if I could get rid of a lot of clutter in my life, you know? I feel like I need...I saw these two paths, you know? I saw in my work with corporate advocacy that I could look just like the corporation. I mean, I could.

"There are people who are in this work of advocacy—they look just like the corporate world, and I can feel myself wanting to look nice, have nice things, because, of course, then the people in the corporate world would listen to me—because I look like them.

"Then, I hear this other voice that says, 'What? Would Jesus today look like corporate America? And what is this in you that wants to look corporate?' So I can either go like that—I mean, that's a path that a lot of people, good people, take—and then I say, 'no.' I don't want that. I want...Would Dorothy Day look like corporate America? No.

"There is an identification with the poor that's a message of what's in my heart, that I want an alternative to corporate America, you know? Not that corporate America's all bad, but there's a look, and I can feel myself, when I go to these meetings with the corporations. I dress up in a suit. I have my briefcase. I look just like the CEOs that I'm talking with."

Sister Marge's reflections illustrate how heroes function for those who have them. Sister Marge does not actually want to be her heroes but, as she says, to emulate her heroes. Clearly, Sister Marge recognizes her heroes' faults. Even with their faults, however, Sister Marge's heroes center her in a calling, a calling that leads Sister Marge to transcendental horizons beyond ordinary life. Sister Marge's heroes are for her an ideal reference group, by the standards of which she is able to separate herself from the attractions or temptations of more ordinary paths. Sister Marge's heroes are inner beacons calling her back to her true self. Definitely, in Sister Marge's case, having heroes is not childish or weak but a source of moral strength.

Martha Schmidt and Sister Marge were not my only interviewees to have heroes. We saw that in having an articulated worldview, Sister Marge was much like the secular black activist, Lawrence Patterson. Sister Marge and Lawrence Patterson are alike in another way. Like Sister Marge, Lawrence Patterson also has heroes. Who are Lawrence's heroes?

"Uh." Lawrence thinks a moment. "Malcolm X, George Jackson, Toussaint L' Ouverture, Nat Turner, Jack Johnston, Angela Davis. Freedom fighters in general, you know? I'm inspired by people who struggle and fight against injustice. Wherever that is, you know? Wherever it may be. Those are my heroes...Mao Tse-tung."

Lawrence certainly cites enough heroes to form an entire reference group. "Do you think about these heroes?"

"Yeah, I think about them."

"Can you tell me what you think? Do you consider yourself an
activist?"

"Not now. At one point I would. At one point I was."

If Lawrence has difficulty thinking about himself as an activist now,
it is in part because he feels his current life fails to meet the standards
of his heroic exemplars. As is true for Sister Marge, Lawrence's heroes
call him beyond ordinary life.

"What does it mean for these people to be your heroes?"

"It means...What I think about is the struggle against injustice,
political oppression, social, cultural, and economic deprivation.
Meaning that people are just deprived so much of what is inherently
theirs. These things are being taken from them. Not all at once, a lot
of the time, but systematically.

"You know, particularly among African American people. You
know, today, slowly but surely, everything about us that makes us
unique and makes who we are is being taken away. Taken away,
degraded, assimilated, you know?

"We mentioned earlier about the movie *Malcolm X*. I liked the
movie. What I didn't like was at the end, all of those super-rich bas-
ketball players, actors, you know? The people who helped finance the
movie were the ones who were—at the end of the movie—were laughing. You know that was a hell of a commentary on such a man's life.
You know that was a hell of a way to leave that movie."

"They were laughing?"

"Well, I mean, they were sitting around enjoying...like Magic
Johnson and Eddie Murphy, I think, was in there. The point is, it was-
n't attached to any struggle. The point it was attached to was the purse
strings. It's not attached to any struggle. That man's life meant
more...It was make a movie and make money off of me, you know?
That man's life meant more.

"So on the one hand, it was a good movie. Kids of today could take
a look at what it was like then, and what we were able to accomplish,
what he was able to accomplish in terms of his strengths and his convictions. The way that he controlled and the way he refused to bend in
the face of the police and all the other pressures that he...he
remained uncompromising until his death.

"And ah, I think that was a great point to make with the movie, but
again, the assimilation part of that is just a movie, you see? And peo-

ple aren't armed with a sense that we have to continue the struggle and move forward, you know? The same way Malcolm did.

"If he were alive today, what would he be doing is the question. Would he be sitting back, an armchair philosopher, talking about what needs to be done or would he be out there in the streets kickin' butt? He'd be out there in the streets kickin' butt. That's my belief.

"Mao Tse-tung. Would he be sitting back talking about the Little Red Book or would he be out there, creating another book? And taking the struggle further. I mean that's why they're my heroes."

Lawrence's heroes function for him in much the same way as Sister Marge's function for her. Like Sister Marge, Lawrence, in examining his own life, asks how his heroes would behave. Because like Sister Marge's heroes, Lawrence's represent supererogatory ideals, Lawrence is unsatisfied with how his own life compares with those of his heroes. That dissatisfaction in turn functions like a call, urging Lawrence to exceed himself.

"When you say these people are your heroes, do you just mean you...Do you mean something more than that you admire them?"

"Yeah, I mean I try to live by their example." Lawrence laughs. "I'm being honest. At one point, I tried very hard to live by their example. In the recent past, I've fallen way short."

"Does that make you feel guilty?"

"Yeah, I feel guilty as hell. Guilty in a sense, but I also feel like I'm not living up to potential, and that's why I ask, What would Malcolm be doing right now? What would Mao Tse-tung be doing right now? What—what would George Jackson be doing right now, you know? Would they be sitting around, talking about, philosophizing, going to summits and meeting about things? Or would they be in the streets organizing people to oppose oppression? I believe they would be opposing oppression. In a real living way, not in a philosophical, wait-'til-the-moon-comes-around or something like that."

At the end of his life Mao was hardly out in the streets organizing people to end oppression. What matters here, however, is less the historical Mao than the mythic Mao Lawrence has come to idealize as a hero. Since we first met Lawrence in chapter one, he and I have continued talking in the same all-you-can-eat diner. I finally ask him if we should get up and get something else.

"I want to get something else," Lawrence says. As I rise to follow him to the buffet, he offers some trailing remarks. "What makes...what makes them heroes? My heroes? Because I believe if they were living today, they would still be active. They would not be armchair philosophers. They would not be armchair philosophers."

Lawrence clearly feels he should be out organizing now and not talking to me. In part, it is Lawrence's heroes who make him feel that way. Lawrence feels he belongs with his heroes, and that feeling calls him from everyday concerns to a higher, political purpose.

Earlier we saw that both Sister Marge and Lawrence Patterson shared something with Christian fundamentalists. Like fundamentalist Christians, both Sister Marge and Lawrence Patterson had more articulated worldviews than most people. We may not be surprised, therefore, when we find that again, like Sister Marge and Lawrence Patterson, Christian fundamentalists tend to have heroes. When I ask Matt Bennett, for example, whether he has heroes, he answers affirmatively and with an entire pantheon of heroes, who, he tells me, are all either from the Bible or church history. I ask him to name some.

"Hudson Taylor, a missionary to China; E.T. Studd. Both were early missionaries, and I'm just impressed with the way they left everything behind, education and wealth and family, left it all and went to do what God told them to do."

As was the case for Sister Marge and Lawrence Patterson, Matt Bennett's heroes represent supererogatory ideals that call him away from ordinary life. For those who experience such a call, it is an ever present demand to lead a heroic rather than an ordinary life. Indeed, sometime after my interview with him, Matt Bennett himself went to Africa as a missionary.

"Uh, who are these people? Hudson Taylor is...? They're both missionaries? To China?"

"Yes. E.T. Studd went to China and Africa."

"And so, what you find heroic in them is that they left everything behind...Could you repeat that again?"

"In order to do what God called them to do, to build the kingdom of God, and to leave behind the pleasures of this world."

"Who—who else, you said some figures from the Bible? Who would be..."

"The apostle Paul. I appreciate the way God used him to basically start the early church. He suffered for Christ. He just taught, explained who Christ was and how he fulfilled the Old Testament. He wrote most of the New Testament."

"Um. What virtues does Paul embody?"

"The truth of the Bible, the truth about God. Much of the New Testament, a lot of his writings are sort of the foundation for what Christians today believe."

"Well, how could Paul be your hero? I just want to make sure we're talking about heroes in the same way. So far, I think we are, but I just want to make sure. I mean a hero...You could do like E.T. and Hudson Taylor did. I can see how they can be heroes for you. You're not going to write another testament, so how...What could you...In what way could you follow...A hero is someone you emulate. Would you agree with that?"

Matt laughs at my questions. "I can't write another New Testament, but I can study what Paul's written and have the same commitment to sticking to the truth, to what God has said."

It is striking that among those I interviewed, the people who tended to have heroes were those emotionally grasped by an encompassing meaning of life. That is not to say that all who articulated a worldview had heroes. As we have seen, Jason Fishman, for example, did not. Yet, among those I interviewed, the relationship between heroes and meaning began to suggest a pattern. I began to suspect that in their purest form, heroes are a marker of the transcendent, calling us to supererogatory ideals. Whereas conventional role models show us how to live ordinary life, heroes, I hypothesized, represent exemplars of moral idealism through whom we ourselves are called beyond the ordinary.

At this point, I needed to know how representative were the people I interviewed. Was it really the case that most people tended not to have heroes? Did those with heroes generally tend to have a different orientation to overall meaning? Such questions could not be addressed practically by more in-depth interviews. I needed a larger, more systematic sample.

How Many People Have Heroes?

Surprisingly, when I looked to find literature on the prevalence of personal heroes, I found very little. Some research had been done on the personal heroes of children and adolescents, and one study had examined the heroes of public figures.[22]

John Gardiner and Katryn E. Jones, for example, examined hero-identification among prominent figures in education and government, finding that such public figures often cite other public figures—both living and dead—as personal heroes, public figures such as Anton Chekhov, Meriwether Lewis and William Clark, Winston Churchill, and John F. Kennedy (whose *Profiles in Courage* likely identified his personal heroes).[23] For those who had them, the heroes identified symbolized such moral ideals as humility, integrity, dedication, vision, and courage. Presumably, by identifying with such heroes, public figures seek to embody the same ideals themselves.

No study, however, has examined the heroes of ordinary American adults. A few national public opinion polls have asked about respondents' heroes, but the questions are all constrained in one way or another. One question, for example, asked whether any family members were heroes. Two others asked whether there were any heroes alive today in America.[24] None asked simply whether respondents have any personal heroes—alive or dead, American or non-American, family members or not. Aside from essays lamenting the loss of heroes, most sociological studies examined only how heroes were portrayed by the media.

Thus, if I just wanted to know, as I did, whether having personal heroes was a rare or common trait, I was on my own. Accordingly, in each of the two Philadelphia surveys we conducted, we asked respondents whether they had any heroes and, if so, who those heroes were. When the results of the two surveys were combined, we were able to hear from a random sample of 627 Philadelphia residents. How many had personal heroes?[25]

In both the spring and fall surveys, only 44 percent of respondents said they had heroes. When the heroes named were examined and invalid responses such as "I'm my own hero" were removed, it turned out, again consistently, that only 40 percent of the respondents had heroes.[26]

It appears that at least in metropolitan areas like Philadelphia, while hero-identification is not uncommon, most people do not identify with heroes. On the positive side, that is one indication that, contrary to some fears, most people are not identifying with mere celebrity. Of course, on the negative side, if people are not identifying with celebrities, it is largely because they are not identifying with personifications of any values.

Of course people still have values even if they do not identify with personifications of those values. Yet, insofar as heroes personify certain types of values, namely supererogatory ideals, drawing us to one or another standard of moral greatness, a lack of heroes is one more indication that modernity or postmodernity simply is not very oriented toward transcendental or supererogatory ideals.

Let us not, however, be too hasty in our assessment of hero-identification in modern society. We find that 40 percent of those asked say they have heroes. How accurate is that 40 percent figure? Might we not have undercounted some people who, while they deny having heroes, do actually identify with personages who function as heroes for them?

We must admit that likelihood. Conversely, we must also presume that some respondents reported having heroes when they actually do not have heroes in the sense we mean. We gain a better feel for the true prevalence of heroes if we consider whom we likely undercounted and whom we likely overcounted.

Surveying people about their heroes over the phone has its problems. In particular, we need to wonder whether the respondents had the same understanding of what is meant by a hero. As we have been talking about them, heroes are not just role models but charismatic role models, who model not just a single role but an entire life, who inspire us to pursue supererogatory ideals. Thus, for Lawrence Patterson, heroes are people who inspire him to struggle against injustice and by whose example he attempts to live. Similarly, when I asked Sister Marge what the word *hero* meant to her, she replied "a role model par excellence." It is people who have heroes in this sense whom we properly want to count as having heroes.

The problem is that not everyone understands the word *hero* this way. Some people deny having heroes because they think a hero connotes an impossible figure, free of faults. To Joe Barboso, calling someone your hero places too great a burden on him or her.

"I try not to call anybody heroes because I think that's a big thing to put on a person. I mean, that's a really big thing to go up to somebody and say, 'Hey, you're my hero,' or something like that. 'I try to do everything like you.' And that's a big responsibility.

"Like, I don't have heroes but I think I have some role models. And so my role models would be my grandfather for, like, responsibility, for doing what you had to get done. For doing what had to be done, because it needed to be done. My grandfather, he had no education. He barely got through high school. He finished high school later in his life, and he went back, and he worked his whole life.

"He was in the navy. He fought in World War Two, and he lost a lot of friends there. He came back. He worked his butt off. He raised four kids, and you know, he did, like, a really good job, and when I ever talk to him now, I mean, he still has that ethic about him of, you know, here's what you're doing, here's what you have, here's what needs to get done, and he can just build that bridge to do what needs to get done. And like he just—he just showed me how to find a way to do things that needed to get done and, like, I don't know, dealing with the problems and stuff like that.

"I guess my mother's a role model because she always did what had to get done even when it wasn't what she wanted to do herself. She always did—she could have went out and partied all the time like when we...like when she was raising me and my two sisters. My two sisters are two years and three years older than me respectively, so when we were growing up, it was just her raising us, and I'm sure there were times she wanted to go out and party with her friends or go out and dance or something like that."

Joe Barboso also distinguishes between heroes and role models. He says he does not have heroes, but he does have role models. Joe, however, suggests that heroes must be perfect whereas our conception does not require that. So despite what Joe believes, might not his role models actually conform to our conception of heroes?

At some point, role models may shade into heroes. Joe's role models particularly seem to model not any specific role but rather more general moral ideals such as responsibility and perseverance. True, these are not supererogatory ideals that bespeak a specific calling, but Joe's particular heroes, nevertheless, portray substantial courage. Joe's heroes thus represent an ambiguous case.

Joe's case actually raises two concerns. First, the distinction between heroes and role models is a subtle one. Although it is a distinction to which Joe Barboso is sensitive, not everyone may be. When we look at the ordinary people often cited as heroes, we need to wonder whether, when asked if they have heroes, many respondents cited instead what are more clearly just ordinary role models. To the extent that they did so, our 40 percent figure of people with heroes may well be inflated.

The second concern is that because for some respondents, like Joe, the word *hero* connotes an impossibly perfect figure, they might deny having heroes when in fact they do orient their lives around personages who function just as we have conceptualized heroes as functioning. If we are unsure whether or not Joe should be counted as having heroes, there are other cases that are less ambiguous. If Eric Sawyer, for example, had denied having heroes over the phone, he should probably have been counted as having heroes nonetheless.

When I interviewed Eric, the tape had stopped without our knowing it. When we discovered that calamity, we reviewed some of what he had just told me.

"Oh," Eric begins, "I said, I thought I had come of age at the end of the sixties or early seventies, when there were a lot of...when music...It seemed to make a major factor in a lot of people's lives a lot more than it does now, and the words in that music and everything about that culture was an important thing to people. It wasn't entertainment. People were exploring, and other people were excited by that exploration."

"And what were they exploring?"

"They were exploring themselves. They were exploring their limits. They were exploring the meaning of life. They were...Everything was open to question, and that created some anxiety, but also everything, everything was possible."

"Okay. And you said that..."

"And being a songwriter, I identified extremely strongly with people like Joni Mitchell and Neil Young and James Taylor, people who were taking that direction, that focus on meaning and heavy songs and that kind of thing. So that was my coming of age."

"And these people...so you said served as mentors to you."

"Right. You had said, 'Who are your heroes?' And I said, 'They're more like mentors.' I gave the example of James Taylor's song about being a lonely lighthouse, and people coming there just to stay away from him, that he was a beacon: Don't go this far; it's the lighthouse, flashing on, flashing off, fading away. But that was a very important guidepost for someone living their life. There's this richness in life that was manifest through his lyrics. There was this aspect of it that even he thought had gone too far in a certain direction."

Eric cites certain figures with whom he identifies extremely strongly, people who serve him as beacons of a moral path beyond convention. Yet, he too is uncomfortable with with the word *hero* and prefers the word *mentor*. Interestingly, that same word, *mentor*, is preferred by others I interviewed—Hannah Gottlieb, for example.

When Hannah talks, she makes still another important distinction, the distinction between personal and cultural heroes. If we ask people whether they have personal heroes, they may tend, instead, to cite cultural heroes, heroes of the group—Harry Truman, for example. Although we may value what Harry Truman did and stood for, we do not necessarily model our own lives around cultural heroes like him.

Hannah laughs when I ask her about heroes. "One of the courses I took this summer, interestingly enough, was called 'Who Is a Hero?' And it went back to rabbinics. What did the rabbis define as a hero?"

"The rabbis had a discussion on heroes?"

"Right. In this way: A hero is a multicultural term applied to the person..." Hannah laughs. "Why am I telling a sociologist what a hero is?"

"No. No. Please tell me."

"I should take my notes from my course to share with you, but, 'The person who embodies the values of...that the society values.' This person has the values and is held up, and one of the things we looked at in this course was in ancient literature, what were the characteristics of the hero. And we went through and looked at that. So, for example, the hero was often abandoned at birth. The hero was self-sacrificing. The hero does things to benefit the...you know, whatever.

"And then we took a look at rabbinics, and although the rabbis did not have the term *hero*—that was not part of their vocabulary, what they did do was go back to biblical sources and ask what did the people in there either embody or what should they embody.

"And so what they would do, for example, is for somebody like Moses...There's so many...Abraham is probably easier. You don't know why Abraham was chosen, and there's so much information you don't know about Abraham. What the rabbis did was write countless what we call midrashim, which are stories that explain why Abraham was chosen. He weaned himself in ten days, and could talk, and he walked on the mountain, and he was monotheistic. He looked at the stars in the sky and said, 'You're not my God. There's a God that...' You know?

"So what they were doing was creating this character to create a fuller...really a hero, because what you see is a character who embodies all the qualities that they wanted. And so what we did at the end of the course was to list, What are these qualities? What are the heroic qualities that the rabbis were trying to tell us?"

"Do you remember what any of these qualities were?"

"Oh, yes. Actually, the top-notch ones are to have Torah knowledge, to have knowledge and through Torah knowledge and spiritual connection to God, you make the difference. So, for example, a woman like Deborah who is a judge, and she led them into battle and they won. The rabbis don't write anything about, oh, she was a good military leader. They write, She knew Torah. She taught people Torah.

"Because she knew Torah—and they show verses how she could figure out when they should go into battle. So this is one of the great qualities."

"This is in the Talmud?"

"Well, the Talmud you would say is a limited book. The Talmud plus...There are many other midrashim—collections of stories the rabbis wrote besides just the Talmud."

"Well, that's really...fascinating."

Hannah nods. "That came by your asking me if I have heroes."

We both laugh. "Yes, well, what you've described to me are cultural heroes, heroes of the group."

"Hm-hm."

"But what about personal heroes? Do you personally have heroes? Your own personal heroes?"

"I probably don't use that word in my vocabulary. Probably what I think about are mentors."

"Okay." As we have seen, the same distinction between heroes and mentors was made by Eric.

"Because a hero somehow raises somebody—for me, at least—out of reality, but a mentor…that's a closer connection for me. And, yes, I have had many mentors and people that mentor different things for me. I can't say there is one person who embodies all the qualities that I aspire to, but I have lots of people along the way who I feel have been nurturing to me and who I have been able to watch and say, 'Oh, that's good or I like that.' And you know, try and be like them. To be like my mentor, to be like my hero."

Hannah is another person with a very deep, articulated worldview that encompasses the whole of life and imbues it with meaning. Although she too resists the word *hero*, like Eric, she identifies with mentors who conceptually function in much the same way. In fact, like many who are more comfortable with the word *hero*, Hannah has not one mentor but a whole pantheon of mentors. Although both Eric and Hannah disclaim the use of the word, *hero*, if people like them are not counted among those who have heroes, they probably should be.

Hannah clearly distinguishes between personal heroes and cultural heroes. She includes none of the biblical figures she mentions, for example, among her personal mentors. Others, when asked about their heroes, do not make such a fine distinction between personal and cultural heroes—Eli Cohen, for example, when I ask him whether he has heroes.

"Well," Eli says, "I believed in heroes, yeah."

"Who are your heroes?"

"I believe in great, great leaders."

"Like?"

"Like…Churchill…Truman…Ben Gurion…Golda Meir. They are my heroes."

"Why?"

"Because they did for their—for their people. They did for their country. They give their life for their country. People learn from them. People respect them. And that's why they're heroes."

Eli does not actually model his own life around these great leaders. Instead of identifying his personal heroes, he has identified, rather, cultural heroes of the group. When we ask people over the phone who their heroes are, many likely are inclined to do the same. Like those who cite ordinary role models rather than true heroes, those who cite cultural heroes rather than their own personal heroes will inflate our estimate of people with personal heroes.

I mentioned earlier that theoretically one does not actually wish to be one's hero but only to stand with one's hero. Theory, however, is sometimes confounded by practice. When I ask Diane Norris about her heroes, she fears I will laugh at her.

"I have three heroes at the moment."

"I would love...okay, tell me about them. Who are they?"

"You'll laugh."

"I won't."

"You promise?"

"I promise."

"Let's see. One hero is Jane Fonda. My second hero is Princess Diana."

"Okay." These do not seem so laughable. Perhaps Diane thinks I will laugh because her heroes are celebrities.

"How long have they been your heroes?"

"Oh, ten, fifteen years."

"Okay. So tell me why they're your heroes."

"Well, Jane Fonda is easy because she's a successful independent woman, and I guess I identify with her because she actually went too far and she's had to take a lot of flak for going to Vietnam, and so I admire her for her various careers, for her movie career and her fitness career, and I had a little trouble when she married Ted Turner, 'cause I find him a kind of a sleaze but..."

"Princess Diana, I guess, because she's beautiful and I love style and fashion. And I like...oh, the idea of being a princess is sort of neat and—and having enough money to do whatever you wanted, but I mean, obviously her life has turned out horribly. I can't really...but still, I can admire her image, her style and her fashion and her beauty, you know?"

"Let me ask you a different question. What does it mean...Now, you say they're your heroes. What do you mean they're your heroes? What do you mean by a hero?"

"Well, they're people that I admire and read about and would like to be."

"You would like to be?"

"Yeah. I'd like to be."

"They're not guides? Are they guides for you?"

"Well, in a way Jane Fonda is, I think, because of the way she's lived her life. And she's—you know, she's got a lot of attractive qualities, too."

"You follow them, you read about them."

"Oh, yeah. I mean I would read anything that was published about them."

When we ask people over the phone whether or not they have heroes, 40 percent say yes. In light of all we have just heard, however, what does that figure mean? Is it an inflated estimate of those who have personal heroes in the sense we mean or is it, rather, an undercount?

Probably undercounted are some people like Eric and Hannah who, while they resist the word *hero*, nevertheless have mentors who function in a similar way. If some people like Eric and Hannah are undercounted, many others are probably overcounted—overcounted if what we are really after is people with personal heroes by whose supererogatory example they attempt to live their entire lives. Asked over the phone whether they have personal heroes, many, like Eli Cohen, may cite cultural heroes instead. Similarly, in contrast with Joe Barboso, many people may not distinguish heroes from ordinary role models like their parents.

According to how we have conceptualized heroes, people do not actually want to be their heroes but, rather, to stand with or emulate their heroes. Moral emulation, at any rate, is the heroic function in which we are interested. As we have seen, however, some people, like Diane Norris do, actually want to *be* their heroes. Diane tells me she actually wants to be Princess Diana because she would like to live Princess Diana's life. Our 40 percent figure will include people like Diane Norris as well.

People who actually want to be their heroes are probably uncommon. Probably more common are people who reject the word *hero* in favor of *mentor*. Probably much more common, however, are people who cite cultural rather than personal heroes or who do not distinguish between heroes and ordinary role models. If the first two, less common categories of people were undercounted by our phone survey, the more common, latter two categories were likely overcounted.

If, therefore, what we are really after is people who seek to emulate the supererogatory behavior of their heroes, the 40 percent figure more likely represents an overcount rather than an undercount. If so, then while 40 percent may be taken as an upper bound on people with personal heroes, the actual percentage of such people is likely lower. In the absence of any other data, we may tentatively surmise that most people do not have charismatic heroes by whom they are oriented toward transcendental horizons. That surmise receives some confirmation when we examine who the people surveyed said their heroes are.

WHO DO OUR HEROES TEND TO BE?

Between the spring and fall surveys, 162 heroes were named by 246 people. The heroes named ranged from Albert Einstein and Abraham Lincoln to Oprah Winfrey and Oliver North. Almost half the respondents who said they had heroes mentioned more than just one.

I classified people's heroes as one of six different types, and Table 5-1 shows how frequently each type was mentioned. "Celebrities" encompasses sports figures and popular entertainers, those whom Lowenthal refers to as "idols of consumption." Any hero whose claim to fame resides in the political arena was classified as a "Political" hero. Political heroes include Hillary Clinton and Martin Luther King Jr. Saints and other exemplary religious figures such as Mother Teresa were classified as "Religious" heroes. "Local" heroes are heroes of ordinary life who are personal acquaintances of the respondent—local socially if not always spatially. Among others, local heroes included family members, particularly the respondents' mother and father— the two heroes most frequently named; teachers; clergy; and friends. The "Arts" is a somewhat heterogeneous category that includes scientists such as Einstein or Linus Pauling; philosophers such as Socrates; and painters, poets, and novelists such as Pablo Picasso, Maya Angelou, and Norman Mailer. Finally, heroes not fitting any of the first five types were classified as "Other."

In Table 5-1, the first column shows the percentage of respondents who mentioned each hero type. The second column presents the actual number of these respondents. Since each respondent could mention more than one hero, there were more heroes mentioned than respondents. Column 3 shows the percentage of all heroes mentioned who belong to each type. Column 4 shows the actual number of these.

Whether we look at the percentage of respondents mentioning each hero type or we look at the percentage of all heroes mentioned belonging to each type, the data presented in Table 5-1 indicate that when adult Americans have heroes, their heroes tend not be celebrities. Fewer than 16 percent of respondents with heroes cite celebrities as their heroes (Column 1). Similarly, celebrities account for only 14 percent of all heroes named (Column 3). Finally, when we include

Table 5-1. Hero Types

	Respondents Mentioning Heroes of Each Type as a Percentage of		Mentions of Each Hero Type as a Percentage of	
	Respondents With Heroes*		Total Hero Mentions	
	(1)	(2)	(3)	(4)
Hero Types	%	N	%	N
Local	47.2	118	39.5	144
Political	28.8	72	26.0	95
Celebrities	15.6	39	14.0	51
Religious	14.0	35	10.7	39
Arts	6.4	16	4.9	18
Other	5.2	13	4.9	18
Total	100%	293	100%	365

* Percentages do not sum to 100% because some respondents name multiple heroes.

those who have no heroes at all, only a little over six percent of respondents identify idols of consumption as heroes.

Not even comparatively does the general public tend to equate heroes with celebrities. Idols of consumption or celebrities are not among the most frequently cited hero types. Instead, celebrities rank third in frequency after local and political heroes. Among those with heroes, the number of respondents who mention local heroes (47 percent) is about three times greater than the number of respondents who mention celebrities (16 percent). Similarly, the number of respondents who mention political heroes (29 percent) is almost two times greater. Likewise, in terms of mentions, the percentage associated with celebrities (14 percent) lags far behind the percentages associated with local heroes (40 percent) and political heroes (26 percent). Celebrities, in fact, do not rank that much higher than religious heroes (11 percent).

Boorstin and Lowenthal are undoubtedly correct that radio, television, and popular magazines pay undue attention to mere celebrity, crowding out the veneration of true heroism. The media's crowding out of heroes by celebrities may well leave people with a dearth of heroic exemplars with whom to identify. That may explain partly why only a minority of respondents say they have heroes.

On the other hand, the low frequency of celebrities identified as heroes suggests that the public has not fully succumbed to the media bias. People certainly remain enamored of celebrities and gossip concerning them. Adolescents may even idolize celebrities as heroes. Yet when adults choose their personal heroes, it is not celebrities they tend to choose. When we speak therefore of whom our society identifies as heroes, we must distinguish between the public and private aspects of culture. On the one hand, the media and their discourses have great public visibility. Far less visible are the heroes honored privately in our individual hearts. Yet our own private heroes are as reflective of who we are as a society as the heroes more publicly celebrated by the media. When public and private values diverge as they evidently do in the case of heroes, it is important for analysts not to mistake the public values for the values of the culture *tout court*.

The literature on heroes frames the current dimunition or actual lack of heroes as a loss. To do so is to suggest that vibrant heroes were more prevalent some time in the past. Perhaps such a case can be made for cultural heroes. As no public opinion polls were conducted in the distant past, we are unable to make the same determination for personal heroes.

What can we say? Remember that Nietzsche thought heroes might replace God as exemplars of larger calling. Similarly, according to Campbell's heroic monomyth, the hero is one who, in response to a call, leaves the familiarity of ordinary life to enter a sphere of transcendental conflict; in returning, the hero raises the level of ordinary life itself. One implication is that this is an existential journey we are all supposed to take. Another is that heroes serve to orient us to transcendental callings.

Do we truly need personal heroes? Most people do not think about heroes as a social phenomenon. Those who do have one of two reactions. First, some people think of hero-identification as a childish pursuit. However, there are several considerations that count against this supposition. First, there is the previously mentioned finding that those in public life frequently have heroes to guide them. Second, in the analysis of my own survey data, there was a statistically significant relationship between hero-identification and education. Having heroes was associated with more rather than less education. Having heroes thus seems to have less to do with childishness than with vocation. Indeed, we saw something of this in the people I interviewed.

The other reaction to heroes people sometimes have is that it is not the childish but society's elite that tends to have heroes. Certainly, if we think of who might have had heroes in, say, the Middle Ages, we may be more likely to think of knights and other members of the court than commoners, whose roles were more circumscribed. That today public figures and the more educated are also more likely to have heroes lends further support to this opinion.

Against this opinion is that the people I interviewed and surveyed were hardly elite in any strict sense; yet, many had heroes. Further, we must ask what it is about being elite that would make one more likely to have heroes. The answer that immediately comes to mind is a sense of public vocation. We are back to associating heroes with the larger sense of purpose of a transcendental calling. Although social factors may prevent some people from developing a larger sense of purpose, it is not something confined to the very elite. On the contrary, if a sense of public service is something we are now trying to foster among all citizens, then the number and types of heroes with whom we identify personally may be one measure of success.

Unfortunately, no such success is indicated by the data before us. Instead, what is indicated is a cultural withdrawal from transcendental horizons in favor of an affirmation of ordinary life. If heroes do represent transcendental callings and if 40 percent is the upper bound on people with heroes, then heroes and heroic callings appear to be peripheral to our culture.

The affirmation of ordinary life is further indicated by the types of heroes with whom people identify. From Table 5-1, we see that local heroes—personal acquaintances from ordinary life—were by far the most frequent category of hero mentioned. In fact, there were as many mentions of local heroes (40 percent) as there were of the next two most frequently mentioned categories combined: political heroes (26 percent) and celebrities (14 percent). The same pattern obtains when we look at respondents. Almost half of the respondents who had heroes (47 percent) mentioned personal acquaintances as among their heroes. Again, this is more than the combined number of respondents who named either political heroes (29 percent) or celebrities (14 percent).

Earlier we raised the possibility that when asked to name heroes, many respondents named ordinary role models instead. The high percentage of local heroes named lends credence to that possibility. To the extent that many respondents named ordinary role models rather than heroes, our true percentage of people with heroes may be far below 40 percent. On that interpretation of the local heroes named, we are left with much a smaller percentage of people who respond to transcendental horizons by hero-identification.

On the other hand, even if we accept all the local heroes as true heroes and not just ordinary role models, it still seems to be ordinary life rather than transcendental horizons that is being affirmed. To the extent that local heroes represent the values of ordinary life, it appears to be ordinary life that is affirmed by our heroes.

Finally, the contemporary affirmation of ordinary life is indicated by what is absent from the data: much mention of historical figures. Instead, the data display a striking ahistoricity in hero choice. Of the 162 different heroes mentioned, only ten lived prior to the twentieth century: Jesus, Washington, Jefferson, Lincoln, Bach, the Virgin Mary, Columbus, Saint Paul, Saint Francis Xavier, and Socrates.

Commentators may lament the dearth of heroes among our contemporaries, but there is no reason our personal heroes must necessarily be contemporary. Indeed, if people were actively looking for transcendental heroes, history is replete with them. All ten of the historical figures named, for example, represent ideals that transcend ordinary life.

It might be said that of course people tend to choose contemporaries as their heroes simply because it is their contemporaries with whom they most identify. This objection misses the point: Why is it just contemporaries with whom people most identify? We may attribute the lack of historical heroes to a general lack of historical knowledge. On the other hand, the causal connection may well go the other way. If people saw their lives as situated within some kind of ongoing tradition or project, then they likely would identify with the historical exemplars who symbolize the ideals of that project. The historical knowledge, then, would presumably follow. The ahistoricity of our heroes is thus another indicator of a postmodern, emotional disengagement from transcendental metanarratives.[27]

WHO TENDS TO HAVE HEROES?

We have been examining the extent to which heroes signify transcendental callings of one or another metanarrative. While we have so far gathered some evidence suggesting that heroic callings are now dim, we need to examine more closely this connection between heroes and metanarratives.

In the early years of this century, sociologist Charles Horton Cooley was also fascinated by the subject of heroes. He too suspected that heroes represented transcendental ideals. Specifically, Cooley believed that heroes were connected with a basically religious sensibility. "Hero-worship is a kind of religion," wrote Cooley, "and religion...is a kind of hero-worship."[28] Cooley thus connected hero-identification with religion and other transcendental metanarratives. For Cooley, too, hero-identification was a way for the individual to mark self-transcendent aspirations associated with moral idealism. If Cooley is correct, then we should expect to see a relationship between hero-identification on the one hand and religiosity and other indicators of an orientation toward transcendental meaning on the other.

We have observed that people who describe themselves as "very religious" are different. In particular, we saw that they tend both to think a lot about the meaning of life and to be more frequently in possession of some ultimate meaning. In this chapter, too, the in-depth interviews seemed to suggest that religious people are different. Interviewees with heroes tended either to be religious or, like Lawrence Patterson, to be oriented at least toward secular metanarratives that are equally transcendent. The survey data allow us to test this relationship between heroes and meaning more systematically.

There was not much in our survey that helped to explain who was more or less likely to have heroes. Having heroes was unrelated to gender, race, income, or age. Men and women, blacks and whites, and people of all ages and incomes were equally likely to be with or without heroes. In fact, education was the only demographic characteristic at all related to having heroes.

Beyond education, having heroes was related only to measures of transcendental concern. Recall that the survey contained three such measures: how often one thinks about the meaning of life; certainty about the meaning of life; and self-perceived religiosity. Recall also that in the spring survey, respondents were asked how often they think about the ultimate meaning of human existence, to which the possible responses were: "Always," "Often," "Sometimes," "Rarely," or "Never."

In terms of hero-identification, the minority who always think about the meaning of life are once again distinct. There was no difference between those who think about the meaning of human existence sometimes as opposed to rarely or never (see Table 5-1a in Appendix). In each case, 37 percent have personal heroes. In contrast, of those who always think about the meaning of human existence, close to 62 percent have heroes. We thus obtain initial confirmation that having heroes is related to transcendental concern.[29]

Certainty about the meaning of life provides a second confirmation. Recall that in both the spring and fall surveys, respondents were asked, " Which of the following statements best describes your attitude toward the ultimate meaning of human existence?" The possible responses were:

(1) There is no meaning to our existence. We are just lucky to be alive;

(2) Our existence must have some meaning, but I don't know what it is;

(3) We are here on earth for a purpose and I feel I have *some sense* of what that purpose is;

(4) We are here on earth for a purpose and I feel *I know* what that purpose is;

(5) I have some other attitude toward the meaning of life.

Respondents choosing response 1 were combined with those choosing response 5. They represent an anomalous group who reject the equation of meaning and purpose that the question presupposes (see Table 5-1b in Appendix).

Responses 2 through 4 indicate degrees of increasing certainty about the purpose of human existence. Those who chose one of these responses believe that human existence has some purpose. They just differ in their certainty about what that purpose is.

It appears that the more certain one is about the purpose of human existence, the more likely one is to have personal heroes. Of the 27 percent of respondents who think human existence purposeful without knowing what the purpose is, a little over 30 percent have heroes. Of the 41 percent who say they have some sense of what the purpose of human existence is, 42 percent have heroes. Finally, of the 20 percent who say they know what the purpose of life is, almost 56 percent have heroes. Again, a connection is confirmed between hero-identification and transcendental metanarratives.[30]

Let us now return to those who either deny that human existence has meaning or who have some other attitude about human existence. Forty-three percent of them have heroes. This is approximately the same percentage as those who say they have some sense of life's purpose.

Why do the respondents in this category have a greater tendency toward heroes than those without any sense of life's meaning but a weaker tendency toward heroes than those who say they do know what life's purpose is? Without more information, we can only speculate. There may of course be some additional motivation for hero-identification other than what I have identified.

The finding, however, is not inconsistent with what we have established so far. Recall that these respondents are a mixed group. Likely

Table 5-2. Hero-Identification and Religiosity

	Do Respondents Have Heroes?		
How Religious Respondents Are	No	Yes	Total Cases
Not Very Religious	67.3%	32.7%	113
Somewhat Religious	62.0%	38.0%	284
Very Religious	46.4%	53.6%	153

among them are adherents of metanarratives like Buddhism or Taoism, which render life meaningful without according it a purpose in the Judeo-Christian sense. Thus, even if these respondents reject the way the question was posed to them, they still subscribe to metanarratives having their own transcendental ideals. It would then follow for a portion of respondents in this category to personify their ideals through heroes.

We have been examining Cooley's contention that hero-identification is an expression of transcendental ideals. It is supported by the relationships between hero-identification and the survey's two measures of meaning—how often one thinks about the meaning of life and one's felt knowledge of what the meaning of life is. Those more oriented toward transcendental meaning do seem more likely to have personal heroes. If Charles Taylor is correct that ours is a disenchanted age that affirms ordinary life over transcendental meanings, then these findings also suggest why most respondents do not have personal heroes.

Given the close association between religiosity and the two measures of meaning, we would expect to find that religiosity is also related to hero-identification. As Table 5-2 indicates, this expectation is borne out. Almost 53 percent of the very religious respondents have personal heroes, compared with 37 percent of the somewhat religious respondents and 32 percent of the respondents who are not very religious.[31]

The effect of metanarratives on hero-identification is even clearer when we examine the combined effect of religiosity and frequency of thought about the meaning of life. In the spring survey, 23 (9 percent) respondents described themselves as both very religious and always thinking about the meaning of life. One hundred fifty-nine (64 percent) respondents said they were neither "very religious" nor "always thinking" about the meaning of life. Of these 159, only 30 percent had heroes. In the former category, however, composed of very religious people who are always thinking about the meaning of life, 70 percent had heroes. If a personal sense of the heroic survives today, it is likely among the very religious or otherwise ideological that we will continue to find it.

How do we put all these findings together? Traditionally, heroes are the protagonists of myths, metaphorical or figurative accounts addressed to the ultimate questions: Who are we? Where did we come from? Why are we here? Addressed to ultimate questions as they are, myths relate to a sacred plane of existence, a plane that transcends profane, everyday life. In the sacred plane, heroes personify transcendent ideals and transcendent visions of the good.

Throughout this book, we have been exploring the demythologized or profane nature of modern culture, the ways in which modernity is alienated from transcendental horizons. Ours is, as Charles Taylor has said, an age in which everyday life is valorized, not some higher plane of transcendent purpose. Ours is a bourgeois culture, in which the good is found in ordinary acts of work, domesticiy, and leisure.

Without a transcendent plane on which we are required to orient ourselves, we may feel little cultural need for personal heroes. As the mythic dwelling place of heroes is culturally marginal, its heroic residents are marginal as well. Most people do not have personal heroes, and among those who do, most frequently cited are the local heroes of ordinary life.

It is likely no accident that people with personal heroes tend to be both religious and attuned to grand metanarratives. If in their most vibrant form, heroes relate to concerns that are ultimate, then it will be those still consciously directed to the ultimate who continue to have heroes.

CHAPTER 6

Callings, Journeys, and Quests

I am I,
Don Quixote,
The lord of La Mancha.
My destiny calls And I go.

—*"The Man of La Mancha"*

Set out, then, accoutered lightly or heavily, and strive
with your possessions and your selves in the way of God. That is best
for you, if only you knew. Had their compensation been swift and the journey
undemanding, they would have followed you;
but they found the long haul arduous.

—*Qur'an 9: 41-2* [1]

When Cervantes first wrote *Don Quixote*, his intention was to spoof the age of chivalry. The idea was to portray a character whose mind had become so befuddled by the heroic rhetoric of knights errant that he goes off to make an utter fool of himself.

Four centuries later, in Dale Wasserman's play, *The Man of La Mancha*, Don Quixote's life comes to serve the entirely opposite point. In the play, Quixote is still mad, still suffering delusions of grandeur. Yet, this time, we are not supposed to remain laughing at Quixote's antics. This time, ridicule is meant to be replaced by a growing sense of respect.

As absurd as Quixote still is, we are meant to observe in the man from La Mancha a certain nobility of purpose. Indeed, the entire play expresses a nostalgia for purpose. The signature song is a catalogue of cosmic callings: "To right the unrightable wrong…To fight for the right without question or pause/To be willing to march into hell for a heavenly cause."

In the end, the very point of the play is to turn our initial condescension toward Quixote back onto ourselves. Quixote has returned to idealism; we have not. We are cynical about idealism. We consider it naive or foolish. We are all sober realists now. Yet, by the end of the play, we are meant to wonder whether, out of his madness, Quixote has not recovered something vital, something we have lost to our own detriment. In the end, we are meant to cheer the idealistic impulse, latent in all of us, that Quixote represents.

There is something ennobling about a life in service to ideals, to concerns morally weightier than our own commodious existence. Thus we miss the point of Quixote's story if we think the message is just to follow one's dream. It is not just any dream Quixote pursues. He specifically does not pursue what might be described as a morally neutral preference or desire. What makes Quixote an idealist is his dedication to a specifically moral purpose of larger significance. That pursuit in turn endows Quixote's life with larger significance. It becomes a life that participates in a cosmic project.

Quixote's idealism is a response to a call. Quixote himself says that it is his destiny that calls him. Yet how does his destiny do that? More basically, how does whatever it is that Quixote calls his destiny come to be owned by him? What makes that destiny his?

Sociologically, Quixote's idealism actually exemplifies the point of the previous chapter. As Joseph Campbell has observed, the hero's journey is always begun in response to a call.[2] For us to feel called, there must be someone or something that calls us. Calling Quixote are the heroic exemplars with whom he has filled his head. Those heroes become for him a transcendental reference group toward whose standard he now feels compelled to strive.

It is because Quixote is morally moved by the code of his heroes that he experiences himself directly addressed by it. The heroic code calls Quixote specifically for a response. The direct address to himself that Quixote experiences is what makes the call and the destiny his. By moving us morally, by demanding like behavior from us, our heroes may call us and, in the process, furnish us with a destiny.

Sociologists are very familiar with the concept of calling. It was central to the thought of Max Weber, one of sociology's founders. In *The Protestant Ethic and the Spirit of Capitalism*, Weber argued that Protestantism had developed the idea of calling as a way of universalizing the Catholic *vocatio,* or vocation.[3] Within the Catholic tradition, the vocation was a call from God to leave everyday life to become a priest, nun, monk, or brother. The word *profession* originates in this context, denoting a profession of commitment to take the vows of poverty, chastity, and obedience.[4]

Catholicism erected a dichotomy between the ordinary life of the laity and the transcendental service of a charismatic elite, called by God specifically to that vocation. Luther and Protestantism abolished this dichotomy. According to Protestantism, it is not just clerics who are called by God. Accordingly, there is no need to enter a clerical order to respond to God's call. Each of us, in the midst of ordinary life, is called by God to do something. Each of us has his or her own individual calling, his or her own task or mission here on earth. The Protestant calling thus universalizes the Catholic vocation.

According to Weber, the concept of calling gained prominence from Luther's translation of the Bible and use of the word *calling* in particular. Luther made it clear that long before Catholicism, God's call was reaching out to us all. Abraham is called by God to be the father of Israel. The disciples are called by Jesus to become fishers of men.

Weber defines a calling as a task set by God. Today, the word *calling*, like the words *vocation* and *profession*, is generally identified with certain kinds of occupations. The occupations honored by association with the religious words *calling, vocation,* and *profession* were originally occupations one pursued not just to earn a living. One pursued such occupations because one was called to do so. One became a teacher, a lawyer, a minister, or a physician not just because one was attracted to that endeavor, not just because one had special gifts making one potentially proficient in that line of work, but because one had been called to pursue the spiritual purpose entailed by that activity.

In Weber's formulation, a calling involves a specific task or mission. One is not just vaguely called to realize one's potential. Task or mission is essential to the idea of calling. In the classical tradition, Cincinnatus is called away from farming for the specific purpose of saving Rome.

As people actually experience callings in their lives, however, we understand the concept too narrowly if we always identify callings with occupations or other equally specific tasks. There are ways we can be called more broadly. We may also be called to live a specific kind of life. We may be called, for example, to follow Jesus, to take up his cross as our own. Moslems likewise experience a call to follow Muhammad, who, in turn, felt called to acknowledge the oneness of God. Although such callings still align our lives as whole to a particular purpose, that purpose is hardly as concrete as a specific task or occupation.

We likewise understand calling too narrowly if we follow Weber in construing calling as a purpose necessarily assigned by God. Cincinnatus was not called by God and, arguably, neither was Quixote—at least not directly. Ideals other than God can call us.

What remains important is that a life's calling retain cosmic significance. If it is not God who calls us, it must at least be the cosmos. More broadly understood, a calling is a task or purpose of cosmic significance.

In the language we have been using, a calling represents a kind of hypergood, a first principle of a life to which other goods are subordinated. As such, a calling unifies a life. A called life is like a soldierly station, a post the called one does not desert despite sacrifices to the self, despite the need to subordinate or even abandon other goods.[5] Response to a call therefore affords the self a kind of unity, a unity of purpose. Underlying that unity of purpose is the unwavering disposition of commitment.

We have observed that a hypergood is not so much something we choose as something that chooses us. The very word *calling* connotes a relation between the called self and the hypergood it serves. We do not choose one calling or another. Instead, a particular hypergood impresses itself upon us as an emotionally experienced ideal. By the passion it evokes in us, the hypergood calls us out of our former life to a new life of service to the hypergood. It is the hypergood that is initially the active agent and not we ourselves.

The hypergood calls us. We ourselves are either called or not. If a call goes out to us, we either hear it or not. If we hear the call, we do or do not respond. In all ways, we react to rather than initiate the relation between ourselves and a hypergood.

Calling is not the only way to understand the spiritual unity of our lives. I said earlier that in the signature song of *The Man of La Mancha*, what we have is a catalogue of cosmic callings. In the song, Quixote refers to these callings collectively as his "quest." Alternatively or in addition to experiencing ourselves as called, we might also capture a sense of spiritual unity by imagining our lives as a journey or quest.

Calling and quest are not mutually exclusive categories. Indeed, as we have noted, Joseph Campbell says that the "hero's quest" or journey often begins with an initial call, a summons to embark. Yet the metaphors of journey or quest can also have independent resonance. We may resonate with the metaphor of life as a journey or quest without necessarily experiencing ourselves as called to anything in particular.

The metaphor of life as a journey certainly figures in Christian symbolism. We need think only of *The Pilgrim's Progress*, which explicitly represents life as such. Yet, the metaphor is by no means limited to Christianity. Through the stories of Israel's exodus and Muhammad's hejira, Jews and Moslems likewise understand themselves as existential pilgrims. Indeed, John Renard observes that "of all the world's religious traditions, none has maintained so strong a sense of its members as a community on pilgrimage as has the Islamic tradition."[6]

There is something universal, then, about Hermann Hesse's *The Journey to the East*, which depicts life as a great sacred pilgrimage in search of meaning, a pilgrimage that encompasses all religious traditions and even secular routes.[7] The journey, as Hesse describes it, is timeless and spaceless. It is a journey we undertake with our souls rather than our bodies. He depicts the journey as a pilgrimage, a collective enterprise rather than an individual quest. By joining the pilgrimage, we walk with others and not alone.

In *The Journey to the East*, the unnamed protagonist has abandoned the pilgrimage, believing it to have foundered. He has succumbed instead to the world's cynical rationalism, which dismisses all quests for ultimate meaning. The protagonist is meant to represent the modern sensibility. In contrast, we again meet Quixote as one of those still on the road.[8]

By the end of the book, the protagonist has come to realize that despite appearances, the great pilgrimage continues—even in his absence. At first mortified to learn that the pilgrimage did not betray him but rather he the pilgrimage, the protagonist finally understands that despair and abandonment, too, are part of his particular journey, part of its manifold paths. In the end, he responds to a call to resume the pilgrimage in a more conscious, humble way.

Does the great journey continue even today? Without us? Whether or not we ourselves are part of it, the pilgrimage does proceed. There are those still on the road. I speak, for example, with Alexander Wenig, who has himself wandered long and far to arrive at where he is when I encounter him. Alexander is a practicing Catholic who also on occasion still attends Quaker meetings. During two years in Iran with the Peace Corps, he was introduced to Islam. On his return, he joined an American Sufi order and is to this day a Sufi "healer."

"Oh, journeys," Alexander says. "Life as a journey is very important to me. It is a metaphor that just really works for me. When I lose sight of where I am going or of what I am doing, it helps me get back on track.

"We are all on a journey. And there are so many ways in which this metaphor can be used. We can talk about highways and byways."

"What do you mean?" I ask.

"Well, our path isn't straight. We don't go straight to where we are going."

"Where are we going?"

"To death."

"To death?"

"Well," Alexander explains, "death may not be the end of the journey, but it is one point where we all will arrive. I don't have a clear picture of what will happen after death. But you can speak of journeys even in that context."

I nod, thinking of the Egyptian and Tibetan books of the dead.

"I didn't originate these concepts, this metaphor. I think it comes from my involvement with the Sufis."

I nod again. Alexander then goes on to show me just how powerful the journey metaphor can be.

"And to me, accompaniment is important. You can't accompany people on their whole journey. Much of it we must walk alone. But we can stop and walk a short distance with each other. That accompaniment is really important. That to me is the meaning of a faith community. In a faith community, you accompany each other on the journey."

Accompaniment for Alexander means attending the baptism of newborn babies and the funerals of those in his faith community who have died. It means being there with others at the important passages of their lives. "Ninety percent of life," Alexander says, "is showing up." Alexander shows up at other places, too. He carries the Eucharist to those in prison and to those alone, dying from AIDS.

"We are here to hold each other's hands," Alexander tells me, "to accompany each other on this journey. And that to me is the meaning of life. We are here to take each other home."

Veet Raj and Anand Naveeno, the couple who had traveled with the Bhagwan Sri Rajneesh, are influenced by Eastern philosophy.

"Do you think of life as a journey?" I ask them.

"Yes," Anand responds.

"Veet, do you think of life as a journey?"

"Yeah. A moving…"

"So where do you think we're all journeying to?"

Anand responds first. "To happiness."

Veet answers differently. "Like the river to the sea."

Anand continues. "I think like relaxation."

"Relaxation?" I ask Anand.

"Mm-hm. Like when we have problems in life, if you—maybe because we want something else than what we are given so we swim against the stream instead of just go with the stream. And, uh, when we have reached a state of a total relaxation, we accept the stream."

Veet now adds a comment. "All, you know? That's all that is: accepting your life, accepting, just being accepting...all that come with acceptance. Flowing with the stream."

"It sounds a lot like—"

"Right," Veet interrupts. "Yeah, in that Eastern group."

"We don't know the particulars," Anand says.

"Yeah," Veet continues. "And we're not particularly any—we're a synthesis of all of them."

"Say that again," I ask.

"We're a synthesis of all of the...including Western religion, although it's...in Western religion...one has to really—really, how do I say? Imagine it, be very imaginative to find it there."

If Anand and Veet have difficulty resonating with Western conceptions of life as a journey, it is perhaps because in the Western traditions, particularly Christianity, the journey metaphor is often subordinated to prior understandings of life. That is certainly true in the case of fundamentalists John Wasserman and Matt Bennett.

"Sometimes," I say to them, "life is compared to a journey. If you think of life that way, where are you going on this journey?"

Matt looks at John. "Would you go first?"

"You always let me go first," John replies. "Okay, life is a journey up a stream. As they say, even a dead fish can swim downstream. All the world has fallen into sin, and a lot of people are just being sucked along, not thinking about the meaning of life, just going with whatever meaning suits their fancy or just what other people are doing. But God wakes some people up and calls them to swim the other way, and it makes the journey difficult if you are a minority and doing things that other people think are strange, but God is waiting at the end. That's the end, the upstream end, and judgment is waiting at the bottom end."

"Yeah," Matt affirms, "I would say something similar...though I would elaborate on one important thing. Because I've thought about the journey illustration before, and I like and dislike it."

"Really? Why?"

"Because I would say there is a journey and yet...well, actually, one thing I like about the model John mentioned with a downstream and an upstream...I think a lot of the world thinks we're all in a journey together, and some of us are a little further ahead than others. Some of us are a little bit better than others, and, you know, a lot of us are pursuing God, and at some point, we will probably cross a magic line in the sand or something that will say, 'Now, now I am acceptable to God. I am headed for heaven.' If I haven't crossed that line, you know, then, kind of, well, we're on a spiritual journey, and we're hoping that we get close enough to God that we get accepted into heaven versus those that aren't close enough to God or aren't really trying on their journey and will end up failing."

"And this is the way the world thinks?"

"That's the way I think a lot of people look at it, you know? I'm kind of on this journey. At some point, I cross over into what would be acceptable to God or, you know, you might have the grace piece in there that, you know, God, you know, it's not really my work except you still see it kind of as a lifelong journey.

"I think the Bible paints a different picture. I would paint a much different picture of it, which is the world...We're all headed away from God. And there's a point at which God grabs some people and turns them around. And once you're turned around, it is a journey of growth in what it means to follow God, but there's a very definite turning point in that journey that's a hundred-eighty-degree turn.

"And until that point, you are journeying straight to judgment, and there is no other thing that's going to happen at the end. That is the end. And once you've turned around, you're...Heaven is the end of the journey no matter what, whether you are one of the slow walkers, whether you are one of the fast runners.

"Once you've turned, once God has turned you around, heaven is the end. So there's kind of two journeys going: one to destruction and one to heaven. And there's a point in time when people get turned from one to the other and put on the other journey, but it's not kind of one long journey that some people make it to the end of and some people don't happen to make it to the end of, as I think it is often painted."

CALLINGS TODAY

I observed earlier that the concept of calling was central to one of sociology's three founders. It is remarkable, therefore, that within sociology it has received so little empirical attention. Robert Wuthnow asked some questions about callings in a large, national survey and treats the results briefly in his book on religion and money in America.[9] Beyond Wuthnow's brief glance at callings, there is nothing empirical. Thus, what follows here must still be regarded as an exploratory foray into a long overlooked subject.

Over the previous few chapters, we have been trying to determine what links remain to tie us, not so much horizontally to the community as a whole but vertically to a larger sense of purpose. Whether or not it is mediated by community, we have been seeking experiential connection with what is ultimate or transcendent. We have been seeking moral idealism and emotional connection with the cosmos itself.

So far, we have seen God become emotionally remote. We have marked the fade-out of heroic consciousness. We have observed how even the question of life's meaning has receded from us. Like heroes with whom they are closely connected, callings and journeys are two more almost universal ways through which people have connected emotionally with cosmic purpose and thereby lent unity to their lives. Popular books are still written today with allusions to calling in the title, Robert Coles's *The Call of Service*, for example, or Daniel Gordis's *God Was Not in the Fire*, subtitled *A Call to a Spiritual Judaism*.[10] Yet, with how many today does the word *calling* in these titles resonate? How common today is any sense of calling? Do people still think of life as a journey? When people do feel called or think of life as a journey, to what do they feel called? To where are they journeying? The extent and content of sacred experience are what we are after.

The results of my own empirical research are equivocal. They indicate continued popular resonance at least with the concepts of calling and journey. Some, like Alexander Wenig, can articulate the personal import of those words with eloquence and emotional power. For many others, however, the resonance is all that remains. For them, calling and journey are, like God and the meaning of life, floating signifiers, evocative signs without clear referents. Many others respond no longer even to the signs.

Not surprisingly, Sister Marge O'Hara is one who does experience her life as a response to a call. She explains to me how she was first called to the sisterhood.

"My home was directly behind the convent of my elementary school, so we shared the back hedge. The sisters were young because it was close to the mother house, and they were always sent to my home parish as their first mission, so I was exposed to a very positive image of the sisterhood in my formative years.

"I responded to that very positively. I also think my rank in the family—I was the oldest daughter of a family of seven—I always felt a sense of responsibility and leadership. I felt that from an early age, and I saw the sisters in a position of leadership, and then when I had this feeling of I want to give my life to the glory of God, how could I then do that?

"At that time, the alternatives were not as varied as they are today, but I saw it as, well, I could do it in marriage, and I loved, I loved the idea of being married. I loved the idea of being a mother, of having a family. I mean I felt drawn to that, and I felt I didn't want to have to give that up in order to have a life that would give glory to God.

"But something said to me, If you follow this way and you're willing to make that sacrifice, that's what I'm asking you to do. So there was an element definitely an element of resistance and feelings that I was giving something up that I really felt drawn to. And I loved having boyfriends and friends of my brother's that I would—I was always in love, you know?

"From the time I can remember in kindergarten, I remember having, you know…flirting and having crushes and always having significant others in my life, and I used to think, Oh, gosh, that's going to be hard. So and then of course I was eighteen when I made the decision, so as I reflect now I can see that's how I developed.

"But then through several significant stages of my life with the sisters, I have had to come to grips with direction in my life, you know? Is this…am I really happy, you know? Is this really good for me? Is this the life, after thinking about it, because I was only eighteen at that time? Is this really what God's calling me to do now?

"And I've had those kind of times that come about and—say, a thirty-day retreat, a twenty-fifth anniversary, times when I would fall in love and feel like why did I do this in the first place? Why did I get myself into this?

"Each time I went through significant examination of my vocation, I would come up with, No, I think this is what God wants me to do, and I think I'm good at it. And I am really deep down happy in this life, even though I have, I can't have everything, so I have the feeling of…When I look at married couples and I say, Yeah that is a really nice life, and I would like that, but I can see that I have a really good life too, and they have had many sacrifices. I see in my sister and brother-in-law the sacrifices they made, and then I go home at night and have…I had sacrifices, but then I had the benefit of a certain amount of independence, a certain amount of time for solitude that a life with a significant other wouldn't provide. So the life of community has given me a lot of opportunity for growth as well as a sacrifice."

"You talk about being called, and you still feel called? The same calling as you had originally?"

"I think my sense of call has changed. I think basically having the feeling that I'm doing what I believe, as far as I can figure out with the reflection from other people that I respect, that I'm doing what God wants."

"Well, what is your calling now? What is your…what are you called to do now?"

"I feel called to a life in community for the sake of the gospel but with a special relationship to God that calls me to attend to that relationship as my primary relationship so that I work on cultivating contemplation and my prayer life and attending to a life with God that is different because I have the luxury of attending in a more focused way than I would if I were in a marriage relationship or in a career as a single woman, but I say publicly to the world that I have a commitment to making my relationship with God my most significant relationship."

As we might expect, Sister Marge's call is very specific. She not only feels called to put God first but to put God first in a very particular way. I ask her, however, whether we are not all called to put God first in one way or another.

"I think we are," she says, "because when Jesus said, you know, 'Leave everything,' that is meant for everybody. That's for every baptized person, you know?

"I think what it means is that God needs to be first, and the way I would interpret that in marriage would be that God has to be first and the marriage relationship is…that a couple see each other as a reflection of God's love for them. You know? That how you respond to your wife, how she responds to you is an expression of your love for God.

"Mm-hm."

"So that is different from celibacy in that the celibacy is a calling for that direct communication. But also like I feel that the expression of God through Christ is my brothers and sisters…"

"Mm-hm."

"In, you know, especially those most in need and that the beloved of God is that person who is most in need, reflected in a family. Like if a father has a child who is blind—I saw this, you know? I saw this in a family who has like ten children. One child is blind and the parents' love for all the children, you know, was beautiful, but everybody had to focus on that little one, and now you can think, that's how it is with

God. That those who are most vulnerable, those who are—are most unsupported by material things and other things are those that we need to kind of rally around."

It is not surprising that Sister Marge feels called. Her entire life is explicitly devoted to a specific Catholic vocation with a sense of calling at its heart. Yet it does not require such organizational structure to feel called. Fundamentalist Christians John Wasserman and Matt Bennett tell me what calling means to them.

"It means," John says, "basic underlying peace is following Jesus Christ wholeheartedly and learning to be like him. He called those who followed him closely his disciples. He called his other followers to be disciples in the same fashion. What it particularly means in the context of my life is also finding more mature Christians that I can follow after. I am following them as they follow Christ because I am following Christ. That's what discipleship is rooted in, that's what its purpose is—to know Christ, to make him known."

"So it's a call to know Christ?" Again, the calling here has a very specific content.

"Yes, and that's—that is and should be common to those who follow scriptural teachings, you know? I specifically believe I belong here at this place and this time. Obviously, not everybody else does. So I guess the fundamental call is to follow Christ."

"So there is like a fundamental call and more specific calls, where you are called right now?"

"Right."

I turn to Matt. "Do you have anything to add?"

Matt responds. "It's very God-centered. I think we have a call, which is not just a euphemistic way of saying that that's what we just think we should do. We really believe that this is what God has initiated in calling us to be Christians, to follow Christ. And more specifically, to know God's will. Specifically, what he wants us to do with our lives."

Matt affirms a point I made earlier that when we experience ourselves as called, it is not we who take the initiative. A calling is not the same as an inclination that originates with us. We experience a call as something independent of us to which we respond.

The ideas of calling and journey are supposed to be prominent in Christian—and particularly Protestant Christian—discourse. Yet even among those attached to that discourse, many evidently go through life without feeling they have received a call. That is true for Frederick and Martha Schmidt, conservative Lutherans.

"Okay," I ask them, "do either of you feel like in your life you have some sense of calling?"

"I wondered about that," Frederick replies. "I have no idea what it could be."

"You never felt you were called to something?"

"No."

"And you, Martha? No?"

"I thought there might have been some stuff in the Bible but never called. I can't think of anything. I don't know."

I change tacks. "Do you see life as a journey at all?"

"As a journey?" Martha asks. "It's been a journey and sometimes a pretty tough road."

"You ask us—" Frederick begins, but Martha interrupts.

"We'll be married fifty-five years this year in December, and we had a tough road."

"I wonder why?" Frederick muses.

"And some people," Martha continues, "have it real easy, but we've had, we had lots of problems."

"You wonder why," Frederick says. "Why am I here? What am I here for?"

Frederick and Martha are not the only Christians who experience no sense of calling. I ask Robert Zimbruski whether he experiences himself as having a calling. "No," he tells me. I ask Ellen Smith the same question. She does not have any sense of calling either.

I have a slightly more extended conversation on the topic with Betty Enders. "Do you feel any sense of calling in life? Do you know what I mean by that?"

"Yes."

I realize I had asked Betty to respond simultaneously to two separate questions. Thus, now, I don't know what her affirmation means. "Yes, you know, but you don't..."

"Yes, I know what you mean, but I don't think so."

"Suppose we think of life as a journey."

"Oh my God."

"Do you ever think of life that way?"

"As a journey? No, I don't think so."

"Okay. How about as a quest?"

"As a quest. I don't think so either. I don't...I never really thought about it, to be honest with you."

Sometimes it is not that people have never thought about the idea of a calling. Instead, some people familiar with the concept consciously reject it. Bruce Gonzalez is among their number. I interview Bruce along with his friend, Sharon Traub. Both in their thirties, they work together for an international relief agency. Sharon is a practicing Catholic. Bruce is a Unitarian Universalist. Unitarian Universalism is one of the least dogmatic of Christian denominations. Of course, along with that tolerance comes a certain thinness of doctrinal belief. It is therefore not surprising that Bruce would have trouble with the concept of calling. What is surprising—or at least ironic—is how aptly the concept of calling nonetheless applies to him.

"Okay," I begin. "Some people experience a sense of calling in life. Do you have any sense of calling in your lives? Anything in particular?"

Sharon answers first. "Nothing in particular. At least, I haven't figured it out yet. I mean, I believe in that sense of calling, that people can have that, but I don't, and I've searched for that. Like, I don't think I have a calling for specific things. I don't really feel that."

I turn to Bruce. "Do you?"

"A calling. See, calling strikes me again as a word that's rooted in some sort of...religious background, and so I'm not sure that I could, that I can buy into that exact spirit of the word."

"Okay."

"But this is a story that Sharon knows about a guy I was talking with once when I was looking for a job. He asked me...well, we were on the phone. He said, 'Well, you know, what do you do?'"

"And I started reciting my resumé...you know? And he says, 'Oh no, that's not what I mean. I don't mean what you've done. I mean more what do you...what do you do? What are you?' He said, 'What are you?'"

"Well," I say to Bruce, "I was going to ask you that myself."

Bruce continues. "I had no idea where to go. He said, 'Well, you know, are you a salesman? Are you a writer? Are you a counselor? Are you a builder? Fundamentally, what are you? What is it that you do?'"

"And I...It was a mind-boggling question at the time, and I latched onto one of the things he said. 'Well,' I said, 'I'm a writer.'"

"I always felt comfortable explaining myself that way. So I said, 'I'm a writer.' So that moved the conversation forward and we went on and talked about things. But his question stayed with me for a long time, and I realized that my answer was not sufficient, wasn't accurate. And it took me months, but it finally came to me one day. Not with sweat over it, but it came to me, that I'm not fundamentally a writer but more fundamentally a storyteller.

"And every time in my life when I've been, when I felt most successful with other people or successful at work or...self-satisfaction or the sense that I'm doing, contributing something unique, that it is of me, it's when I'm telling stories. And that's the case right now in my current job, when I'm up in front of the board, you know, inspiring them about what we do. So I think that that's what I am, in answer to his question."

Quite unexpectedly, Bruce is one of the few people able to tell me who he is essentially, who he is in the cosmos. He is a storyteller. It is by invoking a paradigm of almost mythic significance that he is able to do so.

"You know, I took Sharon to this storytelling conference. It was the National Storytellers Conference, and those people who are part of that association really believe in storytelling as an incredibly important form of human interaction and of learning and spiritual development. And I buy into that. I definitely buy into that.

"I'm attracted to stories, and I'm fascinated with...Yeah, it's part of me. It's an—I don't view it as something...I don't know. It's just what I'm...what my interests are, and I'm fascinated with it, and I do believe in the value of it, and in the...Like, I think when you just say stories or storytelling, there's an instinctual kind of, 'Oh, a story,' you know? There's something, there is something mythical about it. I think that's the word you wanted to use."

"Mm-hm." I had asked Bruce about the mythic element in the type of the storyteller.

"And, you know, Homer and all this other business and it's the same thing. That's fundamentally what Homer was before someone wrote down his stories. And so, yeah, I—I believe in all that. Definitely. I believe in the value of it, and that motivates me in what I want to do with my future."

Andrew Greeley, a sociologist and Catholic priest, would particularly approve of the value Bruce places on stories. According to Greeley, religion originates in the poetic stories we collectively create to express our deeper experiences.[11] Expressing deeper experiences appears to be what Bruce feels called to do.

We have seen that some people orient themselves in relation to exemplary personages even while rejecting the word *hero* as a designation for those exemplars. We wondered then whether we should or should not say that such people have heroes. In relation to callings, Bruce presents us with a similar conundrum. On the one hand, Bruce's identification of himself as a storyteller is precisely what we would mean by someone with a felt sense of calling. Yet, Bruce himself rejects that word. If we are interested in the number of people who respond to the specific word *calling*, then, of course, we ought not to count Bruce as one with a calling.

We are, however, less interested in the specific word *calling* than in the relationship between a self and the cosmos that this word captures. Despite Bruce's contrary judgment, is his relation to the cosmos captured by the word *calling*?

I said earlier that in order for us properly to say that one is called, there must be someone or something that calls. What is it that calls Bruce? Clearly, it is not God. Bruce makes no reference to God in this context.

If anything calls Bruce, it is the mythical image of the storyteller itself. The storyteller image does seem to call Bruce to a particular place in the cosmos. In so doing, the image lends a conscious unity to the spiritual aspirations of Bruce's life. If so, then we probably should classify Bruce among the called.

Those who have so far expressed a calling have been connected in one way or another with a religious discourse. Even Bruce, who rejects the word *calling*, is familiar through Unitarian Universalism with multiple discourses of ultimate meaning. Probably both a sense of calling and the recognition of it as such are more likely among those who are conversant with discourses of ultimate meaning, particularly discourses that explicitly employ the concept of calling. Yet, as in Bruce's case, some people may have a sense of calling even without that word for it. They may have a sense of calling even without a strong connection to discourses of ultimate meaning.

Jason Fishman appears to be one such person. Jason is a political activist. Jason is Jewish, and Judaism is not a religious tradition in which the idea of calling figures prominently. Even if the idea of calling did figure in Judaism, Jason's religious background in Judaism is meager. Nevertheless, the idea of calling still holds some resonance for Jason.

I ask Jason about this. "Some people feel as if they're here for some purpose or mission or experience themselves as called to do something. Do you have any such experience like that?"

"I would say more in a negative sense. In that when I've been in a situation where I was not either politically active or not involved in work that I felt was contributing to the good of humanity in some way, that I have like serious problems with alienation. Like, what am I doing here? What is the point of all this?"

"Okay." Jason is telling me that when he is not contributing to humanity in some way, he feels disconnected from the cosmos, possibly disconnected as well from what he feels called to do.

"And I don't have those...when I'm, you know, working hard and..."

"You experience something when you're not doing what...You experience calling in the absence rather than in its presence?"

"Yeah. Like I don't go to work every day thinking, you know, like I am committed to doing public health work...But I did housing and community development stuff before that, and I liked that, and I made the change for...really to pursue my intellectual interests and really wanted to work more with human...kinds of level issues than financial issues and that kind of stuff."

"Okay."

"But," Jason laughs, "I mean, I don't go to work every day thinking like, 'I'm doing the Lord's work here.'"

I laugh too, thinking to myself how presumptuously I sometimes regard my own work.

"But," Jason concludes with a laugh, "I also don't go to work thinking like, 'I have no idea what the point is.'"

How Prevalent and Strong Is the Sense of Calling Today?

Judging from the people I interviewed, a sense of calling appears neither prevalent nor strong today. Among my interviewees, only the very religious seemed actually to utilize the concept on their own. A few others such as Bruce Gonzalez and Jason Fishman seem to respond to a sense of calling, although *calling* is not the word they would naturally use to describe it. The rest appear neither to invoke the word nor to feel the feeling.

How representative of our wider society are the people I interviewed? To find out, I conducted two surveys. One survey constituted the senior research project for my undergraduate student, Theresa Greto. Together, Theresa and I collected a sample of three hundred undergraduate students from ten different classes at our institution. This sample had the advantage of numbers and a virtually complete response rate. On the negative side, it was a sample exclusively of largely white college students at one institution.

To obtain a more representative sample, I again went through our survey research center. There, through random-digit dialing, we obtained a sample of 182 Philadelphia residents. The disadvantage of this sample was its much lower response rate and smaller size.[12]

Despite their respective shortcomings, the two surveys together give us at least an initial sense of the prevalence of calling in the general population. Both surveys asked respondents whether they feel any calling in life, whether there is any cause or mission to which they feel they were devoting their lives.

The survey results contained a few surprises. In both, larger percentages than I had expected resonated with the word *calling*. In the student survey, 40 percent of respondents said they felt some calling in life. Forty-five percent (45 percent) of the respondents in the Philadelphia survey said the same. In comparison, 30 percent of the respondents in Wuthnow's national survey said they felt called to their particular line of work.[13]

Many people feel called, however, without being able to identify what they are called to do. This finding introduces a conceptual puzzle. Can one feel called without knowing what one is called to do? In this context, *call* would seem to be a transitive verb. Just as one cannot properly be said to have an intention without an intention to do something in particular, it is hard to understand how one can properly say one is called without knowing what one is called to do.

A little later, we will come to a better understanding of this paradox. For the moment, let us confine our discussion only to those who can actually say to what they are called. In the student survey, only 30 percent of respondents both said they felt a calling and could identify what it is. Among the Philadelphia respondents, 40 percent both said they felt a calling and could identify what it is. What are the kind of things that people say they feel called to do? In both surveys, respondents' callings were classified under four broad categories, and the distribution of responses is presented below.

Calling	Student Survey	Philadelphia Survey
Family/self/success	29%	40%
Work/vocation	30%	13%
Religion	11%	11%
The Social Good	30%	36%
Total cases	101	193

The categorical distributions of callings in the two surveys were remarkably similar. In both surveys, only 11 percent of respondents cited specifically religious callings. These were not specific callings to adopt clerical vocations. Instead, they were more general callings to follow Jesus or serve God.

Comparable percentages in the two surveys reported a felt call to contribute somehow to the social good. As a category, the social good broadly includes callings ranging from the diffuse to the highly specific. Among the more diffuse callings cited were "to make a difference" or "to be a better person." Among the more specific callings were conserving the environment; attending to the homeless, the underprivileged, or disabled; fighting discrimination; and championing the rights of women.

Among those who reported being called to contribute to the social good, age seems to make a difference. Students were more likely than Philadelphia residents as a whole to feel a call to conserve the environment. They were also more likely to express the vaguer calls to be a better person or to make a difference. More specific callings seem to come with age.

The major difference between the student and Philadelphia surveys, however, was that students tended more to respond to occupational callings whereas the Philadelphia residents as a whole tended more to respond to callings in the category of self / success / family. Again, however, there were differences even within these categories. Within the category of self / success / family, the Philadelphia residents tended much less to respond to callings focused on the self and to respond much more to callings related to children or family in general. Students were much more likely to feel such diffuse, personal calls as "to be the best I can be," "to be successful," or "to realize my potential."

The occupational callings were especially interesting, particularly among the Philadelphia residents as a whole. The occupational callings cited were professions or tasks that also clearly serve the general good. For example, people cited medicine, law, and education, the occupational callings traditionally associated with professional vocations. In addition, other people cited music, AIDS research, teen drug abuse, the military, and politics.

How do we interpret these results? If we consider just the percentages of people who say they feel called and the tasks to which they feel called, it appears as if a sense of calling has not completely disappeared. As a first guess, a sense of calling appears to survive among at least a third of the population.

If some sense of calling survives among at least a third of the population, then, on this matter, the people I interviewed seem to be unrepresentative of the population as a whole. Fewer than a third of the people I interviewed expressed any definite sense of calling. Here, however, we must be careful. The surveys indicate only that at least a third of the respondents can respond appropriately to questions about callings if asked. This does not mean the concept of calling is very operative in their lives. Asking about callings introduces a concept that may not otherwise organize respondents' lives. It is not clear whether all those who can interpret their life goals in terms of calling actually do so on their own. If they do not, then the people I interviewed may not be as unrepresentative as they seem. For some minority of the population, a certain resonance with the concept of calling remains. How important that concept is to their lives, we do not know. As in the case of heroes, we have managed only to place an upper bound on the contemporary importance of calling.

As in the case of heroes, we must wonder who is more or less likely to experience a sense of calling. As in the case of heroes, not much predicted who is more or less likely to experience a calling. In neither survey was calling related to gender. In the student survey, calling was unrelated to major. In the Philadelphia survey, people of all incomes or educational attainment were equally likely or unlikely to experience a calling.

For both surveys, one of the most interesting findings was a nonfinding. Given the historical origin of the concept of calling, we might expect Protestants more than Catholics to experience themselves as called. In neither survey was this the case. Wuthnow, similarly, found no difference between Protestants and Catholics.[14] Calling now seems a culturally diffuse concept, equally familiar to all Christians—and even to non-Christians.

Yet, as in the case of heroes, so too in the case of callings: the very religious are distinct. In the student survey, respondents were again asked how religious they would say they were. Among those who said they are very religious, 70 percent also said they experienced a calling (see Table 6-1 in Appendix). That percentage is not only high absolutely but also substantially higher than the percentages with callings among all other levels of religiosity. Clearly, the vocabulary of calling persists forcefully among the small minority in our culture who are not only cognitively connected with religious discourses but emotionally connected as well.

The student survey also contained a number of questions about philosophical reflectiveness. Students were asked how often they thought about God, how the universe came into being, and the purpose of life.[15] As we saw was also true for heroes, such meaning variables were efficacious predictors of spirituality. As we would expect, there was a statistically significant relationship between religiosity and how often one thinks about God and the origin of the universe, although the relationship between religiosity and life goal just fails to be significant.[16] Further, if one frequently thinks philosophically about life's ultimate questions, one is much more likely to be one who also experiences a sense of calling (see Table 6-2 in Appendix).

As we found before, the philosophically or existentially reflective tend to be the same people who consider themselves very religious. Once again, therefore, we receive confirming evidence that in religious discourse and in our emotional connection to it, our moral vision is lifted to broader horizons. In the great loss of emotional connection to discourses of ultimate meaning, religious or otherwise, what contracts is the horizon of questions we pose to ourselves.

In the Philadelphia survey, only two factors on their own were statistically related to calling. One was frequency of attendance at religious services, which in this survey was asked instead of how religious respondents considered themselves to be. Among those who attend religious services once a month or more, over 60 percent also expressed some sense of calling in life. In contrast, among those whose attendance of religious services is less frequent, only 43 percent expressed some sense of calling.[17]

Race was the other factor in the Philadelphia survey that was statistically related to calling. Blacks were more likely to express some sense of calling in their lives than whites. Whereas only 37 percent of whites both expressed a sense of calling and could say what it was, 57 percent of blacks both cited a sense of calling and could say what it was.[18] Of course, the independent effect of race disappears when we try to predict calling, controlling for all different factors simultaneously (see Table 6-3 in Appendix). Then, the only factor that continues to have an independent effect on calling is reflection on the meaning of life. Presumably, if race matters to calling, it matters through a differential sense of ultimate meaning.

Following the publication of Cornel West's *Race Matters*, there was much public attention to the question of "black nihilism."[19] West, a sociologically informed theologian, coined the term to describe the loss of values and moral purpose among young, male African Americans living in the poorer sections of our inner cities. In the ensuing public debate, there has been some danger of forgetting how narrowly specific West's original reference to black nihilism was.

In this context, it is well to consider, therefore, what has been documented here. First, if there is a question of nihilism in our culture—

and I think there is—it goes well beyond black nihilism. Indeed, insofar as most of my interviewees are white, we might almost regard what I have found as the pervasiveness of white nihilism. Second, all the surveys I conducted for this book were done in Philadelphia, where the large black population is mostly poor. Yet, on most measures of religiosity or philosophical reflectiveness, there was absolutely no difference between black and white respondents. The only exception was here in the case of calling, and on this measure, African Americans appear more religiously connected than whites.

My interview with Tandra Waters may, perhaps, be regarded as an illustration of black spirituality, although, as we will see, it illustrates much else besides. In her late twenties, Tandra is one of the first black women to pursue a career in neuropsychology and is very committed to giving back something to the local community.

To begin with, I did not expect my interview with Tandra to be as instructive as it turned out to be. Tandra is one of those who feels she has a calling but does not know what it is. As we have seen, I thought I had such people figured out.

"Why do you say you have a calling," I ask Tandra, "if you don't know what it is."

"Because. I feel God has something planned for me to do. I just don't know what it is yet."

"You consider yourself religious?"

"Hm-hm."

"What denomination are you?"

"Methodist. United Methodist."

"And do you attend religious services?"

"Yes, I usually go to church."

Tandra tells me she is familiar with the concept of calling, and I ask her where she learned it. She tells me she must have heard of it in church but cannot provide a specific example of how it would have been used in church. I now want to ascertain what Tandra's conception of a calling is.

"A calling," Tandra tells me, "is what God has planned out for you to do." Tandra has articulated exactly what we in sociology understand a calling to be. Tandra goes on. "God has planned out something for everyone. God plans out everything—every moment, even your death."

"God has planned out everything?" I ask.

Tandra nods in affirmation.

"Well, even bad things? Like the Holocaust? You think God planned that?"

Tandra is not a theologian and has evidently not thought about this question. "Well, no. I don't want to say that God planned bad things. He doesn't plan the bad things, but he knows it. He knows they will happen."

I nod. "Is it possible not to do what God has planned out for you? I mean, God plans out something for you to do, and you don't do it. A missed calling?"

Tandra nods. "If you don't have a relation with God, you can miss your calling. If you don't listen to God, you can not do what God has planned."

I ask Tandra whether she feels she has a relationship with God, and she tells me she does. "I have a strong foundation with God. I never feel alone. I don't worry about what will happen. I can talk with God, and that makes me feel okay. I always remember what my mom says: 'Do your best; God will do the rest.'"

"So is the meaning of life to accomplish the purpose God has planned for you?"

"Yes. Our purpose is to be good, to do good. Jesus is a model. Of course, we're not perfect, but to strive to live our lives as Jesus did: help others, be honest, not gossip or speak badly about others behind their backs."

Aside from doing good, which is morally purposive, Tandra, like so many others, has associated goodness mostly with procedural norms. I ask her whether all these virtues are on a par. Is any one more important than the others? Tandra's answer gives me pause.

"Well, I would say helping people, but not if you lie." Tandra laughs. "They're all interrelated. It's no good if you're honest, but you don't help people if asked." In contrast with many, Tandra seemed about to give priority to a moral purpose—that is, helping people, but she explains how and why various moral virtues are all of a piece. The interrelatedness of moral virtues is a quality to which I have not given much attention, but I definitely agree with Tandra that it does not do much good to be morally purposeful if one neglects to be procedurally moral as well.

Impressed by what Tandra has told me so far, I try to see if I can gain even further insight from her on the notion of calling. Accordingly, I ask her for examples of callings, of the kinds of things God might have planned for us to do.

"Establish a school for underprivileged children; to be a champion of animal rights; to be a lawyer who goes against companies that mess up the environment; start a homeless shelter."

That is a list that is interesting not just for what it includes but for what it excludes. First, the callings Tandra cites are all very specific rather than diffuse. I follow up on this point. "This is an interesting list. You've named very specific callings. You know, most people, when I ask this question, aren't as specific. Can a calling be less specific such as 'Be all you can be?'"

Tandra laughs. "You mean, like the army?"

"Well, yeah, or some people say they are just called to realize their potential. Can those kinds of things be callings?"

"No," Tandra says. "Because a calling is specifically to do something. God wants us all to do our best, but you can be the best fry maker at a MacDonald's, but that isn't your calling. I think it has to be deeper."

The paradigmatic callings Tandra cited above are not just specific; they are also, as she would put it, "deep." Strikingly, they are all ways in which we exceed ordinary life, ways in which we go beyond business as usual. I wonder whether Tandra also recognizes callings to which we might respond in more ordinary ways.

"Can it be a calling to be a parent?"

"Yes, a good parent. Although I would say more adopting children. It's easy to love your own biological children. It's taking it a step further to adopt someone else's child and love him or her."

Here, again, for Tandra the paradigmatic calling has a supererogatory nature that takes good behavior a step further. We are called not just to do the good things we ordinarily do. When we are called we are called to exceed the bounds of conventional life.

That may be true for the paradigmatic calling, but as Tandra is not a theologian who has thought about these questions before, Tandra revises her statement. Later she tells me, "You know, parenting can be your calling. I think about my own grandmother. I wouldn't say she hasn't reached her calling in life. Maybe that was it: to raise her children and produce good people."

Parenting is an important task, the value of which we often overlook. But parenting too is a task of cosmic significance. The results of the Philadelphia survey indicate that many people feel called to be good parents. Melinda Whiting, for example. I ask her whether she experiences a sense of calling in her life.

Melinda nods her head affirmatively. "Uh-huh."

"You do?"

"Uh-huh."

"How?"

"My husband and I just talked about this not too many months ago."

"Oh, really?"

"Yeah."

"You're like one of the few people who answered that affirmatively. So I've just been asking that sort of routinely. Uh, could you…"

"I feel that part of my reason to be here is to be a parent."

"Uh-hum. And this is a calling?"

"Yeah."

"Okay."

"To try to help my son along in life and to be a teacher and disciplinarian and everything rolled into one."

"Huh." At the time, evidently I could not believe I had found someone who actually responded to the concept of calling. "And would you use the word *calling*?"

"Uh-huh. Uh-huh." Melinda definitely does respond to the word.

"Can you tell me how you would use the word. Like—do you understand what I'm asking you? I mean…"

Melinda understands. "I understand a calling as to be like when people say they are called to be a preacher…"

"Oh, okay." I'm convinced.

"Or called to be a nurse or…"

"And you feel called to be…"

"A parent."

"Okay. Hmm. And you—you were discussing this with your husband?"

"Uh-hum. Uh-hum. That that's what I feel like my job is supposed to be."

"Huh. And what did he say?"

"He said then maybe I should be a teacher."

Contemporary Journeys

If, for most people, the contemporary sense of calling is not strong, how strong is the contemporary sense of life as a journey? Like the concept of calling, the journey metaphor is an idea that may lend a spiritual unity to a life, a way of making sense of life as a whole. We have already seen that the journey metaphor was important in this way to some people. It was important to Alexander Wenig, to Anand Naveeno and Veet Raj. In their cases, the journey metaphor originates in spiritual discourses. The journey metaphor in fact is one of the spiritual resources that discourses of ultimate meaning seem distinctly to afford.

Thus conversant with discourses of ultimate meaning, two of the other people I interview actually invoke the journey metaphor without my bidding. Stephen Hertz refers to the journey metaphor when I ask him about his love for Jesus.

"What do you mean, you love Jesus?"

"Well..."

"How can you love..."

"Someone you can't see?"

"Yeah."

"Well," Stephen explains, "when I think about it, I'm able to love someone I can't see, especially Jesus, because of his word and the way it speaks to me. Um, sort of grabs my heart and takes it places, where in one sense, I'm longing to go to those places, but in another sense I'm really afraid, and they're sort of uncharted in my being. In that sense...he takes me on this, like, journey, but maybe that's not really answering the question."

"Where does he take you? And where are you longing to go? What is that journey?"

"I think that journey is a real healing journey...I notice a lot of broken relationships in the world, not just on personal levels but social levels, racial levels, economic levels. And to me, Jesus is one who breaks those barriers down and allows people to relate to one another and to heal the breaches between people. And to me, I think that healing has come in a very—in a very incredible personal experience in realizing that healing in my life, where I feel like he's brought me to a place where I can now accept myself for who I am because he has accepted me for who I am. And that took quite a long time to get to that point."

Stephen's journey is consciously a journey of spiritual healing, and he has already traveled far on that road. Accordingly, Stephen has a clear sense of where his journey is taking him.

Prem Prakash is one of the followers of the Bhagwan Sri Rajneesh. He, too, raises the journey metaphor himself in our interview. Talk of journeys arises as Prem is telling me of his interest in art.

"I was always interested in art. My mother saved all the drawings and stuff I did, you know? I mean, I didn't know what I wanted to do, and a friend of the family down there suggested I go to art school because I'd always been interested in it. And looking back, I feel like if a thing you're really interested in is so natural to you that you don't think of it as this is what I want to do, you know? It's just there, and you're just doing it. And I think part of that, too, is the search thing, call it a search or a quest or whatever. At this point, I feel that nobody—everybody has religion, so nobody needs a religion, meaning everybody has religion, has a quest, has a search, even atheists."

"Hm-hm."

"Right? And so nobody needs a religion, meaning the organization, full of people telling you what to do, you know? And looking back, you realize more and more that parents tell you what to do; teachers tell you what to do; politicians do; ministers, priests whoever; rabbis. Until maybe one day you realize, Well, is that what I want to do, you know? Is that me?

"You know, we're so conditioned by all this stuff that…People used to talk about finding oneself. We've been so lost in doing what everybody else says that you don't take time to think about…especially if nothing rocks your boat, you go along. If people can lead your life for you and it's fine if, if it's fine with you, you know? Uh, so anyway, that's…it's why people drink a lot or do drugs…because that's a bothering thing in the back of their mind. What am I doing here? Where am I going? Why am I here, you know? All those questions."

I nod. All those questions are the point of my research. Without direction from me, Prem has taken our interview where I wanted it to go. In *The Journey to the East*, the protagonist has abandoned the journey, the grand quest for meaning and spiritual wholeness. He has instead succumbed to rationalism, despair, and the concerns of daily life. Prem goes on to tell me that people abandon the journey because it is too unnerving to think about ultimate questions. It is much easier, Prem maintains, to allow our souls to be channeled by the natural flow of society.

Perhaps when we are channeled by society's flow, it is less that we actively avoid thinking of ultimate questions than that those questions do not even occur to us.

The journey metaphor is a readily available feature of Christian discourse, but the ready availability of a discourse does not necessarily mean it will speak to us. For a discourse to speak to us, it is not enough that we cognitively know the words. More important is that we emotionally resonate with the reality behind the words. When we lose emotional contact with the reality, the words themselves become empty. Thus, even for those cognitively conversant with Christian discourse, it can seem completely foreign to think of life as a journey. I ask Diane Norris, a church-going Methodist, for example, whether she ever conceives of life as a journey.

"Not really," Diane replies, "because I take a lot of journeys. And journeys are fun. Life is sort of just getting through."

"Okay, how about a quest? Sometimes life is compared with a quest. Does that image at all resonate with you?"

"Probably not, because I'm not really looking for anything."

Tom Brown, raised Catholic, concedes that life might be likened to a journey, but it is unclear whether he makes any spiritual use of that likeness.

"All right, let me...Do you think of life as a journey?"

Tom thinks a moment. "Well, yeah, it's a type of a journey."

"So where are you going on this journey?"

"Where am I going?!"

I nod. "Where's the journey to? Why do you say it's a type of journey?"

"I don't...well, you know, I don't know. I don't know why I said that."

"Okay."

"I don't know. As far as where I'm going, well, how's it going, I don't know how my life's going to end up."

"Uh-huh."

"What's going to happen in the next thirty years, so I—you know? As far as...I don't know what's...how to answer that."

"A lot of people have a lot of trouble with these questions. I have a lot of..."

"Well, yeah, I mean, these are, these are either hypothetical or..."

"Sort of abstract."

Tom nods. "Abstract, and I have trouble with abstract questions. I don't know how to deal with them, with abstract questions."

In Tom's case, it is almost as if the journey metaphor is a solitary vestige of spiritual discourse lodged in his psyche. He finds the metaphor inside himself but is without any feel for how to put it to spiritual use.

The journey metaphor resonates more strongly with Julie Cates. "All right," I say. "Let's try this. Life is sometimes compared with a journey."

Julie has begun to laugh at my introduction, and I laugh with her. "Do you ever think of life that way?"

"Yeah. Most of the time."

"Most of the time? Why? Well, forget why. Where are you going on this journey? Where is this journey leading you?"

"Sitting on a porch in Iowa in a rocking chair. "

"That's where it's leading you?"

"Yup...cornfields in the distance."

"What does that mean? That must mean something to you...more than it sounds."

"Yeah. It does."

"Okay. What does it mean? What does that mean to you?"

"If I get to the point in my life when I am old and I am enjoying being old and sitting on a rocking chair, and I have, I have accomplished...some of the things that I'd set out to do—maybe not all of them, but I've maybe done some dreams and I have a family, a wonderful, caring family, and I have grandchildren, and I can sit on my porch, and rock, and sort of think about things and not...not regret too much—I mean everybody regrets things."

"Hm-hm."

"But I feel strongly that...We're asked this question a lot. If you could go back and change something in your life, some pivotal point, would you do it? And in that sense you regret something so much that you'd change it. I don't think I would. I mean, I've done—I've made some mistakes, but at the same time, if I had not made those mistakes, I wouldn't be here...And so, I would hope to be able to sit on that porch and not wish I had taken a different path."

I have some regrets. I regret I had asked Julie to forget about why she views her life as a journey and to focus instead on where her journey is taking her. It is not that I am disappointed in the destination to which Julie alludes. Julie's destination connotes a fulfilled life, lived without major regrets. That sounds like a life that would measure up to Nietzsche's criterion of "eternal return." My regret, instead, has a different source. I no longer think that the destination is the most relevant question to ask about someone's journey. It is not the destination that gives the metaphor its symbolic power but how we understand what happens along the way. That insight dawned on me only after my subsequent conversation with Alexander Wenig and my interview with Bruce Gonzalez and Sharon Traub.

After I had spoken with Bruce and Sharon about callings, I went on to ask them whether either viewed life as a journey.

Bruce speaks first. "It's absolutely a journey. There's no question in my mind it's a journey."

"And where are we going?" At the time of our interview, I still thought that what is important to the journey metaphor is the destination.

"I don't know."

"Why is it a journey if there's no destination? Why is it like a journey?"

Bruce laughs. "Well, someone said that if you don't know where you're going, you're going to be sure to get there. Um, I don't know. I have...my mind's a blank, but that's my answer to that."

"Okay," I say, turning to Sharon. "And you agree that life is a journey?"

"Yeah, I mean, I believe in more of a journey concept, but I think I've always experienced life as more of a—well, a quest is too dramatic, but I think that I've always thought more in terms of the future and like a goal that I was trying to achieve until the last five years, when I didn't feel like I really had a goal. And I think, and I think..."

"What was your goal when you..."

"Well, it was always like something career-related, I guess, like, you know?"

"Oh."

"I graduated from high school, graduated from college, and then I had plans beyond that, which kind of didn't happen, but I think, I think it's just been more in the last five years that I probably started being present and experiencing life as more of a journey and, you know, not being so fixated on future goals."

Bruce now interjects. "Well, you know, journey...Look, the word *journey* is a metaphor."

"Mm-hm." I wonder now whether it was Bruce who first made me think of journey specifically as a metaphor.

Bruce continues. "Life as a journey. It's not exactly a journey, it's metaphorically speaking..."

"But what does that, what does that..." I have begun to stammer.

Sharon now answers. "Well, to me, journey means more of an adventure or more of a...To me, it somehow connotes something more about the present, like you're just living, you're experiencing life, you know, day to day and..."

"You're taking experiences as they come?"

"Yeah. Right. Right. As opposed to just being focused on the future and not really experiencing the present or just really, you know? I don't know if that—does that make sense?"

It does make a great deal of sense, and I say so. "It makes sense, but you're saying...I just want to be clear."

"It's just an experience," Sharon says.

"Do you think of it as destination, is that important to the metaphor?"

"Absolutely not. No." Bruce is adamant. "I don't think that. Just—again speaking of the metaphor, I don't think that the destination is an important part of the metaphor at all."

"Okay. What's the important part of the metaphor?"

"That—that the journey goes on, meaning the experience of the...the effort to reach the destination, even though you may not know what it is. You'll never get there. Like the movement, the movement. The journey suggests that...suggests a deliberateness..."

I nod, and Bruce continues.

"And you're ethically engaged in something. And I believe this. I believe in that somehow."

"You do believe in...what?"

"In the activeness of life, that we're not—we're not passive. I don't think we're just passive. I think that we're engaged in it."

"Okay, the movement," I venture.

"The movement," Bruce affirms.

"Okay."

"And the deliberateness of that movement."

"Okay."

"You know," Sharon now interjects, "I have to say something that reverses what I said before, but there is an element of it, I think, that's a quest to me too. It's a quest for truth. I mean, I always feel like I'm continually searching for that or trying to."

"The truth?"

"Yeah, a truth...but also the wholeness, the quest for wholeness, you know?

"Wholeness?"

"Yeah."

"What do you mean by wholeness?"

"Being fully who you are, being like free or in some ways free completely of who you are overcoming. I don't know."

It seems to me, whether she knows or not, that Sharon has said something profound. She speaks of truth not just as a linguistic relation between our claims and the world but as the ultimate reality we seek to encounter. Further, the journey toward truth is, she says, a journey toward spiritual wholeness, toward becoming who we authentically are and overcoming who we are not. Such a journey is undertaken by Eric Sawyer.

A NATIVE AMERICAN SPIRIT QUEST

When Native American boys came of age, they were sent out on a spirit quest, a search for their identity, to find out who they really were. A suburban marketing analyst, Eric Sawyer, tells me he too once went on a spirit quest.

"My wife and I were going to counseling for a while to a therapist who had been recommended to her by a gynecologist, and I stopped going for a while, and then we continued, and she happened to mention to my wife that she was doing this...uh...something called vision quest."

"Really."

"This was after our band had broken up. I hadn't been able to get the motivation to do music for six years, maybe seven years. And I felt kind of, like, a big gap in my life, so you know, the idea of vision quest and crying out for a vision for your life, that whole thing."

"Yeah. Well, actually, can you talk a little bit about that vision? Some people...What I'm really looking for is people's vision quests. So, I mean, so that's something I'm familiar with directly and the new-age stuff, but..."

"Well, I don't know a lot about it. I know that it's based on kind of a Native American thing, where, when a man, when a boy came of age, he went through some rituals, and then went out into the wilderness to fast and to cry out for a vision for his life, and when he came back, he had an animal name, you know? And had this identity."

"So did you do this?"

"I did, like, a very suburban version of it, and the preparation was, for me—and the therapist said it was long for me—was this eight- or nine-month preparation that involved a lot of dream analysis, imagery. During that time, it became obvious that, like, music was, like, vital to who I was and one of the ways where I was really me, rather than kind of, like, putting up some kind of front to..."

"Say that again," I ask. "Sorry."

"The music was her...When we would talk, there would be—I would bring up lines from songs. I guess I started to do that a lot, maybe. And most of the stuff I had written was very personal stuff, which is probably why I was bringing up lines from songs. And she said, 'Well, you'll have to bring in your guitar sometime and play some of these songs.' So I did. I played one song, and she was, like, kind of knocked over with how, like, this was, like, a strong statement of personhood, of who I was."

"Huh."

"And so I gave that some thought, and then traveling, I got some lyrics at a certain point, and I was writing again. This song developed, and that started me doing music again, that whole preparation period, some of the things I went through.

"So did you...she prepared you for the vision quest or she helped you prepare for the vision quest."

"Right. That was the idea. And it was during this preparation that this stuff was happening. At the end of the preparation, there was a...I forget what it was called, but I came to a place, and I invited friends, and there was send-off and really, I mean, the suburban version of it was I rented a cabin at Lake Nachawana in winter, when there wouldn't be anybody around. I went there and fasted for three days."

"You fasted for three days?"

"Yeah. You know? Drank juices during that time period, took something to record my thoughts and, like, waited for something to happen, basically."

"And did something happen?"

"Uh, it didn't knock my socks off, I mean. It kind of reminds me of the first time I did cocaine and people said, 'Well, it's very subtle.'

"I did have this sense, though, and it was the last morning I was there, of walking down to see the lake because it was frozen. It was just an incredible visual thing, walking down to see the lake, and seeing this movement in the bushes, and looking, and kind of standing there, and all of a sudden there was a...I don't know whether it was one bird or several birds, but the bird was, like, heavy, fat. And this line from the Bible came into my head, some mutation of it. 'Consider the fowl of the air neither toil nor reap, yet your heavenly father provides for them.'

"There was this bird in the middle of winter snow and, like, this bird was doing okay. And the message was, 'Don't worry about being able to survive. Do what you want to do.'

"Okay, that was the interpretation I took of that. The bird was, you know, the bird was being taken care of. The universe was taking care of this bird."

"So did you, um, get an identity from that experience?"

"No, no. I wasn't looking for an identity so much as a vision for how I could lead my life, what to do."

"And did you get it?"

"That was always the central question for me: What to do?"

"That was always a central question for you?"

"Yeah, even back in 'seventy-four, I wrote a song, you know? And it had this theme about what do you do. Is it really you that's making you?"

"Is it really you that's making you?" I like it. A question for postmodern identities.

"Yeah. Or is it somebody else? But what do you do, you know? How do you spend your time?"

"That's really the whole issue of identity. That's really interesting."

"Now, I couldn't totally buy it. I mean, I couldn't say I want to quit my job and play guitar. And I don't know whether that was weakness or, like, I felt a little bad that I wasn't doing that. Like that was what I was supposed to do, but I couldn't decide whether it was what I was supposed to do or what I just felt like I should be doing. If you know what I mean.

"It was actually in that preparation for that vision quest that I got the message really strongly that it didn't matter whether I made a living playing music or not. I should be playing music, 'cause it's important to who I am for me to be expressing myself that way."

With callings and quests now behind us, we mark a milestone on our own journey. We began by arguing that although metaphysically we always remain single, undivided selves, it is another matter whether we phenomenologically experience ourselves as such. We noticed that those who seem better able to articulate a coherent sense of self are those who also acknowledge a sense of larger purpose. A sense of larger purpose, we concluded, is vital to a larger sense of self.

With this conclusion, we undertook over the past few chapters to search for larger purpose in America, a sense of purpose somehow grounded in our place in the cosmos. In callings, quests, heroes, and so forth, we have examined different spiritual routes of cosmic connection with larger purpose. Throughout, we continued to find people who remain connected with larger purpose in these ways. More frequently, however, we found an emotional alienation from the cosmos with an attendant loss of moral purpose. If, therefore, we have lost ourselves phenomenologically, it is perhaps because we have first lost our bearings in the universe.

The underlying problem goes beyond discourse, on which so much social theory today focuses its attention. In fact, if we remain exclusively at the level of discourse, we will not even see the problem. After all, in terms of spiritual discourse in America, we have belief without emotional engagement. Thus, it is hardly that the relevant discourses have disappeared. They are there, and people believe in them. Many people just are not emotionally engaged by the realities signified by the discourses.

Alternatively, we could say that our spiritual discourses have lost their power. This in fact is what was said by the so-called death of God theologies in the 1960s. There is nothing wrong with this way of talking—unless it is intended to dismiss relevant features of the problem. If it is asserted that our spiritual discourses have lost their power, there are two questions we need to ask: The power to do what? And for whom?

The power in question is the power to comprehend and evoke a certain reality, and the whom for which the reality is evoked are individuals. If we really want to understand the lost power of our spiritual discourses, then we must examine the opposite ends discourses tie together: individuals and reality. Because it is the function of discourse to relate individuals to reality; without both individuals and reality, discourse alone is empty. It is a typically empty analysis I have been resisting by bringing individuals and reality back into our account.

If we have discovered a loss of contact with ultimate or sacred reality, the fault lies not exclusively or even principally with discourse. It is not as if better words will reestablish the missing connection. More fundamentally, the problem is a failure of experience. It is as if we are without an ability to listen in a certain key, to resonate with a particular rhythm. We continue to invoke the words but without feeling, without being touched by the realities the words convey.

Throughout the past few chapters, we have been paying particular attention to the category of experience. We have tried to understand what it means to experience a calling, to have a hero, to be grasped by God or a meaning of life.

Although sociologists speak endlessly of experience—of the experience of the marginalized or the oppressed or of this group or that one, experience is not something about which sociologists have thought much conceptually. Sociologists often equate experience with a perspective, but the two are distinct. A perspective is what results from certain experiences. Nor is experience just a history of happenings in which we have been involved.

An experience is the impact on us of something independent of us. Experience thus has three components: the subject of experience, the quality of the experience, and the object of experience. The subject of an experience is the one experiencing it, and the object is what actually is experienced. In any genuine experience, the object of experience contributes something to the quality of experience. Otherwise, the putative experience is not a true one at all but only an illusion. Thus, to the extent that sociologists ignore the object of experience, they treat all experience as illusion. And that is a mistake we must avoid.

What does this mean when the experience we are considering is religious? The object of experience is always one reality or another. Am I saying then that sociologists must assume that the objects of religious experience—God, for example—necessarily exist? No. But I am saying that sociologists also cannot proceed methodologically—as they so often do now—as if God or other objects of religious experience can be ignored.[20] At least sociologists cannot do so and still pretend to be examining religious experience.

The issue here is of concern not just to sociologists but to all. I have been arguing that what we observe in postmodernity is a failure of religious experience. We now see that this formulation is apt only if there is a religious object of experience with which we are failing to connect. Is there? Can we even rationally discuss whether there is? These questions bring us to critical space and ultimately to the role of community. Before going there, however, we have one last stop to make.

CHAPTER 7

Resources of the Self

The characteristic prophet is a lonely man who
has discovered his truth about the world, the cosmos,
ethics, God, and his own identity
from within, from his own experiences, from what
he would consider to be a revelation.

—*Abraham Maslow*

The cohesion of our lives is not an all-or-nothing proposition. Thus, besides moral purpose, there are other resources that avail toward cohesion. Thinking of our lives as a story is one such resource, but there are others as well. Hence, even in the absence of moral purpose, we may achieve some cohesion in our lives through other routes. Even without moral purpose, we may yet not be as utterly fragmented personally as postmodernism suggests.

The comparison of our lives with a story is particularly important to consider. We need to conceptualize our lives this way. We are historical beings whose lives unfold as a narrative. In principle, therefore, it might be unreasonable to expect people to capture completely who they are at a single moment. Even when people cannot so verbalize who they are, in the narration of their lives vivid selves may yet materialize before us. One troubling loose end in our account is the relation of larger purpose to the temporal nature of the self.

Experience, we will see, is one of the central elements that mediates between narrative and purpose. Peak experiences in particular furnish both purpose and the threads that tie together the stories of our lives. Of course, when a peak experience is distinctly religious, questions of truth immediately arise. We will begin to address those questions along the way. Whereas postmodernists jettison truth altogether and, in the case of religious experience, sociologists try to ignore it, we will pursue a more daring path.

ALTERNATIVE RESOURCES OF THE SELF

Even with the widespread loss of moral purpose, there are yet depths to the self that need to be plumbed, resources of the self from which we manage to fashion internal coherence. How individuals identify with the political or demographic categories to which they belong has been well studied by sociologists: race, class, and gender, for example. There are, however, other, more sacred resources of the self, such as astrology or the occult, that have been less studied by sociologists concerned with identity.[1]

Intellectuals are wont to dismiss astrology as a practice for fools. How can anyone believe that the stars above have any connection to our personal lives here on earth? Perhaps, however, we do not fully understand the use that people actually make of horoscopes and ouija boards. Certainly, as our once worshiped sacred sun sinks beneath the horizon, the urge for sacred contact remains. It is not surprising, therefore, that in the ensuing night, people seek new heavenly bodies to mediate such contact.

Even sacred contact, however, may not be what people principally seek from the symbols of the new age. It may be that many readers of horoscopes do not actually believe in astrology. They may simply use the signs of the zodiac to organize an internal sense of who they are. Julie Cates supplies a hint toward such a conclusion.

When I ask her who she is, Julie laughs. "I always kind of identify with...it's silly, but astrology."

"Astrology?"

"Yeah."

"Stars?"

"Yeah."

"Virgo..."

"Yeah! Because I'm a Gemini, in May. And I always think it's...pretty accurate, as weird as it is. I don't know. I don't know if I believe in the whole astrology thing in predicting your horoscopes and stuff, but...how a Gemini is always too different. It explains in the sense that they're alike and that they're different. Because I think the basic parts of me are...wonder."

"Are what?"

"Wonder."

"Wonder?"

"I really love the things about the world. I go out and I love the dew on the trees, and I love children's faces, and I love playing in the playground and doing stuff like that. And I really derive a lot of pleasure out of the little things in life."

For Julie Cates, the truth of astrological theory seems of minor importance. Of primary importance is the way the various astral signs represent different kinds of selves and offer to her a single, "too different" Gemini self with which she can identify. In identifying with the self represented by Gemini, Julie brings her own self into focus. She comes to know better who she is and who she is not. Astrology, for Julie, is a resource for self.

Tarot cards seem to function similarly for Anand Naveeno. Although, unfortunately, I captured on tape only a fragment of our exchange on this topic, Anand had told me that the tarot is a way for her to communicate with herself.

"You do tarot cards just for yourself? You don't like to do them for other people?"

"Yeah. It's not...there's nothing objective about it, you know?"

"Why do you do it?"

"Because it's...it answers something for me."

"What does it answer?"

"Hmm?"

"What does it answer for you?"

"Well, whatever I ask. Usually I ask about certain situations. For example, should I buy a good house, you know? And then a certain card comes up and the card represents something for me: either the first look represents yes or it represents no or sometimes I don't know. And I see a link."

"Well, you were...you were saying something to me that I thought was really interesting about each card for you...It sounds like you're saying...you used the card to get in touch—the cards to get in touch with yourself?"

"Yes. I said that the card represents a stage of life."

"Yeah."

"Through our lifetime. For example, certain stages of childhood and certain stages of adulthood. And they represent us on a journey."

It does not matter whether or not Anand attributes any mystical attributes to the tarot cards. Through her interaction with the tarot cards, Anand is able to conceptualize better where she is on her own journey. The tarot provides for Anand a form of meditation, a device for the self-reflexive monitoring of her life. As astrology is for Julie Cates, the tarot is for Anand Naveeno a resource of self.

For two of those I interviewed, the martial arts function similarly. I first ask Adam Schuster what he derives from the martial arts. "What do you learn? What are you learning, beyond fighting?"

"Well, ultimately it's a fighting technique, but I think that it helps you intellectually and spiritually as well. Physically, intellectually, and spiritually."

Adam has learned, he tells me, not to pigeonhole reality, including himself. Things don't fall into neat boxes or categories. He sees himself particularly not as a distinct point in the past, present, and future but as a flow in a continuum.

Roger Rossiter is early in his career as a philosophy professor. He, too, has devoted several years to the martial arts. When I ask Roger about his worldview, his martial arts experience makes itself felt.

"I have a definite concept of the structure of reality and a teleological view of the world. In part, my view is scientific and philosophical…However, thanks to a couple odd experiences and several years in the martial arts, I also accept a certain spiritual element.

"In terms of what humans should do, I buy into a view of my own that is close to a Platonic-Taoist concept of human nature and of the proper human ends. In short, human beings have definite natures, and acting against those natures will result in harm, while acting in accord and harmony with one's nature leads to benefits. I would say that my martial arts training has influenced my views here quite a bit. There simply seem to be ways of life that are harmful to individuals and society and other ways of life that lead to the flourishing of individuals and society."

The martial arts seem to have sensitized Roger, like Adam, against Western "pigeonholing" and toward Eastern concepts of flow. The Taoist concepts of yin and yang receive direct application in many martial arts, where one learns not to resist force but to flow with it.

"Some days I accept a Taoist view that 'good' and 'evil' are labels placed by man that actually lead to more trouble and prefer to talk about nature and acting in accord with or against nature. On these days, I would say that 'good' is acting in accord with one's nature. In everyday terms, 'good' is being truly what you are to the fullest extent."

Partly from the martial arts, Roger derives the concept of an authentic self with which he may or may not be in harmony or flow. There are many alternative resources of the soul, some of which we may not even be aware of employing. Thus far in this book, we have asked people to tell us—Western style—who they are at one point in time. The caterpillar's question seems to ask, *Who are you right now?*

As I have suggested, it may not be so surprising that people cannot answer this question. We are, as even the Western existentialists have counseled us, historical creatures, creatures whose being unfolds in time. The temporal nature of our being is the import of Sartre's dictum that existence precedes essence. We become who we are essentially by how we live, existentially.[2] Perhaps, then, at any given instant we are no one. Perhaps we become who we are only by how we live the entirety of our lives.

LIFE AS STORY

If we are seeking the identities of actually living people, perhaps we need to be instructed by literature. Literature presents us with clearly distinct identities: Jean Valjean of *Les Miserables*, Dinah of *Adam Bede*. If we know their stories, we know them. We know them not as singular points in time but as temporal unfoldings that, over a narrative canvas, preserve a unity through change.[3] Who they are cannot be completely captured in an instant.

Imagining our own life story is, then, another resource we might employ to picture for ourselves who we are. We might express who we are by telling our story. But this is apparently not a resource that many people employ. Although everyone can tell specific stories associated with their lives, most either never think of the entirety of their lives as a story or, if that idea occurs to them, it is not a story they can imagine enjoying. I ask Ellen Smith, for example, if her life were made into a novel or a movie, what that novel or movie would be about.

"It would be kind of boring," Ellen answers.

"What would it be a story about?"

"What would it be a story about?"

"If they made a movie of your life."

"Somebody shy, I guess, on their way to school and then, got a little...got married and, I don't know, doesn't sound very interesting.

Became an accountant. When I think of the image of me, it doesn't sound too exciting."

Other people, however, do respond to the metaphor of life as a story. Diane Norris, for example, responds to the same question.

"If I were to write a novel in which I was the central character, I would sort of be this person that tried to hold things together and various things would happen, and various things would be going on, and I would just sort of be trying to get through, holding everything together."

Presented as an abstract concept, the story of Diane's life does not, perhaps, tell us much about her. Like Ellen Smith's story, it does not sound very exciting. It is only when Diane supplies some of the actual narrative that her identity becomes vivid.

"We have an adopted son. He's twenty-three. And it's been a very difficult adoption. He was nine years old when we adopted him."

"Ah." Already the story becomes interesting.

"He's currently going through a bad period. He was in jail for five months this year for selling marijuana."

"Hmm."

"He got out of jail and was doing fairly well for about five months, but just last week he got fired and gave up his apartment, and he's gone back to running around with his...He knows his natural family."

"Huh."

"And his little brother, who everyone says has been selling cocaine, is the person who he's running around with now."

"Might be he has some sense of identity with him."

"He does, yes."

"And he feels the need to act with him."

"Uh-huh. And he kind of goes back and forth between the two families, and he tries out our way for a while, and then feels he can't make it and goes back to their way."

"Must be difficult."

"Yeah, I think I'm getting used to it. I didn't get as upset this time as I have before."

There is an engrossing story here to be sure, and even from the little we hear of it, Diane begins to emerge as a kind of heroic figure.

Iris Barbuda has a story too. "If your life were a story," I ask Iris, "what would it be a story about? Either what would it be a story about or what would be the theme?"

"The evolution of the spirit."

"Ah."

"How life's lessons, I guess, teach you and make you grow if you let them. And you don't become calloused by some of the bad things that happen to you. So I guess my theme would be living life to its fullest, lessons learned, and getting old."

"That's great."

"It is?"

"Yeah, well, it's great that you even have an answer. That's really good, and it's a good...That's a good story for your life to be about."

Without prompting from me, Betty Enders announces, "I'd love to sit down and write a book, but I've never really sat down and made an attempt at it, but, you know, my life story reads like a book."

"Well, it's funny that you said..."

"I mean it does, and it would make very entertaining reading."

"If your life were a story, what would be it's theme?"

"Oh, God."

"What would be the theme of the story?"

"The theme of the story would be, I think, just luck. Like Erma Bombeck. I love Erma Bombeck. Have you ever read her books?

"No, not her books." Other people's stories, too, may be a resource of the self. In identifying with other people's stories, we come better to know our own. That is the case for Betty.

"Oh, read her books. I mean she's hysterical. And it's hysterical because she writes about life and how life really is. You know what I mean? Like everything she talks about: her kids, and her husband, and traveling, and the problems and everything. You're laughing because you can relate to it. It's things that happen in everyday life, and I think a lot of the problem is people can't laugh at themselves. If you can't laugh at yourself, then you're in sad shape, and I basically laugh at myself."

"So the theme of your story would be life?"

"It would be life."

"Okay."

"Just life in general."

"That's interesting." It is interesting, but, again, we don't learn much about Betty just from the concept. It takes the actual narrative material to bring Betty alive as a character.

"Well, I've been a waitress and a bartender most of my life, and I always said I wanted to write a book called *Up the Night Shift*. Just...like I've always worked during the day, and the night-shift people always kind of got away with murder. You know what I mean? Shirking their duties and stuff like that, and just funny things that happen when you're a waitress and you meet different people.

"I love people. I love to meet different people and, you know, you just have funny things that happen to you. I mean that would be funny, and my life is really funny.

"I mean people, you know, you think everybody's life is the same: the mother, the father, and two-and-a-half kids and the dog. You know what I mean? And it's not. Everybody, you find out, I guess, as you go on, everybody has had some problems. There is no such thing as being—having the perfect marriage and so happy that you never have an argument. And you know, if you've never had an argument, then one of you has just decided to lay down and be so passive that you're going to let this other personality dominate you.

"And you know, everybody is individual and you have to keep your individuality. I mean if everybody was exactly alike, wouldn't it be boring? If we all thought alike and, I mean, I think it would be a boring world to live in if we all felt the same way about everything. It would be boring. You need that."

Betty has maintained her humor despite some trying experiences. But again, we learn Betty's character not from her abstract description of her life story but from actual narrative.

"It's funny because my husband is an only child, and I'm one of five. That's a tough combination right there. But both his parents are alcoholics. His mother died at fifty-three years of age from cirrhosis of the liver, and when she died, my son, Karl, was in fifth grade. His sister, Mary, was older.

"We had a lot of problems, you know, with him. We couldn't figure out, what the heck…what's going on.

"Well, they brought in a child study team, and they talked to Karl, and they had him go through whatever it is that they do, and one part of their interview with him was drawing a picture of his family. Well, we were all in proportion to the picture, but Karl was just this little, tiny person in the great scheme of things, and it was just that he had no self-confidence or anything.

"So then they recommended that we go see this counselor, a wonderful man, a fantastic man. We went to see him, and we went as a family."

"We were there for an hour, and after the hour was over, he said to Karl, 'Karl, it's great meeting you. Maybe I'll see you again. Mary, it was nice meeting you. Maybe we'll get together again.'"

"And he turned to Phil and I and he said, 'I want to see you two again.'

"We were like, 'Oh my God, what did we do?' You know? I mean in an hour's time, what could he have possibly learned?"

Even in a miniature narrative like this one from everyday life, suspense may build.

"But here, and that's the first time I'd ever heard the word *dysfunctional*. And after that, it was like I was hearing it all the time. I'm the product of a dysfunctional family. Well, in going through counseling, and then he had us attend AA meetings, mainly for Phil, because of being a child of alcoholic parents.

"You learn so much. I mean, Phil learned things about himself and his life that he had totally blocked out of his mind altogether. It was a scary, very emotional and upsetting experience, but I think it made us both better people and a little bit more understanding, you know? What goes on."

In Betty's narrative, there is drama, challenge, and response. There is also character development and change. Yet, through that development and change, there is also continuity. It is one and the same Betty whose character develops and changes. That continuity through change of a unitary person is what arrests our attention.

When, in chapter one, I asked Eli Cohen the caterpillar's question, he replied, "I'm an ordinary man." I remarked then that this did not tell us very much about him. As we will see, *ordinariness* and *normality* seem to convey more meaning to Eli than we usually attach to those words. Eli was at Auschwitz. And he survived. There is a story there that is hardly ordinary. Eli, himself, suggests that the story is a powerful one.[4]

"I'll tell you," Eli declares. "If you would come with a story, I should tell you my whole story since I was born...till today."

"Yeah?" If Eli were to tell his story, it would include how, at the camps, he had heard of his sisters being torn apart by dogs; how, after the war, he met Guzia at a displaced person's camp; how he and a friend crossed the Alps on foot to locate Guzia's brother in Italy. As Eli would tell it, the story would end happily with his achievement of an ordinary life in the United States.

"This would be the most beautiful book," Eli tells me.

"Why?"

"Because I would tell you every little thing, every little detail, what happened to me and to our family and the past and the present and the future. What happened to me till now. This is—if you would write a book on this whole thing, you would make a terrific...it would be a best-seller."

Well, perhaps it would not be a best-seller if Eli told us every little thing. Then it would be an indiscriminate log. What we want to know are not all the details but all the details that matter. We would want Eli to tell us only about his significant experiences. Guzia affirms this from the kitchen.

"People wouldn't find it so interesting," Guzia says.

"You would be surprised," Eli retorts.

"Why would they be interested?" I ask.

"Because it's a true story. People like true stories. Fiction, I don't like fiction. I like true stories. And my story…"

I ask Eli what it means to be a plain, ordinary man, as he says he now is.

"To be nice. Honest. Very, very important, a very good family man, take care of your kids."

"Why is that so important?"

"Because this is a part of life."

"Why is it good, so good to be a good family man?"

"Because this is part of life. This is a part of normal life."

The ordinary is what we take for granted. Eli does not take ordinariness for granted. Achieving ordinariness was for him a gift. How and why such simple ordinariness is so precious a gift is the story Eli might tell.

Eli describes himself as nice, but we come to appreciate what this means only when it, too, is embedded in a story. When Eli tells his story—or, rather, his multiple stories—we come to recognize that contrary to postmodernist opinion, a crucial, coherent part of Eli persists from one social context to another.

"I say the main, important thing in life is to be nice and…nice to somebody else, the next, the next people. I feel all my friends, people I associate with, they all like me for one reason: because I'm nice to them. They're…they are nice to me. All my friends what I know. If somebody is not nice, I don't bother with them."

Like many older Philadelphians, Eli and Guzia make weekly pilgrimages to Atlantic City, where Guzia plays the slot machines at the casinos and Eli walks along the boardwalk. For Philadelphia's senior citizens, a casino bus is the usual means of transportation to Atlantic City, but they still need to get themselves to the bus stop.

"There's a woman. She goes with us to Atlantic City. So I take her home all the time, because she lives a block away. So I leave her over…so, one time was Sunday. I see her stand there. We were going some place. She stays there.

"I say, 'Why are you staying here?'

"She says, 'I gotta go to my sister. She's in a home.'

"I say, 'Come into the car. I'll take you.'

"This lady couldn't get over. She don't know me too well. I'm just...you know, I know her from Atlantic City. And then she came home, she call up another lady, another friend, you know? And she told the story about how I took her. To me, it wasn't a big deal. It wasn't, you know, a big deal. It's just ten minutes, but she couldn't get over it.

"I took her because I felt that if she could stay on corner, waiting to go to her sister, you know? I felt good! I felt real good. It was a pleasure for me. It wasn't a big deal. This is life. This means being good to the next person. Don't you think I'm right?"

"Yes, I do."

"Mr. Dryer calls me up. He says, 'Eli, please, my wife's got to go to the hospital, and I don't have nobody to take me. I called a taxicab, and they didn't show up.'

"I took her. They couldn't get over. When they had a seventy-fifth anniversary, we were the only ones invited there." Eli laughs.

"The only ones from all the neighbors. And he was...he told everybody, 'This is my neighbors. They're wonderful people.'

"This is a wonderful satisfaction. And then he gave me two bags full of stuff to take it home. His son came from Florida. He said, 'This is Eli and Guzia. They are wonderful neighbors.' This is life. This is to enjoy life."

"Hmm."

"Mrs. Schumacher calls me up, and she says, 'Eli, please take me to the doctor.'

"I'll do it in the middle of the night. And I do. I did already something like that, different kind of people. And I do it in a modest way...not because I'm real...just a modest way. But an enjoyable way. This means good deeds." In the Jewish tradition, such good deeds are called *mitzvot*.

"Some people wouldn't do it. Some people ask for others favors. They're not going to do it to you. They enjoy not to do a favor. With me, just the opposite. If I do something for somebody or help out with something, this is my greatest pleasure. I love it."

Eli's stories reveal himself. They contextualize his life and his world, the people around him and what they do. And we see a narrative unity to Eli's behavior, a unity that gainsays postmodernist talk of fragmented selves. It is a unity that Eli himself recognizes as the core of who he is.

"Okay," I ask Eli. "If...what—what would you like it to say on your tombstone? If you had..."

"I know, I know."

"Is there anything…"

"Well, the same thing what I been saying till now: 'That here's a person that respect…respect everybody. And he did good deeds. And that's all.'"

Perhaps now we are in a better position to begin connecting purpose and story in relation to identity. At an abstract level, the concepts of purpose and story are interconnected. A purpose is something we pursue, and a pursuit only unfolds in time. We pursue a purpose in our actions and their consequences, and in our subsequent reactions to those consequences. An account of such a process is a story. Conversely, human stories imply purposiveness. That is why after telling us that existence precedes essence, Sartre immediately introduces the concept of a "project." A human story is just a concrete account of the projects people pursue and their effects on themselves and others.

From a different angle, a life's purpose is related to a life story as the abstract is to the concrete. In their preceding accounts, Diane Norris, Betty Enders, and Eli Cohen all articulate some sense of purpose that summarizes their lives. Diane Norris tells us her life is about holding things together. Eli Cohen describes himself as an ordinary man who respects everyone and who does good deeds. These formulations do capture something essential, but they remain abstract. We only vividly appreciate what the speakers are talking about when the narrative detail is filled in. Narrative supplies the concrete detail that gives body to abstract purpose.

It is narrative detail that supplies individuality as well. Betty Enders says life would be boring if everyone were alike. Indeed, it would be. Yet, at the level of our abstract purposes, many of us are alike. Recall our conversation way back with Matt Bennett and John Wasserman, when both described themselves as followers of Christ. I asked at that time how, then, the two were different, and we struggled to answer. Part of the answer involves story. Clearly, Matt and John are different in being two distinct centers of conscious experience. It follows that they have two distinct narrative histories. Thus, although their goal may be the same, their stories are not. Narrative detail is part of what makes each of us the unique selves we are.

If purpose without narrative remains an empty abstraction, narrative without purpose lacks shape. By saying what our lives stand for as a whole, we instruct others—and ourselves—how to shape the narratives of our lives. When Eli Cohen suggested that his life narrative would include every little thing, we countered that it would not be relevant to know what he typically has for breakfast or the hour at which he retires for bed. As a narrative does not indiscriminately include everything that happens, a narrative of character formation includes only what is relevant to character.

Still, a question remains. Where our lives are governed by an overriding purpose, it makes sense for this purpose to be the theme around which our life narrative is constructed. Suppose, however, our lives is not governed by any overriding purpose. A narrative of our lives will still reveal a vivid self. If so, is our life story more fundamental to who we are than moral purpose?

To answer this question, we must return to the distinction between our ontological and phenomenological selves. Even if we lack moral purpose in our lives, we remain coherent selves ontologically, unique centers of conscious experience. Thus, insofar as narrativity is part of our ontological makeup, even should we lack moral purpose, a story will still capture who we are. After all, a coherent story can be constructed even about one whose life lacks any moral cohesion whatsoever.

It is to the cohesion of the self as we ourselves experience it that moral purpose is essential. Without moral purpose, we may have no idea ourselves how to compose the story of our lives. This is part of what it means for us to lack a coherent sense of self. Even if we are able to compose a life story, we face a question that does not arise for characters whose lives are entirely fictional. In the case of real people like ourselves, we have to ask of a life story whether it is true or apt. Does it fully capture who we are or does it, rather, miss vast reaches of what we are about? Only if we construct our life story in relation to what is ultimate to us can we be sure to capture in our story what our lives are ultimately about.

PEAK EXPERIENCES

Purpose and story are connected in still another way. In my interviews it became evident that an entire life story can be profoundly shaped by a single core or peak experience. Such peak experiences engage the emotions and the intellect in ways that fuse together the disparate parts of a self. For those who have them, peak experiences become like anchors of the soul, lending coherence to our life stories.[5] Transcendental or entirely secular peak experiences similarly furnish enduring purpose.

We often see something of this in literature. Consider how in Joseph Conrad's *Lord Jim*, the whole aftermath of the protagonist's life is shaped by his experienced shame at his abandonment of his ship. Consider, likewise, the integrity of Jean Valjean's life after his encounter with "the good bishop." In each case, a profound experience unites the soul of the literary character over time . The power of such literature derives from the manifest parallels in real life.

One of my favorite interviews was conducted with Ernst Dorfburg by electronic mail. Then in his eighties, Ernst had a doctorate in chemistry and spent his working life in industry. We originally met in an electronic chat room, where we had taken different sides in a philosophical dispute over free will and determinism. We corresponded and shared articles, and eventually I asked Ernst if I could interview him for my book.

After retiring from chemistry, Ernst had gone on to pursue a master's degree in philosophy and seemed to be as obsessed with philosophical questions as I. As I communicated further with Ernst, he became increasingly intriguing. Originally from Austria, Ernst had grown up in Vienna as a contemporary of Sigmund Freud and Ludwig Wittgenstein.

I ask Ernst what drives him, what makes him so philosophically obsessed. He tells me that it all goes back to a certain deep experience sixty-eight years ago.

"You are the first person I have met," Ernst electronically writes to me, "who is interested in what I have to say, not only about my deep experience but also about what motivates me to pursue all the wider reading from basic science to biblical criticism. You also ask whether I am searching for something.

"I made several attempts to answer these questions. Every time I tried, I found myself typing several pages without reaching the end of my story, which spans the sixty-eight years that have elapsed from my 'experience' to the present. The present includes our discussions and your questions that brought things to light that had been buried in my subconscious. I realized that, short of an autobiography, I could not fully answer your questions. So I decided to shorten my answer, which, as you will presently see, is still quite lengthy.

"The year was 1927, and I was sixteen years old. I was sitting in our living room and had tuned in a certain radio station to listen to 'Die Schoene Muellerin,' a group of songs by Franz Schubert.

"The reason I had selected this program was that I wanted to learn to appreciate and enjoy classical music, and I felt that I was missing something because it was almost painful for me to have to sit through any musical performance of classical music.

"I was listening to the music and was looking through the open window at a tree in the garden, when something strange happened. I felt that I had left my body and had become one with the tree in the garden, with the pebbles on the garden paths, and with everything else in the universe. I felt some mild amusement seeing my body sitting there in the living room. I had a feeling of indescribable bliss, a feeling that everything was, is, and forever will be as it should be and could not be any other way, and that time did not pass, that the future was contained in the past and the past contained in the future, and there was only one time, the present. That I was at one with the universe, that the universe was within me, and I was inextricably linked to the universe."

The reflection is a bit uncanny that in the same year in the same city, Freud had just published his *The Future of an Illusion*, having not yet addressed the experience of "oceanic feeling" Ernst describes.

"I don't know how long this state of ecstasy lasted. It might have been a few seconds or several minutes. One thing I am sure of: it is that it could not have lasted for more than half an hour, because the Schubert program I had listened to was still on. But the music that came over the radio waves now was no longer the classical music that I had found so boring. It was heavenly music such as I had never heard before.

"The above description does not do justice to what I experienced. Much later, some forty years later, I found a much better description in R.M. Bucke's *Cosmic Consciousness*. Here is an excerpt: 'There came upon me a sense of exultation of immense joyousness accompanied or followed by an intellectual illumination impossible to describe. Among other things, I did not merely come to believe but I saw that the universe is not composed of dead matter, but is, on the contrary, a living presence; I became conscious in myself of eternal life. It was not a conviction that I would have eternal life, but a consciousness that I possessed eternal life then; I saw that all men are immortal; that the cosmic order is such that without any doubt all things work together for the good of each and all...The vision lasted a few seconds and was gone; but the memory of it and the sense of the reality of what it taught has remained during the quarter century which has since elapsed. I knew that what the vision showed was true.'"

Many besides Bucke and Freud have acknowledged the reality of such experiences as Ernst's. Psychologist William James was equally aware of it. Theologian Paul Tillich calls it "the eternal now." Long before any of these thinkers, it had become the definitive religious experience of Hinduism and Buddhism.

What was true for Bucke has been true for Ernst as well. The memory of cosmic consciousness has remained a strong experiential core of Ernst's identity long after the actual event. It motivated not only his reading but his eventual pursuit of a degree in philosophy.

"It is now 1995, and sixty-eight years have elapsed since my experience of cosmic consciousness, to use the term used by William James and R. M. Bucke rather than the term *epiphany*, which has a religious connotation. In retrospect, this experience consciously or subconsciously explains my lifelong search for an answer to the question: Does my life have a meaning?

"For a while, I was able to put myself into a state of bliss, a trance, so to speak, by just thinking about my experience. Gradually, over a period of perhaps two or three years, I lost this ability and all that was left was the memory. Then came Hitler, the occupation of Austria, emigration to the United States, the war, and the Holocaust.

"By that time, not much was left of the beauty, peace, and bliss of my dream/experience, except that cosmic feeling that everything was the way it had to be and could not be any other way.

"It was easy for me to find confirmation of that part of my dream/experience in math, cosmology, evolution, science, and even in my own field, chemistry. The great discoveries made in these fields in my lifetime provided me with incontrovertible evidence that the universe and I, as an integral part of the universe, were not here by accident and were, therefore, predetermined events."

I began to see why the doctrine of determinism, which we had originally disputed, was so important to Ernst today. Whereas I had at first attributed Ernst's belief in determinism to scientific positivism, I found, rather, that it was motivated by a humanistic worldview that had arisen from a mystical experience sixty-eight years ago.

Ernst's deep experience became a resource for his soul. It provided him with both a morality and a worldview. It positioned him in moral and cosmic space. And with those positionings came a coherent and enduring identity as well.

Ernst's case coincides with our earlier observation that it is in the emotion of personal experience that we find—or fail to find—evidence for life's sacred dimension. Yet, as we also observed, while personal religious experience may provide us with prima facie grounds for belief in a particular view of the sacred, personal experience is not infallible. It may sometimes be the illusion Freud suggests it always is. Precisely because our personal experiences and our interpretations of them are all so different, they cannot all be equally correct.

While our convictions may begin with personal experience, we still must enter the critical space of argument and counterargument over our beliefs. We still need to subject our personal experiences—or, at least, our interpretations of them—to more objective scrutiny. Because he is such a reflective individual, Ernst realized this early on. That is how he came to debate determinism with me over the internet. His life models the quest for truth we undertake in critical space.

"But that certainty, that everything was as it had to be, was only part of my dream/experience. Where was the other part, the part that everything was in harmony and that all things worked together for the good of each and all? Where was the Grand Design I felt was a part of it?

"While I was working, I did not have the time to address these questions. But consciously or subconsciously, I knew that neither math nor science could give an answer to these questions and to the question as to whether my life had a meaning beyond the fact that I was an integral part of a law-determined universe. So I looked everywhere to find where such questions had been asked and discussed, and, of course, the best places to explore were the various religions.

"And here, finally, is my answer to your question, 'What motivates you to pursue all the wider reading you have been doing—from basic science to biblical criticism?'

"To me, religions are a branch of philosophy, the branch that deals with questions such as, 'Does my life have meaning?' 'Why is there evil in this world?' 'Why do good people suffer and bad people prosper?' And other related questions.

"The Bible is a good example of how some of these questions have been answered. But biblical criticism is essential for an appreciation of the prose and poetry in which some of these answers have been presented. Without such criticism, the Book of Job, for example, cannot be properly understood, and its power, poetry, and, above all, its message are completely lost."

At the core of Ernst Dorfburg's life is a religious experience, what psychologist Abraham Maslow has termed a "peak experience." While Maslow tends to think that all peak experiences are ultimately the same, William James counsels us rather to appreciate their variety.

Ernst's experience of cosmic unity reflects the characteristic religious experience of the East. In that experience, there is no distinction between self and other. Instead, we actually become the mind of

Brahma, the very universe comprehensively conscious of itself. The characteristic religious experience of the West tends to be different, a theistic experience in which a certain differentiation remains. Ultimate reality is not so much experienced as a whole that inextricably includes us but as a thou to whom we relate personally.

It is such a typical Western peak experience that Stephen Hertz relates to me. As in Ernst's case, Stephen's peak experience was also one that brought his life into coherence and thereafter positioned him in both moral space and cosmic space. Phenomenologically, from then on, he had a new identity that continues to cohere across time and space. Mention of Stephen's peak experience surfaces when I ask him if he feels called.

"Mm-hm. I feel called to share this experience, this life that I've…I feel like God, like, woke me up from the dead. Because of what hap— It was, like, high school, and in my freshman year I was sexually addicted.

"I really was, and it really brought me to the point of, like, just spiritual death. Like numbness. There's nothing worse than being numb. Gosh, that you can't feel pain; you can't feel happiness; you're just there. Just going through the motions. You're just…you want to die, but you're scared to. But you can't really feel the pain so you think that death is the best way and the only way out.

"I mean at that point, a lot was going down in my life. So a real spiritual longing…See, what had happened is I got so fed up with my parents' Christianity that I told Christ to prove himself. If he was God, he had to show it to me. And until then, I was just going to say F.U. to your Christ, you know? To you, Christ, because nobody hears…I don't see you in these Christians. I don't see you at all. Where are you?"

Stephen confirms one of the points I have been emphasizing. Belief withers when unaccompanied by experience.

"And I went out, I guess, in kind of a hippie sort of way on a quest for love. I wanted to find out what that was. Where it was. I guess I'm still on the same quest. I've just taken a different…well, not a different…back on the track of Christ. But love at one time, almost—well, it equaled sex.

"Mm-hm."

"And I found that that wasn't love at all."

"Did you find that on your own? I mean, actually, you know, I don't want to get too personal, so…"

"Yeah."

"Anything I raise, by the way, you can say 'I don't want to talk about that.'"

"No, I don't mind talking about it...Well, what was I saying? Oh, when I figured out sex didn't equal love, that's the point, I mean..."

"And love was important?"

"Love was—yeah, probably the most important."

"And so how did Jesus prove that he existed to you?"

"Well it came...First, I figured out that love didn't equal sex, sex didn't equal love, and that led me to the point where I found I was in real spiritual poverty, kind of at the bottom, when I really realized my numbness to what was going on around me."

"This is like sophomore year of high school?"

"No, this is like my freshman year at college."

"Oh, okay."

"The end of my freshman year, the beginning of my sophomore year, kind of like September 'ninety-one. It got to the point where all my girlfriend and I did was fight or have sex. And we were supposed to be in love.

"I knew that we weren't in love anymore. I tried very hard to have her fall back in love with me, but I knew that it wasn't going to work. I tried so many different things for a whole summer that it always ended up an argument or being in bed, and sex got to be just like going through the motions. It just—I mean, just was like filling up a physical need, a desire, a lust.

"And it got to the point where one...I mean, one night we're having sex, and she wouldn't even kiss me. I was like, 'Shit!' I was like, 'Oh, my lord! What the hell is happening to me? I am so fucked up.'

"And I was like, 'She is so fucked up. We are fucked up, and she doesn't see it, and I see it now.' And I just, like, I just rolled off her and, like, totally, I was beside myself, and she didn't get it. She didn't care even to get it.

"Mm-hm."

"And then I knew we were really...something was wrong. And the next...Well, the next night...See, I was down visiting her for like a few days, so I was staying with her. The next day, I was going home, and I was just having...I mean, after something like that happens, it's like your whole world is, like, coming down in on you.

"So I was back in my own bed in my parents' house, and I was thinking about a lot of things. Suicide is one of them, and, I was just like, 'Jesus, are you there?'

"And I heard this voice and it was like completely...Like this isn't supposed to happen. Like, I'm not one to hear voices, you know?

"I grew up Christian. No one ever heard voices. No one. No one. No one.

And, and it's something that only happens in the Old Testament: look at Moses, you know?

"And this voice said, 'I never left you. You left me.'

"And I was just like under my covers, like hysterical, like shaking, crying, shaking, scared, because I thought he was going to judge me. I thought that was it. I mean...but he didn't.

"And right after that, I felt this overwhelming sense of love, and I was just...was like, 'Uh, don't let me leave you again. I just want to follow you. Just don't let me leave you. I want to follow you. I'll go wherever; I'll do whatever as long as I can follow you.' It blew my mind. I was still struggling with the addiction a lot. I broke the relationship off like that. I explained things to her. She thought...well, before that, I equated God with Jerry Garcia, so when I told her that I had this, like, revelation, she thought I was full of it. And I can't blame her. I totally couldn't blame her, and I was, like, well, you know, I really need to go. I can't help it."

"She probably was happy to have you go at that point."

"No, she made life hell. She called for months, for a few months. Like, we tried to do the friend thing. At first, she would call and curse me out. I mean, and, then, other days she would be like, 'I love you. I want you back.' And then the next day she'd curse me out. It made me nuts."

"Well, did you start doing something, practicing something different then? I mean, all right, so you had this revelation..."

"Well, I started really looking...I experienced such a great love, and it came through calling on Jesus and him answering. This was new. I mean this, like, didn't happen before.

"So I really started...I was reading my Bible like crazy, like, especially in the Psalms because there's an incredible sense of poverty in a lot...personal poverty."

"Hmm."

"A brokenness. A real humility, and I was attracted to that because I felt so down and out."

"You identified with it."

"Yeah. But then I saw this God in the Psalms who was more than helping this person, this broken person. I mean he was providing, he was enabling, he was causing this person to grow, causing this person to reach out to others and heal, and trying to help heal others and was, like—I couldn't read enough. The words, like, wouldn't come off the page and..."

"You were just doing this on your own?" I ask because sociologically I am wondering what the larger social context was in which this was happening.

"I was doing this on my own. This would happen—like, I would have nightmares. I would have crazy stuff about what would happen. I mean, what happened with me and my girlfriend being addicted, and I would get up at two o'clock in the morning and just read until I could sleep again. And it was wild. It was really wild. And that was pretty much the story. I guess you can call it a conversion."

Whether we call Stephen's experience a conversion or not, his experience was certainly a powerful one, an experience that radically altered the subsequent trajectory of Stephen's life. If conversion means just that—*metanoia*, a life reorientation, then Stephen's experience did produce conversion.

On the other hand, Stephen's experience appears also to represent a developmental stage in the religious life characteristic of a certain kind of conservative Christianity. I hear accounts very similar to Stephen's from other Evangelical Christians, accounts of eventually reaching a personal impasse at which one finally submits oneself to the life management of Christ. This is the classic "salvation" experience of more fundamentalistic Christianity, the experience of being personally saved.

We might almost say that the experience of personal salvation is a possibility afforded by the tradition of Evangelical Christianity for which its followers are previously groomed. I hear, for example, from some young people raised in the Evangelical tradition that, while they accept the doctrines of Evangelical Christianity, they themselves have not yet accepted Christ as their personal savior.

How can they not have? To an outsider and particularly an intellectual outsider, it seems strange for one to believe that one must accept the personal salvation of Christ and yet not to have done so. How can one believe in the need for salvation without acting on it? To academics especially, who so emphasize the intellect, the failure to act on such a belief is mysterious.

The academic mistake is to overemphasize the cognitive element of religion. What the pre-saved Evangelicals may mean is that while they abstractly recognize the need to accept Jesus as their personal savior, they have not yet themselves personally experienced this need, this call. Even prior to this experience, however, the Evangelical tradition has already prepared its followers with the intellectual categories to interpret this need when confronted with a certain kind of personal crisis. It is this element of preparation for an experience the tradition itself affords that makes me hesitate to label Stephen's experience a conversion rather than a stage in the experiential life of the Evangelical religious tradition.

In contrast, the experience of personal salvation is much less char-
acteristically associated with either more liberal Protestantism or
Catholicism. Indeed, as a practicing Catholic, I can report neither having felt personally saved nor ever resonating even abstractly with a doctrinal need for personal salvation. In fact, as I often tell Evangelicals
with whom I speak, the very concept of salvation is foreign to my own
religious outlook. In the tradition I reflect, there is instead much more
resonance with what Stephen had to say about participating in Jesus's
call to realize the reign of God on earth.

One point I am trying to make is that it is difficult to separate the
cognitive and emotional qualities of religious experience. There are
no uninterpreted experiences. It is not as if we first have an experience and only after, in cool reflection, an interpretation.

The very experience itself is already partially constituted by inter-
pretive categories. Stephen claims to have heard the voice of Jesus. He
is as certain that this is what he experienced as Bucke and Ernst are
that they actually experienced cosmic consciousness. What we experience profoundly impresses such certainty on us with this kind of force.

How does Stephen know that his experience was of a reality and
not a hallucination? How does he know that it was the voice of Jesus he
heard and not the voice of Satan? The Evangelical tradition supplies
both the categories through which the experience already comes interpreted—an interpretation without which the experience itself might be
fundamentally different—and the criteria of authenticity. To verify and
examine his experience, Stephen consults the Bible. Had what the
voice said contradicted the Bible, Stephen might well have concluded
that he was holding congress not with Jesus but with the devil.

Was it truly Jesus speaking to Stephen? This is a theological question. The theological nature of the question goes overlooked by secular sociologists who would be quick to dismiss—or explain
away—Stephen's experience as entirely a social construction. Such a
sociological interpretation of Stephen's experience assumes either
that there is no resurrected Christ to speak to us or, even if there is,
that the resurrected Christ is restricted in the way he speaks—specifically, that he cannot or will not speak through the dynamics of our
individual psychologies. In its very denial of the reality posited by religion, social constructionism inadvertently enters the arena of theological debate.

Yet, have I not myself already supplied social constructionism with
all the ammunition it needs? Didn't I just argue that experiences such
as Stephen's are nothing more than mental constructions, socially pre-

pared by a certain kind of religious tradition? Experiences such as Stephen's may depend on social categories, but they also reflect something more. There is a saying, now popular among sociologists, that social institutions enable as well as constrain.[6] Scientific experiments, for example, are social constructs that enable us to identify real causal processes we could not otherwise detect. It does not follow from the fact that scientific experiments have been socially devised that what they reveal is not a reality independent of us.

The same principle applies to religious realities. It is entirely possible that there exists independently of us a multifaceted, transcendental reality, certain facets of which different religious traditions enable us to see. That is not to say that everything every religion tells us is a part of the truth. It is not even to say that all religions necessarily reveal some portion of the truth. Religious doctrines, just like scientific theories, can also be wholly wrong.

Which religious doctrines are wholly or partially wrong and which are correct? We only discover the answer by subjecting religious claims to the arguments of critical space. Contrary to popular—and even academic—opinion, we will see that such debate can be undertaken. We can argue—and argue persuasively—even about religion.

The typical sociological approach to religious experience is simply to ignore the reality to which the religious experience is but a response. Sociology hopes thereby to exclude distinctly religious questions and avoid theological debate. The problem is that if religious experience truly is a socially mediated response to something beyond the social, then to disregard this sacred reality is to ensure that a full understanding of religious experience always remains beyond sociology's ken.

There is one further point I would like to press about Stephen's religious experience. About 30 percent of Americans believe the Bible is literally the very word of God. To outsiders, this fundamentalism appears irrational. To outsiders, its implications are also often offensive. Particularly offensive is the fundamentalist belief that one must accept Jesus as one's personal savior in order to avert hell in the next life. Yet, as indicated by the responses to the following question in a national survey, the necessity of salvation through Jesus alone is a conviction held by a sizable portion of the American public.[7]

Do you think that a person who doesn't accept Jesus can be saved?

Yes	49%
No	38%
Other/Not sure	13%

In our current climate of multiculturalism, it appears insensitive to hold, as fundamentalists do, that one must believe in Jesus in order to share God's favor. I myself side with those who think the fundamentalists err on several counts. I do not believe the Bible represents the very word of God. Even if it did, I do not think that all of the Bible would best be interpreted literally. As Ernst suggests, God, too, might sometimes choose to speak in metaphor and hyperbole. Finally, I certainly disagree with the view that one must accept Jesus in order to save oneself from hell, the very existence of which I also question.

Nevertheless, there is a widespread tendency, especially prevalent among academics, to withhold their usual multicultural sensitivity from fundamentalists. Many who insist on politically correct speech in relation to all other groups feel quite free to speak disparagingly of fundamentalism.[8] They thereby betray, despite their words, some adherence to objective, cross-cultural absolutes. Fundamentalism is castigated for its intolerance. As I have argued, tolerance is the cosmogonic value arising from postmodernist multiculturalism. For postmodernist multiculturalists, tolerance, at least, appears to be accepted as a standard eligible for cross-cultural application.

It may be erroneous to believe that the Bible is the actual word of God, which, as such, must be interpreted literally. This belief is not mindless, however. To outsiders, it appears mindless because it seems inexplicable. It appears inexplicable in turn because, on matters of religion, we tend to focus too much on beliefs. We tend to regard religions as just different sets of beliefs and ignore altogether religion's experiential component. It is, however, the connection between the emotional and cognitive elements of fundamentalism that rationally explains the tenacity of fundamentalist religious beliefs.

Peak experiences such as Stephen's impress themselves powerfully on the psyche. We come away with a certainty about the reality of what we have experienced. In addition, just like crystals forming around initial seeds, our identities frequently form around peak experiences. In such cases, our peak experiences are vital to who we are. Our very selves are invested in them.

If our peak experiences are so vital to who we are, if we come to have so much invested in them, then it stands to reason that we will be especially protective of the intellectual categories that both interpret the experience and, more fundamentally, make the experience what it is in the first place. The fundamentalist experience of personal salvation is one such experience.

The fundamentalist experience of personal salvation depends on a certain reading of the Bible. Even before one actually has such an experience, one knows from that reading that experiencing oneself as saved is necessary to escape hell. The intellectual categories of the biblical interpretation form an intellectual shape into which alone the salvation experience can eventually fit. Without the hole created by those intellectual categories, there can be no such experience. After the experience, moreover, it is further literal reading of the Bible that confirms the experience to be what it is.

Challenges to the authority of the Bible therefore become as well challenges to the authenticity of one's personal experience of salvation, challenges to a peak experience that has both impressed itself with certainty on the believer and become the seed around which the believer's subsequent identity has formed.

For those who have experienced personal salvation, therefore, much is at stake in the defense of the intellectual categories that create and preserve the meaning of the peak experience. That means much is at stake in the defense of the Bible as the literal word of God. This must be appreciated. There is something else operating here other than what appears to be a density of mind.

It is not easy for us to entertain debate about the worldviews to which we have an experiential connection and which, thereby, have become so central to our very identities. It is, rather, psychologically dangerous. Although to accept such risk, to live dangerously, as Nietzsche admonishes us to do, is important to our intellectual and spiritual growth, we must nevertheless appreciate the stakes.

The validity of the fundamentalists' experience of personal salvation could be preserved, albeit with modification, even without a literal interpretation of the Bible, but this would lead the fundamentalist away from the conservative and more toward the liberal tradition of Christianity. This path remains difficult and emotionally dangerous.

The fundamentalists I interviewed are not all typical, even within their own tradition, but several wrestle with the intellectual consequences of their experience. Stephen, for example, struggles within the tradition over what it means to accept Jesus.

"You have missionaries, you know? And they've gone to very different sorts of people in the most, you know, far out places of the world, and they tried to bring their Christ into a culture that doesn't ask those questions. I think every culture needs their own Christ. I think the things in the story are so universal that everyone can identify with them, but often in, like, traditional and missionary work, it's sort of donning an attitude of American U.S. supremacy or superiority. It's become more of a culture thing than a Christian thing: You have to be born again in this way, in the way we say. I think faith is a lot more being a child, and God is a lot more than just one experience."

Brad Caldwell also struggles with the implications of his core experience of salvation. I ask him whether he believes that people who do not accept Jesus are all destined for hell.

"Yes," Brad affirms.

"You do."

"Yeah."

"Do you ever think you're wrong about that?"

"No. I mean, my relationship with God is really so real to me, and I mean, I guess when I see doubt coming, and I see that is a very good tactic from the enemy, from Satan, using to doubt my faith so..."

"Hmm, okay."

"I guess one thing I wanted to say before I forget is just—maybe this won't help you out any, but when I come across passages in the Bible that I have trouble with, you know, it's my, my inclination not to believe it and..."

"Your inclination is not to believe it?"

"Yeah, but then I start questioning my own thoughts and, you know, to discover, What am I missing here? Is there something that I am not seeing? I go in trying to think, Just read into the passage more and get other people's...so it's something...I don't really question the Bible. I really question me."

"Hm-hm."

"I don't know if that helps."

"Yeah, that helps. Do you ever wonder whether it's true that all non-Christians will go to hell? Do you ever think, Well maybe..."

"Yeah, I wonder, I mean..."

"Like God will at the last minute say, 'Yeah...'"

"No. I don't think he's going to change his mind at the last minute."

"No, not at the last minute. But maybe a reprieve. I mean..."

"I wonder about the babies. How he's going to handle that?"

"Well, how?"

"I don't know."

"How is that handled?"

"I mean, you hear of these children who cannot make a decision, you know? Not having that ability so that would be something that..."

"Do they go to hell?" It was precisely to handle this question that the Catholic church invented infant baptism and, for those infants who miss even that, limbo.

"I don't know. I don't have an opinion on that. I'm not sure. That would be something I...work through."

Brad is a young Christian, only recently saved. John Wasserman and Matt Bennett have been Christians longer. Accordingly, they have thought longer about my questions. I ask them whether God does not appear arbitrary, saving some people from hell and not others.

John answers first. "There is one specific passage...well, probably more than one, but one that I can think of off the top of my head, a specific passage where that gets addressed. It's one of those passages that is kind of disturbing, that I think is probably the heart of the matter, which asks the question specifically, Why does God give mercy to some and not to others?

"And the answer is, 'Who are you, O man, to question God?' And that...the potter has the right to make some clay for noble purposes and some for purposes that are not. And you know, in one sense that can, that's a slightly disturbing passage."

The passage is disturbing because it suggests that just as a human potter can legitimately do what he wants with the pots he himself creates, so can God justly do what he will with his own creations, namely us. So if God wants to destine some people to hell and others to heaven, this is his prerogative as creator. To me, this image of God is not very pleasing, but John goes on to offer an interpretation through which he deals with it.

"But in another sense, I think, you know, the passage does suggest that I'm not going to have the answer to that question as much as I want the answer to that question at times and as much as a lot of people are going to ask me the answer to that question."

John laughs. "I'm not going to have it. The answer lies with God. And he hasn't chosen to say a whole lot about it."

"Well, you know," I continue, "that's a stumbling block for a lot of people like me. It matters to me that in this view God is very arbitrary, too arbitrary for me, so that I can't accept it. I can't deal with that arbitrariness."

Now Matt enters his opinion. "Well, first of all, like, I wouldn't use the word *arbitrary*. There's a reason we don't know. Ultimately, we are not the masters of the destiny of the universe and just have to accept that God is, and we don't know enough how he chooses or why he chooses...to say that God is arbitrary. Then the other thing is people often ask questions like this: I mean, if God is ultimately in control, if he's sovereign, then why do my—why do my choices have any significance?"

"Hm-hm."

"And it's tough to get a handle on, but you could ask it another way: If God is not in control, then God's not sovereign. How much less do your choices have any significance? In your short amount of time, small amount of space in the light of the universe you don't affect its destiny, and a lot of us like to think that we're important, that our choices are the ultimate choices. So I guess if God were not in control, what sense would it all make? If God were not there, it's just biochemical reactions in this world of chance. What significance would our choices have? And so while it's disturbing to think that much is not completely up to me, it's awful comforting to know that all our choices are in the context of God's will and that he's a good and a wise and a just God. And we don't know his reasons."

We have been asking how fundamentalists can reconcile God's goodness with the relegation to hell of what turns out to be most of God's human creation. We may not be satisfied with the fundamentalist answers, but that is not the point. The point is that fundamentalist theology is constrained by its own core experience—the experience of personal salvation.

Fundamentalists experience themselves as personally saved—saved specifically from hell. It is difficult to preserve the reality and authenticity of that personal experience if one comes to admit after all that one did not need to be saved from hell by Jesus, that other avenues of salvation are possible or that hell does not really exist. To make such admissions diminishes the experience. It is experience, therefore, that lies at the core of fundamentalist belief.

Although Maslow equated peak experiences with religious experiences, our identities may also crystallize around deep experiences that are not specifically religious. Peak experiences of a nonreligious variety can also anchor our identities.

Gerry Storr tells a story in which he discovers that his entire life has revolved around the intense experience associated with a forgotten note. We may recall that the ethical guideline of Gerry's life is a particular form of the golden rule: "Don't lay hands on anybody, and no one lays hands on you." Gerry's story reveals the experiential origin of this operating principle.

"My principle always was don't lay hands on anybody and no one lays hands on you. Is that the golden rule? Yeah. I treat people the way I want to be treated. I'm not going to hassle, I'm not going to threaten you, but don't threaten me. Okay? That to me is, is you know, that's how I've always lived my life. I mean, from day one. Okay?

"I can't remember—I can't remember a time I didn't live my life that way, and I can actually go back and tell you why. When my...I did age regression with my psychiatrist when I was being—getting divorced.

"When I got divorced, I went to a psychiatrist and did age regression. I actually did, and my mother confirmed this. I think age regression to some extent is...People get carried away. Okay? But for me, for this one...for two instances...for two recollections, it was incredibly vital to me. One in a very positive way, a very warm feeling, and another very painful, but extremely important.

"The warm one: The psychiatrist took me back to a time when I felt warm and content with my father. I remember that, and the interesting thing was I actually felt those emotions. Sitting in the car with him and doing stuff. It was—it was really..."

"This was under hypnosis?"

"Yeah." The psychiatrist had evidently offered to implant a post-hypnotic suggestion that would prevent Gerry from remembering any emotional pain experienced while under hypnosis. Gerry, however, refused this measure.

"I wanted to remember everything, you know? I wanted to remember everything. I wanted to remember every emotion. I wanted to remember everything. Why do it if you don't remember? I mean, why go through this shit if you're not going to...

"At first, I couldn't believe in it. Of course, I had to do it intellectually. I had to read all the articles. I studied the stuff. I mean, I went into a real study of it for about a month before I agreed to do it. And I also made the psychiatrist sign a thing to say that she would not make me act like a chicken."

"Yeah?"

"She was a Filipino. She thought I was very bizarre, okay? No, I asked her to, but she thought it was a joke. Actually, I was kind of serious."

"Well, I can understand that actually."

"You know, I mean, I did not want to find myself videotaped acting like a chicken. Anyway, she created what she called an affective bridge."

"Say that again."

"Affective, you know? She called it an affective bridge. Actually, there was an article, several articles..."

"Affective British?"

"Bridge."

"Oh, bridge."

"Bridge." An affective bridge is evidently a positive emotion associated with a childhood memory that allows one to think back to childhood without having to break through defense mechanisms.

"So I said warm, caring. She wanted me to get some really positive feelings. So then she said, 'Are you really ready for a negative one?'

"And I said, 'Well, you know, if it's there, let's do it.' Okay?

"So she took me back to the last time I saw my father. I had no recollection of this at all. Actually, the first time we did it, I remember saying this was the last time I talked to him. My father was giving himself shots of painkillers. We lived in a small tenement apartment, and I said it was like seeing my parents through the wrong side of binoculars, you know?

"I remember I was seven years old and seeing this, okay? Very telling. I think, actually, the metaphor was very correct. They were both...my father's dying, but my mother was being taken away from me too because all her time was being spent with my dying father, right? And we had no money for...So it was...Actually, I thought the metaphor was looking through the wrong end of...you know? I saw both of them there, far, far away.

"But that wasn't enough for Angela. She said there's more there.

"So she said, 'When was really the last time?'

"So we went back and looked at the last time, and it turned out the day before my father died, I was in the hospital. I knew I couldn't be there. They didn't let eight-year-olds, you know, in the hospital, certainly not in a 'fifties, VA hospital.

"And it was unbelievably painful. My father died. He had lung cancer. He was like six foot six, two hundred thirty pounds, dark, black hair when he was younger, you know? I take after him a lot as you can see." Gerry laughs because he is considerably shorter than six foot six, a lot lighter than two hundred thirty pounds, and has blond hair.

"And when he died, he weighed like—you know, typical fifties lung cancer—weighed eighty pounds. Couldn't talk.

"So I was actually in the room with him the night before he died. And he wrote me a note, you know? And of course I remembered none of that, okay? None. Talk about repressed.

"So you know, I'm a skeptic, you know? So I—I cannot tell you, I cannot convey, I would never encourage anyone to do this. I thought...See, I was stupid. I thought that I would be what I've always been all my life: the observer. I thought I'd see the eight-year-old child and the dying father in a room and I'd observe. Take notes. I could analyze the behavior, okay? No.

"I was that eight-year-old, and I experienced those emotions, and I experienced the pain. It was—it was actually one of the most frightening...I was actually out of control. I was sobbing out of control. Actually, she had to stop the thing.

"And of course, you know, I remember all of it. So I got to enjoy the pain and suffering, and then I got to remember all of it, and then go through it again, over and over again. I mean it was really...When you think about it, it's like, whoa! Let's take the club and beat me over the head."

Gerry pauses. "It was so valuable. And they sent me a note from my father, which read, 'You have to take care of your mother. And never back down from anything.'

"'Never back down from anything, okay?' And here I am now in my thirties and I'm sitting in this room and...Oh God, the irony! I mean, the irony's the thing. A woman in Blue Bell, Montana, comes to the town. She's a female Filipino—the only one—and she has her office in a motel room! Circle T Motel. This is true! Could I make this up? A friend of mine says to me, 'Gerry, the strangest things happen to you.'

"And the walls have roaches on them. So it looks like a really cheap, tacky whorehouse, okay? Not that I've ever been in one. Um, doing age regression with a Filipino female psychiatrist at the Circle T Motel in Blue Bell, Montana. I mean, it's not the way Woody Allen does psychoanalysis, okay?

"So I'm sitting in this hotel room, absolutely out of control, you know? Sobbing, the whole bit. I mean, and she has to stop the thing and calm me down and go back. But see, I was still so skeptical. So I called my mother that night, and she said everything was true! Exactly. That she got special permission to get me there because they knew he was going to die the next day. Took me in there, that he wrote the note, that he couldn't speak, you know?"

I ask Gerry why this experience was so valuable to him.

"Because of how I live my life. That note was absolutely...When he wrote me that note, it is exactly the way I lived my life. Absolutely. Still, today, at forty-seven, but when...but the revelation was when I was thirty-one years old, and I'm sitting there and saying, 'Fucking A.'

"You know? It was like, This is it? Twenty-four years of my life have been determined by a scrap of paper? Whoa! I have not been in control of my destiny, you know? Then, if you're already inclined to be an existentialist, then it sort of moves you to the next level."

"So you think it's absurd?"

"I think that, yeah. I think the human mind is very complex, and

I think that emotions are…" Gerry shakes his head. "I've lived my life based on a note."

Perhaps. The story is a powerful one, and it powerfully illustrates a number of points I have been trying to make. Like Ernst's before it, Gerry's story reveals a unity of self even across a span of many years. It further illustrates the origin of that unity in a peak experience involving intense emotion. The story thereby illustrates as well the relation between narrative unity, experience, and emotion.

Yet, there is a final point the story also illustrates. I observed earlier that there are questions to be posed about our own life narratives that do not apply to the narratives of fictional characters. In our own case, we need to ask whether a particular story of our lives is true or apt, whether it fully captures who we are. No doubt some important aspect of Gerry's life has been based on a forgotten note. The narrative unity is there. But is this the whole story? The most important story that could be told about Gerry's life? We have to wonder.

Emotions experienced in the political arena can also be powerful. They also can become a seed around which an identity crystallizes. Consider Ken Ambrose, one of my first interviewees. At the time I had interviewed him a few years ago, Ken was an economics major in college, just about to graduate. He had also been a strong political presence on campus, one of the co-founders of the College Republicans.

I almost idly ask him whether his young conservatism had been influenced by Reagan.

"Oh, of course. Yeah."

"The Reagan administration had an effect on you?" I am actually surprised by Ken's affirmation.

"Absolutely."

"Can you explain. I mean, one thing I'm interested in, if you could talk about it, is, I think…Well, growing up, the administration in office does have an effect on us, but it's often unclear what that effect is."

"Well," Ken replies, "you don't think about economics when you're a youngster. But you are aware of what's going on around you. You know that in the late seventies you go to get gas with your parents, and there are gas lines."

"You remember that?"

"Oh yeah. I remember the late seventies. You remember things…you start to recall inflation was high, the double-digit this, the double-digit that, the misery index. And then, you know, then all through, what was it, 'eighty-three, the end of 'eighty-three through to when Bush screwed it up…everything was fine. You know, all the interest rates were low, everything was low, and it just...instills you with a feeling of goodness. Like Republicans in office, my parents have a job. I'm happy. Everybody's happy. Lower taxes, stuff like that."

This exchange had occurred at the beginning of the interview. I had dropped the topic and had gone on with my usual questions.

"What would you say are the moral principles you live by?"

"The moral...principles...I live by?" Ken laughs.

I laugh, too. "Do you have moral principles?"

Ken continues laughing. "Stalling for time. I have no morals...No, seriously, like in—like in what facet? I need more specifics here."

"Interpersonal relations," I say. This doesn't help. Ken remains silent.

"Okay," I say, "let me..."

Ken interrupts. "What are we talking about? The Catholic virtues: don't lie, cheat, steal or..." Ken has gone to Catholic school.

I nod. "Do you buy that?"

"No, never."

"No? So what do you buy? Do you buy anything?"

"I buy the me-first principle. Whatever I do...uh...should be...I'm not going to do anything that's going to jeopardize my life or my personal well-being for the sake of an acquaintance."

"Say that again?"

"I'm not going to sacrifice my own well-being or my own personal welfare, personal interests just to do something for somebody else."

"Even a friend?"

"This is on a scale, though. Obviously, it's relative. If—if the guy's going to..."

"How much sacrifice as opposed to..."

"Yeah. It's the old risk versus return portfolio theory. Like, if I ask...if the guy's going to die, and I don't stand to lose much. Yeah, cost-benefit trade."

I nod, and Ken returns us to the Reagan administration. "I do think that those views..."

"Which views?"

"The views of the me-first principle."

"Hm-hm."

"I do think those were probably shaped due to the Reagan era."

"You do?" Again I perk up. "How?"

"Just because of the anti-collectiveness of the attitude of the government, the laissez-faire. Like give everything back to the people. We don't want to create a big government. Less government."

"So in reaction, you became sort of..."

"Well, it transferred power from the central government to the people. It makes us more powerful. They set up a system of, like, an economy where the me-first principle had more rewards. The level of reward you were going to get for each increment of me-first was more than—than..."

Ken seems to be speaking of the marginal returns to egoism, but at the time of our interview, I am not getting it. "It sort of authorized the me-first type of approach?"

"Right. It authorized it and made it more—more beneficial to have that approach."

"Well, maybe it was more beneficial. Would you say the Reagan administration also made a me-first approach more, I guess, legitimate?"

"Right."

The political economic reality we experience when we come of age often becomes the baseline from which we assess politics and economics throughout our lives. If so, then Ken certainly will employ a baseline markedly different from that employed by those of us who came of age in the sixties. That partially explains the generation gap between Ken's generation and the generation of baby boomers.

Age cohort, however, is not destiny. In the sixties, I was out of step with the radicalism of my agemates, and, once again, I appear to be out of step in midlife as my agemates become more conservative and I more radical.

If it is experience that consolidated the me-first principle for Ken, it is also experience that threatens to deconstruct it. Ken went through college on a track scholarship, and, as he contemplates his future, his experience with the team unsettles the personal identity he has previously composed.

"You know," Ken tells me, "actually I've been thinking about coaching. I mean, I don't know if this fits into my personality, but I've been doing a lot of coaching here. I coach the distance runners on the team because our coach is inept."

"But at least he evidently recognizes he's inept."

"Uh, no, he thinks he's..."

"He doesn't know you're..."

"Well, he knows I'm coaching them but..."

"He thinks the results are due to him."

"Yeah. Actually, I don't know what he thinks, but anyway, the results have been extremely positive since I picked these guys up five weeks ago. They're all setting personal bests, week after week, and most of it's mental, and a lot of it's the workout that I'm giving them, and it's gratifying to me to see them do well."

"Why?"

"I don't know. I can't explain it, and I don't think it fits my personality."

"Well, it doesn't reflect what you say is your personality."

"And it's—it's frightening me. It really is."

"That's very interesting. Is this the first time you've done something that's really, well, you've gotten a lot, substantial gratification from…"

"Like, it is charity work. I'm obviously not being paid for it. I've never done charity work." The fact that Ken finds he enjoys doing "charity work" is what bothers him. It unsettles his self-concept and his operating principle to experience fulfillment doing something for somebody else without personal gain.

"Actually, here's another example, which again frightens me. But I attributed this to just getting old. You know, when you're little, it's Christmas time, you receive more satisfaction receiving gifts than watching others receive what you've given them."

"Mm-hm."

"Well, over the past year or two, I'm more…I've become more excited watching other people open the gifts that I have gotten for them than actually opening the gifts that they have gotten for me. Now I don't know what this means on a Freudian couch, but…"

"When you get to be my age you don't get excited about any of it."

"That's what my mother says. She hates the holidays."

"I love the holidays, actually, but I hate the gift-giving."

"I don't know where that fits my personality. I mean, I don't think it fits at all."

"So these—these things have given you some pause."

"They make me, they make me stop, take a step back, and try to look at me objectively from like, from like an outsider's position and then say, What's going on here? Why do you feel this way when in another situation you feel something…"

"You're experiencing in the latter case a sense of community."

Ken is not ready to accept this. "Don't say that. *Community* comes from that same Latin base, *commune, communist.*"

Far be it from me to attribute to Ken a growing communist sensibility. Yet, coaching may become for Ken what the three ghosts were for Scrooge. Ken eventually did go on to become a professional track coach. It would be interesting to see several years later how that experience has affected him.

Experience, especially the emotions associated with experience, is a powerful thing. It can be the seed around which our identities crystallize. As in Ken's case, it can also be a solvent, capable of dissolving a previous worldview. In such cases, emotional experiences can speak to us more rationally than formal rationality can. If to be a prophet is to experience a revelation within, then we are all prophets receiving our own individual revelations.

As powerful and important as they are, however, experiences are never infallible. They may provide the prima facie grounds for our beliefs, but we must acknowledge that experiences will differ not only from person to person but, over time, also for one and the same person. The same person will undergo profound experiences that turn out to be contradictory in their implications. Rational reflection remains necessary to adjudicate among our experiences—not just from person to person but even for ourselves alone.

How do we know which of our experiences fully capture reality and which do not? The only way is to explore our experiences in concert with others, particularly with others whose experiences radically differ. We need to place ourselves in communities of discourse.

CHAPTER 8

Communities of Discourse

God is real because he produces real effects.

—*William James*

Tom Brown, remember, believes in God but describes his belief as shaky. Tom considers his belief shaky because he sees no physical evidence for God. As we have observed, however, Tom has done little to look for such evidence. To look for the evidence and to evaluate it, Tom would have to join a community of discourse on the topic of natural theology. He would have to examine what others have cited as evidence for God and how that evidence has been assessed. To evaluate truly whether or not there is any evidence for God's existence, Tom would have to enter a conversation that, for ages, has been going on without him.

To enter such a conversation requires intellectual effort. For Tom to exert such effort, the question of God's existence must sufficiently matter to him. Does it? At the moment, probably not. Tom further tells us that in addition to seeing no physical evidence for God, he has no personal experience of God. Without any personal experience of God, why should the question of God's existence be a priority for Tom? More likely, God's existence remains an academic issue of little relevance to Tom's life. Tom does not investigate God's existence because Tom does not currently experience God's existence as a pressing issue in his life.

Tom reflects the general dynamic I spoke of at the opening of this book. We asked there whether the retreat from transcendental horizons is due principally to a contemporary skepticism about ultimate truths. I denied that this was the case. I argued instead that our skepticism about ultimate meaning itself already reflects our emotional retreat from meaning. The emotional retreat comes first, the skepticism second. Over the course of this book, we have documented the emotional retreat. It remains to see the skepticism unfounded. Now we will see that if we reason together from our disparate experiences, we can move closer to ultimate truth. We simply need to expend the effort. When we do, we enter critical space, the space of argument and counterargument.

There are two things Tom Brown lacks. He lacks emotional connection with ultimate reality, which he believes to be God. Tom also lacks an ability to say whether or not this belief about ultimate reality is true.

Both these needs are availed by what sociologists call communities of discourse.[1] A community of discourse on a topic is a community that maintains a conversation on that topic. For example, philosophers of religion constitute a community of discourse that collectively assesses the evidence for and against God's existence. The discourse of this community is an evaluative one of argument and counterargument.

Not all discourses are disputative, and communities of discourse serve functions other than evaluation. More basically, a community of discourse may provide us with the initial vocabulary we need even to identify and talk about a phenomenon.

Tom suggests that he believes in God merely because he was brought up to believe, that he is more or less just mindlessly following the programming of his childhood. Tom may be right. There may be no more to Tom's belief in God than habit. On the other hand, Tom's persistent belief in God despite his doubts might also rest on something that Tom just lacks the vocabulary to express—even to himself.

We have seen that there is a sort of power inherent in names. The ability to name is the ability to fix the flux of reality and order it. Through names, we first take cognitive charge of the reality in which we find ourselves. Through names, we are able to pick out a piece of reality and examine it with heightened awareness.[2]

A vocabulary of names is the first service to us that a community of discourse provides. Vocabularies are not developed in isolation. There are no private languages. If the ability to name heightens awareness, such heightened awareness comes only from the discourse or talk of a community. Accordingly, those isolated from all communities of discourse on a topic will be without a vocabulary relevant to that topic and consequently without the heightened awareness on that topic such a vocabulary allows.

A vocabulary does more than just heighten our awareness of what it initially names. By enabling us to reflect on what is named, a vocabulary also enables us to see new relationships and develop new concepts. A vocabulary thus becomes a conceptual floor on which further thought can be built.

A vocabulary avails even more. As our conceptual understanding deepens, so does the range of what is possible for us to experience. By expanding our vocabularies, communities of discourse become vehicles through which new experiences become possible as well. We saw that fundamentalist Christianity is a community of discourse that affords the experience of personal salvation through Jesus. Because this experience requires a certain conceptual framework for it even to be interpreted as such, it is not an experience that is generally available outside a fundamentalist or evangelical community of discourse.

Although communities of discourse avail emotionally strong experiences of the ultimate, an experience of the ultimate is only one of the two things I suggested Tom Brown lacks. The other is an ability to assess critically whether or not our beliefs about the ultimate truly follow from whatever we experience of the ultimate. This, too, can be done only in communion with others, especially with *haverim*, study partners who challenge us to consider what we might otherwise neglect.

Is critical evaluation really necessary? Is it not enough that together with one or another community we hear the call of the ultimate and so raise our sights to transcendental horizons?

Certainly, throughout this book I have been championing the need to raise our vision to ultimate horizons, but no, I do not think it enough to do simply that. My point all along has not been that we all should find one or another faith that suits us. Nor has it been that we all should just become more community-minded or root ourselves in the consensus values of our community. All along, I have been after bigger game.

If I have been calling for larger vision it is because I think there is an ultimate meaning to our existence and because, like Jason Fishman, I believe that one thing we all were meant to do here is search out what that meaning is. Our distinct communities are but a vehicle toward that end, not the ultimate object of our search. When we come to the end of our search, it will be the truth that sets us free. Not faith or just community consensus.

If not by consensus, how do we know the truth? On this earth even in community, we see only in part as through a glass darkly. To correct our vision we need *haverim*, especially *haverim* from different communities with different experiences of the ultimate. Even with *haverim*, we can never know the truth infallibly. What we can do is argue our way to the soundest conclusion so far and remain ever open to new arguments that will take us farther still. It is a demanding task and one that we must do together. Yet if we truly take seriously our beliefs about the ultimate, we cannot neglect to scrutinize them in critical space.

There are two things then that remain for us to do. We must see how communities of discourse afford certain sacred experiences it is otherwise difficult to have, and we must see how in communion with others we can reason our way to truth even about ultimate matters—even about Jesus and even about God.

THE PRIMACY OF EXPERIENCE

Beliefs, experiences, and emotions are all interconnected. Beliefs afford certain emotional experiences that in turn foster and expand our beliefs. Over time, however, it is the emotional experience that becomes the driving element. If the emotional experience withers, the associated beliefs become shaky as well.[3] This primacy of experience is illustrated by my conversation with Hannah Gottlieb, who, as the religion director of a synagogue, draws on the rich vocabulary of the Jewish tradition.

I tell Hannah that I want to talk with her about God. "You believe in God?"

"Believe is the wrong word," Hannah tells me.

"Okay."

"I think," Hannah continues, "*believe* is what kills it for everybody. I experience God. And I'm a strong believer in...what Judaism has done, what everybody has done—you know? We talked about it—post-Holocaust science. Everything has to be proven. That's belief. You know, prove it to me. That's belief.

"That's not faith. That's like believe and skip over it. What I try to do for the kids in the school, what I feel like I've done for myself is experience God and offer people opportunities to experience God.

"I could tell you all about love—oh, it's about flowers, it makes me feel warm, and it's nice. But once you're in love, you know. Same thing with God. I could tell you all about it. It will help you if I tell you. It will help you if I do this and that.

"But once you've had that experience...Ah! And you talk to people who have had that experience. They know."

I nod. What Hannah is attempting to express is what I am attempting to express. I try to enlist her help in my endeavor. "Well, what does it mean to experience God? How do you experience God, and how do you help people have the opportunity to experience God?"

Hannah laughs. "God. You know, it's like you're going to take a button out, and it's all going to go 'whoosh.' There's just so much. So I'll try to speak logically.

"There's two questions then. One is how have I done it. The other is how do you help other people do it."

"Okay," I say. "Start with how you have done it."

"Okay. Start with there is a God, I believe in God, young teen. Mother dies at nineteen. Within a week, there is no God. That didn't pull me away from Judaism, but it's clear that there is no God.

"And then you see this slow path of coming back to something else. Like, the first thing is to get rid of this image that God is this master—the puppeteer kind of thing. So that's real good *never* to give to anybody.

"And we try not to give that to our children. I remember when I first got into Jewish education, the rabbi said, 'Be very careful. Do not create God as the white-bearded man on the mountain who, when you need someone, miracles will come.' Because that is a guarantee to turn people off.

"So the first thing is to get rid of childhood baggage. That's something that children generally create themselves. That's a connection that children are able to identify."

"What's the connection?"

"That image. That's the connection. We know that image. Kids create that for themselves. So when my young son comes in and he's trying to tell me that God parted the Red Sea, and I'm trying to tell him, 'Well, there are other ways to understand that; we don't have to understand that literally,' he's telling me I'm wrong, you know? So that's one problem. Kids are very concrete."

Thus, just as there are beliefs that permit deeper experience, there are beliefs as well that hinder it. Part of what communities do is accumulate the wisdom to discern the difference. Hannah goes on.

"So that's one thing—to get rid of that. So where do I go? I did get involved in Jewish education, and one thing I did was become a teacher, both of children and adults. And in my adult teaching, I began to learn.

"We read together as a group of adults for a long time."

I nod. Hannah is describing the creation of a mini-community of discourse.

She goes on. "Like, we began to look at the Bible. And one of the questions that everybody came to as adults was, Is there a God? You know? And they're looking at the texts for an answer.

"And the answer they saw in the texts was really the opposite of what they would be comfortable with. It would lead someone not to believe in God. It was inconsistent with what you could be comfortable with.

"But through that process of study—and I can't pinpoint how it happened, windows of connecting...links—let me just say—like, little sparks of connection to this God force started happening. Why? By hearing the words of the text—now, I do not believe that these are the words of God. You were talking about biblical criticism. I don't think these are literally the words.

"I think it is the possibility that this has helped people experience God and try to put it into words. The Jewish notion that these words are metaphoric and not representation of what actually happened.

"Another thing that we did—and this was, like, a critical moment for me. Prayer is another thing that alienates people to no end. We decided that every morning and every night, we would say the Shema, which is the prayer that God is One.

"And in this group, we did that. And in this process of doing this every morning and every night, I knew that everybody in my group was doing it. I knew that I was doing it.

"And I had this wonderful experience that went through time and space and was like...touching a force that really went through time and space. And it was so neat to me. And I've spoken to other people who through other moments have been able to do that. So that was really a very pivotal moment of experience."

The experience Hannah describes is not new to sociologists. The sense of transhistorical, trans-spatial connection achieved by shared ritual is real and powerful. Durkheim said it is the experience of community itself, making God just the external symbol of community.[4] It is a naturalistic bias, however, to assume necessarily that what Hannah experiences here is only the bond of her own community and not also something more ultimate.[5] Perhaps the experience of community is but a window of connection to something larger yet, the God force Hannah suggests or the entire comos itself.[6] Community may be like a telescope, concentrating and focusing energy that typically remains too faint for us to detect on our own. In that case, community is but a vehicle for connection with ultimate reality, not the ultimate reality itself. Hannah goes on to illustrate how a religious community of discourse can further attune its members to experience ultimate reality.

"There is," Hannah says, "an exercise that we do with the kids in the school: 'Everybody eat the snack!' You know? 'Just shove the food in your mouth, and everybody eat it. Go ahead.'

"Okay? Then, we give everybody the same snack, and we say, 'Now, say a *brucha*, say a blessing—and then eat the snack. Okay? Now, we're going to compare and contrast those two experiences.'

"'Oh,'" says Hannah, mimicking the children's response.

She then resumes speaking as as if she were an adult teacher. "'What's the difference when you stop to connect to this force when you're doing this snack? What's your experience like as opposed to...It's the same thing living life.'

"This is what Judaism does. You're supposed to say a hundred blessings a day in Jewish life. Well, I don't say a hundred blessings. The point of the hundred blessings is that in everything you do and touch, this is a way to experience God."

What Hannah is telling us is crucially important to a proper understanding of religion's potential. Religion is potentially a vehicle through which we can connect with another plane of existence.

Done with the right understanding, the Jewish blessings are not pro forma, mechanical rituals. Nor are they merely devotions to the creator taken to obsessive excess. Done with the right understanding, the blessings are not even performed primarily for the creator. Primarily, they are performed for ourselves—to sensitize ourselves to a certain experience of cosmic connection. In creating that connection, the blessings sacramentalize ordinary, otherwise meaningless acts into holy occasions to celebrate meaning and experience who we really are. As sensitizing devices, the blessings and the exercise belong to a whole spiritual technology culturally developed by the Jewish community of discourse.

Hannah herself goes on to say the same thing. "Judaism," she says, "creates this notion of, you know, experiencing God. The blessing is only the technique, the vehicle to help you do that."

Is God truly what is being experienced here? This is a theological question that requires examination in critical space. We cannot just dismiss the possibility. It does not follow from the social effort religious experience requires that the object of religious experience is just what sociologists would term a social construction—a projection of the

group. To experience a marijuana high also requires social attune-
ment, but no one would deny that marijuana also has a real, independent effect that one only learns to detect. So it may be with
religion. In that case, religious experience would be better described
not as a social construction but as a social achievement.[7]

We have seen that when it comes to values, many people are inar-
ticulate. It is not so much that they lack values. What they tend to lack
as a result of their dissociation from any community of discourse on
values is a certain valuational depth. Many people's values tend to be
conventional and superficial and unrooted in any larger sense of
meaning. In contrast, Hannah's values have layers, through all of
which she is able to say who she is within a grander, cosmic order.

"You said," I say to Hannah, "the values of Judaism were charity,
helping others..."

"There're many, many, many...There are so many..."

"Where do the values of Judaism come from?"

"They come from two places. One, you would say, it begins with
law, with the *mitzvot*. That's the term. And it is said that in the Torah,
there are 613 *mitzvot*. Laws like you don't put a weak animal...you
don't yoke a weak animal and a strong animal together to pull. So
that's one place. So what do you learn from that? To be thoughtful and
kind to animals. Okay? So that's one place where values come from."

"They come out of the law?"

"They come out of the laws that were stated in the Torah. And
then what the Jewish tradition did was...They needed to understand
and expand on that. And that's where you get rabbinics. That's where
you get Talmud and all the rest.

"That's one expansion. Then, there's mysticism. One of the values
we're throwing around in school this year is called *tikkun olam*, mend-
ing the world. Where did that come from? It came from the mystics
who had this notion of God and light and of containers, and it's broken and you have to mend it, whatever.

"So where do Jewish values come from? It's this wonderful...They
call it a chain of tradition. You know, it's rooted in law, and then it's
just layers and layers built...And part of what we try to do in the school
is...Our kids get great, humanist values, you know? So what we do for
them is help them put it within a Jewish theology, a Jewish framework...which is really important."

Hannah ends with a comment that takes me aback. It so powerfully confirms what I have been saying about the cosmogonic origin of
values that it is almost as if I had put Hannah up to saying it. What

Hannah explains to me is how her personal values are more than just an expression of her individual personality but, rather, an embodiment of something greater.

"When I'm nice to you," Hannah tells me, "it's not just because I'm a nice person. I get to connect somebody to a much bigger picture. One, I'm nice to you because for thousands of years, that's my tradition, and also by being nice to you, I get to create something...I get to create a light, and I also get a window to connect to the force of God."

In the end, religious communities of discourse afford more than just discourse. They additionally afford the possibility to experience emotionally realities generally inaccessible outside a group and more specifically inaccessible outside a religious group. Because the experiences afforded by a religious community are specifically experiences of the ultimate, they are charged with the power to morally unify a life.

As important to us as these deeply emotional experiences may be, we still must wonder whether they are not all just social constructions, illusory group effects. I have resisted the sociological tendency to make them so by definition.[8] Yet they could still turn out to be so in fact. Like Tom Brown, we all must retain some doubts. If we care about the truth about what we experience, then we must subject our experiences to critical scrutiny. In that undertaking, communities of discourse again assume a central place.

CRITICAL SPACE

How do we know whether a religious experience reveals a deeper truth about our existence or whether instead our experience is just an effect of more mundane social processes? All our experiences have the feel of revealed truth. Yet we know that what our various religious experiences seem to reveal cannot all be true if only because so many of these supposed revelations conflict. They cannot all be entirely true simultaneously.

To assess the truth of what we personally experience, we cannot remain at the level of our own personal experience. As each of our own personal experiences is fallible, we must each submit our personal experiences to the scrutiny of public argument. Christian physicist Sandra Moreno says as much when I ask her about doubt.

"Do you ever doubt?" I ask her. "It sounds like your Christian beliefs are really founded on some sort of deep personal experience."

"That's what started..."

"Okay."

"But—but if that's where it stays, then what is…My experience is no better than anybody's else's experiences, and I have to believe that what I have found is true. And so how do I know that it is something more than just, 'Well, this feels good to me and that feels good to you, and we'll just all kind of go together?'"

Sandra's comment illustrates the point I made about Tom Brown at the opening of this chapter. Because Tom lacks any personal experience of God, his belief in God is not emotionally compelling enough to motivate him to ascertain the truth of his belief. Because, in contrast, Sandra does experience an emotionally fulfilling relationship with God, she has a pressing need to satisfy herself that what she experiences is real. Thus, at bottom, what makes Sandra different from Tom in relation to God is less intellectual style than a difference in emotional experience.

"I've looked into the evidence in the Bible," Sandra goes on. "You can look at many different manuscripts, evidence for how it was transmitted, and my belief is, I believe, along with other Christians, that it was transmitted by God—through man, that man was the one that wrote it down on the papyrus or whatever and it got copied over thousands of years and transmitted.

"And if you look at all…When I've taken some time to study that, you look at all the different evidence, and there is a long tradition of, for example, in the Jewish…Early on in the Old Testament, the tribe, the tribal condition and everything, it's very solid."

I am not entirely sure what Sandra means by solid. If she means that the Bible is not simply a collection of fables and folklore, that it contains genuine history as well, she is right. On the other hand, of course, the Bible does contain its share of myth and fables and, in addition, even where it purports to be historical, its share of historical inaccuracies as well.

"It's very, very solid," Sandra continues, "and the New Testament documents are more solid than, as far as I know, other documents from the same period. We have tremendous, excellent evidence that Jesus Christ existed and that he did what the Bible says."

Again, I would agree that the evidence for Jesus's historical existence is quite strong. I would further agree that we also have considerable evidence that Jesus did in fact say and do much of what the Gospels record him saying and doing. On the other hand, and I am not sure what Sandra would say about this, we also have compelling historical evidence that Jesus actually did not say and do quite a number of the things the Gospels report of him.

"There are," Sandra continues, "eyewitness accounts, consistent...And if you look at other manuscripts within the hundred or thousand years around that time, the biblical evidence...Actually, there's more of a record that has survived than for any of the Greek tragedies or the histories of Rome and Greece.

"They have a fragment the gospel of John, dated around 125 A.D., which is the earliest fragment of the gospel of John. And that's less than a hundred years after Jesus's death, and so that is a pretty short span of time. So the short period of time between when the events happened and when the fragment was written is pretty small."

What is striking about Sandra is that she has submitted her personal experience of Jesus to public argument. Although not a biblical critic herself, she has listened in on the discourse of biblical scholars. Biblical scholars form an epistemic community of discourse.[9] An epistemic community is one that maintains an ongoing, evaluative discourse on one or another aspect of reality.

The nature of evaluative discourse is argumentative. On empirical matters, there are never any deductive proofs that establish truth with absolute certainty. Instead, there is only a preponderance of the evidence on behalf of one claim or another. Establishing a preponderance of evidence is a community undertaking. It takes an entire community to advance different points of view. It takes a community to attack and defend all the different lines of argument until it eventually becomes clear which are untenable dead ends and which continue successfully to resist counterattack. The arguments themselves achieve a social facticity in the critical space the epistemic community maintains. Like tangible lines of force, the arguments must be considered by both partisans and antagonists of any position.[10] Over time, the members of an epistemic community come to know which arguments and evidence are strong and which are weak.

All of this can take a great deal of time. A frequent complaint of students taking undergraduate philosophy is that by the end of the course, they have been offered no resolution to any of the issues to which they have been introduced. They easily reach the conclusion that philosophical argument can never resolve anything, that for any argument, there is always an equal and opposite counterargument.

The students fail to realize that on the issues to which they have been introduced, they have been exposed only to the opening moves. They are like novices at chess who have been taught the standard lines for a range of openings, each consisting of just the first twelve moves. Naturally, the first twelve moves of any chess game will determine neither a winner nor even the strongest opening. To determine the latter requires a great number of games with many promising lines ruled out only by playing to the end. In this regard, intellectual debate is much like a chess game. It takes time and multiple players.

In the end, not even the consensus of an epistemic community establishes the truth once and for all. A consensus only represents the community's best judgment so far. Sometimes, that best judgment is later overturned. Sometimes, it is the dissenters who were right all along. Community consensus does not decide the truth like some kind of fiat. What is true is a determination we each must make for ourselves—with or against a consensus. And yet it is not a decision we rationally make on our own. To decide what the truth is, we need others for the same reason we need others to learn how to play chess effectively. We need to test our arguments against other members of an epistemic community so that we can see for ourselves which of our beliefs hold up under fire and which instead need to be revised or abandoned.

When we find ourselves isolated from an epistemic community's discourse on a topic, we are generally unaware of the powerful lines of argumentative force already trained on that topic. At most, we have experienced only episodic conversations that failed to resolve anything. Accordingly, we come to believe mistakenly that no progress on the topic is at all possible.

On ultimate matters, Peter Nighting finds himself in this position. As a computer analyst, Peter is well connected to technical discourses relating to computer information systems. When it comes to God, values, and religion, however, he has been discursively isolated.

When our formal interview ends, Peter and I continue to talk about what can be known about ultimate matters. "You can't even know," Peter tells me, "whether Jesus really existed."

I raise my eyebrows. "Yes, we can know that. I think it is almost certain that Jesus existed."

I go on to tell Peter that our beliefs are not just preferences because there are better or worse arguments for our beliefs. The weight of argument adds up for or against the beliefs we might prefer.

Peter grabs a book and holds it up. "Jesus's existence will never be as certain as the existence of this book. And if you cannot have that level of certainty, the effort isn't worth it."

I concede some ground to Peter. "That may be, but we can know of Jesus's existence with somewhat less certainty, say seventy percent. We can be seventy percent certain."

"That's not good enough," Peter replies, "because some doubt will always remain."

Peter's argument is significant. When it comes to matters of ultimate concern—the existence of Jesus, for example—Peter seems suddenly to adopt an absolutist criterion of truth. This is a criterion we do not normally employ in other contexts. Of course, we always search for greater certainty on issues of importance to us. However, if we expect to achieve absolute certainty, we never will find it. Because Peter has decided that on questions of ultimate significance it is absolute certainty we need, he considers fruitless any effort to explore such questions. Instead, they remain for Peter just matters of faith to be decided by one's preferences. Ironically, it is Peter's absolutist criterion of truth that leaves him radically skeptical about ultimate matters. Accordingly, Peter rarely thinks about ultimate questions. Peter's mistake is widely shared.

One mistake Peter makes is trying to consider the question of Jesus's existence in an argumentative void. As always, the proper question is comparative: How strong are the reasons for thinking Jesus actually lived in comparison with the reasons for denying Jesus's historical existence? Of course, to assess these reasons comparatively, one first needs to be aware of them. Such awareness comes only if we at least listen in on the scholarly discussion about Jesus. If we do not listen in on that discussion, it will likely appear to us, as it does to Peter, that there is nothing we can say beyond what we individually prefer to believe.

I suggest to Peter that he revise his criterion of truth. "Are you," I ask him, "as certain about the truth of evolution or of electrons as you are about the existence of that book?" I tell Peter that although I am less sure of evolution and electrons than I am of the book's existence, I am still fairly sure of both.

Peter is taken aback by the question. "Well, now, I don't know about evolution, but I am sure electrons exist."

"How do you know electrons exist?"

"Because you can see them."

I assure Peter that no one has ever seen an electron and that in fact electrons may not be there to be seen. What has been seen are the traces of electrons—signals on an oscilloscope.

Peter finds this extremely unsettling and wonders now whether he should believe in electrons. This was not my intention, and I again advise him to adopt a different criterion of truth. What Peter fails to see is that through argument with others, a social process, we can challenge each other to consider the preponderance of evidence and so come to a better take on the truth. We can manage to change and even unsettle each other through argument. Argument has just had this effect on Peter himself.

WHAT CAN WE KNOW ABOUT THE HISTORICAL JESUS?

Whereas Sandra considers the biblical account of Jesus very solid, Peter is radically skeptical of our ability to know anything about Jesus. Is their difference of opinion just a matter of rival faiths, Sandra's belief in Jesus versus Peter's disbelief? That is the common assumption, that about ultimate matters there are no grounds for saying anything persuasive to one another. This is an assumption to hide behind. If there are no grounds for rational argument about the ultimate truths we hold, then everyone is safe. We can each be left to believe what we want without challenge. Of course we are also left not taking very seriously our beliefs in those ultimate truths.

For this reason, I want to unmask this assumption. I want to show that about Jesus or about God there is plenty we can rationally say to each other that could potentially alter what we believe. That leaves us in a much more dangerous world. It means the beliefs we grew up with might be wrong—either wholly or at least in part. If so, then by daring to question, we could potentially lose our faith or watch it alter in unforeseen ways. Yet if we truly are serious about Jesus or God, then it is the truth about them we should desire and not just what we find implanted in our heads. The quest for truth is a journey many of us have too long delayed.

One of the people I had an opportunity to interview was Hal Taussig, a distinguished biblical scholar and founding member of the Jesus Seminar.[11] The Jesus Seminar began as a group of liberal biblical critics who met to reach consensus on what we can know about the historical Jesus. One of its recent publications, *The Five Gospels*, includes, in addition to the four canonical gospels, the noncanonical gospel of Thomas.[12] One of the seminar's controversial claims is that the gospel of Thomas contains as much history about Jesus as the canonical four.

What makes *The Five Gospels* so controversial, however, is not just its inclusion of the gospel of Thomas. In *The Five Gospels*, every gospel saying attributed to Jesus is color-coded to indicate the seminar's assessment of that saying's historicity. The colors range from red (a saying that almost certainly goes back to Jesus); through pink (a saying that Jesus probably said something like) and gray (a saying close to Jesus's thought); to black (a saying that almost certainly *does not* go back to Jesus).

The membership of the Jesus Seminar actually votes on how a saying of Jesus is to be colored, and only about twenty percent of the
gospel sayings are colored red. The seminar's practice of voting on the
Bible appears blasphemous to fundamentalist Christians, and even
many non-fundamentalist scholars have deep reservations about it.
Accordingly, the procedures and criteria of the Jesus Seminar have
been attacked from a whole range of perspectives.[13]

In effect, the seminar represents the skeptical wing of professional
biblical scholarship. Yet even it concedes that at least twenty percent of
what the Bible records Jesus as saying he actually did say. If he said all
that, plus more that the Bible merely paraphrases, then clearly Jesus
must have existed. The truth, we see, may be somewhere in between
what either Sandra or Peter believes. Should both seek further truth,
both may have to change their views in crucial ways.

The seminar's coding of the words attributed to Jesus in the Bible
is not done at whim. The seminar scholars employ established criteria,
most of which are accepted by all professional biblical scholars. The
gospels, for example, contain memories from multiple traditions that
differ in age. All things being equal, it is generally agreed, a greater
claim to authenticity attaches to a saying found in an earlier rather
than a later stratum of tradition. Similarly, if a saying is attested by
more than one independent tradition, it also has a greater claim to
authenticity. Sayings that are both early and multiply attested are
among the most likely to go back to the historical Jesus.

As I begin my interview with Hal, I have Peter Nighting in mind.
"People think we really can't know anything about Jesus. Isn't it all a
matter of faith?"

"Well," Hal responds, "I personally believe we can know some. And
what we've worked on collectively over the past ten-plus years in the Jesus
Seminar illustrates a cautious approach to what one can say in good conscience as historians about the historical person of Jesus. And so, yeah, I
think we can say some things. It would be nice if we could say more.

"But we can say some things—and you know, that is within the relativity of all knowledge. But what we can say about the historical Jesus,
right now, is at least as reliable as the morning newspaper."

"Say that again." I'm not sure I heard Hal correctly.

"What historians can say about the historical Jesus is, I think, at
least as reliable as the morning newspaper. Now—and I hope you get
the irony of that."

I laugh, and Hal laughs with me. I do get the irony. Nevertheless,
I ask Hal to explain.

"What I read in the newspaper every morning is...I have some trust in and some skepticism about. So, you know, when I read it, I assume that about seventy percent of it is very reliable and you know the rest of it is somewhere between not reliable at all and yet to be determined. So, I would claim that what historians can say about Jesus is similar."

"Well," I continue. " Can I push you on a specific question?"

"Absolutely."

"What is the most certain thing we know about Jesus?"

"That he was crucified."

"And how do we know that? Why is that so reliable?"

"Well, there are a number of sources from within Christianity and from outside of Christianity that tell us that. It is something that people would not have been proud of. There are a whole bunch of noble death traditions in the hellenistic Mediterranean, where you tell a story of someone who died to make them look noble, and there are a bunch of things within the stories about the death of Jesus that rely on the noble death tradition...but you wouldn't want to enhance somebody's death by putting him on the cross. It was one of the most ignominious ways of dying. Also, if you were in the line of followers of somebody like that, it immediately held you in suspicion with the imperial government because crucifixion was the explicit punishment for insurrection. So in other words, multiple sources and the fact that it's not something of which legends are made."

"Obviously," I comment, "multiple sources here mean as well as gospel sources, extra-canonical sources."

"Yeah, right. We have very little outside of Christianity that talks about Jesus directly, but in this case we do. We have the Jewish historian, Josephus, and, perhaps, a Roman historical record that says he was crucified. And then we have the letters of Paul. The sayings gospel of *Q* alludes to crucifixion and all of the noncanonical gospels, and...Oh, and the noncanonical gospel of Peter. All have Jesus crucified."[14]

I press Hal further. "It also sounds like you were alluding to the criterion of embarrassment?"

"Right."

"I sort of had gotten the impression that the Jesus Seminar...that the scholars associated with the Jesus Seminar were reluctant to use that, that they emphasized more multiple textuality."

"No," Hal answers, "I would say both of them are reasons. Yeah, there is a criterion of embarrassment."

The criterion of embarrassment refers to any event that would have embarrassed the early church—such as Jesus's baptism by John or the accusation that Jesus was in league with the devil. Many scholars consider such events likely to be historical on the grounds that the church would hardly have gone out of its way to invent any event so embarrassing as to require damage control. According to Hal, the crucifixion itself meets this criterion.

"Well, let me ask you this. Fundamentalists would say, 'Aren't you just picking and choosing what in the Bible you will accept?' How would you respond to that?"

"Right. Well, first with appreciation. By saying, 'Yes, on some level we are.' But of course fundamentalists pick and choose all the time—as to what they emphasize and what they don't.

"So in appreciation of that I would want to say, 'Yeah, we all do.' And any hard or social scientist who says they aren't is fooling themselves. You do pick and choose. That's a tendency everyone…Nevertheless, there is something you can do to subdue that tendency, and biblical scholarship—mainstream biblical scholarship—has a number of ways of trying to reduce the tendency of scholars to pick and choose. But they do."

I nod at Hal. "Well, I understand why you responded like that, but I'm sort of surprised. It seems as if you are not just picking and choosing, you are picking and choosing according to criteria."

"Right," Hal affirms.

I continue. "In preparation for this interview, I was reading *The Five Gospels* and noticed that…one of my favorite passages in the Bible is the "sheep and the goats…"

"Right."

"It was colored black!"

Hal laughs. "It's a great passage."

The passage about the sheep and the goats appears in the twenty-fifth chapter of Matthew's gospel. It concerns the last judgment, in which Jesus separates the sheep from the goats, those who recognized Jesus in the poor and oppressed and those who did not. It is a passage for social activists. However, its being labeled black means Jesus likely never said it, that it was probably a creation of the early church.

"I was," I say, "charmed but dispirited to see the note that this was a passage the scholars all agreed they wished Jesus had said."

Hal laughs again. "Yeah, exactly."

What the note illustrates is very important. Despite their personal preferences, the scholars of the Jesus Seminar reject the historicity of the saying about the sheep and the goats. Thus, however individually we assess the truth, our own personal preference is not the final arbiter. On the contrary, there are times when with courage we must admit to ourselves that what we would prefer to be true is not. The very admission acknowledges truth as something independent of us.

I continue to press this point with Hal. "So, I mean, we don't just pick and choose at whim."

"Oh, of course. Yes, right. No, not at all. According to criteria. But I just have to say it is one of the most fundamental dimensions of current historical work to be conscious of your own relativity. It seems to me that it's time historians stopped pretending total objectivity. We have relative objectivity.[15]

"And yes, we have criteria that we establish that try to reduce our tendency to pick and choose. But we in fact do. And I would say that in twenty-five years, if you look at the criteria...Twenty-five years from now, if you looked at the criteria that we established in the Jesus Seminar, we would notice some cultural bias that we ended up having. Now, we think they're perfect."

As I listen to Hal, I wonder what Peter Nighting would say about all this. Would he dismiss the efforts of the Jesus Seminar because its knowledge is only relatively objective? Then again, what would postmodernist philosophers say?

There are strong reasons for thinking that Jesus lived and was crucified. There is multiple attestation from both within and without Christianity about the crucifixion, some of which goes back very early after Jesus's death. In addition, we must consider that the crucifixion would initially have been embarrassing to Jesus's followers and therefore not something they would have been likely to invent had it not actually happened.

Against all these considerations, what are the reasons for denying that Jesus was crucified? Just radical skepticism? Certainly, in this terrain there are no deductive proofs that establish absolute certainty. It hardly follows, however, that no rational judgment is possible. Even in the absence of a deductive proof, we can still evaluate the weight of rival arguments. In this case, the preponderance of evidence falls heavily on the side of Jesus's crucifixion and his historical existence.

Is There Physical Evidence of God?

Perhaps in the end we might not consider it so remarkable that we can establish certain facts about the historical Jesus. Even if Jesus did live 2,000 years ago, we are still considering the life of a human being. It is wholly another matter when we turn our attention to God. Are there really any considerations we could count as evidence for or against the existence of God?

Again, we will never be able to prove deductively with absolute certainty that God either does or does not *exist*. No empirical truth can be so proven. At most, we will have to content ourselves once again with a preponderance of the evidence.

So far, on the question of God, we do not yet have even any preponderance of publicly observable evidence. That being the case, believers and disbelievers alike are rationally justified in placing at least initial trust in their private experiences.[16] Those who experience God's presence have good grounds to place the burden of proof on atheists. Those who experience God's absence are equally justified rationally in placing the burden of proof on theists.

Things do not stay static, however. Theists and atheists both should be ever watchful to see whether the other side's burden of proof actually is being borne. Although no definitive conclusion can yet be drawn, the current evidence is enough to disconcert both believers and disbelievers alike. Among other places, this evidence has surfaced in physical cosmology, the discipline that studies the origin and development of our universe.

I explore the issue with physicist Sandra Moreno, who did some important early work in this area. I tell Sandra that among the people I interviewed, most are only vaguely aware of new developments in cosmology and that most see little relation between their own lives and what caused the big bang fifteen billion years ago. I ask her whether she sees any relation between cosmology and the ultimate questions of our lives.

"Myself," Sandra answers, "I do think that, and I think that it's funny. I was just looking over something, thinking about your questions last night. I looked over Stephen Weinberg's book, *Dreams of a Final Theory*.[17] It's fascinating. There's a chapter in there called, 'What About God?' And he is groping and grappling with these things, and one of his interesting remarks was that many scientists don't think there's any relationship at all. And I think that there are some scientists that feel that way.

"It's very interesting. I was totally unaware. I'm amazed that I have been so unaware of these questions since I was a child. I mean, I've been interested in cosmology, I've been fascinated by it, and I don't really think I ever really made the conscious statement that it has to do with who we are and where we came from, but it's always been there.

"I mean, and it's very clear that to a lot of people, it's a very important issue.[18] And what we're doing, what the cosmologists have found—the people who do the data, that do the observations and along with it the people that do theoretical work—have found that all the data and all the theories that agree with the data point to the creation of the universe. A beginning.

"And if there is a beginning, then who started this?"

"Say that again."

"If there is a beginning, who started it?"

"Um…" Sandra is asking the philosophical question once asked by Leibniz: Why is there something rather than nothing?

"There is," Sandra continues, "there is this 'problem of the initial conditions.' And it seems to me now, I never thought that there was a problem. I always just assumed that God did it."

"You did? You…"

"Oh, yeah. I always just sort of assumed like, What do you mean? I can't believe that I'm so dense that people were…Of course, there's a problem. The problem with the big bang model is the initial conditions. I said, 'Well, what problem?' You know? I never could understand why people had a problem with that. I mean…"

"When you say people, you mean physicists?"

"Oh, the people at my…my colleagues. There is a general sense of a problem of the initial conditions, and I think that the problem comes from…The theory can't explain it. In other words, if there is an initial state, the theory can't somehow explain the initial state. It can't explain the beginning."

One point Sandra is making is that physics cannot explain why there is a universe at all. That question remains only in the background if we assume the universe has always existed. The question becomes salient when the evidence becomes overwhelming, as it is now, that the entire universe originated out of nothing at a particular point in time. Why did it do so? This is one question, Sandra suggests, that has her fellow physicists disconcerted.

The temporally contingent nature of our universe is not its only disconcerting feature. Even more disconcerting is the growing appreciation that ours is not just any old universe. On the contrary, to the hard-nosed physicists who study it, this universe of ours looks increasingly as if it had been designed. And if it was designed, must there not be a designer? No wonder physical cosmologists today often speak of uncovering the fingerprints of God.

That design proves a designer is one of the classic arguments for the existence of God. Early on, we heard it cited by Iris Barbuda. There I said that the argument from design did not deductively prove God's existence. The argument from design was originally applied to the biological order. It was observed that the component parts of organisms all seem carefully designed to work together for the survival of the whole. Insofar as biological organisms seem constructed according to a purpose, did this not imply a designer who purposely constructed them this way? Not necessarily, which is why the argument from design cannot be considered a deductive proof. What Darwin showed is that such apparent design can be achieved without a purposeful designer. It can equally be achieved through the principle of natural selection. Although today there are some biochemical considerations suggesting that not all design can be dismissed from biology, a preponderance of evidence has certainly accumulated for natural selection as a general mechanism for biological evolution.[19]

After Darwin, the philosophical consensus considered the argument from design demolished. Until now. From the ashes, the argument from design has arisen anew, this time from observations in physics. We see here why all our knowledge remains provisional—or, as Hal Taussig put it, only "relatively objective"—and why even consensus cannot be equated with truth. Because the truth remains separate even from community consensus, we can never rest easy with what we think we know but must remain ever open to new arguments.

What are the elements of design in the universe? The nature of the universe is determined by its basic parameters—the strengths of forces and the masses and charges of fundamental particles. Theoretically, these parameters could all have had values very different from what they actually are. What we actually see, however, are what physicists call "anthropic coincidences." It turns out that were any of a great number of the universe's parameters even minutely different, we would not be here. There would be no life not just on earth but anywhere in the universe.

The existence of stars like our sun, for example, depends on certain delicate balances such as that between the forces of electromagnetism and gravity, which is 10^{39} times weaker. A balance between two forces of such vastly different magnitudes is itself an indication of astonishing sensitivity.[20]

Yet such a balance is critical to our existence. Were gravity only slightly weaker or electromagnetisim only slightly stronger, stars like our sun could not exist. Instead, all stars would be red dwarfs. With similarly slight changes in the other direction, all stars would be blue giants. Neither red dwarfs nor blue giants are hospitable to life.

We would also have ended up either with all red dwarfs or blue giants if the electron-proton mass ratio differed only slightly. As it happens, the electron is about one ten-thousandth as massive as the proton. An electron only slightly less massive would have produced all red dwarfs, and an electron only slightly more massive would have produced all blue giants.[21]

It is truly startling that something as gigantic as a star could depend on a balance between particles as infinitesimal as the electron and proton—a proton, after all, is only one ten-trillionth of a centimeter in size. Yet, there are still other examples like this. The universe would contain none of the chemical building blocks of life if the neutron did not outweigh the the proton by a tenth of a percent—approximately the mass of two electrons.

That all the universe's many parameters just happen to coincide to make life possible cannot be due to chance. That any one parameter alone happens to turn out right is astronomically improbable. That by chance alone they all simultaneously turned out right defies belief. It has been estimated that the odds against the pattern we actually see are greater than one followed by a billion trillion zeros.[22]

As our appreciation of the anthropic coincidences deepens, we begin to see why atheists should be disconcerted. It does almost appear as if intelligent life were meant to be here. Astronomer Fred Hoyle was prompted to declare, "The universe is a put-up job."[23] Similarly, in his autobiography, Nobel laureate Freeman Dyson writes, "The more I examine the universe and study the details of its architecture, the more evidence I find that the universe in some sense must have known that we were coming."[24] If Tom Brown were actually to look for physical evidence of God's existence, he would not come up empty-handed.

Still, the evidence is not conclusive. If there are considerations to disconcert atheists, there are also considerations to disconcert theists. True, the anthropic coincidences are a puzzle that needs to be explained. They are not a pseudoproblem dreamt up by theologians. Physicists themselves take the puzzle seriously.

The physics community, however, is currently betting on a nontheistic solution. The solution is a theory called cosmic inflation. The inflationary theory postulates that for a fraction of a second after the big bang, the infant universe underwent a period of exponential expansion in which it ballooned in size by a factor of 10^{50}. If a BB were to expand at this rate, within the merest fraction of a second, it would assume the size of the entire visible universe.

Such an extraordinarily rapid expansion would itself explain some but not most of the anthropic coincidences. Yet, the theory of cosmic inflation has another payoff that could finish the job. On the standard model of cosmic inflation, ours would not be the only universe to be generated. The inflationary process would instead generate an almost infinite number of different universes.

If ours is only one of an infinite number of distinct universes, the anthropic coincidences lose their mystery. Across these many universes, the force strengths and particle properties vary. The vast majority of universes do not possess parameters making them ever capable of supporting life. In a sense, most are "junk" universes, destined never to become conscious of themselves.

If the number of actual universes is truly infinite, then there will always be at least a few like our own that exhibit the perfect balances necessary for life to evolve. It is then no mystery why we find ourselves in a universe that appears so finely tuned. It is only in such a fine-tuned universe that we could possibly find ourselves. The law of large numbers removes all the mystery from the apparent fine-tuning.

The theory of cosmic inflation can be tested, and physicists now are actively testing it. It is a rather remarkable development. Although physicists themselves do not generally think of it this way, they are in effect empirically testing for the existence of God. So far, our choice is between an almost infinite number of other universes or a solitary universe that then looks inescapably as if it has been designed. Because the inflationary theory is so theologically pivotal, I ask Sandra about it.

"Well," Sandra tells me, "there's one major problem with the inflationary model that is mentioned only very quietly...and it's not said too often although it sticks out like a sore thumb to others. Inflation makes one really big prediction—about the density of the universe: that the density should be equal to the critical density. Nobody's measurements come close to that. That's the problem. That's a big problem."

According to the standard inflationary model, the total mass in the universe should exactly equal the critical density between openness and closure. In a closed universe, one with too much mass, the force of gravity will eventually cause the universe to collapse back into the single point from which it originated. In an open universe, one with too little mass, the universe will just continue to expand forever. At the critical density to which Sandra refers, the universe is on a knife edge between open and closed. What Sandra is saying is that so far not enough mass has been found in the universe to reach that critical density. If the missing mass is never found, it would be an important setback for inflation—and for the theory of multiple universes. The designer's image would then reappear.

Sandra continues. "Right now, the way it stands, most people seem to say that without having the density—the critical density, you really can't have inflation. That's one of the things that inflation really does require. Most of the observations say the density's probably at 0.1 of the critical density, maybe 0.2 or 0.3, but nobody's up there really close to 0.9 or 1.0. Nobody is up there.

"The point I want to make is that inflation makes a prediction that the density equals certain values. Okay. Now you go to the people that measure the density of the universe, and you say, What do you find? And nobody says they find what inflation predicts. Therefore, it would appear that the data on the density of the universe rules out inflation."

The data may rule out the standard inflationary model. Since I spoke with Sandra, however, newer inflationary models have been developed that may not require so much mass. And since our interview as well, further observations suggest that the missing mass really should be there to be found. Perhaps some or all of it is associated with a newly discovered repulsive force that seems actually to be accelerating the cosmic expansion. How this all will end is too soon to say. The argument, the chess game continues.

The central point I have been trying to make here is that, contrary to what postmodernists suggest, contrary to what is popularly maintained, there definitely is evidence we can examine both for and against the existence of God. The claim that nothing can challenge our views about ultimate matters has been debunked. If so, should we not check in to see what challenges there are? Should we not join in the cosmic conversation?

I am not suggesting that we all need to become both biblical critics and physical cosmologists. I am suggesting that we all need at least to listen in on the conversations from these quarters and weave them in with our own. We must do so if we care about the ultimate truth behind our existence. We must do so if we possess the proper humility about our own beliefs, the humility to admit that our own beliefs about the ultimate may be partly or even wholly wrong. We must do so if it matters, for example, that we do what the historical Jesus really wanted and not just what we have come to think he wanted from a distance of 2,000 years away. As frightening as it may be to do so, it is only by questioning our own beliefs that we grow in our beliefs, that we move closer to the truth. Truth is calling us. Will we respond?

CHAPTER 9

The Human Vocation

If not now, when?

—*Hillel*

There is a wide sense today of moral malaise. Thus, from both the political right and left, many moral calls are issued. The political right calls us back to virtue or family values. The political left calls us to democracy, community, or active citizenship. My call in this book is more radical, for each of these other calls is subordinate. To the extent that each calls us to something good, each is good only by virtue of something more ultimate. My call is for us to return to the Most High.

Is there a human vocation, something we all were meant to achieve here on earth, not just individually but together? Is there a human destiny we were meant to fulfill? To ask these questions is to ask about the meaning of life. It is simultaneously to ask how we are to live. For if there is some great project humanity is meant to realize, then each of us should be part of it.

There are those, especially within the academy, who would scoff at the very idea that humanity has been entrusted with a cosmic vocation. They would sneer as well at the notion that we in any sense were meant to be here. We heard this view expressed by Lawrence Patterson, the African American Marxist. To Lawrence, our existence on this earth is the chance outcome of blind, physical forces. It was chance that evolution progressed in such a way as eventually to generate human intelligence. It was chance that this universe of ours just happened to be so put together as to make evolution even a possibility in the first place. Since we are here only by chance, our existence has no objective meaning beyond the individual meanings with which we endow it. There is nothing we have been charged to do except what we charge ourselves to do.

This view may be right. At the moment, it hardly can be said to command a preponderance of the evidence. For all its hegemony among intellectuals, it remains a rationally nonbinding sensibility that privileges the personal experience of God's absence.

Outside the academy, most people do not share Lawrence's view. Most people, we have seen, believe that we are each here for a reason. They seem certain that there is some deeper meaning to our existence. Most Americans in fact go even further. Most Americans believe that in one way or another, we were put here by God. And if there is a God who put us here, then, as even Tom Brown finally concedes, God must have had a reason for doing so. Whatever the meaning of our existence, for most Americans this meaning originates with God.

What does it mean for the meaning of our existence to originate with God? In the Western view common to most Americans, meaning—as in the meaning of our existence—relates to purpose. In this sense, to say that our lives have meaning is to say that they serve some larger purpose. If then we associate the meaning of our lives with God, the suggestion is that God placed us here for a purpose. As Sister Marge put it, our being here coincides with a plan of God—or at least a hope of God.

What might that plan or hope be? It is at this point that Americans exhibit a profound spiritual alienation. Alienation is a condition of separation or estrangement, especially a separation or estrangement from what is actually close to our own being. Specifically, we are spiritually alienated from the plan or purpose or hope of the God in whom we profess to believe.

If we believe that God had some plan or purpose for putting us here, should not our part in that plan or purpose be the most important thing in our lives? Should we not trouble ourselves just a little to discern what this plan or purpose might be? Evidently, we do not. For many Americans, belief in God is what Hannah Gottlieb describes as just something to accept and skip over. In fact, many skip over it so fast as never to consider what God might want of us. Joe Barboso, the young physics student, imagines that if God had once had a reason for creating us, God has since lost interest in it. More likely, Joe is projecting his own lack of interest onto God.

When I ask Tom Brown why he thinks God put us here, he tells us that as he is not God, he does not know. Tom goes on to suggest that it would be arrogant for him to presume to know the mind of God. In itself, Tom's humility about ultimate matters is an important virtue. We differ widely in our experiences of the ultimate. Thus, we get at the real truth only by remaining so open to correction from others that we are willing to be taken beyond what we currently believe. Even by this standard, however, Tom's humility is excessive, reflecting rather the same kind of incuriousness expressed by Joe Barboso. If God truly wants something of us, would it not have been reasonable for God to let us know what it is? Tom has done little to find out.

Joe and Tom's lack of interest in God, like that of outright atheism, reflects not higher reason but a personal experience from which God is absent. Conservative pundits bemoan the loss of belief in God. In America, however, there is little loss of belief. Except perhaps for our intellectuals, nearly all Americans believe that in one form or another, God exists.

The real religious divide in America does not concern belief. It concerns emotional attachment to the sacred. There are those who are emotionally attached to God and those who are emotionally alienated from the God in whom they believe. This emotional divide in turn derives from a more fundamental divide in religious experience. According to public opinion polls, between a third and a half of Americans report some religious experience, although not necessarily of God.[1] From what we have seen in the course of our inquiry, we would expect those who personally experience God to be emotionally attached to God. Conversely, we would expect those—even believers— who do not experience God to be emotionally detached. The latter will tend to conceptualize God as some vague force or mysterious Other that takes no personal interest in human affairs.

Paradoxically, we may remain alienated from God's plan or purpose even when we do experience God. Even then, we may still miss our human vocation. This happens when we interpret God's plan too individualistically and especially when we share none of Tom Brown's humility. Personal experience confronts us with the force of revealed truth. That is why we say seeing is believing. The temptation of direct experience is to believe it puts us in possession of absolute truth. Often, our own religious communities abet this temptation by enjoining us not to question our shared experience but to have blind faith in the community's orthodox understanding of it. We end up devoted not to God's plan but to one very human, very fallible understanding of it.

There is a role for faith in our lives. We should not abandon our strongly held beliefs with every doubt. If we did that, we would become like reeds shifting in every wind. Yet, given the diversity of religious experience and religious belief, Tom Brown rightly judges it hubris for us to presume a priori that it is we alone who know the mind of God. We may have a piece of the truth. We may even have a bigger or more important piece than anyone else. But we cannot know this a priori. We can only know it if we subject what we believe to critical scrutiny. If what we believe is the truth, then it will stand up to debate. But we can only know this if we do in fact debate.

We may think that unquestioned faith is a loyalty we owe God. Certainly, if our faith is in God alone, then it is a loyalty that is owed. There is a difference, however, between faith in God and faith in any particular doctrinal understanding of God. Our faith in God must transcend our faith in all human doctrines concerning God. That includes faith even in the Bible as the very word of God. This too is a human doctrine.

Our faith must be in the God who continues to be with us even when we lose what we thought we knew of God. Only that faith gives us the courage to separate what is human from what is divine. If we do not perform this task, then our faith will lead not to growth but to rigidity. Faith in human doctrine is not the path to God. Such faith leaves us fearfully clinging to what is only a way station along the road. In the end, it is to offer God less than what is due.

I have spoken repeatedly in this book of our need for *haverim*, for study partners who challenge our beliefs and so urge us further along the road. Our study partners must come not only from our own faith community. We have been speaking of a human vocation, not the vocation of Catholics, or of born-again Christians, or even of Americans. If it is to a human vocation we are called, then we are also called beyond the confines of our home communities.

The point of *haverim* who differ from us in experience and belief is not to put together some composite blend. It is not as if we are out necessarily to take something from every religion, mix, and stir. How would we even know what and how much to take from each? What we are after is not to incorporate all views but to entertain all arguments. Only then can we know how firm is the rock on which we stand.

In the end, it may be that we retain in essence much of what we originally believed. We may be fortunate in starting out with a big piece of the truth. Even then, however, it will be surprising if along the way we do not also learn something from others, something that somehow changes what we believe. Although it is not the point of the great conversation for us all to incorporate one another's views, in the give and take of conversation, something is awry if we invariably win all the arguments.

It may seem now that I am calling only for greater intellectual rigor. We all should question our individual faiths, read, and discuss. Yes, I am calling for that but much more than that. That is only the beginning. If I were calling only for greater social-mindedness or participation in the larger community, such intellectual rigor might be unnecessary. However, although such may be the call of others, it is not mine.

I am calling us back to the Most High. I want us to assume our human vocation. Yes, that requires intellectual effort. It also requires intellectual courage. It requires us with humility to pursue with each other an ever better understanding of what our vocation is. It requires us always to learn anew what our own understanding leaves out. It requires us to take very seriously our lives on this planet.

At the moment, in many ways, we do not take either our lives or our vocation seriously enough. Instead of engaging each other on ultimate matters, we assiduously leave each other alone. It is as if we have all signed a mutual nonaggression pact stipulating that if we allow everyone else to believe whatever crazy thing he or she wants to believe, he or she in turn will allow us to believe whatever crazy thing we want to believe.

Of course we should allow people to believe what they will. I am not advocating a new Inquisition. But where others are willing, we should challenge them in the hope that they in turn will challenge us. As *haverim*, we should be helping each other to grow.

As it is, under our mutual nonaggression pact, we come to treat our opinions like sacred objects, immune from challenge. Paradoxically, our most sacred opinions get reduced to trivialities. We come to think of them as fictive, personal myths, not worth arguing about because they have no public consequence.

At the same time, we leave each other unprovoked with understandings of our human vocation that are too small. Americans particularly are wont to think of our human vocation much too individualistically. When in this book we asked people about the meaning of life, it was about the meaning of their own personal lives that they tended to speak. Few voiced any grander picture that encompassed our common humanity.

Nevertheless, there is something of a standard, American understanding of our common, human vocation. The understanding is that we are all here to work out our personal salvation so as to make our way privately to heaven. Stephen Hertz alluded to this understanding when he spoke of Christians who experience a great personal transformation but who neglect the widows and orphans of this world.

The standard American understanding of the human vocation is too small, too individualistic. It further tends to undervalue this plane of our existence. We ask, Why are we here? Not just our specific selves but all of us collectively. Whatever our answer, it must match the grandeur of all that prepared for our arrival. That grandeur is not honored by viewing the entire universe as just a launch pad for our eventual flight to heaven. This universe is just too magnificent to bear no value in its own right.

Consider the cosmic preparation our existence required. It was a labor longer than seven days. First, perhaps an untold number of different universes had to be exploded even to achieve just one that could eventually support intelligent life. Then this promising universe had to realize its promise. It had to expand and cool, allowing atoms and molecules to form. It took several billion years for stellar clouds to aggregate. These took another several billion years to coalesce into the star clusters we know as galaxies. A whole first generation of stars had to manufacture carbon and the other organic building blocks of life. Once these organic compounds were manufactured, those stars had to explode so that their organic debris could fertilize space. From the organic debris, a second generation of stars could form, this time with planets containing what was needed for life. All this took billions of years more.[2]

Carl Sagan popularized the view that the universe is teeming with life. Newer assessments indicate that it may have taken a universe as gigantic as ours to produce intelligent life even just once. The odds against life more complex than microbes are astronomical. It took a planet of just the right size and of continuously just the right distance from just the right kind of star in one of just the right kind of spots in one of just the right kind of galaxies. It took many other conditions besides.[3]

For us to appear, even this special planet first had to be prepared. Among other things, it had to cool, and the atmosphere had to become just right. That could not happen immediately. Most likely, the earth's first atmosphere was blown into space from the impact of celestial collisions. After the collisions ceased, the second atmosphere was created by volcanic outgasing, producing concentrations of water vapor and carbon dioxide. From the condensation of the water vapor, the first oceans formed.[4]

Once the oceans cooled, it took close to a billion years for the first life to form. Prokaryites converted the carbon dioxide into oxygen, which first reacted chemically to reduce the ammonia and methane in the atmosphere. Only when these noxious gases had been largely eliminated did the atmosphere begin to accumulate the free oxygen on which more complex animal life depends.[5] It then took another three and a half billion years for evolution to generate us.

Call all this chance if you will. The striking thing about our universe is that it has not been static all these 15 billion years. Like us, our universe has a history. That history, morover, has been going somewhere. It has been moving toward us. We are the universe become conscious of itself. Surely there is an important vocation just in that. Whatever the reason for our existence, part of it must be to bring the universe to completion. It is time we began to act collectively as befits our station.

Jason Fishman was the health-care professional we heard from early on. Because Jason is very ecologically minded, he distrusts the suggestion that we humans are so important. Such a view, he considers, has made us wanton with the earth. Yet, if we are the universe become conscious of itself, then we are an integral part of the the universe, its very soul. It follows that we should treat the earth not as we have done and as we are doing now but rather as a soul treats its body. Still, our human vocation demands more than this as it takes more than this to bring the universe to completion.

What would it take to bring the universe to completion? Before addressing this, let us take a moment to reflect on what it means for our individual identities if there really is something we can call a human vocation. We established early on that however we think or behave, each of us always remains a unique center of conscious experience, one that cannot be deconstructed out of existence.

What we make out of this bare selfhood is another matter. That does depend on what we think and what we do. We saw that who we end up being is in large part determined by what we stand for. If we stand for the accumulation of material possessions, we are one type of person, and quite another if what we stand for is family values.

Standing for something is the quality of ultimate concern. We stand for those things to which we are ultimately committed and from which we derive our ultimate fulfillment. The objects of our ultimate concerns are that to which our life's purposes are ultimately directed. So who we are comes down to the moral quality of our ultimate concerns and the life purposes we pursue. At the remains of the day, these determine the individual meanings of our lives. At the remains of the day, are our lives to be summed up by shopping or something more? It is what would morally sum up a life in this way that might be expressed on our tombstone. It already says something about the moral seriousness with which we take our lives that few could tell me what they would want their tombstones to say.

Because we Americans tend to think individualistically, we tend to think that it is entirely up to us individually to say what our lives mean. It is not. The meaning of our lives is also determined by what is going on around us. Meaning is always contextual. It always depends on what else is or is not in the picture. Consider two people in an elevator, standing so close together that they touch. Their proximity has one meaning if the elevator is so stuffed with people that there really is no choice how close together the two stand. Their proximity takes on a completely different meaning if in the elevator the two are alone.

The meaning of our lives is equally contextual. Suppose we are exclusively concerned with the welfare of our friends and families. Such an exclusive focus takes on one meaning if all is right with the world. It takes on a completely different meaning if, to take an extreme example, we place ourselves in Nazi Germany. Then an exclusive focus on friends and family cannot help also signifying a wanton indifference to what is going on around us. If what is going on around us is egregious enough, that indifference cannot but negatively affect the meaning of our lives.

Now suppose we all were meant to be here and, moreover, meant to do something specific together with our time on this planet. Suppose in short that we really do have a human vocation. That also would necessarily contextualize the meanings our lives assume. If there truly is some cosmic purpose we are meant to pursue, then we surely should be about pursuing it. To ignore or renounce that purpose carries cosmic significance. Perhaps if we determined that what we were meant to do were somehow immoral or trivial, that would be one thing. That would be a daring, perhaps even a heroic determination worthy of respect.

It is another matter altogether to disregard our cosmic purpose blithely in favor of less weighty or moral concerns. In that case, to say the least, we are alienated from the cosmic purpose of our existence and even from the cosmos itself. To the extent that our cosmic purpose originates with God, we are equally alienated from God.

In the end, we are also alienated from our own souls. Consider the logic. Who we are is determined by the ultimate purposes we pursue.

If there really is a human vocation, then the pursuit of that purpose defines who we authentically were meant to be. Accordingly, if we deviate from that purpose, we are deviating from our authentic selves. It is then from our own higher selves that we are also alienated.

Am I arguing that we all should drop everything we are doing and pursue full-time some yet-to-be specified cosmic purpose? What about people who have no time, who are caring for an invalid, or who otherwise are unequipped to participate in this great cosmic venture? Am I suggesting that their lives are of no account?

I am neither arguing nor suggesting anything so extreme. What I have in mind as our cosmic purpose admits many levels of service. Certainly, it is all some people can do to manage their own affairs. If they do so in the proper spirit, that itself may be a heroic contribution to the human vocation. We must be careful not to consider this issue so individualistically. To the extent that there are people so hard pressed and with so little outside support, that is already a fair indication that collectively we are still far from our cosmic goal. But as Jesus's parable of the talents makes clear, from those to whom more has been given, more is expected in return. Rest assured that if you have managed to get this far in this book, you are among those from whom the cosmos expects more.

Enough of my dark hints. What am I proposing as the human vocation? Nothing not already waiting in our religious and philosophical traditions. As Hannah Gottlieb points out, in each there are layers and layers of accumulated spiritual wisdom. If I have argued that community itself is not the end of our journey, we are certainly not going to arrive there apart from community. As our destination is a collective one, so must be our progress.

Contrary to a popular opinion, all our spiritual discourses are hardly just saying the same thing. Yet, there are important convergences that point in common to a global, ethical purpose.

The monumental eighteenth-century philosopher G. W. Hegel appreciated history—not just our own history but the history of the universe. Although Hegel could not yet know of Darwin or cosmology, Hegel saw the universe as a historical unfolding. According to Hegel, throughout this unfolding, God—or what Hegel called the Absolute Spirit—has been struggling and groping toward self-recognition in physical form. Creation, on this view, was not a one-time affair but a continuing, almost artistic process. In the inert world of matter, the Absolute Spirit failed to recognize itself fully, and so, like a painter tinkering with a canvas, it overlaid the inert world with organic life. Yet not even organic life fully captured what the Absolute Spirit was trying to express. It went back to the drawing board and added humanity.

In humanity, the Absolute Spirit came closer to recognizing itself, but not in humanity's original condition. From then on, according to Hegel, the Absolute Spirit went to work on human history. For Hegel, our human history is going somewhere—or at least meant to be going somewhere. It is meant to reflect finally the self-image of the Absolute Spirit.

What could we possibly offer back to the Absolute Spirit as its self-image? It could only be a universal order of peace and justice, an order in which peace reigns because justice reigns. The justice we are speaking of here is not bourgeois fairness, with its emphasis on merit. The biblical tradition has always understood justice as the way we collectively treat the widows and orphans among us. When Israel began to neglect its widows and orphans, prophets always arose to upbraid it. In the twenty-fifth chapter of Leviticus, written long before the common era, let alone Karl Marx, Israel is enjoined to hold regularly a jubilee year in which all land is redistributed, all debts forgiven, and all indentured servants set free. The jubilee prescription does not ask how fairly the land was originally exchanged, how properly a credit came to be owed. It was the resultant inequality—and its effects—that constituted the injustice, and the Jubilee was meant to repair it.

According to biblical historians, the Jubilee was likely never practiced. It remained but a vision. It still remains a vision of what we respectably could offer back to the Absolute Spirit. In short, it is our human vocation universally and together to realize Utopia.

But that is so idealistic! Yes, of course. What other than an ideal could be fit to be called the human vocation? What else could worthily be offered back to the Absolute Spirit? If idealism puts us off today, it is precisely the profound loss of idealism this entire book has been about. This loss is the measure of our cosmic alienation.

The Hegelian idea that we are to bring the universe to completion we may take as a myth or metaphor. It happens—not accidentally—to coincide with Christian tradition. Let us return to Stephen Hertz, the accountant who is also an Evangelical Christian. Against those who see religion and politics as two separate domains, Stephen reminds us that Jesus had a program, which he called a kingdom. The word kingdom, Stephen further explains, implies a political dimension. Many Christians want to distance religion from politics because they think politics is something dirty and religion something pure. Politics is dirty. The dirt comes of practicing politics in an alienated world. On the other hand, politics is also the domain in which we practice prophetic justice. It is the politics of Christ's reign that Christians should take up.

What is the reign of God preached by Jesus? In Luke, Jesus quotes Isaiah to the effect that God's reign means good news for the poor, pardon for prisoners, and release of the oppressed. Does this not sound like the Jubilee year? In fact, the last sentence Jesus quotes is, "To announce the acceptable year of the Lord." The acceptable year is the Jubilee.[6] Jesus evidently was an idealist too.

Like Hegel after him, Jesus understood the reign of God in historical terms. Jesus described it as a mustard seed that would appear insignificant at its start. Yet it would eventually grow, and grow so prodigiously that one day it would envelop the world. For this to happen, Jesus's disciples had to work at it. Wherever the poor have not received good news, wherever prisoners remain enthralled and the oppressed still burdened, there the reign of God has not yet reached.

Jesus showed us how to begin. All were welcomed to the table without hierarchy. All were healed even without professing any specific doctrine. Women as well as men were considered fit to discuss scripture. Foreigners were called neighbors, and even enemies were loved. Is this reign of God not also another name for Utopia?

We are told that Jesus's first disciples held all things in common and gave to each according to his or her need. This is reminiscent of still another name for Utopia, although few Americans today will believe it. Nevertheless, not all who labor for our vocation do so under the same banner.

However the communist experiment turned out, its egalitarian vision remains a worthy one. The failure of the communist system no more signifies the futility of that vision than the early failures of the Wright brothers meant we were never supposed to fly. We simply need to put into our human vocation as much effort as we put into planes.

In the early 1990s, there was a political cartoon that pictured two Soviet officials conversing together. "The good news," said one, "is that there are plenty of Marxists left. The bad news is that they all are in American Universities." Yet, why should Marxists remain even there? Can we professors not see what everyone else can?

Yes, we can see what everyone else can, but we have also read what Marx actually said. Americans mistakenly think that Marx spent his time writing blueprints for a better society, flawed blueprints that obviously could not be implemented. This greatest of Hegel's followers did no such thing. In fact, in all the volumes that constitute Marx's collected works, there is precious little that describes what a communist society should look like. Instead, what Marx spent his time doing was analyzing history and criticizing capitalism. Those analyses and criticisms retain their force even today, which is why they continue to be considered by those in the academy who still call themselves Marxists. Overcoming the continued defects of capitalism must remain on our historical agenda.

It is also something of a mistake to suppose that Marx was intransigently opposed to religion. In fact, Marx once even paid religion an oblique compliment. "Religion," he said, "is the sigh of the oppressed, the heart of a heartless world." Let me return the compliment with one equally oblique. Marxism is the prophetic voice of religion detached from its sacred ground.

The point I have been making is that a number of different secular and religious traditions all point to a common human vocation, the realization of a truly just and loving order. It is a vocation the Kabbalah calls *Tikkun ha Olam*, the repair of the world. In that task, we become co-creators with God in the effort to bring the creation to completion.

We need to practice *Tikkun ha Olam* because this world of ours is in sore need of repair. If individually many do not personally experience any higher calling, it may well be because we live in a world so collectively sunk in alienation. It is to the collective level that we need to direct our attention.

Jesus denied that people can serve two masters. In particular, we cannot simultaneously serve both God and money. We will end up, Jesus said, honoring one and despising the other. We American Christians solemnly nod our heads and say amen. Yet in our deeds, we presume Jesus got it wrong. Our lives are devoted to accumulation and consumption. To overspend, we overwork, and not even that is enough. We also overborrow.[7] In the end, we prove Jesus's point. We have chosen our master, and it is not God.

We say amen willingly enough because we all think the message applies to others and not to ourselves. In one study, most of the personnel in a large corporation described 90 percent of their co-workers as materialistic. They claimed in contrast that they themselves were not. These numbers do not add up. If 90 percent of the personnel are described by others as materialistic, then more than a few must be fooling themselves.[8] Our alienation comes with a fair share of denial.

The real problem resides at the collective level. If we are individually materialistic without knowing it, it is because ours is a materialistic society. That means more than just that the majority of people in this society are individually materialistic. More fundamentally, it means that as a whole, this society actively impedes our ability to be anything other than materialistic. It is materialistic, for example, to own two cars. Yet we often lack the public transportation to do otherwise. It is in large part our society itself that makes us individually materialistic. Jesus's message applies not just to individuals but also to entire societies. They, too, cannot serve two masters. Again, it is very clear which master our society has chosen.

The capitalist order is now global in extent. It is a reign not of God but of desire. It has been called McWorld.[9] McWorld is the reign of corporate power. It is a reign in which we come to view even democracy as nothing more than consumer choice. As long as we are free to buy as much of whatever we want at the lowest price, we are happy. We cease to notice that the real choices—what is made, by whom, where, and how—are no longer up to us. Seduced into civic mindlessness, we accept what we are served. McWorld is a reign in which we are encouraged to identify our very souls with market segments. Like Circe, McWorld everywhere magically transforms human dignity into something swinish. This is a profound alienation. Celebratory postmodernism is its sigh of contentment.

The religions of the East have a word for our condition. They call it *avidya*. *Avidya* is such fascination with the superficialities of life that we fail to turn our attention to anything higher or deeper. *Avidya* is no longer just an ineliminable feature of the human condition. McWorld is a social order that thrives on *avidya*. And because it thrives on *avidya*, it secretes *avidya*. McWorld produces surplus *avidya*.

It would not be so bad if what we do, we do only to ourselves. McWorld, however, is a global reign. We in America reside in its capital. While we are pacified with surfeit, much of the world toils in sweatshops to supply our want. It is folly to suppose that with enough toil, they too will eventually attain our wantonness. As the earth cooks, the United States already consumes far more than its proportionate share of the earth's bounty.[10] Were it even possible, it would be environmentally unsustainable for everyone everywhere to do the same. What will happen to the earth when a billion Chinese all start driving Jeep Cherokees?

Again, this is not principally a matter of our individual choices but of the collective way we have organized our lives. Whereas some countries of the world are underdeveloped, ours is overdeveloped. Things must change. Individually, perhaps, we cannot be blamed for inhabiting McWorld. Individually, this was not our choice.

In contrast, we can be held individually to account for what we do to change things. That is our choice. At the moment, we in America seem inclined to relinquish all popular power to the market, which we endow with an omnipotence to make everything right. The religions of the West have a name for this. They call it idolatry. The market is the golden calf of postmodernity, before which we sacrifice our forests and seas, the earth's depths and its heights. How long before we feel God's wrath? According to latest reports, not long at all.

Against McWorld, I am not urging a *jihad* that privileges the perspective of any one faith community. But to the extent that *jihad* means holy undertaking, I am urging a kind of *jihad*, one that calls for return to our human vocation. In relation to that vocation, not even complete justice within our own community is good enough. Unless our righteousness exceeds even that of the Communitarians, we are not yet resident in God's reign. McWorld is not the image to offer back to the Absolute Spirit. Our call is to fashion a world order that is. Children of the world, let us awake from alienation and resume our cosmic task.

Appendix A

Theory

As scholars, we try to write in a way that clearly lays out arguments and central concepts to advance our theoretical understanding of the world. We do this because we are committed to its importance to the larger society. Often, however, our jargon and associated references make us inaccessible to a wider audience. The ideas contained in this book are important to both scholars and the popular reader. To engage both audiences, I left the arguments and references more implicit in the text. Although most of the references appear in the footnotes, scholars will need to be more alert to what is at issue. This appendix seeks to make that task easier by laying out some of the theoretical controversies canvassed.

The book's principal antagonist is a postmodernist philosophy that denies truth, meaning, and our coherent subjectivity. That includes a social constructionism that treats reality as something that can be bracketed out of our accounts. Particularly opposed is the application of social constructionism to religious experience. In any true experience, the object of experience must contribute something to the content of the experience. Thus, if social constructionism intends to bracket out from analysis the object of religious experience, it is no longer analyzing experience at all.

Experience cannot be admitted as a category without simultaneously readmitting the coherent persons who are the subjects of experience. Thus, equally opposed here is the new cultural Durkheimianism that in favor of discourse would do away with individual actors as surely as the old structural Durkheimianism. However much religious experience, commitment, and emotional attachment are phenomena about which we can discourse, they all find operative location within the individual.

Against rational choice theory, no distinction is made between rationality on one side and emotion and experience on the other. The book seeks to show, furthermore, that the rationality applicable to religious experience is epistemic rather than instrumental. About epistemic rationality, rational choice theory knows nothing.

On the positive side, this book represents an empirical application of critical realism. Critical realism is a postpositivist philosophy of science, now most associated with Roy Bhaskar.[1] Critical realism presumes an alethic rather than an epistemic conception of truth that reseparates ontology and epistemolgy.[2] This separation makes truth something possible to attain without foundations. More distinctly, critical realism breaks with the old, positivist understanding of causality as involving deterministic, nomothetic laws. For critical realism, causal explanation instead refers to underlying mechanisms that in the human sphere are never deterministic.

The principal mechanisms discussed in this book are personal experience and emotion. In its attention to these elements, the book seeks to reframe the secularization debate away from just belief and practice. Clearly, finally, I do understand that I have produced a book that not only addresses the sociology of religion but that also quite definitely is what might be considered religious sociology. Attribute this daring move to postmodernism. Postmodernism champions the voice of the excluded Other. The academy's Other has long been religion. Perhaps postmodernism's invitation was not meant to include religion. Nevertheless, this truly uncanny guest has now tagged along behind deconstructionist literary theory.

Appendix B

Tables

Table 4-1. Religiosity and Reflection the Meaning of Life*

How Often
Respondents
Think About
Meaning of Life

	How Religious Respondents Are			
	Not Very	Somewhat	Very	Total
Rarely	15.3%	18.6%	13.2%	N = 46
Sometimes	76.3%	69.0%	52.9%	N = 178
Always	8.5%	12.4%	33.8%	N = 47
Total	100%	100%	100%	N = 271
	N=59	N=123	N=68	

χ2 = 19.948   α = .0005

* For results of multiple regression analysis, controlling for demographic variables, see Chapter Four, note 13, p. 327.

Table 4-2. Religiosity and Attitude Toward Meaning of Life*

Respondents'
Attitudes Toward
the Meaning of Life		How Religious Respondents Are		
	Not Very	Somewhat	Very	N
No meaning or other attitude	27.2%	8.5%	10.5%	73
Don't know meaning	33.0%	27.4%	11.8%	161
Some sense of life's purpose	33.0%	46.2%	36.8%	242
Know the purpose of life	6.6%	14.2%	40.7%	117
	100.0%	100.0%	100.0%	
Total N	152	281	121	593
$\chi2$ = 84.8	α < .001			

* For results of multiple regression analysis, controlling for demographic variables, Chapter
  Four, see note 14, p. 327.

Table 5-1. Hero-Identification and the Meaning of Life

a. Hero-Identification and Reflection on the Meaning of Life.

How Often Respondents
Think About Meaning of Life | | | Do Those Respondents
Have Heroes? |
| --- | --- | --- | --- |
| | No | Yes | Total Cases |
| Rarely/Never | 63.0% | 37.0% | 46 (17%) |
| Sometimes | 62.9% | 37.1% | 178 (66%) |
| Always | 38.3% | 61.7% | 47 (17%) |
| Total Cases | 160 | 111 | 271 (100%) |

(*Table 5-1. Continued*)

b. Hero-Identification and Certainty about Meaning of Life.

Respondents' Certainty About the Meaning of Life	No	Yes	Do Those Respondents Have Heroes? Total Cases
Don't know meaning of life	69.6%	30.4%	161 (27%)
Have some sense of life's purpose	57.9%	42.1%	242 (41%)
Know the purpose of life	44.5%	55.5%	117 (20%)
Life has no meaning/ Have other attitude	57%	43%	117 (12%)
Total Cases	247	346	593 (100%)

Table 6-1. Student Survey Results

Calling by Religiosity (N = 321)

	How Religious Are You?*			
Have a calling?	Very Religious	Somewhat Religious	Not very Religious	Not at all Religious
No	29%	61%	70%	59%
Yes	71%	39%	30%	41%

*$\alpha < .001$

Table 6-2. Student Survey Results

Percentages of Respondents with Callings by Measures of Philosophical Reflectiveness (N = 320)

	How Often Do You Think About:		
	Always	Often	Rarely
The existence of God	61%	37%	34%**
How the universe came into being	73%	43%	27%*
What is the purpose of life	59%	38%	34%***

* α < .001
** α < .002
*** α < .020

Table 6-3. Who Is Most Likely to Have a Calling?*
Stepwise Multiple Regression Analysis

Independent Variable	Final β	Cumulative R	Cumulative R2	Change in R2	Significance
Reflection about Meaning of Life	.217	.278	.077	NA	.014
Religion	.032	NA	NA	NA	.784
Service Attendance	.162	NA	NA	NA	.143
Education	.078	NA	NA	NA	.489
Age	.064	NA	NA	NA	.566
Income	.012	NA	NA	NA	.889
Race	.188	NA	NA	NA	.091

* Calling defined here as "true calling," a sense of calling combined with an ability to say to what specifically one is called.

NOTES

INTRODUCTION

1. Bloom 1987, p. 25.
2. Porpora 1990.
3. Pirsig 1972.
4. Random sampling of interviewees is an ideal few in this kind of research are able to achieve. See, however, Hart (1992) and Lamont (1992). In contrast with most research in this area, Hart and Lamont both employ random samples.

   Random sampling has at least two major advantages. First, it gives us a sense of how representative our interviewees are. I attempt to address this question by comparing what my interviewees say with the responses of random samples to questions on both national surveys and surveys I conducted myself locally in Philadelphia. By way of such methodological triangulation, I, too, although less directly, am able to offer a sense of my interviewees' representativeness.

   The second major advantage of random sampling—whether simple or complex—is its avoidance of bias. By not sampling randomly, there is always the possibility of systematic bias in the types of people I chose to interview. The most visible kinds of potential bias were avoided by choosing to interview a cross section of the population that varied not only in terms of outlook but in terms of socioeconomic and demographic characteristics as well.

   Still, less visible kinds of bias may remain. At this exploratory stage of inquiry, however, that seems a minor problem that can be corrected by further research. According to the critical realist philosophy of science this study reflects, objectivity is not a property of the individual study but a result that emerges from multiple studies in critical engagement with each other.

Even with the greatest methodological sophistication, a single study rarely attains the full truth on its own. All studies require the correction of further research. Hart's work, for example, is an excellent piece of sociology that tries to find out the varying ways in which Christians' political views stem from their religious views. In fact, Hart's book partly inspired me to undertake mine. Originally, I had wanted to do something similar. Yet, as Hart himself admits, while he sampled randomly, his sample largely consisted of people very active with their churches. It turns out that these people tend to be more reflective and articulate than others about the connections between their political and religious views. When I began questioning Christians less involved with church activities, I found they could not trace their political views back to their religious views because they had neither well-articulated political views nor even well-articulated religious views. Both were fragmentary. This is a side of our population that still needs to be heard from when we talk of the religious and political views of Christians.

The point is that the truth rarely springs full-blown from a single, perfect study. Waiting for such a study amounts to waiting for Godot. Instead, we arrive at truth—if at all—through a cumulative and collective process of correction and reformulation. For that dialogical process to proceed, however, it must begin somewhere with some initial formulation, which may not tell us the whole truth. On the matters discussed here, it is only the initiation of such a dialogue that this book represents. Just as my data add a perspective to Hart's findings, other researchers responding to me will undoubtedly refine and correct the picture I present.

5. Tillich 1957.
6. Pincoffs 1986.
7. For some exceptions, see Gaita 1991; Kekes 1988; Nussbaum 1990, 1994; and Solomon 1983.
8. MacIntyre 1981, *op. cit.* Taylor 1989.
9. Aristotle 1991: 1072a-1072b.
10. Nussbaum 1990.
11. Lovin et al. 1985.
12. Taylor, *op. cit.*
13. Harrington 1983, Wolfe 1989.
14. Porpora (1987) was a critique of the Durkheimian approach to social structure.
15. Wuthnow (1987) and Coulter (1989) are influential champions of this kind of cultural Durkheimianism, although Campbell (1996) demonstrates that today, cultural Durkheimianism is almost sociological orthodoxy. Barbalet (1998) eschews the new cultural turn in a sustained

treatment of the relation between experienced emotion and social structure. Langman (1999a; 1999b) is also in this tradition.

16. Bellah et al. 1985.

17. The word *metanarrative* seems to have been coined by the French thinker Jean-François Lyotard (1984). It has since come to be widely used by postmodernists to designate both the loss of any grand meanings and the virtual impossibility of such.

18. Bellah et al., *op.cit.*, p. 219.

19. *Religion in America* (1993), a publication of the Princeton Religion Center.

20. *U.S. News and World Report* poll, March 7, 1994.

21. World Values Survey, 1990–91.

22. Yamane 1998.

23. Although emotions are not just feelings, they are also not just talk as social constructionists (Coulter 1989; Harre 1986) would have it. Solomon (1980), I think, comes closest to what emotions are when he defines them as a kind of judgment. Not even Solomon, however, comes close enough. Solomon's conception of emotions as judgments is too cognitive. As not all judgments are emotions, we must at least distinguish emotions as judgments that are felt. Even better perhaps is to retain what Solomon is attempting to capture without reducing emotions to another mental category. Thus, following Heidegger (1962), I construe emotions as orientations of care toward the objections of emotions. Our different emotions specify our different ways of caring about things and as such are relational postures in which our entire selves are oriented toward the world.

24. Wolfe, *op. cit.*, p. 234.

25. Taylor, *op. cit.*

26. Susan Tridgell in the literature department at the Australian National University has been one of my biggest supporters and closest readers in the preparation of this book. She nevertheless takes issue with me on various points, and one is on the importance I assign to argument. She admonishes me at least to distinguish what I mean by argument from the point-scoring exercises in which academics often engage. I am happy to oblige. Although something can be learned even from an exchange with a point-scorer, argument ideally should be a mutually supportive experience.

27. Tillich 1952.

CHAPTER ONE. THE CATERPILLAR'S QUESTION

1. See Margolis 1987.

2. Margolis, *ibid.*

3. Watts 1957, p. 44.

4. Heidegger 1962.
5. Ishiguro 1988.
6. On work and calling, see Sullivan 1995. On the concept of a moral career, see Greenwood 1994.
7. Mead 1964.
8. Sartre 1956.
9. Upanishad *katha*. Prabhavananda and Manchester 1948, p. 17.
10. Upanishad *Chandogya*. *Ibid.*, pp. 63–79.
11. On the I's reflexive blind spot, see Wiley 1994a, p. 45–46.
12. Larana et al. 1995.
13. Althusser 1969 and Althusser and Balibar 1970. Collier (1989) argues for a less antihumanist reading of Althusser, but his is a decidedly minority interpretation.
14. See, for example, Derrida 1973, 1976, 1978.
15. Lacan 1977.
16. *Ibid.*
17. Foucault 1972, 1977, 1980.
18. Laclau and Mouffe 1985.
19. Gergen 1991; Lifton 1993.
20. Deleuze and Guattari 1977.
21. Mark 5: 9.
22. See, for example, Butler 1990; Flax 1990, 1993.
23. Buber 1970. See also Wiggins 1976.
24. Anderson (1988) coins the phrase, "exorbitation of language" to connote the elevation of language to an exorbitant position, a position that swallows up the human self.
25. Margolis 1987, *op cit.*
26. Durkheim 1951, p. 212.
27. Margolis 1987, *op cit.* See also Margolis 1978. The position Margolis outlines is called "nonreductive materialism" and is more nuanced than I have presented it here.
28. Margolis 1987, *op. cit.*
29. Following post-Wittgensteinian philosophy, many sociologists would argue that mental states are not attributable to individuals but are, rather, public rules that members of a culture use to make sense of each other's behavior. For programmatic statements of this position, see Blum and McHugh 1971, Coulter 1989, Harre 1986, Rubinstein 1977. I (Porpora 1983, 1997) and others (Campbell 1992, Davidson 1963, Margolis 1970, 1979) have extensively criticized this position elsewhere. Here, it must suffice to say that by so emptying persons of their mental states, the post-Wittgensteinian position leaves us bereft of any theory of individual motivation that can explain why people perform one culturally acceptable action rather than another.
30. A distinction between our ontological and phenomenological selves has

also been drawn recently by Wiley 1994a and Lemert 1994. It is particularly interesting that Lemert and Wiley should happen on this important distinction simultaneously since Lemert's sensibilities are postmodern while Wiley's are closer to modernism.

31. Porpora 1990.
32. There are four primary Jewish traditions in the United States today: Orthodox, Conservative, Reformed, and Reconstructionist. To some extent, the differences among these traditions refer primarily to liturgical and ritual strictness. Theologically, there is more overlap. The Conservative tradition, for example, encompasses synagogues that are both socially and politically quite liberal.
33. Nietzsche 1969.
34. Wilder 1938, p. 54.
35. Buber, *op cit.*

Chapter Two. The Further Geography of the Soul

1. Weber 1976.
2. Scrooge is an example of a more general phenomenon. Barbalet (1998, pp. 29–64) shows how the hatred of distracting emotions serves to focus rational asceticism.
3. Aristotle, 1985, 1147b. See also Rachels 1988, p. 21.
4. As noted in Chapter I, Solomon (1980) interprets emotions as a kind of judgment. Trying to preserve the important cognitive element in Solomon's characterization, I consider emotions, rather, as sui generis orientations of care.
5. Eliade 1957.
6. Miller 1993; Belk 1993; Kuper 1993; Nissenbaum 1996.
7. Taylor 1989, p. 28.
8. In sociology, the explicit distinction between instrumental and ultimate goals goes back to Weber 1947.
9. See Bellah et al. 1985; Lamont 1992.
10. Diamond 1987.
11. Lyon 1985. See also Kuper *op. cit.*, p. 157.
12. Gordis 1995, pp. 85–87.
13. *Ibid.*
14. Feuerbach 1957. For a contemporary, Christian interpretation of Feuerbach, see Robinson (1963).
15. Aristotle 1985, pp. 1–24. See also Aristotle 1952.
16. Procedural ethics are one manifestation of the "instrumentalist" orientation of modern life, an orientation that first came under criticism from Max Weber 1976. The general critique of instrumentalism subsequently became thematic for the Frankfurt School. See, for example, Horkheimer and Adorno 1972. In the domain of ethics in particular,

criticism of instrumentalism has been made by Taylor 1989, 1992; by Bellah et al. 1985; and by Sullivan 1995.

17. This is one of the main findings documented by Wolfe 1998.

18. On the secularized nature of public discourse, see Carter 1993. Although Bellah (1970) argues in contrast that public discourse presupposes a "civil religion," civil religion turns out to be metaphysically shallow.

19. As does postmodernism in general, Robert here commits a version of what Bhaskar (1989) refers to as the "epistemic fallacy," which is to conflate reality with our knowledge of it. The need to keep the two distinct is evident here in the conceptual difficulties afflicting Robert's position. In critical realist terms, our transitive, epistemic understanding of human rights is one thing and the intransitive, ontological reality of human rights is another. See Bhaskar 1975, 1989.

20. For representative versions of this point of view, see Denzin 1986; Richardson 1991; and Seidman 1991. More seminal is the work of Michel Foucault, for example, Foucault 1980b, and Jacques Derrida 1976. Foucault and Derrida in turn draw on Nietzsche. See, for example Nietzsche 1958, 1967.

21. Vonnegut 1973, p. 67.

22. Camus 1955.

23. *Ibid.*, pp. 88–89.

24. Sartre 1975.

25. Watts 1957, pp. 47–48.

26. Thoreau 1993.

27. Schor 1998.

28. See Wight's (1997) brilliant critique of postmodernism's incommensurability thesis.

29. Albert Schweitzer's (1968) monumental *The Quest of the Historical Jesus*, written at the turn of the century, left fifty years of pessimism about what could be known of the historical Jesus. Making a virtue of necessity, both the neo-orthodoxy of Karl Barth and the liberal, existential theology of Rudolf Bultmann held the true object of Christianity to be not the historical Jesus but the mythic Christ of faith. (See, for example, Barth 1957; Bartsch 1966; and Bultmann 1958.)

    By the 1960s, biblical scholars regained their confidence and applied new critical methods to what would be termed the "New Quest" for the historical Jesus (see Robinson 1979). We are now in the midst of yet a "third quest" in which, this time, biblical scholars carefully incorporate sociological insights; in which they root Jesus much more in his first century, Jewish milieu; and in which they attempt more thoroughly to go beyond the evaluation of individual deeds and sayings to an overall comprehension of Jesus's ministry. Wright (1996) represents one of the more exciting innovations along these lines. For an unusually accessible, thorough, and critical introduction to this new quest, see Witherington 1995.

30. What exactly we mean by Jesus's resurrection is open to various interpretations. It need not mean simply a revived corpse such as that of Lazarus. Instead, Jesus may have returned to his disciples in some kind of spiritually transformed body. See Pannenberg 1970.

31. From a survey of "unchurched Americans" conducted by the Gallup Organization in 1978. See question identified as USGallup.77121N, R24 in Roper Archives, *Public Opinion On-line*. Although the poll I cite was conducted almost twenty years ago, there is no evidence that public opinion has changed much on this matter. On the contrary, according to a 1993 survey entitled "Total Confusion," the Barna Research Group found 74 percent of Americans "strongly agreeing" that Jesus "was crucified, died, and rose from the dead." See question identified as USBarna.93Jan, R45 in Roper Archives, *Public Opinion On-line*.

32. See Williamson 1998.

33. On the impossibility of a "God's eye view," see Putnam 1981, pp. 54–56.

34. Again, see Seidman *op. cit.* for a representative version of this position, although the phrase *hermeneutics of suspicion* can be traced as far back as Ricoeur 1978, pp. 32–36.

35. In what is overall a book with which I am very much in sympathy, Craig Calhoun (1995, p. 11) argues against theories that attempt to assume "the umpire's chair," which, in effect, adopt what he calls "a view from nowhere." It is difficult to know what theories Calhoun has in mind here, for as he very usefully mediates between modernism and postmodernism, he ineluctably assumes the umpire's chair. He gives us his own best judgment, supported by arguments, about where modernism is stronger than postmodernism and vice versa.

    Calhoun wants to argue in favor of a "Critical Theory" that always remains cognizant of its own fallibility. I have no problem with that, but I do have a problem with the way Calhoun puts it. As I think Calhoun's own treatment demonstrates, whenever we base our conclusions not on our own person but on the strength of argument, we are offering a view from nowhere. We are in essence asking others to evaluate what we say not on the basis of who we are or who they are but on the objective merits of the argument made—as if the argument were made by nobody.

36. Again, see Wight *op. cit.* for a penetrating critique of the interparadigm silence induced by postmodernism's incommensurability thesis.

CHAPTER THREE. THE EMOTIONAL DETACHMENT FROM THE SACRED

1. See Murchland 1967.
2. See Berger 1969.
3. Buber 1952.
4. See Lyon 1985.

5. Finke and Stark 1992.
6. Eliade 1957.
7. *Ibid.*
8. *Ibid.*
9. Tillich 1952.
10. The "numinous" is defined by Otto (1958) as that which is totally other. Our experience of the numinous is multifaceted, ranging from fascination to dread and feelings of uncanniness.
11. The Nazgul are the nine unholy riders from "Mordor" in Tolkien (1954). More universally familiar, perhaps, is the otherworldly villain, Darth Vader, from George Lucas's *Star Wars*, which actually borrows much of its numinous qualities from Tolkien.
12. Otto, *op. cit.*
13. *Ibid.*
14. Eliade, *op. cit.*
15. See Bhaskar 1993, p. 251. Bhaskar makes the alethic conception of truth central to his "Dialectical Critical Realism." My views on alethia were developed in conversation with Ruth Groff, who nevertheless comes out in opposition to this development in critical realism. See Groff (1999).
16. See Lovin and Reynolds 1985.
17. Gordis 1995, p.189.
18. Nietzsche 1967, p. 20. Max Weber is the sociologist most responsible for the thesis that the West experienced a distinct and protracted process of cultural disenchantment, beginning with the ancient Jews. See Weber 1927. pp. 232–270.
19. Lyotard 1984.
20. Poll conducted by Gallup Organization in November 1990. USGallup.122008, R2 on *Public Opinion On-Line* at Roper Center, University of Connecticut.
21. Question asked in February 1991 as part of General Social Survey (Module 1991), National Opinion Research Center. USNORC.GSS91S, Q1583C on *Public Opinion On-Line* at Roper Center, University of Connecticut. In a 1990 World Values Survey, NORC also asked this question, although in this case, the only response categories were Agree, Neither Agree nor Disagree, Disagree, and Don't Know. Asked in this form, 58 percent of respondents agreed that life is meaningful only because God exists. Only 7 percent neither agreed nor disagreed. Three percent did not know how to respond. Thirty-one percent disagreed. See USGALLUP.90WVAL, Q135 on *Public Opinion On-Line* at Roper Center, University of Connecticut.

For some reason, the response categories of the 1990 question elicited many fewer people than in 1991 who neither agreed nor disagreed with the statement posed. Many more made up their minds one way or the other, about an additional ten percent agreeing and about an additional six percent disagreeing.

Regardless of the exact numbers, both the 1990 and 1991 results indicate a substantial portion of the population—between a third and a half—for whom God is not the ultimate meaning of existence. Those who accord God ultimate meaning are far fewer than the between 85 percent and 95 percent who say they believe in God.

22. Question asked in September 1985 by *U.S. News and World Report*. USROPER.640019, Q30 on *Public Opinion On-Line* at Roper Center, University of Connecticut.

23. The title of this section is obviously a variation on James (1961), whose emphasis on experience I am clearly following.

24. Both Tracy (1975) and Kung (1980) interpret the affirmation of God as an affirmation of the meaningfulness of life.

25. The notion of a limited God who suffers along with the creation is particularly associated with the "process theology" of Whitehead 1929.

26. Roof (1993) argues that religious alienation is partly a generational phenomenon, particularly affecting baby boomers like Tom Brown, who grew up in the centers of the sixties counterculture. Religious alienation may have been more pronounced among those growing up in the midst of the sixties counterculture, but as can be seen from the people I interviewed, religious alienation is also found in other age cohorts as well. Religious alienation is thus a more culturally pervasive phenomenon.

27. Berger 1974.

28. There are exceptions. See, for example, Berger 1979; Greeley 1996; Hay and Morisy 1978; Neitz 1987; Neitz and Spickard 1990; Yamane and Polzer 1994; and Young 1997.

29. Polkinghorne 1994.

30. This is documented by a number of studies. For example, see Stark 1996, p.167.

31. See, for example, Barrow and Tipler 1986; Leslie 1989.

32. Jastrow 1978, p. 15.

33. Freud considered religious belief irrational for just this reason. Against rational choice theory, Neitz and Mueser (1997) stress the sense-making rationality involved in religious belief. Young (1997), on the other hand, characterizes religious experience as either "nonrational" or "precognitive." In contrast with Neitz and Mueser, I am arguing that sense-making is not just a rational approach to belief alternative to instrumental rationality but that in applying instrumental rationality to belief, rational choice theory totally confuses the rationality of belief and the rationality of action. In contrast with Young, I consider religious experience to be epistemically both cognitive and rational—although certainly not calculative.

34. This point goes back to Davidson 1973 and Stroud 1969 and is conceded even by Rorty 1982. It gained currency in sociology from Giddens

(see, for example, 1979, pp. 71f). It rather decisively counts against any kind of Lacanian position (see, for example, Clough 1994), according to which our experience is so pervaded by unconscious impulses as to be globally unreliable.

35. Alston (1991) presents a similar line of argument.

Chapter Four. The Meaning of Life

1. An enormous literature on the meaning of life in psychology and sociology is comprehensively compiled and reviewed by Baumeister 1991. Yet, very little of this literature addresses the question at the metaphysical level considered here. Instead, the concern is with the more concrete issues of daily living: happiness at home and work, whether or not one has long range goals, and so forth.
2. See Klemke 1981.
3. See Berger 1969, Kearney 1984.
4. This was a question in the May 1990 World Values Survey conducted by the Gallup Organization. See USGALLUP.90WVAL, Q133 on *Public Opinion On-Line*, The Roper Center, University of Connecticut.
5. We have already seen that for some theologians such as Kung (1980) and Tracy (1975), the affirmation of life's ultimate meaningfulness is one of the primary functions served by an affirmation of God. Perhaps many of my interviewees are doing just that.
6. The difference between the two response patterns is statistically significant (a < .001). In a paired difference t-test, the average difference in responses was greater than one category.
7. Generally overlooked in the United States, for example, is the role of grassroots religion in the Central American revolutionary activity of the 1980s. See Berryman 1984 and Lernoux 1980.
8. Giddens 1991.
9. Teilhard de Chardin 1959.
10. See Perrin 1967; Crossan 1992; Meier 1994; and Wright 1996.
11. Altogether a little over 27 percent of the Philadelphia sample regarded themselves as very religious. This is comparable to the 22 percent of very religious respondents found by Lamont 1992, p. 57. Lamont, of course, was examining the upper-middle class. Religiosity, however, may not be a class dependent trait. I ran a multiple regression analysis with religiosity as the dependent variable and age, race, gender, education, and income as independent variables. In this analysis, age ($\beta = -.17$; a < .0001), race ($\beta = -.16$; a = .012), and gender ($\beta = .12$; a = .012) were all significantly related to religiosity. Age, surprisingly, was inversely related to religiosity; blacks were slightly more religious than whites; and women were slightly more religious than men. Neither education ($\beta = .03$; a = .50) nor income ($\beta = .04$; a = .37) was significantly related to religiosity.

12. On the multidimensionality of religiosity, see Glock and Stark 1965.

13. Quantitatively oriented scholars will want the results of a multivariate analysis. I ran a multiple regression in which the dependent variable was how often one thinks about the meaning of human existence. The independent variables were age, gender, education, income, race, and religiosity. In this analysis (R = .333), age (α = .58), gender (α = .09), education (α = .31), income (α = .28), and race (α = .23) were all insignificant with ß's all lower than 0.1. Only religiosity (ß = .334; α < .0001) was significant—and highly significant. Religiosity explains about 11 percent of the variation in the meaning variable, even controlling for demographic categories.

14. Again, the bivariate relationship between religiosity and ultimate meaning persists even when controlling for demographic categories. I ran a multiple regression analysis with attitude toward the meaning of human existence as the dependent variable. To do that, I first had to make this variable at least ordinal, which meant removing those who said either that life has no meaning or that they have some other attitude toward the meaning of life. Such respondents, as we have seen, reject the framework posed by the question. Their removal left three categories of increasing clarity about the meaning of life.

   Again, there was no relation between the meaning variable and any of the demographic categories; age (ß = .11; a = .08), education (ß = -.10; a - .83), income (ß = 1.02; α = .83), race (ß = .06; α = .33), and gender (ß = -.06; α = .41) were all insignificant. Only religiosity (ß = .18; α < .001) explained any of the variation in the dependent variable with statistical significance (R= .33).

15. Such an explanation is suggested by Rodney Stark's rational choice approach to religion. See Stark 2000.

16. Again, critical realism speaks of such ultimate reality as *alethia* or alethic truth. See Bhaskar 1993: 63–64.

17. Weber 1947.

18. The designation, *silver rule*, comes from Bull 1969, pp. 155–56 and Rost 1986, pp. 65–66.

19. The distinction was drawn in the fourth century by John Chrysostom. See McArthur 1967. On the linguistic insignificance of the difference between the golden and silver rules, see King 1928.

20. Leviticus 19:18.

21. See Bull *op. cit.*, and Rost *op. cit.*, pp. 64–65.

22. See Wattles 1996.

23. Wuthnow 1991.

24. See Funk et al. 1993, p. 156. But see also Wattles *op. cit.*, pp. 52–54, for a defense of the authenticity of the golden rule saying. According to Wattles, what may have been startling is the original, radically deeper meaning Jesus attached to the golden rule. Still, Wattles concurs that

Jesus preached an ethic far loftier and far more demanding than the reciprocity or procedural respect we familiarly associate with the golden rule today (pp. 55, 60–66).

25. See Klingaman 1990.
26. On the reign of God in Jesus's ministry, see Crossan and Meier *op. cit.*
27. Albert Schweitzer (1906 / 1986) was the first to call our attention to the radical nature of Jesus's ethic. Jesus's ethic, Schweitzer argued, was meant to be an "interim ethic" until the reign of God came in power. Today, although scholars continue to acknowledge the radical aspect of Jesus's ethic, they no longer regard it as interim. Instead, the view today is that Jesus regarded his ethic as appropriate to the reign of God, which Jesus considered already in some fashion present in his ministry. See Crossan and Meier *ibid.*
28. Urmson 1971.
29. Matthew 5:39–42. These words are among the most attested of Jesus's actual sayings and are found in the earliest written layers of tradition. Even the highly skeptical Jesus Seminar considers them authentic. See Funk et al., *op. cit.*, p. 143.
30. Perrin *op. cit.*, p. 146.
31. See Vermes (1973) for an account of how Jesus intensified rather than contradicted the Jewish holiness code.
32. Matthew 5: 44–48.
33. Funk et al., *op. cit.* p. 147.
34. See Wright 1992, p. 97, but also Wright 1996 for a more extended and quite compelling treatment of Jesus.
35. Chadwick 1967.
36. Roth 1975.
37. Taylor 1987.

CHAPTER FIVE. HEROES

1. Eliade 1959. According to the *New American Dictionary*, the word *hero* is now gender-neutral and can refer to women as well as men. Empirical study suggests, moreover, that female respondents in particular hear the word *hero* as gender-neutral. See Hakanen 1989a. Thus, throughout this chapter, the single word *hero* is used to designate both male and female heroic figures.
2. See, for example, Keen 1994.
3. Durkheim 1951, pp. 208–16.
4. Nietzsche 1969.
5. See Hakanen *op. cit.* See also Hakanen 1989b.
6. Fishwick 1983.
7. *Ibid.*
8. Becker 1973.

9. Campbell 1968.

10. Warner 1959.

11. Emerson 1940.

12. Becker, *op. cit.*, p. 1.

13. Boorstin 1968, p. 325.

14. Schlesinger 1968, p. 341.

15. Glicksberg 1968, pp. 357, 362.

16. Campbell *op. cit.*, pp. 387–88.

17. Fishwick *op. cit.*

18. Lowenthal 1943.

19. Boorstin *op. cit.*, p. 334.

20. *Ibid.*, p. 336.

21. See Coles 1993.

22. For studies of adolescents, see, for example, Hakanen *op. cit.* Likewise, see Balswick 1982.

23. Gardiner and Jones 1983.

24. See, for example, Patterson and Kim 1991 and Smith 1986.

25. The response rate in the spring was 41 percent and in the fall 38 percent. These response rates yielded a sample of 277 cases in the spring and 350 in the fall for a combined sample of 627. For a more technical, methodological discussion of this study, see Porpora 1996.

26. As we have conceptualized heroes, one cannot be one's own hero. I similarly removed responses like "Mickey Mouse," which, I presume, were facetious.

27. For what it means theoretically for us to situate our lives within an ongoing narrative, see MacIntyre 1981.

28. See Cooley 1964, p. 314. See as well Schwartz 1985.

29. $\chi^2 = 19.948$; $\alpha = .0005$. See Porpora 1996 for multivariate analysis.

30. $\chi^2 = 84.8$; $\alpha < .001$. Again, see Porpora 1996 for multivariate analysis.

31. $\chi^2 = 14.2$; $\alpha = .0008$. Again, a multivariate analysis is presented in Porpora 1996.

CHAPTER SIX. CALLINGS, JOURNEYS, AND QUESTS

1. This translation is found in Renard 1992, p. 61.

2. Campbell 1968.

3. Weber 1976.

4. Sullivan 1995, p. 12.

5. See Goldman 1988, p. 122. Goldman's study is one of the few pieces of anglophone sociology since Weber to examine the concept of calling.

6. Renard 1992, p. 59.

7. Hesse 1956.

8. *Ibid.*, pp. 30–31.

9. Wuthnow 1994, pp. 67–73.

10. Coles 1993; Gordis 1995.
11. See Greeley 1996.
12. The response rate was about 44 percent. As in the other surveys conducted through the center, this one was administered by trained students. The low response rate is in part explained by insufficient time to track down all respondents who declined to be interviewed at the time.
13. Wuthnow 1994 *op cit.*, p. 69.
14. Wuthnow *ibid.*, p. 68.
15. These questions were adopted from a study done twenty years ago by Wuthnow 1976, pp. 260, 270.
16. For the relation between religiosity and how often one thinks about God, the significance level was $\alpha < .0001$. The significance of the relation between religiosity and thought about the origin of the universe was $\alpha < .009$. The relationship between religiosity and lifegoal just fails to be significant ($\alpha = .08$).
17. The significance level was $\alpha = .03$. The finding corroborates Wuthnow's 1994 *op.cit.*, p. 69. He also found the sense of calling more pronounced among churchgoers.
18. The significance level was $\alpha = .019$.
19. West 1993.
20. See, for example, Berger 1979, who presents such a position despite religious sympathies.

CHAPTER SEVEN. RESOURCES OF THE SELF

Note: The title of this chapter is clearly in homage to Taylor's (1989) *Sources of the Self.*
1. But see Luhrmann 1989.
2. Sartre 1962.
3. The importance of narrativity to our sense of identity is one of the seminal contributions of MacIntyre 1981. I also spent considerable space on narrative explanation in Porpora 1987, an effort that goes quite unnoticed now that narrative has finally been discovered by sociology. The obvious lesson is that it is as critical a mistake to be too far ahead as too far behind.
4. Jacobson (1994) collects many such stories of Holocaust survivors that likewise bear powerfully on issues of identity.
5. Maslow 1970. Wuthnow (1976) also notes the importance of peak experiences.
6. The terms *enablement* and *constraint* in reference to social structure were popularized by Giddens 1979.
7. Poll conducted by Yankelovich, Skelly and White for the American Jewish Committee in 1981. In 1993, the Princeton Religion Research Center likewise asked a national sample whether they agreed that "the

only assurance of eternal life is personal faith in Jesus Christ." Fifty-nine percent (59%) agreed completely and 17 percent agreed somewhat. Only 21% disagreed.

8. See Carter 1993.

CHAPTER EIGHT. COMMUNITIES OF DISCOURSE

1. See Wuthnow 1989.
2. The sociological classic on this point is Berger and Luckmann 1966.
3. Generally, sociologists ignore not only the relation between religious belief and religious experience, they generally ignore religious experience altogether. Neitz (1987) is one of the few contemporary sociologists even to treat religious experience. Yet not even she treats the relation between belief and experience.
4. Durkheim 1951.
5. If sociologists are reluctant to speak of religious experience, it is partly because they wish to avoid addressing the object of religious experience. To do so would implicate them in theological debate. To avoid that, sociologists take for granted Durkheim's naturalistic thesis that the object of religious experience is just community itself. However, if Durkheim treated the religious as social, he also tended to regard the social as religious. As Turner (1999, p. 134) recently put it, quoting a passage from T.S. Eliot, "We have to face the strange idea that what is part of culture is also a part of our lived religion 'so that from one point of view religion is culture, from another point of view culture is religion.'"
6. Berger (1979) speaks of such experiences as "intimations" of transcendence.
7. Becker 1953.
8. Berger (1974 *op. cit.*, p. 128) speaks of sociology's "quasiscientific legitimation of the avoidance of transcendence." The ruse works, Berger says, by "assassination through definition." Any transcendent object of religious experience is rendered nonexistent by definition alone. In its place stands a social construction. Unfortunately, Berger (1979 *op. cit.*, pp. 36–37) himself inadvertently commits the same assassination. To separate sociology from theology, Berger would have sociologists methodologically bracket out of analysis the object of religious experience. In any true experience, however, the object of experience must contribute something to the content of experience. Thus, if sociological analysis is to ignore the object of religious experience, it is hardly an analysis of experience at all.
9. The term *epistemic community* comes from Assiter 1996.
10. On the social facticity of what appears in public space, see both Berger and Luckmann *op. cit.*, and Taylor 1982.
11. I spoke with Hal primarily to solicit "expert testimony" and, therefore,

with his permission, saw no reason to disguise his name. Hal Taussig is the actual name of the biblical scholar I spoke with.

12. Funk and Hoover 1993.

13. Witherington (1995) presents a cogent Evangelical critique, Johnson (1996) a critique from the historically skeptical wing of liberal theology, with Wright (1992, 1996) and Meier (1994) criticizing the Jesus Seminar on more common ground.

14. The so-called *Q* document has never been found, but biblical critics are certain it existed—and fairly certain as well about what is in it. It is known that in addition to their own independent sources of information, the gospels of Luke and Matthew copied extensively—sometimes word for word—from both the gospel of Mark and from another common written source. That other source is labeled *Q*, which stands for the German "Quelle," or source. Obviously if both Luke and Matthew copied from *Q*, *Q* must have been written before either of them and thus represents an earlier layer of tradition.

15. Hal's comment about relative objectivity coincides with a distinction drawn by critical realism between "epistemic relativity" and "judgmental rationality." Bhaskar 1975; 1989, p. 23; Manicas 1987.

16. For a defense of the epistemic value of religious experience, see Alston 1991.

17. Weinberg 1992.

18. Sandra is not the only physicist to think the new cosmology has an important bearing on the meaning of our lives. For a compendium of scientific opinion on this subject, see Margenau and Varghese 1992.

19. Hume 1991. For an excellent account of how evolution explains the origins of species without a designer see Dawkins 1987. For a cogent argument that ineradicable elements of design remain in biology, see Behe 1996.

20. Davies 1982, p. 73.

21. *Ibid.*

22. Leslie 1989. There is now a vast literature on this topic, from the more technical (Barrow and Tipler 1986; Leslie 1989; Davies 1982 *op. cit.*; Dressler 1994; Morris 1990; Rowan-Robinson 1993) to the more popular (Davies 1984; 1994; Greenstein 1988; Gribbon and Rees 1989). The issue has even surfaced prominently in two recent novels: Updike 1986 and Sawyer 2000.

23. Cited by Davies 1984 *ibid.*, pp. 223 and 242.

24. Dyson 1979, p. 250.

CHAPTER NINE. THE HUMAN VOCATION

1. Yamane and Polzer 1994. See also Hay and Morisy 1978.

2. Ward and Brownlee 2000.

3. *Ibid.*
4. *Ibid.*
5. *Ibid.*
6. Yoder 1972.
7. Schor 1998.
8. *Ibid.*
9. Barber 1996.
10. *Ibid.*

APPENDIX A

1. See Archer et al 1999; Bhaskar 1975; 1979; 1989; 1993; Manicas 1987; Porpora 1987.
2. Although he himself does not go by the name of critical realist, I adopt Alston's 1996 formulation of an alethic conception of truth. I am equally indebted to his 1991 defense of the epistemic status of religious experience.

References

Adams, Douglas. 1979. *The Hitchhiker's Guide to the Galaxy.* New York: Pocket Books.

Alston, William. 1991. *Perceiving God.* Ithaca: Cornell University Press.

————. 1996. *A Realist Conception of Truth.* Ithaca: Cornell University Press.

Althusser, Louis. 1969. *For Marx.* London: New Left Books.

———— and Etienne Balibar. 1970. *Reading Capital.* London: New Left Books.

Anderson, Perry. 1988. *In the Tracks of Historical Materialism.* London: Verso.

Archer, Margaret, Roy Bhaskar, Andrew Collier, Tony Lawson, and Alan Norrie (eds.). 1999. *Critical Realism: Essential Readings.* London: Routledge.

Aristotle. 1952. *Metaphysics.* Ann Arbor: University of Michigan.

————. 1985. *Nicomachean Ethics.* Indianapolis: Hackett Publishing Company.

Assiter, Alison. 1996. *Enlightened Women: Modernist Feminism in a Postmodern Age.* New York: Routledge.

Balswick, Jack. 1982. "Heroes and Heroines Among American Adolescents." *Sex Roles* 8 (3): 243-49

Barbalet, Jack. 1998. *Emotion, Social Theory and Social Structure: A Macrosociological Approach.* Cambridge: Cambridge University Press.

Barber, Benjamin. 1996. *Jihad vs. McWorld.* New York: Ballantine.

Barrow, John D., and Frank Tipler. 1986. *The Anthropic Cosmological Principle.* New York: Oxford.

Barth, Karl. 1957. *The Word of God and the Word of Man.* New York: Harper.

Bartsch, Hans Werner. 1966. *Kerygma and Myth: A Theological Debate.* New York: Harper & Row.

Baumeister, Roy F. 1991. *Meanings of Life.* New York: Guilford.

Becker, Ernest. 1973. *The Denial of Death.* New York: Free Press.

Becker, Howard. 1953. "Becoming a Marijuana User." *American Journal of Sociology* 59: 235-42.

Behe, Michael. 1996. *Darwin's Black Box.* New York: Touchstone.

Belk, Russell. 1993. "Materialism and the American Christmas." Pp. 75-104 in Daniel Miller (ed.), *Unwrapping Christmas.* New York: Oxford.

Bellah, Robert. 1970. *Beyond Belief: Essays on Religion in a Post-Traditional World.* New York: Harper and Row.

———. Richard Madsen, William M. Sullivan, Ann Swidler, and Stephen M. Tipton. 1985. *Habits of the Heart: Individualism and Commitment in American Life.* Berkeley: University of California Press.

Berger, Peter. 1969. *The Sacred Canopy.* Garden City, N.Y.: Anchor.

———. 1974. "Some Second Thoughts on Substantive Versus Functional Definitions of Religion." *Journal for the Scientific Study of Religion* 13 (2): 125-33.

———. 1979. *The Heretical Imperative: Contemporary Possibilities of Religious Affirmation.* Garden City, N.Y.: Anchor.

———, and Thomas Luckmann. 1966. *The Social Construction of Reality.* Garden City, N.Y.: Doubleday.

Berryman, Phillip. 1984. *The Religious Roots of Rebellion: Christians in Central American Revolutions.* Maryknoll, N.Y.: Orbis.

Bhaskar, Roy. 1975. *A Realist Theory of Science.* Leeds: Leeds Books.

———. 1979. *The Possibility of Naturalism.* Atlantic Highlands: Humanities Press.

———. 1989. *Reclaiming Reality.* New York: Verso.

———. 1993. *Dialectic: The Pulse of Freedom.* London: Verso.

Bloom, Allen. 1987. *The Closing of the American Mind.* New York: Simon and Schuster.

Blum, Alan, and Peter McHugh. 1971. "The Social Ascription of Motives." *American Sociological Review* 36: 98-109.

Bonhoeffer, Dietrich. 1997. *Letters and Papers from Prison.* New York: Touchstone.

Boorstin, Daniel. 1968. "From Hero to Celebrity: The Human Pseudo-Event." Pp. 325-40 in Harold Lubin (ed.), *Heroes and Anti-Heroes: A Reader in Depth.* Scranton, Pa.: Chandler.

Brecht, Bertolt. 1966. *Galileo.* Translated by Charles Laughton. New York: Grove Press.

Buber, Martin. 1952. *The Eclipse of God.* New York: Harper and Row.

———. 1970. *I and Thou.* New York: Charles Scribner's.

Bull, Norman J. 1969. *Moral Education.* London: Routledge & Kegan Paul.

Bultmann, Rudolf. 1958. *Jesus Christ and Mythology.* New York: Charles Scribner's Sons.

——— 1962. "The Study of the Synoptic Gospels." Pp. 7-78 in Rudolf Bultman and Kark Kundsin, *Form Criticism.* New York: Harper Torchbooks.

Butler, Judith. 1990. *Gender Trouble: Feminism and the Subversion of Identity.*
New York: Routledge.

Calhoun, Craig. 1995. *Critical Social Theory.* Oxford: Blackwell.

Campbell, Colin. 1992. "In Defence of the Traditional Concept of Action in
Sociology." *Journal for the Theory of Social Behaviour* 22: 1-24.

———. 1996. *The Myth of Social Action.* New York: Cambridge.

Campbell, Joseph. 1968. *The Hero with a Thousand Faces.* Princeton:
Princeton University Press.

Camus, Albert. 1955. *The Myth of Sisyphus.* New York: Vintage.

Carter, Steven L. 1993. *The Culture of Disbelief.* New York: Basic Books.

Chadwick, Henry. 1967. *The Early Church.* Baltimore: Penguin.

Coles, Robert. 1993. *The Call of Service: A Witness to Idealism.* New York:
Houghton Mifflin.

Collier, Andrew. 1990. *Socialist Reasoning: An Inquiry into the Political
Philosophy of Scientific Socialism.* London: Pluto Press.

Conner, Steven. 1989. *Postmodernist Culture: An Introduction to Theories of the
Contemporary.* Oxford: Basil Blackwell.

Cooley, Charles Horton. 1964. *Human Nature and the Social Order.*

Coulter, Jeff. 1989. *Mind in Action.* Atlantic Highlands, N.J.: Humanities
Press.

Crossan, John Dominic. 1992. *The Historical Jesus: The Life of a Mediterranean
Jewish Peasant.* Harper SanFrancisco.

Dawkins, Richard. 1987. *The Blind Watchmaker.* New York: Norton.

Davidson, Donald. 1963. "Actions, Reasons, and Causes." *Journal of Philosophy*
60: 685-700.

———. 1973. "On the Very Idea of a Conceptual Scheme." *Proceedings of the
American Philosophical Association,* 17: 5-20.

Davies, Paul. 1982. *The Accidental Universe.* Cambridge: Cambridge University
Press.

———. 1984. *Superforce.* New York: Simon and Schuster.

———. 1992. *The Mind of God.* New York: Simon and Schuster.

de Chardin, Teilhard. 1959. *The Phenomenon of Man.* New York: Harper
& Row.

Deleuze, Gilles, and Felix Guattari. 1977. *Anti-Oedipus: Capitalism and
Schizophrenia.* New York: Viking.

dell'Arco, Maurizio Fagiolo. 1982. "De Chirico in Paris, 1911-1915." Pp. 11-
54 in *De Chirico.* New York: The Museum of Modern Art.

Denzin, Norman. 1986. "Postmodern Social Theory." *Sociological Theory* 14:
194-204.

Derrida, Jacques. 1973. *Speech and Phenomena and other Essays on Husserl's
Theory of Signs.* Evanston: Northwestern Unversity Press.

———. 1976. *Of Grammatology.* Baltimore: Johns Hopkins University
Press.

———. 1978 *Writing and Difference.* Chicago: Chicago University Press.

Diamond, Cora. 1987. "Losing Our Concepts." *Ethics* 98-99: 255-77.

Dressler, Alan. 1994. *Journey to the Great Attractor.* New York: Knopf.

Durkheim, Emile. 1951. *Suicide.* New York: The Free Press.

———. 1955. *The Elementary Forms of the Religious Life.* New York: The Free Press.

Dyson, Freeman. 1979. *Disturbing the Universe.* New York: Harper & Row.

Eisenstadt, Shmuel N. 1982. "The Axial Age: The Emergence of Transcendental Visions and the Rise of Clerics." *Journal of European Sociology* (22): 294-314.

Eliade, Mircea. 1957. *The Sacred and the Profane.* New York: Harcourt, Brace & World.

Emerson, Ralph Waldo. 1940. "Heroism." Pp. 249-60 in Brooks Atkinson (ed.), *The Complete Essays and Other Writings of Ralph Waldo Emerson.* New York: Random House.

Feuerbach, Ludwig. 1957. *The Essence of Christianity.* New York: Harper Torchbooks.

Finke, Roger, and Rodney Stark. 1992. *The Churching of America.* New Brunswick: Rutgers University Press.

Fishwick, Marshall. 1983. "Introduction." Pp. 5-14 in Ray B. Browne and Marshall Fishwick (eds.), *The Hero in Transition.* Bowling Green: Bowling Green University Press.

Flax, Jane. 1990. *Psychoanalysis, Feminism and Postmodernism in the Contemporary West.* Berkeley: University of California.

Foucault, Michel. 1972. *The Archaeology of Knowledge.* London: Tavistock.

———. 1977. *Discipline and Punish.* London: Allen Lane.

———. 1980. *A History of Sexuality.* New York: Vintage.

———. 1980b. *Power/Knowledge.* New York: Pantheon.

Funk, Robert W., Roy Hoover, and the Jesus Seminar. 1993. *The Five Gospels: The Search for the Authentic Words of Jesus.* New York: Macmillan.

Gaita, Raimond. 1996. *Good and Evil.* New York: St. Martin's Press.

Gardiner, John, and Katryn E. Jones. 1983. "Leaders of the American West: Who Are Their Heroes?" Pp. 285-94 in Ray B. Browne and Marshall Fishwick (eds.), *The Hero in Transition.* Bowling Green: Bowling Green University Press.

Gergen, Kenneth J. 1991. *The Saturated Self: Dilemmas of Identity in Contemporary Life.* New York: Basic Books.

Giddens, Anthony. 1979. *Central Problems in Social Theory.* Berkeley: University of California Press.

———. 1991. *Modernity and Self-Identity: Self and Society in the Late Modern Age.* Stanford: Stanford University Press.

Glicksberg, Charles I. 1968. "The Tragic Hero." Pp. 356-66 in Harold Lubin (ed.), *Heroes and Anti-Heroes: A Reader in Depth.* Scranton, Pa.: Chandler.

Glock, Charles, and Rodney Stark. 1965. *Religion and Society in Tension.* Chicago: Rand McNally.

Goffman, Erving. 1959. *The Presentation of Self in Everyday Life.* Garden City, N.Y.: Doubleday.

Goldman, Harvey. 1988. *Max Weber and Thomas Mann: Calling and the Shaping of the Self.* Berkeley: University of California Press.

Gordis, Daniel. 1995. *God Was Not in the Fire: A Search for a Spiritual Judaism.* New York: Scribner.

Greeley, Andrew M. 1996. *Religion as Poetry.* New Brunswick: Transaction.

Greenstein, George. 1988. *The Symbiotic Universe.* New York: William Morrow.

Greenwood, John. 1994. "A Sense of Identity: Prolegomena to a Social Theory of Personal Identity." *Journal for the Theory of Social Behaviour* 24: 25-46.

Gribbin, John, and Martin Rees. 1989. *Cosmic Coincidences: Dark Matter, Mankind, and Anthropic Cosmology.* New York: Bantam.

Habermas, Jurgen. 1987. *Philosophical Discourse on Modernity: Twenty Lectures.* Cambridge: MIT Press.

Hakanen, Ernest. 1989a. *Adolescent Identification of Heroes: A Study of Media Exposure and Perception of Public Figures.* Unpublished Ph.D. Dissertation, Temple University.

————. 1989b. "The (D)Evolution of Heroes: An Expanded Typology of Heroes for the Electronic Age." *Free Inquiry in Creative Sociology* 17 (2): 153-58.

Harre, Rom. 1986. "An Outline of the Social Constructionist Viewpoint." Pp. 2-14 in Rom Harre (ed.), *The Social Construction of the Emotions.* Oxford: Blackwell.

Harrington, Michael. 1983. *The Politics at God's Funeral: The Spiritual Crisis of Western Civilization.* New York: Holt, Rinehart and Winston.

Hart, Stephen. 1992. *What Does the Lord Require? How American Christians Think about Economic Justice.* New York: Oxford University Press.

Harvey, David. 1989. *The Postmodern Condition: An Enquiry into the Origins of Cultural Change.* New York: Oxford University Press.

Hay, David, and Ann Orisy. 1978. "Reports of Ecstatic, Paranormal, or Religious Experiences in Great Britain and the U.S.—A Comparison of Trends." *Journal for the Scientific Study of Religon* 17 (3): 255-68.

Heidegger, Martin. 1962. *Being and Time.* New York: Harper.

Hesse, Hermann. 1956. *The Journey to the East.* New York: Farrar, Straus and Giroux.

Horkheimer, Max, and Theodore W. Adorno. 1972. *Dialectic of Enlightenment.* New York: Herder & Herder.

Hume, David. 1991. *Dialogues Concerning Natural Religion.* New York: Routledge.

Ishiguro, Kazuo. 1988. *The Remains of the Day.* New York: Random House.

Jacobson, Kenneth. 1994. *Embattled Selves: An Investigation into the Nature of Identity through Oral Histories of Holocaust Survivors.* New York: Atlantic Monthly Books.

James, William. 1961. *The Varieties of Religious Experience.* New York: Collier-Macmillan.

Jameson, Frederick. 1984. "Postmodernism, or the Cultural Logic of Late Capitalism." *New Left Review* 146: 53-92.

Jastrow, Robert. 1978. *God and the Astronomers.* New York: W.W. Norton.

Johnson, Luke Timothy. 1996. *The Real Jesus: The Misguided Quest for the Historical Jesus and the Truth of the Traditional Gospels.* San Franciso: Harper SanFrancisco.

Kearny, Michael. 1984. *World View.* Novato, Calif.: Chandler & Sharp.

Keen, Sam. 1994. *Hymns to an Unknown God.* New York: Bantam.

Kekes, John. 1988. *The Examined Life.* Lewisburg: Bucknell University Press.

King, George Brockwell. 1928. "The 'Negative' Golden Rule." *Journal of Religion* 8: 270-79.

Klemke, E.D. (ed.). 1981. *The Meaning of Life.* New York: Oxford.

Klingaman, William K. 1990. *The First Century: Emperors, Gods, and Everyman.* New York: HarperCollins.

Kung, Hans. 1980. *Does God Exist? An Answer for Today.* Garden City, N.Y.: Doubleday.

Kuper, Adam. 1993. "The English Christmas and the Family: Time Out and Alternative Realities." Pp. 157-75 in Daniel Miller (ed.), *Unwrapping Christmas.* New York: Oxford.

Lacan, Jacques. 1977. *Ecrits: A Selection.* London: Tavistock.

Laclau, Ernesto, and Chantel Mouffe. 1985. *Hegemony and Socialist Strategy.* London: Verso.

Lakatos, Imre. 1970. "Falsification and the Methodology of Scientific Research Programmes." Pp. 91-196 in Imre Lakatos and Alan Musgrave (eds.), *Criticism and the Growth of Knowledge.* Cambridge: Cambridge University Press.

Lamont, Michele. 1992. *Money, Morals, and Manners: The Culture of the French and American Upper-Middle Class.* Chicago: University of Chicago Press.

Larana, Enrique, Hank Johnston, and Joseph Gusfield (eds.). 1995. *New Social Movements.* Philadelphia: Temple University Press.

Langman, Lauren. 1999a. "Agency, Alienation, and the Body: Reclaiming Emancipatory Critique in a Postmodern Age." Paper presented at *International Institute of Sociology,* Tel Aviv, Israel.

———. 1999b. "Suppose They Gave a Culture War and No One Came: Zippergate and the Carnivalization of Politics." Paper presented at the March meeting of the Midwest Sociological Society, Chicago.

Laudan, Larry. 1984. *Progress and Its Problems.* Berkeley: University of California.

Lemert, Charles. 1994. "Dark Thoughts about the Self." Pp. 100-30 in Craig Calhoun (ed.), *Social Theory and the Politics of Identity.* Oxford: Basil Blackwell.

Lernoux, Penny. 1980. *Cry of the People: The Struggle for Human Rights in Latin America: The Catholic Church in Conflict with U.S. Policy.* New York: Penguin Books.

Leslie, John. 1989. *Universes.* New York: Routledge.

Lifton, Robert Jay. 1993. *The Protean Self: Human Resiliance in an Age of Fragmentation.* New York: Basic Books.

Lovin, Robin W., and Frank E. Reynolds (eds.). 1985. *Cosmogony and the Ethical Order.* Chicago: University of Chicago Press.

Lowenthal, Leo. 1943. "Biographies in Popular Magazines." Pp. 507-43 in P. Lazersfeld and F. Stanton (eds.), *Radio Research.* New York: Duell, Sloan and Pearce.

Luhrman, T. M. 1989. *Persuasions of the Witch's Craft: Ritual Magic and Witchcraft in Present-Day England.* Oxford: Basil Blackwell.

Lyon, David. 1985. *The Steeple's Shadow: On the Myths and Realities of Secularization.* London: SPCK.

Lyotard, Jean-François. 1984. *The Postmodern Condition: A Report on Knowledge.* Minneapolis: University of Minnesota Press.

Macdonell, Diane. 1986. *Theories of Discourse.* Oxford: Basil Blackwell.

MacIntyre, Alisdair. 1981. *After Virtue.* Notre Dame: University of Notre Dame.

Manicas, Peter. 1987. *A History & Philosophy of the Social Sciences.* New York: Blackwell.

Marcuse, Herbert. 1964. *One-Dimensional Man: Studies in the Ideology of Advanced Industrial Society.* Boston: Beacon Press.

Margenau, Henry, and Roy Abraham Varghese (eds.). 1992. *Cosmos, Bios, Theos.* LaSalle, Ill.: Open Court Press.

Margolis, Joseph. 1970. "Puzzles about Explanation by Reasons and Explanations by Causes." *Journal of Philosophy* 67: 187-95.

———. 1978 *Persons and Minds.* Dordrecht: D. Reidel.

———. 1979. "Action and Causality." *The Philosophical Forum* 11: 47-64.

———. 1986. *Pragmatism without Foundations: Reconciling Realism and Relativism.* Oxford: Basil Blackwell.

———. 1987. "Minds, Selves, and Persons." Pp. 51-100 in Joseph Margolis, *Science without Unity.* Oxford: Basil Blackwell.

Maslow, Abraham H. 1970. *Religions, Values, and Peak Experiences.* New York: Penguin.

Maugham, W. Somerset. 1949. *The Razor's Edge.* London: Heinemann.

McArthur, Harvey K. 1967. "Golden Rule." Pp. 136-37 in John Macquarrie (ed.), *Dictionary of Christian Ethics.* London: S.C.M. Press.

Mead, George Herbert. 1964. *Mind, Self and Society.* Chicago: University of Chicago Press.

Meier, John P. 1994. *A Marginal Jew: Rethinking the Historical Jesus. Volume II: Mentor, Message, and Miracles.* New York: Doubleday.

Miller, Daniel. 1993. "A Theory of Christmas." Pp. 1-37 in Daniel Miller (ed.), *Unwrapping Christmas.* New York: Oxford.

Morris, Richard. 1990. *The Edges of Science: Crossing the Boundary from Physics to Metaphysics.* New York: Prentice Hall.

Murchland, Bernard. 1967. *The Meaning of the Death of God.* New York: Vintage.

New, Caroline. 1998. "Realism, Deconstruction, and the Feminist Standpoint." *Journal for the Theory of Social Behaviour* 28 (4): 349-372.

Neitz, Mary Jo. 1987. *Charisma and Community: A Study of Religious Commitment Within the Charismatic Renewal.* New Brunswick: Transaction Books.

———. 1999 "From the Chair." Newsletter of the American Sociological Association Section on Sociology of Religion (Spring).

———, and James Spickard. 1990. "Steps Toward a Sociology of Religious Experience: The Theories of Mihaly Csikszentmihalyi and Alfred Schutz." *Sociological Analysis* 50: 127-38.

———, and Peter Mueser. 1997. "Economic Man and the Sociology of Religion." Pp. 105-19 in Lawrence Young (ed.), *Rational Choice Theory and Religion: Summary and Assessment.* New York: Routledge.

Nietzsche, Friedrich. 1958. "The Genealogy of Morals." Pp. 147-299 in *The Birth of Tragedy and the Genealogy of Morals.* Garden City, N.Y.: Doubleday.

———. 1967. *The Will to Power.* New York: Vintage.

———. 1969. *Thus Spake Zarathustra.* Middlesex, England: Penguin.

Nineham, D.E. 1969. *Saint Mark.* Baltimore: Penguin.

Nissenbaum, Stephen. 1996. *The Battle for Christmas.* New York: Knopf.

Nussbaum, Martha. 1990. *Love's Knowledge: Essays on Philosophy and Literature.* New York: Oxford.

———. 1994. The *Therapy of Desire: Theory and Practice in Hellenistic Ethics.* Princeton: Princeton University Press.

Otto, Rudolf. 1958. *The Idea of the Holy.* New York: Oxford University Press.

Pannenberg, Wolfhart. 1970. "Did Jesus Really Rise from the Dead?." Pp. 102-18 in Richard Batey (ed.), *New Testament Issues.* New York: Harper & Row.

Patterson, James, and Peter Kim. 1991. *The Day America Told the Truth: What People Really Believe about Everything that Matters.* New York: Prentice Hall.

Perrin, Norman. 1967. *Rediscovering the Teaching of Jesus.* New York: Harper & Row.

Pincoffs, Edmund. 1986. *Quandaries and Virtues: Against Reductivism in Ethics.* Lawrence: University Press of Kansas.

Pirsig, Robert. 1972. *Zen and the Art of Motorcycle Maintenance: An Inquiry into Values.* New York: Morrow.

Polkinghorne, John. 1994. *The Faith of a Physicist.* Princeton: Princeton University Press.

Porpora, Douglas V. 1983. "On the Post-Wittgensteinian Account of Action in Sociology." *Journal for the Theory of Social Behaviour* 13 (2): 129-46.

———. 1987. *The Concept of Social Structure.* New York: Greenwood Press.

————. 1990. *How Holocausts Happen: The U.S. in Central America.* Philadelphia: Temple University Press.

————. 1996. "Heroes, Religion, and Transcendental Metanarratives." *Sociological Forum* 11 (2): 209-30

————. 1997. "The Caterpillar's Question: Contesting Anti-Humanism's Contestations." *Journal for the Theory of Social Behaviour* 27 (2/3): 243-64.

Prabhavananda, Swami, and Frederick Manchester 1948 *The Upanishads: Breath of the Eternal.* New York: New American Library.

Putnam, Hilary. 1981. *Reason, Truth and History.* Cambridge: Cambridge University Press.

Rachels, James. 1988. "Can Ethics Provide Answers?" Pp. 3-24 in David Rosenthal and Fadlou Shehadi (eds.), *Applied Ethics and Ethical Theory.* Salt Lake City: University of Utah Press.

Redfield, James. 1993. *The Celestine Prophecy.* New York: Warner Books.

Renard, John. 1992. *In the Footsteps of Muhammad.* New York: Paulist Press.

Richardson, Laurel . 1991. "Postmodern Social Theory: Representational Practices." *Sociological Theory* 9 (2): 173-79.

Ricoeur, Paul 1978 *Freud and Philosophy.* New Haven: Yale University Press.

Robinson, John A. T. 1963. *Honest to God.* Philadelphia: Westminster Press.

Robinson, James M. 1979. *A New Quest of the Historical Jesus.* Missoula: Scholars Press.

Roof, Wade Clark. 1993. *A Generation of Seekers: The Spiritual Journeys of the Baby Boomer Generation.* San Francisco: Harper SanFrancisco.

Rorty, Richard. 1982. "The World Well Lost." Pp. 3-18 in Richard Rorty, *Consequences of Pragmatism.* Minneapolis: University of Minnesota Press.

Rost, H.T.D. 1986. *The Golden Rule: A Universal Ethic.* Oxford: George Ronald.

Roth, Guenther. 1975. "Socio-historical Model and Developmental Theory: Charismatic Community, Charisma of Reason, and the Counterculture." *American Sociological Review* 40 (2): 148-57.

Rowan-Robinson, Michael. 1993. *Ripples in the Cosmos: A View Behind the Scenes of the New Cosmology.* New York: W.H. Freeman Spektrum.

Rubinstein, David. 1977. "The Concept of Action in the Social Sciences." *Journal for the Theory of Social Behaviour* 7: 209-36.

Rumi, Jal al-Din. 1968. *Mystical Poems of Rumi.* Translated by A.J. Arberry. Chicago: University of Chicago Press.

Sartre, Jean-Paul. 1956. *Being and Nothingness.* New York: Washington Square Press.

————. 1975. "The Wall." Pp. 281-98 in Walter Kaufman (ed.), *Existentialism: From Dostoevsky to Sartre.* New York: Meridian.

Sawyer, Robert J. 2000. *Calculating God.* New York: Tor.

Schlesinger, Arthur Jr. 1968. "The Decline of Heroes." Pp. 348-51 in Harold Lubin (ed.), *Heroes and Anti-Heroes: A Reader in Depth.* Scranton, Pa.: Chandler.

Schor, Juliet. 1998. T*he Overspent American: Why We Want What We Don't Need.* New York: HarperPerennial.

Schwartz, Barry. 1985. "Emerson, Cooley, and the American Heroic Vision." *Symbolic Interaction* 8 (1): 103-20.

Schweitzer, Albert. 1968. *The Quest of the Historical Jesus.* New York: Macmillan.

Scott, Joan W. 1996. "Postmodernism." *Contemporary Sociology* 25 (1): 3-6.

Seidman, Steven. 1991. "The End of Sociological Theory: The Postmodern Hope." *Sociological Theory* 9 (2): 131-47.

Smith, Tom. 1986. "The Polls: The Most Admired Man and Woman." *Public Opinion Quarterly* 50 (4): 573-83

Solomon, Robert. 1980. "Emotions and Choice." Pp. 251-83 in Amelie Oksenberg Rorty (ed.), *Explaining Emotions.* Berkeley: University of California Press.

———. 1983. *Passions.* Notre Dame: University of Notre Dame Press.

Stark, Rodney. 1965. "A Taxonomy of Religious Experience." *Journal for the Scientific Study of Religion* 5: 97-113.

———. 1997. "Bringing Theory Back In." Pp. 3-24 in Lawrence Young (ed.), *Rational Choice Theory and Religion: Summary and Assessment.* New York: Routledge.

———, and William Sims Bainbridge. 1985. *The Future of Religion: Secularization, Revival and Cult Formation.* Berkeley: University of California Press.

———. 1987. *A Theory of Religion.* New York: Peter Lang.

Stroud, Barry. 1969. "Conventionalism and the Indeterminacy of Translation." Pp. 82-96 in Donald Davidson and J. Hintikka (eds.), *Words and Objections: Essays on the Work of W. V. Quine.* Dordrecht: Reidel.

Sullivan, William. 1995. *Work and Integrity: The Crisis and Promise of Professionalism in America.* New York: HarperBusiness.

Taylor, Charles. 1982. "Responsibility for Self." Pp. 111-27 in Gary Watson, *Free Will.* Oxford: Oxford University Press.

———. 1989. *Sources of the Self: The Making of the Modern Identity.* Cambridge: Harvard University Press.

———. 1992. *The Ethics of Authenticity.* Cambridge: Harvard University Press.

Thoreau, Henry David. 1993. "Walden or Life in the Woods." Pp. 1-276 in *Walden and Other Essays.* New York: Barnes & Noble.

Tillich, Paul. 1952. *The Courage To Be.* New Haven: Yale University Press.

———. 1957. *The Dynamics of Faith.* New York: Harper & Brothers Publishers.

Tolkien, J.R.R. 1954. *The Lord of the Rings.* New York: Ballantine.

Tracy, David. 1975. *Blessed Rage for Order.* New York: Seabury Press.

Turner, Stephen. 1999. "The Significance of Shils." *Sociological Theory* 17 (2): 125-45.

Updike, John. 1986. *Roger's Version.* New York: Alfred A. Knopf.

Urmson, J.O. 1971. "Saints and Heroes." Pp. 515-22 in Joel Feinberg (ed.), *Reason and Responsibility*. Encino, Calif.: Dickenson.

Van den Berg, Axel. 1996. "Liberalism without Reason?" *Contemporary Sociology* 25 (1):19-25.

Vermes, Geza. 1973. *Jesus the Jew: A Historian's Reading of the Gospels*. Philadelphia: Fortress Press.

Vonnegut, Kurt Jr. 1973. *Breakfast of Champions*. New York: Dell.

Ward, Peter, and Donald Brownlee. 2000. *Rare Earth: Why Complex Life Is Uncommon in the Universe*. New York: Copernicus.

Warner, William Lloyd. 1959. *The Living and the Dead: A Study of the Symbolic Life of Americans*. New Haven: Yale University Press.

Wattles, Jeffrey. 1996. *The Golden Rule*. New York: Oxford University Press.

Watts, Alan. 1957. *The Way of Zen*. New York: Vintage.

Weber, Max. 1927. *General Economic History*. New York: Greenberg.

———. 1947. *The Theory of Social and Economic Organization*. New York: Free Press.

———. 1976. *The Protestant Ethic and the Spirit of Capitalism*. New York: Scribners.

Weinberg, Stephen. 1992. *Dreams of a Final Theory*. New York: Random House.

West, Cornel. 1993. *Race Matters*. Boston: Beacon Press.

Whitehead, Alfred North. 1929. *Process and Reality: An Essay on Cosmology*. New York: Macmillan.

Wiggins, David. 1976. "Locke, Butler and the Stream of Consciousness: And Men as Natural Kind." Pp. 139-74 in Amelie O. Rorty (ed.), *The Identities of Persons*. Berkeley: University of Califorinia Press.

Wight, Colin. 1996. "Incommensurability and Cross-Paradigm Communication in International Relations: 'What's the Frequency Kenneth'." *Millennium* 25 (2): 291-319.

Wilder, Thornton. 1938. *Our Town: A Play in Three Acts*. New York: Coward McCann.

Wiley, Norbert. 1994a. *The Semiotic Self*. Chicago: University of Chicago Press.

———. 1994b. "The Politics of Identity in American History." Pp. 131-149 in Craig Calhoun (ed.), *Social Theory and the Politics of Identity*. Oxford: Basil Blackwell.

Williamson, Clark M. 1998. "Doing Christian Theology with Jews: The Other, Boundaries, Questions." Pp. 37-52 in Roger Badham (ed.), *Introduction to Christian Theology*. Louisville: Westminster John Knox Press.

Witherington, Ben. 1995. *The Jesus Quest: The Third Search for the Jew of Nazareth*. Downers Grove, Ill.: InterVarsity Press.

Wolfe, Alan. 1989. *Whose Keeper? Social Science and Moral Obligation*. Berkeley: University of California Press.

———. 1998. *One Nation After All*. New York: Viking.

Wright, N.T. 1992. *Who Was Jesus?* Grand Rapids: Eerdmans.

————. 1996. *Jesus and the Victory of God.* Minneapolis: Fortress Press.

Wuthnow, Robert. 1976. *The Consciousness Reformation.* Berkeley: University of California Press.

————. 1987. *Meaning and Moral Order: Explorations in Cultural Analysis.* Berkeley: University of California Press.

————. 1989. *Communities of Discourse: Ideology and Social Structure in the Reformation, the Enlightenment and European Socialism.* Cambridge: Harvard University Press.

————. 1991. *Acts of Compassion: Caring for Others and Helping Ourselves.* Princeton: Princeton University Press.

————. 1994. *God and Mammon in America.* New York: The Free Press.

Yamane, David. 1998. "Religious Experience." Pp. 179-182 in William Swatos Jr. (ed.), *The Encyclopedia of Religion and Society.* Walnut Creek, Calif.: Altamira Press.

————, and Megan Polzer. 1994. "Ways of Seeing Ecstasy in Modern Society: Experiential-Expressive and Cultural-Linguistic Views." *Sociological Analysis* 55: 1-25.

Yoder, John Howard. 1972. *The Politics of Jesus.* Grand Rapids: Eerdmans.

Young, Lawrence. 1997. "Phenomenological Images of Religion and Rational Choice Theory." Pp. 113-46 in Lawrence Young (ed.), *Rational Choice Theory and Religion: Summary and Assessment.* New York: Routledge.

INDEX

Absolute Spirit, 305–6
Action, rationality of, 126–27
Alethia, 101, 103
Althusser, Louis, 40
Antihumanism, 39–45
Argument from design, 89–90
Aristotle
  the good and, 9, 60–61, 65, 69, 71
  knowing and, 59
Astrology, 238
  dialogue about, 238–40
Atman, 26–27
Avidya, 84, 309
Awe, 99

Becker, Ernest, 169, 170
Beliefs. *See also* Religious experience
  open to question, 86–87
  rationality of, 126–27
Bellah, Robert, 14–15, 156, 165
Berger, Peter, 121
Best argument, 21–22
Bhaskar, Roy, 312
Bloom, Allan, 2
Boorstin, Daniel, 170, 171–72, 193

Breakfast of Champions (Vonnegut),
  82
Buber, Martin, 42
Bucke, R.M., 251
Buddhism, 73, 84

Callings, 201–5. *See also* Journeys;
  Quests
  contemporary, 208–9
    survey about, 217–21
  dialogue about, 205–17, 222–25
Campbell, Joseph
  on heroes, 169, 194
  on hero's call, 202, 204
  on modern life, 170–71
Camus, Albert, 83
Capitalism, 309–11
  Althusser on, 40
Catholicism, 203. *See also*
  Christianity
Celebrities, 171–72, 196–98
Celebrity Register, 172
Cervantes, Miguel de, 201
Chandogya, 38
Chardin, Teilhard de, 148

Christianity
  calling and, 203
  as eschatological religion, 162–63
  ethics of, 102
  fundamental
    experience and, 257–62
    heroes and, 182
    identity and, dialogue about,
      46–49
    lack of tolerance for, 260
    moral purpose and, 53–54
    the good and, 65, 70
    human rights and, 74
    resurrection and, 85–86
      dialogue about, 87–92
    supererogation and, 163–64
Christmas, 59
Christmas Carol, A (Dickens), 58–60,
  66
Class system, British, 32–33
Communities of discourse, 274–75
  critical evaluation and, 275–76
  experience and, 276, 281
    dialogue about, 276–81
  truth and, 281–96
    dialogue about, 281–95
Community, importance of, 22
Conrad, Joseph, 250
Cooley, Charles Horton, 196–97
Cosmic Consciousness (Bucke), 251
Cosmic inflation, 294–96
Critical realism, 312
Critical space, 22, 23, 85–94
  communities of discourse and,
    274–76
  religious experience and, 259

Darwin, Charles, 89, 293
Declaration of Independence, 74
Deism, 116
Deleuze, Gilles, 42
Democratic socialism, 11–12
Derrida, Jacques, 41
Dialectical materialism, 141

Dickens, Charles, 58
Don Quixote (Cervantes), 201–2
Dread, 98
Dreams of a Final Theory (Weinberg),
  291
Durkheim, Emile, 12, 43, 278,
  331n5
Durkheimianism, 13–14
Dyson, Freemen, 294

Eliade, Mircea, 59, 97, 168
Emerson, Ralph Waldo, 170
Emotions
  knowing and, 58–60
  moral, 10
End of meaning, 16
Eternal now, 252
Eternal return doctrine, 51
Ethics
  consequentialist approach to, 77
  philosophy of, 9
  religion and, 102–3
Evil, theological problem of, 101–2,
  108, 112
Existentialism, 83–84, 96
  purposelessness and, 140
Experience, 234–36
  communities of discourse and,
    276, 281
    dialogue about, 276–81
  components of, 235
  vocabulary and, 275

Faith, 86, 300
  dialogue about, 122–26
Family values, 65
Feuerbach, Ludwig, 66
Fishwick, Marshall, 169, 171
Five Gospels, The, 286, 289
Foucault, Michael, 41
Fragmentation, of identity, 41–42,
  53, 132
France, antihumanism in, 40
Freud, Sigmund, 251

Fundamentalism. *See* Christianity, fundamental
Future of an Illusion, The (Freud), 251

Gardiner, John, 183
Gauttari, Felix, 42
Giddens, Anthony, 138
Glicksburg, Charles, 170
Goals, morality of, 8–9
God, 97–99
  alienation from plan of, 298–99
  Americans' belief in, 4, 15–16, 96, 299
  "death of," 16, 96, 169
  detached from moral purpose, 104–6
  dialogue about, 106–21
  disconnection from, 17
  evil and, 101–2
  existence of, dialogue about, 87–89, 90, 91–92
  faith in, 300
  dialogue about, 99–102, 122–26
  holiness of, 98–99
  meaning originates with, 298
  in metanarratives, 17–18
  physical evidence of, 290–96
  dialogue about, 291–92, 295, 296
Golden rule, 156–62
  as procedural morality, 72
  trivialization of, 164–66
Good, the, 60–69
  dialogue about, 61–65, 67–69, 70–71
  ultimate, 69–72
Goodness, worshiped, 112
Gordis, Daniel, 102
Greeley, Andrew, 215
Greto, Teresa, 217

Habits of the Heart (Bellah), 14–15, 156

Harrington, Michael, 11–12
Haverim, 87, 89, 276, 300, 301
Hegel, G.W., 305–6
Heidegger, Martin, 31
Heroes, 167–69
  ahistoricity of contemporary, 195–96
  dialogue about, 172–83, 185–91
  evolution of, 169–72
  identification with, 196–200
  survey about, 183–85
  types of, 192–96
Hesse, Hermann, 205
Hinduism, self and, 26–27. *See also* Upanishads
Holiness, of God, 98–99
Holocaust survivors, dialogue about God, 107–12
Homo religiosus, 97–98
Hoyle, Fred, 294
Hugo, Victor, 102
Human rights. *See* Rights
Human vocation. *See* Vocation
Humanism, 38–39, 43
Hume, David, 89
Hypergood, 69–72
  calling and, 204

I-me distinction
  antihumanism and, 39–45
  humanism and, 38–39
I-thou relationship, 42
Identity, 25–26. *See also* Life, as story; Peak experience
  antihumanism and, 39–45
  dialogue about, 34–38, 46–52
  fragmentation of, 41–42, 53, 132
  humanism and, 38–39
  moral space and, 58–73
  names and, 27–29
  self-consciousness and, 26–27, 44
  social position and, 29–34
  vocation and, 303–5
Ishiguro, Kazuo, 32

Islam
    calling and, 205
    the good and, 65, 70

James, William, 252, 253
Jastrow, Robert, 122
Jesus
    eschatology of, 162–63
    ethics of, 164–66
    historical truth and, 282–90
        dialogue about, 281–90
    reign of God and, 307
    salvation and, 259–60
        dialogue about, 262–64
    supererogation of, 163–64
Jesus Seminar, 162, 164, 286–90
Jones, Katryn E., 183
Journey to the East, The (Hesse), 205,
    227
Journeys, 205–8. *See also* Callings;
    Quests
    contemporary, 225–26
        dialogue about, 226–31
    as metaphor for life, 205
Judaism
    ethics of, 102–3
    the good and, 65–66, 69–70
    human rights and, 74
    identity and, dialogue about,
        50–52
    Jubilee Year in, 306
    moral purpose and, 53–54
Judgment, distinguished from toler-
    ance, 81
Justice, 306

Kinship diagrams, 30

Lacan, Jacques, 41
Language
    as basis of self-consciousness, 43
    cooperative advantage and, 42–43
    postmodernism and, 40–41
Les Miserables (Hugo), 102, 250

Levi-Strauss, Claude, 15
Liberal discourse, 93
Liberation theology, 138
Life, as a story, 237, 241–49
    dialogue about, 241–48
Literature, truth and, 10
Lord Jim (Conrad), 250
Lovelace, Richard, 66
Lowenthal, Leo, 171, 193

MacIntyre, Alisdair, 9
Man of La Mancha, The
    (Wasserman), 201–2, 204
Martial arts, dialogue about, 240–41
Marx, Karl, 307–8
Marxism, 307–8
    as antihumanism, 40
    the good and, 70
Maslow, Abraham, 253
Materialism, 308–9
Mead, George Herbert, 38, 39
Meaning of life, 131–32, 138. *See
    also* End of meaning; Vocation
    attitudes about, dialogue on,
        132–35
        no sense of purpose, 142–45
        no purpose, 139–42
        other, 151–52
        purpose understood, 147–51
        some sense of purpose, 145–47
    goodness trivialized, 156–66
        dialogue about, 156–60
    heroes and, 197–200
    life story and, 248–49
    religiosity and, 152–55
    survey about, 135–38
Mentor, 187–89, 191
Metanarratives, 319n17
    disconnection from, 132
    God in, 17–18
    postmodernism and, 14, 16, 54
Metaphysical space, 20–22, 23,
    57–58, 73–84
    religion and, 54–55

Methodology, of author's study, 5–7, 317n4

Mitzvot, 280

Moral proceduralism, 14

Moral purpose, 4–5, 7–12, 18, 57–58

  cosmogonic, 10–11

  effects of lack of, 11–12

  goals and, 8–9

  God detached from, 104–6

  dialogue about, 106–21

  in Jewish theology, 102–3

  Nietzsche blames monotheism for loss of, 103–4

  procedural morality and, 72

  religion and, 53

  ultimate concerns and, 7–8

Moral space, 20, 23

  heroes as center of, 168

  identity and, 58–73, 103

Names, 274

  Althusser on, 40

  identity and, 27–29

Natural selection, 293

Nicomachean Ethics (Aristotle), 60

Nietzsche, Friedrich

  eternal return doctrine of, 51

  heroes and, 169, 194

  loss of moral purpose and, 103–4

  parable of madman, 95–97, 121

Nihilism, 103, 221–22

Nothingness, 38–39

Oceanic feeling, 251

Our Town (Wilder), 52–53

Peak experience, 238, 249–50, 264, 271–72

  dialogue about, 264–71

  religious, 252–53, 257–61

  dialogue about, 250–57, 261–64

Person, self as another word for, 44–45

Physical cosmology, 291–96, 302–3

Physics, faith and, 122–26

Plato, the good and, 9, 60, 65, 69, 71

Political identity movements, 40

Politics

  of Bible, 150

  of identity, 29, 31, 42

Politics at God's Funeral, The (Harrington), 11

Polkinghorne, Thomas, 122

Postmodernism, 2

  denial of self and, 18–19, 44

  lack of values in, 80

  language and, 40–41

  meaning of life and, 132

  metanarratives and, 14, 16, 54

  moral purpose and, 104

  thesis of, 13, 14

  truth and, 90–94

Procedural morality, 72–73

Profane plane of existence, 97–98

Profession, 203

Protestant Ethic and the Spirit of Capitalism, The (Weber), 203

Protestantism, 203. *See also* Christianity

Purpose. *See* Meaning of life

Q document, 288, 332n14

Quests, 234. *See also* Callings; Journeys

  dialogue about, 231–34

Race, calling and, 221–22

Race Matters (West), 221

Religion. *See also specific religions*

  metaphysical space and, 54–55

  sociology of, 121

Religiosity

  calling and, 220–21

  heroes and, 197–200

  meaning of life and, 152–55

Religious alienation, 106
  dialogue about, 106–21
Religious experience, 252–53,
    257–61, 276, 281
  dialogue about, 250–57, 261–64,
    276–81
  sociology and, 331nn3, 5, 8
Remains of the Day, The (Ishiguro),
    32–34, 39
Renard, John, 205
Respect, 158–59
Rights
  dialogue about, 75–76, 78–82
  metaphysical space and, 74–84

Sacred plane of existence, 97–98
Sacred time, 59
Sagan, Carl, 302
Sannyasins, 28
  identity and, dialogue about, 50
  moral purpose and, 53–54
Sartre, Jean-Paul, 38–39, 83
Schlesinger, Arthur, Jr., 170
Science. *See* Physics
Secular humanism, 74
Secularization, self and, 12–18
Self. *See also* Identity
  alternate resources for, 238–41
  denial of, 18–19
  secularization and, 12–18
Self-consciousness, 26–27, 44
  language as basis of, 43
Silver rule, 158–59
Sisyphus myth, 83
Social space, identity and, 19–20,
    23, 25–55
Socialization, 43, 77
Sociograms, 30
Sociology, 11–12
  calling and, 202–3
  as discipline, 12–13
  purpose of religion and, 127
  of religion, 121

Soul, landscape of. *See* Critical
    space; Metaphysical space;
    Moral space; Social space
Sri Rajneesh, Bhagwan, 28
Supererogation, 163–64

Taussig, Hal, 286, 293
Taylor, Charles
  ethics and, 9
  hypergood and, 69
  loss of transcendental horizons
    and, 165
  moral ontology and, 78, 156,
  moral space and, 20, 53, 57
Theology, sociology and, 8
Thoreau, Henry David, 84
Thrownness, 31
Tikkun ha Olam, 308
Tillich, Paul, 7, 9, 23, 69, 252
"To Lucasta, Going to the Wars"
    (Lovelace), 66
Tolerance, 81
Truth
  best argument and, 21–22
  communities of discourse and,
    281–96
  dialogue about, 281–90
  postmodernism and, 90–94
  in secular discourse, 100–101

UFOs, 99–100
Ultimate concerns, 7–8, 9
Upanishads, 27, 38, 39, 40, 42
Utilitarianism, 101

Values. *See also* Good, the; Rights
  heroes as personification of,
    184
  origin of, dialogue about, 117–20
Vocabulary, 274–75
Vocation, 203
  alienation from God and,
    297–301

American understanding of,
301–2
author's call to higher, 297,
305–11
identity and, 303–5
Vonnegut, Kurt, 82

Warner, William Lloyd, 170
Wasserman, Dale, 201
Weber, Max, 58, 157, 170

calling and, 203
Weinberg, Stephen, 291
West, Cornel, 221
Whose Keeper? (Wolfe), 11, 18,
166
Wilder, Thornton, 52
Wolfe, Alan, 11–12, 18, 166
Wuthnow, Robert, 162, 208–9

Yamane, David, 17